THE MUCKRAKERS

East Side scene in Old New York by W. A. Rogers, *Harper's Weekly*, April 9, 1881.

THE MUCKRAKERS

Louis Filler

Stanford University Press
Stanford, California

Stanford University Press, Stanford, California

Copyright 1968 by Louis Filler
New and Enlarged Edition copyright © 1976 by Louis Filler
Preface © 1993 by the Board of Trustees of the
   Leland Stanford Junior University

First published by Harcourt, Brace and Company, Inc., in 1939 as
   Crusaders for American Liberalism
Reprinted by Stanford University Press in 1993
Printed in the United States of America
CIP data appear at the end of the book

Stanford University Press publications are distributed exclusively by
Stanford University Press within the United States, Canada, and Mexico;
they are distributed exclusively by Cambridge University Press
throughout the rest of the world.

CONTENTS

Preface, 1993:
Progressives and
Post-Progressives

There can be little question that we are in a transitional time, toward what consensus cannot presently be determined. How the era designated as Progressive may play a role in coming events is yet to be spelled out in personalities and events.

The Progressive Era was highlighted by a journalism and literature unique in American annals. Although reform has always been a staple in American developments, under several names and rubrics, *progressive* reform differed from both earlier and later reform waves. (See the "Prefatory Note" to my *Distinguished Shades: Americans Whose Lives Live On* [Ovid, Mich.: Belfry, 1992] for a review of the liberal vocabulary.)

It helps perspective to note historical distinctions which, for example, separate pre–Civil War reformers from those in the "Progressive" era, that lasted roughly from 1900 to 1918. Both groups had mighty impact on their times. The earlier reformers coped with slavery and abolition, wrestled with temperance and women's rights, education, and religious unrest. So did the Progressives, even to slavery and "Abolition," to some extent at home (*Muckrakers*, Ch. XXI), certainly in foreign affairs, which Progressives were opening to self-absorbed Americans, as records from the League of Nations to the United Nations show. Such issues mingled with domestic social and ethical unrest, as well as awesome monopolistic drives.

Journalists and litterateurs in the two eras, however, differed.

In both periods they were based on a democratic journalistic readership. But earlier reformers addressed limited audiences. The famous *Liberator*, for instance, edited by William Lloyd Garrison, had a weekly circulation of about 5,000. But copies of the *Liberator* were read by editors, politicians, clergymen, and other strategic social elements. Some of the articles were reprinted in pamphlets: it was a time of pamphlets, collected and read like books. *Liberator* viewpoints drained down from an elite to the masses.

By 1900, when Progressives began separating from Populists to move into the public glare, powerful magazines had developed out of the cultural soil of a mass newspaper press. There had been few magazines before, the best ones mainly for the educated and well-to-do. Magazines for the poor there had been all but none. Such magazines as there were for the shallowly instructed tended toward the cheap and sensational.

New education for the masses and union-won wages and salaries created a demand for national and more intelligent reading matter. Sharp publishers, aided by new printing technology and better trained journalists, fed public hunger for information and ideas. The result was the popular magazine, born to entertain but capable of performing public service. From it came the "literature of exposure," a phenomenon which brought closer a public of magazine readers. Progressives searched the nation for conditions requiring change, because of either corruption or inefficiency—the latter in itself a form of corruption.

Thus emerged the famous "muckrakers" who in their writings supported the work of inspired reform politicians like Robert M. LaFollette and who debated solutions to current dilemmas as critics of reigning conservative apologists. The "Muckraking Era" featured one national sensation after another. It reached its climax during the elections of 1912, which saw former President Theodore Roosevelt and former Governor of New Jersey Woodrow Wilson vying for the Presidency. The Wilson period that followed saw what has been called the most sweeping reform program in American history, though it in fact drew together reforms sought and won over the previous decade.

In comparing Progressivism with later social eruptions and overturns, two important differences want notice. First, Progressives made strenuous efforts to affect as much social change as possible, *while treasuring individual responsibility for society's state.*

Thus, child labor laws were strengthened, but *family* rights in the child were asserted and respected. Citizens as women, as laborers, ethnic groups, consumers pressed their causes while limiting national authority by way of local ordinances, court decisions, and Congressional fiat. Crusaders worked through powerful leaders, but for limited ends. Frances Willard's memorable slogan for women—"Do Everything"—expressed unwillingness to shunt responsibility for their causes into bureaucratic hands.

Not a little of what was developed during later social uprisings drew from the Progressive experience with women, children, the meagerly employed, and others. One theory of the New Deal was that it fulfilled the dream of Edward Bellamy's landmark *Looking Backward*. Arthur E. Morgan, raised in the Progressive tradition, gave impetus to experimental education and created successful incentives for small businessmen resisting monopoly. There were victories, in a time of confusion respecting communism.

However, the youth and ethnic uprisings of the 1960's and after contained novel features, mostly challenging to Progressive interests. A new conservatism in opposition forged alliances which actually brought former rebels and formidable thinkers of the quality of Sidney Hook and Will Herberg into alternative programs resisting the radical challenge.

Leaders in these altercations showed little interest in the Progressives, certainly, but not a few of the issues had roots in such subjects as religion, "family values," education, political standards, and culture which had bemused Progressives as well as their children. Despite the confusion of the times, many names were heard which had once dominated the news—names of such Progressives as James Weldon Johnson, Lincoln Steffens, Ida M. Tarbell, Samuel Gompers, Frank Norris, Jacob A. Riis, Charlotte Perkins Gilman, Harold L. Ickes, Florence Kelley, among others who might emerge from silence to new authority.

Second, social change was argued during the Progressive era through journals of reform in a multiplicity of styles and personalities not later possible. Magazines consolidated or changed their programs, closed down, or lost readers to radio listeners and then television watchers. National reform had been the heart of the reform era; it had turned a sea of local reform efforts into a wave, creating the basic elements of modernity. Special interest publications continued to pour from presses, but they often now had limited circulation or were written in the special jargons of groups. Trade union publications though they might address a large trucker, textile, or steel constituency and be skillfully edited, were too partisan to interest outsiders—or even insiders, who knew beforehand what the publications said.

Great succeeding magazines like *Time* expressed interest in the public good and made extensive "investigative" reports on crime, urban conditions, individuals. But American life was increasingly complex and responsive to far-away circumstances. Events in the then–Soviet Union, Iran, Vietnam, Korea, and elsewhere were no longer remote from such centers as New York and Chicago. Justice for ethnic groups often created national dilemmas. The problems of Mexican Americans, for example, could not be separated from American relations in the Caribbean or Latin America.

Activists in post-Progressive decades had much to learn from the classic figures of Progressivism. Original Progressives had worked effectively in their arguments and appeals to American *traditions*, theirs either by inheritance for those who were members of the highly visible "WASPS," or by adoption for those who came from other ethnic backgrounds, such as Louis D. Brandeis, Booker T. Washington, and Fiorello H. La Guardia. In their speeches and articles, Progressives had appealed to readers and listeners to join them in maintaining the America they loved and in adapting these traditions to needs of later times.

As S. S. McClure, the genius of *McClure's* and himself an immigrant, had written: "There is no one else, none but all of us." This outlook gave older Progressives an eloquence few could match who sought to direct all attention to themselves. It can inspire gifted men and women from any of the new immigrant groups to find common ground with other Americans, new and old, to create social plans serving them all.

The Progressives' love of country enabled them to rise above rhetoric, however powerful. As Edwin E. Slosson wrote (quoted in *Muckrakers*, p. 258):

Literature is more than a tale of facts, as architecture is more than a tale of bricks. [Both] are products of the creative imagination. . . .

Judged by these tests, the recent work of Lincoln Steffens, of Miss Tarbell, of Mr. Lawson, of Sinclair and Phillips, is literature, beyond a peradventure. It has taken the tale of facts from the year books and the official reports, from the statutes and the decisions, and from unwilling witnesses before investigating committees, and has wrought them into narratives that stir the blood. Its writers have seen in the dead materials that which only the imaginative insight ever sees—their significance, their relation to life, their potential striking force.

Ezra Pound put it nicely, for which he can be forgiven much, that literature was writing which was always news. An Ida Tarbell, a Lincoln

Steffens, a David Graham Phillips read today with undulled eyes can be evocative of our later conditions as any one of them was when he or she first astonished the country. The artists of Progressivism are yet to be added up as a movement for a newer generation to appreciate and enjoy.

The cultural dimension is deeper than many today realize, who have not studied it at first hand. The passionate will to write about feelings and relations as well as "facts" was present not only in the patent fiction and poetry and essay writers—O. Henry, Edwin Markham, Hutchins Hapgood, Jack London, Vachel Lindsay, and numerous others—but among all the best observer-journalists of the time. Ray Stannard Baker, a leader of the muckrakers, dreamed of writing a novel, and Steffens actually perpetrated one, *Moses in Red*: a failure of a novel, but with ideas and aspirations which should interest the scholar at least. Beyond such were durable authors like Finley Peter Dunne, creator of "Mr. Dooley," an admitted classic, and Edith Wharton, whose *House of Mirth* belonged to the Progressives. And still others.

There is thus much for the student and educator and those concerned for modern affairs to learn from the world the Progressives and their associates charted, in articles, editorials, tales, and even poems. Edwin Markham may some day be more famous, among those who honor poetry, for his *Ballad of the Gallows-Bird* than for his *The Man with the Hoe*, a poem which went around the world in translations: William James identified it as "reek[ing] with humanity and morality." The *Ballad*, which I have published elsewhere, was not a Progressive achievement, but this would also be true of many of the writings of Markham's associates who dreamed of beauty and brotherhood, and who sometimes attained one and not the other. The *idea* of beauty and the *idea* of brotherhood continue to be the very breath of life in a world which threatens both. Study of the Progressives and of the materials which made up their pattern can profit us in our struggles of the day.

L.F.

The Belfry
Ovid, Michigan

Retrospect, 1976:
With Something About
a Peculiar Utopianism

Reading this book for a new edition has been a startling experience for me in some respects. I have, to be sure, kept up with it as I pursued new researches, prepared new introductions, and checked old views against new experiences. But perhaps it is the uncertain times in which we live which make some of my older formulations seem to me strangely firm. Certainly 1939 was not a year to build upon. The three-year Spanish Civil War, which had cost some 700,000 lives, had come to an end, but all realized that it had been a testing ground for Communists and Fascists who were not about to dissolve their armies. They intended to force the democracies to create their own. I think it may have been a faith in the ultimate integrity of the common people, and in their instinct for good— a Progressive notion—which persuaded me that a certain radical tone was in order, and that the poor merited partisanship *because* they were poor.

With John D. Rockefeller's grandson now Vice President of the United States, and approved by various levels of the population, I am less sure where partisanship belongs, if anywhere. True, I spoke in this book more harshly of the Standard Oil Company than my dear Allan Nevins would have approved, though in his hunger for facts he accepted almost anything in others who claimed to know what they were talking about. I note, however, that I did not question the elder Rockefeller's sincerity. Indeed, I call to mind Jim Rorty, then in his "Marxist" phase, who read my chapter in manuscript on "The Mother of Trusts." He interrupted his reading to ask: "When are you going to start knocking him?"— *him* being Rockefeller. I had an intense interest in personality which made it difficult for me to treat people as pawns, and so able to "knock" them on principle. And it was this which kept my book from becoming part of the "radical" torrent of writing which high-lighted the 1930s and spilled over into the 1940s and beyond in appreciation of "Marshal" Stalin and others like him.

A curious fact about *Crusaders* was that it was almost oddly absorbed in the American scene. It seemed to many of our people at that time that their destiny was being made abroad, and surely in terms of World War II that was the case. My "point" was, implicit in *Crusaders*, that we needed to solidify our character at home, for domestic and international challenges. And this I think it was which distinguished my "radicalism" from that which offered itself with remarkable effectiveness in the Communist *Daily Worker* and *New Masses*. Such "radicalism" was expressed even in the work of the *New York Times* and *Fortune* writer John Chamberlain, whose *Farewell to Reform* (1932) saw muckraking and Progressivism as too little and all wrong, without clearly specify-ing what might be better. Chamberlain's subsequent movement to the "right" should have attracted more interest than it did. I saw him at a meeting of American historians in the 1950s and was amazed at their lack of interest in this really thoughtful man. Yet the Association was far from bereft of conservatives, and it puzzled me why they did not honor his point of view. We all needed to have more insight into the kinds of social philosophy our changing times created. We still do.

But before such shifts as Chamberlain's occurred in historical perspective, the academics were bogged down in conservatism, so far as muckraking was concerned. They treated it as a gaudy in-cident cut short by Theodore Roosevelt's famous 1906 denunciation of it as irresponsible. They kept it separate from Progressivism, which they saw as better rooted in party politics, more worthy of their "research," and forming the soil or sub-soil for Wilsonian idealism. Thus, my very dilation on muckraking as having ramified through social reform and communication gave it to academics a "radical" cast not apparent to those who were excited by revolu-tionary visions.

I myself saw the muckrakers as neither radical nor conservative, but as feeding the several social sectors of society with knowledge and understanding. So the grounds for criticism of my book were not always clear to me. I recall an academic reviewer of one of its printings who complained that the materials were "overwhelming," as though this was a sin. Some problems were in the minds of the critics, rather than in the materials. For instance, it never occurred to me to treat women as separated from the mainstream of American life. Charlotte Perkins Gilman, Ida M. Tarbell, Rheta Childe Dorr, and others made appearances in *Crusaders* because they belonged there, not because they represented womanhood. Indeed, they were very different women, and anyone would have been hard put to find a comfortable formula relating or uniting them. Tarbell was simply as inextricable from the Standard Oil story as Steffens, though he wore pants, was from the story of municipal corruption. Dorr was an individualistic type who spoke for the working woman because she herself was on her own. But Gilman was a radical for philosophic reasons—reasons even less interesting to Tarbell or Dorr than they would be to those equalitarian females with little apparent sympathy for Gilman's austere social standards.

In any event, my mere highlighting of such women gave a "radical" tinge to my work, in the eyes of historians of the time to whom business, politics, and war made up what Robert Browning called "a world of men."

Nor did I realize in 1939 that I had done anything unusual by discussing events and personalities centering around Negroes *as part of* the Progressive era. I was, of course, gratified to be reviewed and approved in the *Journal of Negro History*, and by such people as John Hope Franklin. The point is that it surprised me a bit to find that this feature of the book had been singled out. How did one avoid discussing the role of Negroes in American life? Yet this role was "segregated" in books and studies in ways which created imbalances in social thought: ultimately with "backlashes" of black racism as unfruitful as the conditions they were supposed to correct.

My purpose, such as I perceived it, had been to contribute to a new social criticism: one which would appeal to a higher patriotism, multi-ethnic loyalties appropriate to a nation totally composed of minorities, socio-cultural responses, and the immediate needs of society. American competitiveness inevitably created losers. And though one could ask those who had competed to accept the decisions of referees, still—there were the helpless children. There were also the old: toothless, beaten, nobody to exult over. There were the distorted, the insane, the psychotic, who were nonetheless alive and who constituted a human question which other human beings had to answer in order to be taken seriously themselves. Finally, there were the evil, the malefic, the demonic, who had to be handled with sophistication and sober decision if society was not to live in constant apprehension and disgrace.

Naturally, I expected an interested response from the journalistic community, since my tale dealt so intensely with journalist-litterateurs. And the journalists responded positively to the saga of their predecessors. In fact, the continuity of muckraking has been one of its most striking characteristics, despite the fact that "muckraking" has also been an invidious word applied to shoddy sensationalists, irresponsible snoopers, and the like. Somehow, readers generally and journalists in particular have been aware that there are *two* "muckraking" reputations, and they have discriminated between that of the cheapjack journals and those which assumed a higher public obligation than merely to meet reader expectations. From time to time a writer makes up his mind and, alone or with other writers, decides that the moment has come to impart some new view of social conditions—and another muckraking publication is on the way. Inevitably, it invokes the shade of Steffens and of Upton Sinclair to sustain it in its course.

And yet, since the muckraking era there has been no muckraking era, despite the patently useful labors of such journalists as George Seldes and I. F. Stone. Why has this been the case? If there were a simple answer, we would have fewer problems. But part of the answer, at least, is imbedded in these pages. I well recall an excited young man, now not so young, denouncing "my generation," whatever that meant to him—actually, he was talking of the muckrakers—as having been intent on reforming society. "His" generation, he informed me (this was in 1965), was composed of individuals determined to satisfy themselves. That seemed to him somehow a more honest, or accurate statement of society's needs than the social pieties of the muckrakers.

All well and good, except that in two more years he was himself "researching" the muckrakers, and by shrewd digging had discovered that here and there was a letter by one of them, or by one of their publishers, or by one of their Progressive associates which did not treat Negroes with awed respect. This proved to his satisfaction—and that of his students, no doubt—that the muckrakers were "racists," and so undeserving of the respect of fine, upstanding people like himself.

I kidded him at a professional meeting, asking what difference anything made to existentialists like ourselves, but he was too absorbed in his "researches" to appreciate the joke. He was revising his opinions, he said. But I wondered why, while he was doing all that revising, he could not notice that without the muckrakers and their Progressive associates there would have been no National Association for the Advancement of Colored People. I could not see why he found it painful to remark the fact that the Negro people of the time had, in effect, built up their own Progressive movement tandem to that of their white associates. The career of a James Weldon Johnson was Progressive, or it was nothing. And I wondered why he ignored, rather than welcomed, the lifelong labors in behalf of Negroes of such Americans as Charles Edward Russell in the North and Willis D. Weatherford in the South.

So determinedly invidious and myopic a viewpoint on muckraking as my academic friend held—or *holds*; you never can tell —is a phenomenon that needs understanding. I see it as embodying what I have called a peculiar utopianism, which has all but carved out for itself an American career. We are, to be sure, to some extent a nation of utopians. But I see a difference between our traditional social ventures—the thrilling declaration that "all men are created equal," the effort to make a working society of Brook Farm, the attempt to set up a new Zion in the desert as the Mormons did— and some of our more doubtful millennarian slogans of recent decades. The Founding Fathers came down from heady atmosphere of the Declaration of Independence to create the compromises of the Constitution. And the Brook Farmers and other social experimenters coped with the practical problems of farming and debt payments.

This was a different order of events from those signalled by more recent utopian slogans characterizing Americans on the farm and in the factory as "workers and peasants" who would strike palms with their counterparts elsewhere. American farmers were often crass, but they were not peasants. American laborers were often more muscles than brains, and they often did rotten or no work, but their expectations distinguished them from most laborers abroad no matter what they said during hard times. Such a slogan as "Self Determination in the Black Belt" was cruel in its unrealistic assessment of conditions in the American South. It led ultimately to such sadly destructive and self-destructive slogans as "Freedom Comes from the Barrel of a Revolver": a slogan guaranteed to result in anything but freedom, for its protagonist or any of his or her admirers.

Yet such slogans attracted not only compulsive adventurers but even social leaders, foundations, and publishers. They adorned these catchwords with money, time, and respect—frequently at the expense of past American movements, including Progressivism, which had adhered closer to democratic processes and dialogue, and had shown more substantial results, albeit often at painful cost. At the moment, it seems we have exhausted too many of our options to indulge ourselves in new and potentially bloody utopian adventures. We may hope that in the next years an understanding of our past efforts in experimentalism, reckless as well as responsible, will increase.

Only by examining the strange excrescences of history along with its healthy growth can we set ourselves on more reasonable courses of communication and program-making than we recently have followed. In retrospect, I contend that the Progressivism of the muckrakers is more relevant to solving current national problems than is the peculiar utopianism of the 1960s. I offer two suggestions which might contribute to a fruitful dialogue as we gather data intended to help us make up our minds about this person or that event in the muckraking story.

For one thing, we need to capture a sense of the value of continuity in our historical thinking. And by "continuity" I do not at all mean remembering anything merely because it happened. The muckrakers were not themselves great hands at ancestor-worship. I recall Charles Edward Russell asking me sardonically what "Lincoln Republicanism" meant, if anything. Other muckrakers were skeptical of old wars, of the rags to riches legend, of the beauty of life on the farm, and other established fancies. They were forward-looking, and eager—perhaps too eager—to be modern.

But in their studies of business, politics, and social ways, the muckrakers pondered their own past and that of their families. And they studied the past records carefully in order to ensure the accuracy of their findings. As a result their articles and books on great industries, labor leaders, insurance, the stock market, ethnic problems, children, conservation, and all subjects had a remarkably solid quality which influenced events. We need to consider how we can refine a sense of others' points of view—in the past as in the present—and can learn a technique for communication to persuade the reader that we are not fly-by-night informers, clever word jugglers, and name and data droppers, but rather that we have given every subject thought and hard work.

Actually, our instincts are ready for better rapport with the past. We very properly honored James Stewart's performance in *Mr. Smith Goes to Washington* (1939) as showing how national politics could result in skulduggery dangerous to the national interest, and we laughed intelligently at the exposés of machine politics in *The Great McGinty* (1940). We read as well as watched Robert Penn Warren's *All the King's Men* (1949) and pondered Huey Long's potential for leading an American fascist movement. None of this kept us from severe national blunders, paradoxically as a result of a too easy and too expansive prosperity. But, if we are fated to suffer somewhat as a result, we have at least the means at hand for reassessing our experiences and making something better of them.

So continuity is important. Muckraking is important. But it can never be over-emphasized that muckraking cannot function satisfactorily by itself. It needs to implement and be implemented by a strong Progressive movement, one representative of the broad sections of the population and with leaders who express their best ideals in practical form. Muckrakers and leaders share a common necessity to appeal to the best in people and so to push their social criticism more vigorously than human nature can bear over a long stretch of time. But this does not necessarily impugn the value of what they have accomplished during their best periods. A Robert M. La Follette is a national asset, and has been so recognized. But he needed the realistic understanding and support which a Lincoln Steffens gave him.

A Burton K. Wheeler of Montana was a much more intemperate Progressive talent than La Follette, and in his individualism and western character Wheeler had potential for ill as well as good. He fought the Teapot Dome fraud, and we must thank him for it. But he also saw dangers in the New Deal which led him into empathetic understandings with would-be fascists. And when one recalls that he had some possibilities for becoming Vice President under Franklin D. Roosevelt, and to succeed him in the ordinary course of nature, we are reminded of how necessary to us is a responsible press and political process.

Is another muckraking-Progressive era feasible? Can we look forward to its revival? Certainly we need to avoid wishful thinking. There is a difference between nostalgic appreciation of past glories and an inspired use of past techniques and programs in modern times. But it can be said that other options are not, presently, in the best shape. Many of the ranters of the 1960s have lost credibility and have little to offer in program or achievement. The call of some erstwhile utopians for a "new Populism" is in itself a confession of need for identification with older, grassroots movements.

What the former Vice President Spiro T. Agnew called a "post-Watergate morality" established at least the need for public agreement on an ethic suitable to civic concerns in an increasingly complex social and economic structure. With the demise of "deficit spending," and growing public awareness that the appalling nature of inflation requires new approaches to welfare, civil service salaries, pensions, and other categories which the New Deal had hoped to settle for all time, a new Progressivism could take shape to cope with them. A new muckraking, bold in its analysis, unafraid of offending labor and ethnic shibboleths, could bring to the fore new faces, new pens.

It must, of course, be recognized that dangerous times can inevitably also bring forth new demagogues, answering not to national necessities but to group prejudices. But a strong Progressivism would be able to take the initiative from them, as Franklin Roosevelt managed to do during the early years of the New Deal. It is difficult to know how to characterize that era, in terms of Progressive traditions. We must make adjustments in our thought for change: new times highlight different social characteristics requiring recognition. It is true that survivors of the older Progressive era had generally found New Deal tenets distasteful. And, though the New Deal brought some excellent muckraking of potential fascists, there was less journalistic boldness and enterprise in exposing some of the more doubtful aspects of communism.

In any event, just because the 1930s involved conditions which were not precisely like those of the 1900s, it served no social purpose for New Dealers to derogate the Progressivism of a Theodore Roosevelt, a Beveridge, a Borah, a Norris, without at least giving them full credit for their own varied accomplishments in law and principles. It does no good for us to scorn an Upton Sinclair, a Tom Lawson, a David Graham Phillips, without studying over their words and determining whether we have better ones for comparable situations. In some cases, we have. In other cases, I say, having reviewed the muckraker's words and considered such strictures as I have seen offered, we have not done better, either in method or actual results. Here is the record. You may judge it for yourself.

Over the years I have learned enormously from the muckrakers and their fate. I have shared with them the splendor of their lives and hopes, when they were familiar faces and names to the generality of citizens. I have traced the erosion of their reputations. Upton Sinclair thought that those who died before World War I caught us in its toils were the lucky ones. They departed on the high tide of their faith in American social creativity. They did not have to live to observe, or join in, the aimless gyrations of their fellows in the 1920s which followed American exhibitions of moral righteousness and military victory.

Certainly such a writer as David Graham Phillips—only partly a muckraker, and no muckraker at all following his great muckraking *coup* of 1906—was spared the foolishness which "critics" accorded his work, and the docile acceptance by academics which was generally accorded their "criticism." Upton Sinclair is now in the hands of bibliographers, but there will in time be biographers. Lincoln Steffens already has one, and will have more. And there will be still other biographers for both muckrakers and Progressives, revealed in all their old energy, their old faith in American purpose and potential. One hopes their humanity will not be passed over.

There is always the maverick, the unbought, the curious to turn over old propositions and clichés and study them anew. Such a person will derive much from the muckrakers and Progressives, and pass on new attitudes and perceptions about them to us. They were such a varied lot!

THE MUCKRAKERS

THE WAY OF A CRUSADING LIBERAL:
A COMPOSITE

HE *was born in the Eighteen Sixties, anywhere in the West—
the Midwest, perhaps—where the pioneer had driven stakes and
set about building a city. He was raised in the shadow of momentous events. In his boyhood he felt the tide of immigration rising
about him, and watched the endless building of houses and breaking of new ground. Here he became conscious of large, rude enterprise, of industry, immeasurable and complex, always developing,
restlessly on the move.*

*The boy was of good native stock, of intelligent and hard-work-
ing parents, who brought him up simply, on the old principles of
plain living and high thinking, to respect his elders and do his
work. He did his chores, played, read. He felt inspired by his
early studies in American history and listened attentively to the
tales of those who had served in the War. He accepted Lincoln
naturally as the greatest of the latter-day gods.*

*He was soundly educated and as he grew up, cherished literary
ambitions. Being young and radical in his college days, he was
thrilled by Mark Twain's work and thought it much more important than his professors believed; Walt Whitman, on the other
hand, was a strange experience, a perplexing problem in esthetics.
Like most Western children he had been aware of politics almost
as early as his cradle days, and now he learned to argue the tariff
question and to discuss the greenback and anti-monopolist theories.*

*After college he faced the question of a career. He wanted to
write literature but drifted inevitably into journalism, which was
alive and offered more chances for work. So far as he could judge,
the magazines were practically impenetrable. So he became a newspaperman and was sent about to report the news of the day. Enjoying a first-hand view of contemporary America, he was deeply impressed by the great factories and ships and railroads, the incoming*

3

droves of immigrants, the big city's slums, strikes, and wealth and poverty elbow to elbow. These things were far from literature, but they were life; they were real; and they destroyed forever his youthful desires for the Free Life—life after Murger and the Latin Quarter. This new America needed description and explanation, and perhaps even reform; it was a bad, splendid America; a serious, farcical, gaudy, unsophisticated America, seething with new thoughts and new problems.

Alert and intelligent, our journalist looked deeper than the ordinary man into these things, read widely to acquaint himself with modern political thought, tried to understand the forces working beneath the exterior of American life. Meanwhile he married, lived regularly, worked hard, found little time to squander. He attempted serious writing. He traveled in America mostly on business, and went to Europe to admire the emblems of age-old culture and maturity that were in evidence on every hand. The system and economy that he saw there he wished his own country, too, could show. Yet he loved home and was jealous for her. There were many things he should have liked to say on this score, but he found them hard to formulate in the usual way—the way of the best magazines and books. Some of his ideas sounded, even to him, frightfully serious and quite unprintable.

Our liberal was intensely nationalistic and individualistic, yet watching the steady growth of the corporations, the octopus-spread of railroad power, he tinkered with thoughts of government ownership and regulation. He could see labor's point of view, its need for unified action; he was sympathetic with the problems facing reformers. As for religion, his work and habits allowed him little time or inclination to carry on with the church as his fathers had done, and he thought of it chiefly with disapproval of its unprogressiveness, its tendency to cling to reaction. If the world of affairs was changing, he felt that the church, too, should be modernizing its ways.

With the rise of Theodore Roosevelt, the young journalist gave himself wholeheartedly to the new movement for exposure and reform. These great days kept him busy from morning to night. He bloomed; his powers were free and absolute. An eager public accorded him a hearing, praise and honor, and money. He redoubled his efforts, writing the facts of contemporary life in the style that journalism had developed for him: a clear, bold, straightforward style, concerning itself with facts and figures. Only a few years ago "elegant" qualities had been prized in the literary man; our journalist-reformer sent them into the discard overnight.

He surveyed the "reconstructed" South, visited the factories and townships of New England, explored the far corners of the West and the Territories. He described the men and managements of the great industries and painted vivid pictures of the methods by which they operated. He reviewed the history of the country to find out how we had come to the age of trusts and corruptionists. He recounted with approval the efforts of the new social worker, the new reformer and statesman. And his articles made news that no one could resist reading.

The "muckraker," for so he soon came to be called, dealt with facts and not with theory. Whatever it was he concluded about business and the theory of capitalism—and he reached various conclusions—he made sure to give the facts and details about his subject. He described a lynching with realism, probed the psychology and history of the Rockefellers and Goulds, told intimate stories of the Tammany machine. Conservatives called him a sensationalist; critics and writers in the old tradition, whose stock had fallen low, accused him of being a mere journalist. In his "blue" moments, he was inclined to agree that he was a journalist; but then he would conclude that whether he was or was not, there had never before been such journalism as this.

He began writing novels, essays, and pamphlets, contributing to the unprecedented deluge of reform literature. Though the old school deplored his "pandering to popular taste," he persisted in his work, defiant, and confident of vindication by the "people." For the "people" seemed to understand; careless of whether his work was art or not, they read it eagerly. And the muckraker was satisfied. "The best cure for the evils of democracy," he used to assert, "is more democracy." That was his faith and guiding star.

It seemed, finally, that everything had been described and everything exposed—at least, as much as was necessary. "What are you going to do about it?" Tweed had once asked a New York he had plundered. That question was still worth attention, and our muck-

*raker was still a young man in this second decade of the twen-
tieth century. Sometimes, however, he decided that he had done
his work and retired from the scene. Sometimes he became a Socialist. But more usually he continued to free-lance, standing on
the neutral ground that remained in the new age of outright pro-
union radicalism opposed to stand-pat conservatism.*

*Invariably he supported the War. What else was there to do?
He had time and again declared that America was self-sufficient
and did not have to embroil herself in foreign quarrels. But here
was war, and Junkerism had to be crushed. The persuasion of the
war-machine was irresistible.*

*During the War, our muckraker became better acquainted with
international affairs: now they were his; they had to be taken seriously. He hailed the fall of the Czar with delight, but the second
Russian upheaval was the greatest shock of his life. He had been
able to understand violence under the monarchy as being the desperate resistance of a people tyrannized beyond endurance. But
the Bolsheviks—conscious, intellectual, ruthless—inspired the deepest revulsion.*

*The muckraker emerged from the War days more than ever a
lover of democracy and yet unsure of himself in the new order of
things. He discovered that he was considered outmoded by lively
young men who took him for granted and rather condescendingly
approved his past exploits. They seemed to think him a naïve sort
of person for never having concerned himself with Freud and for
having had no experience worth discussing in Marxism. They forgot how much toil and struggle had gone into his crusades, for
there was now a New Literature, extremely impatient of the old,
which concerned itself with nuances and art. All this was disappointing to the muckraker, for he had once hoped to receive some
recognition among the literary men, or at least among sociologists
and historians.*

*Sociology and literature, in fact, had been carefully separated
since the days of the magazine exposés. The young men who practiced both no longer addressed themselves to the middle-class;
they were intellectual in a new way, pouring their scorn over Babbitt, who had once been Silas Lapham and who had known of
Emerson and Thoreau. The middle-class now remembered nothing of American thought and art but Eddie Guest and "Fra" Hub-*

bard. And to its foot-loose intellectuals there was nothing to reform—or, more accurately—no sense in trying to reform anything.

The ex-muckraker—for now he was truly a figure of the past— established himself comfortably with a corporation or a university. Or he remained his own master. He wrote a few books, served on a number of commissions requiring sane, informed men, thought of Woodrow Wilson with respect and some sadness. To his eyes times became stranger and stranger, a little silly, a little incomprehensible. For now, during the Twenties, there was this fabulous, not entirely satisfying prosperity.

Then came the boom, a cataclysmic crash, and fearful darkness. One tried vainly to see through it, to understand, to help answer the worried questions that filled the atmosphere. The old American heartiness and optimism vanished. One saw gesturing messiahs springing into prominence like dolls. There were riots and strikes that suggested mechanized war. And when one looked about the world there was nothing more inspiriting. One tried to evaluate Russia, itself in convulsion, and to sum up Mussolini; Hitlerism rose like a tidal wave over Germany. Trouble seemed endless and eternal. Somehow, it seemed, we must all go back to school; but there was as much to unlearn as to learn.

Troubled and reminiscent, the ex-muckraker concluded that the old days had been best, that there had been deeds to do and that they had been done. As for today and tomorrow—America was still home; we were still Americans. Perhaps it would all turn out well. . . .

I. THE AMERICAN PLAN

MUCKRAKING came suddenly, unexpectedly, upon the American scene. At the moment when it emerged the nation was apparently in better political and economic order than it had been for years. After all, 1902 was not 1896, when Bryan all but captured the country with a radical program he had borrowed from the Populists. McKinley had been triumphantly re-elected in 1900, and the country had voted support to his domestic and foreign policies. A war had been won, and new territories with it. Capital-labor relations were apparently amicable. Capitalist and worker had even got together in the National Civic Federation, with Hanna, the boss of the Republican Party, as President, and Gompers, the head of the American Federation of Labor, as Vice-President. Nor were the magazines disorderly. There was, of course, B. O. Flower's *Arena*, which was shamefully radical, but the rest of the magazines had only one aim: to be interesting. Their articles and stories were rarely exciting or controversial regarding deep-lying social issues.

Now, suddenly, there appeared in certain magazines a new, moral, radical type of writing by men and women who yesterday had been entirely unknown or had written less disturbingly. These writers savagely exposed grafting politicians, criminal police, tenement eyesores. They openly attacked the Church. They defended labor in disputes which in no way concerned them personally, decried child exploitation, wrote pro-suffragist articles, and described great businesses as soulless and anti-social.

These writers, using the most sordid details to make their points, shocked and bewildered the conservative reader. So far as he knew, they were supposed to be merely writers; it was no business of theirs if someone's factory was a firetrap. He preferred to read his magazines for relaxation, not for argumentative lectures. To the common people, however, the new writing was as gripping as it

9

was educational: they had never known that business and politics could be so interesting. Responding to their rising interest, a dozen magazines were soon competing for popular attention with newer and more vivid exposés, in which they named names and used photographs in order to establish the truth of their claims. Popular magazines had been born twenty years before; now, with this new means of stimulating circulation, they multiplied and grew mature overnight, and infected even the staid periodicals with their new theme.

Reading some of the surprised and indignant articles by respectable people concerning this new writing, one might have thought that nothing had ever been written before in a rousing, critical spirit. Those who felt that magazine standards were being destroyed and literary style ruined by what was evidently a growing fashion, sardonically termed the new writing the "literature of exposure." For its emergence they found many causes, particularly the "yellow" journalism which had been created by men like Pultizer and Hearst and Scripps. Some blamed the new President, Theodore Roosevelt, for the advent of these magazine reformers, holding that he was a radical and an encourager of radicalism. Another theory was that this sensationalism was a craze, an accident, a natural offshoot of Socialist theory and Democratic practice. But whatever the cause there was no denying that the public—not merely scattered, discontented workers and reformers, but the great, ordinary middle-class whose goodwill every business and every political machine had to win—wanted these exposés.

Times were certainly different! It was only thirty-odd years since the Civil War had been fought and won, and already there was talk that sounded to older minds less American than European. It was true that those few decades had been packed with unprecedented events, but grown men educated in the old traditions could see no good reason for social changes. The Republican Party had been the banner-bearer of the Union; it still headed a nation which despite cranks and calamity-howlers had grown stronger, greater, more powerful than any other country in the world. Conservatives remembered when a radical had been a fierce, peculiar individual: if not an anarchist, then some sort of Westerner, obsessed with aims utterly inconsistent with reality.

But now perfectly decent people were approving of caustic articles about men who were the very pillars of society, and were even willing to write such articles themselves. They took extreme stands on the problems of organized government, not in company with sound thinkers, but with Socialists, Single-Taxers, and others who stood outside the pale. What had happened that the American way was no longer good enough for them?

Since the Civil War there had been no such storm of social criticism as this. It was still the mode among Republican orators to make long, ornate speeches on the virtues of the Republic; it was still the style for Republican journals to fly off into ecstasies concerning our glorious past, our glorious present, our still more glorious future. And these spokesmen for our destiny still held their listeners and readers, for the Republican Party was believed to rest on rock—America's ability to increase its population indefinitely and provide it with unlimited opportunities.

The old nations of the earth creep at a snail's pace; the Republic thunders past with the rush of the express. The United States, the growth of a single century, has already reached the foremost place among nations, and is soon to out-distance all others in the race. In population, in wealth, in annual saving, and in public credit, in freedom from debt, in agriculture, and in manufactures, America already leads the civilized world.

That was how Andrew Carnegie, just sixteen years before, had begun an exultant book dedicated *to the beloved Republic under whose equal laws I am made the peer of any man, although denied political equality in my native land.*[1] This book had excited a good deal of attention and had been, in fact, praised as one of the books of the year. Dissenters had not liked its clumsy style; some had found its extreme jingoism distasteful—but there was no denying Carnegie's facts. These were still, insisted the Republicans, the realities. Carnegie might have arranged details of his picture for what he considered patriotic purposes; his army of figures might require revision. But his argument was sound: America *was* rich; it undoubtedly held more opportunities than any other nation in the world. Socialists were welcome to sneer

[1] *Triumphant Democracy: Fifty Years of the Republic,* Charles Scribner's Sons, New York, 1886.

to their hearts' content; England, if she wished, could scorn us
as barbarians. There was indeed a great deal still to do in America, but for the present critics were unwelcome. In good time
America would develop her culture and clean up crime and corruption.

The Republicans and their supporters merely reproduced Carnegie's state of mind. The "American System," now in full operation, was individualism at its finest. It called for an intensive exploitation of national resources and the industrialization of all
America, and for the protection of self-development from foreign
interference. No sober man was going to concern himself with welfare work, factory and mill regulation, immigration, prison reform. Like civic leaders of years past, the Republicans warned
against too much kindness and charity, since these encouraged the
poor to remain poor. Prosperity lay in promoting railroads, digging mines, working machinery: such pursuits should attract the
most capable men in the country. And the American who turned
his eyes the other way was no more than a crank.

It is not to be supposed that the reformer-journalists whose
writings were so discordant with Republican optimism categorically
denied the achievements and promise of American civilization. It
is nearer the truth to say that the indignation they expressed was
a measure of their pride in the nation and their awareness of forces
that were endangering her well-being.

During the post-Civil War years the national economy had experienced an unprecedented orgy of expansion. The Homestead
Act of 1862 had opened free lands in the West to settlers, and
after the War thousands of Americans had poured westward to
prepare the frontier for industry and civilization. The completion
of the Union Pacific in 1869 and the extension and modernization of other roads had at last made the Far West truly a part of
the nation. The matchless natural resources of the West had been
quickly tapped by the farmer, the miner, the stock raiser, the lum-
berman and the oil-well driller. With the multiplication of new
inventions—Philip D. Armour's refrigerator car, the typewriter,
industrial machinery, and office devices—industry and business had
begun that spectacular process of constant modernization that we
know today. In a word, America, which had been no mean power

in the Fifties, had been shooting up to full growth, had become very plainly the nation of the future.

Like the Republican banner-bearers, the muckrakers had been impressed by this evidence of American vitality and genius. But they saw more than this: they saw a nation that would have sorely shocked the Founding Fathers. The new crop of bankers and industrialists that had sprung up during the Civil War days—days which they had found extremely profitable—had been all too often not pioneers but locusts. Men who were making money made enormous sums, but prosperity somehow passed over the heads of common men, and particularly the immigrants who, drawn by the radiance of America's promise, had been crowded into dark factories and indescribably foul slums. The ordinary citizen's feeling that all was not as it should be was shared even by the most discerning among the well-to-do, for they, even more than the less enlightened, realized that the new America had no such statesmen as had served the nation in its infancy. The spoils system had fallen to its vilest level, and despite the efforts of men like Carl Schurz and George William Curtis the stench of corruption arose quite as strongly from politics as from the trust.

The muckrakers were, in fact, long overdue. Decades before, when old Cornelius Vanderbilt was consolidating his railroads in the East, he had been told that he was breaking the laws of New York State, and had demanded in amazement, "Do you think I can carry on business according to New York law?" Evidently he could not, but the scandals that had broken time and again out of the web of high finance had not made better reading for that reason. The plots and machinations of men of his standing had been always so bold as to be not quite believable.[2] In 1869, for instance, Gould, Fisk, and their associates had attempted the flagrant crime of cornering gold, and had effected a partial corner which resulted in Black Friday. Only government intercession had prevented worse damage than was done. In 1872 the oil refiners and producers had been horrified to discover a plot by a few re-

[2] Charles Francis Adams, Jr.'s *Chapters of Erie*, Osgood & Co., Boston, 1871, was a conservative response to the unbridled business warfare which characterized the era. It helps explain the wide dissatisfaction with the new industry on which the muckrakers were able to capitalize.

finers, who included the up-and-coming Rockefeller, to tie up the entire oil industry. Their projection of the Southern Improvement Company, one of the most infamous enterprises of the day, had been an attempt, with the aid of the railroads, to crush all competition. Oil had been discovered only in 1859, had hardly reached its "teething" age, and these men had already tried to monopolize it. The scheme had been smashed, but to what avail the Standard Oil Company, as the muckrakers knew it, stood witness.

Plot after plot, financial and political, reeking with dishonor, had been unearthed during the Reconstruction days. Republican administrations that had taken credit for "prosperity" had been blamed for the spread of corruption, and had pointed to Tammany as an example of Democratic infamy, but that the pot should call the kettle black had given no consolation to reformers. In New York the frankly corrupt Tweed had for a time ruled and although an aroused citizenry had succeeded in unseating him a few had observed that he was only an effect, not a cause, and that his downfall signified nothing—not even that there was a limit to public laxness.

The realization that men like Tweed in politics and Rockefeller in industry were symptomatic rather than isolated figures stimulated the muckrakers, when they finally came, to examine their subjects with care. Those subjects seemed to be simple men of extraordinary boldness. It was easy to understand how they accomplished their vast purposes: at first abruptly and bluntly, by asking and giving no quarter, and later with the same old determination and ruthlessness but with educated satellites who were glad to explain and idealize their behavior. "Nothing is lost save honor," Jim Fisk had said after a particularly sordid deal, and, as the muckrakers soon learned, this was the attitude that informed the principles and purposes of the magnates.

The muckraker realized, too, that the financiers' and promoters' hatred of inefficiency and waste was worth serious attention if not praise, and that few of them were hypocrites in the manner of Daniel Drew. There was, for example, Rockefeller. An early ledger he had kept showed clearly the stamp of the man. In it, he had kept careful accounts of the few dollars he made: how he had given ten cents to the Baptist Church, a few more pennies for a charity, and, meticulously, his other disbursements. Sincerely he cherished, and had always cherished, the pennies and the dimes which he later made famous. But it was not by gathering pennies that he had accumulated his billion, nor was it wholly by industry, diligence and brains. The actual, elemental processes that had produced the Rockefeller and other fortunes included first the arrogant and illegal subjugation of the workingman, the small businessman, and the competitor.

The muckraker could point, for example, to favoritism in the railroad industry. Politics aside, it seemed reasonable that if one company gave a railroad line more business than another, it deserved a lower rate for transportation of its goods, perhaps a secret return on the money which the competitor had paid the railroad, and certainly many incidental favors. But this was only the beginning of a method, ruthless and destructive. It flourished not according to standards of friendship, honor, merit, but on the coldest predatory basis. The rising barons of industry were not interested in the fine shades of ethics that the old-fashioned gentlemen insisted upon. Rockefeller, Armour, Carnegie, and others, using their sheer strength as an instrument of "persuasion," and condoned by the federal government, boldly forced the railroad lines to discriminate in their favor on an unheard-of scale. Railroad lines were cut up into spheres of influence, became pawns in the battle of big business. The ordinary citizen had gradually become aware that a national birthright had been sold for private gain: who owned the railroads owned America, and these super-businessmen owned the railroads. Not only did they threaten the "little" man—the shopkeeper and worker—but the "large" man, the successful man who could not or would not engage in brutal business war, was faced with extinction.

As the liberal crusader looked back over the social carnage of the post-Civil War days, he wondered why the anguish of those who had been under the robber baron's heel—Americans ranging in status from the miner to the defeated oil producer—had produced neither statesmen nor trenchant political critiques, neither poems nor novels—not to mention effective economic action. Periodicals that might have been expected to reflect protest against what was happening in America were still padded with personal reminiscences of the "late War" and with vain attempts to recapture the glory of the great New Englanders—Emerson, Bryant,

Lowell, and other cultured spokesmen of a vanished America. Considering that revolution had threatened during some of these years, considering the magnitude of the railroad strikes of 1877 and 1886 and 1894, considering the bitterness of political warfare —it was of more than passing interest why the nation's troubles should not have found expression in the "best" magazines— *Harper's Monthly*, the *Century*, the *Atlantic*, *Scribner's*. These magazines were "literary"; and their lesser cousins were of the stamp of *Godey's Lady's Book* and *The Police Gazette*. Some social and literary weeklies during a brief lifetime had discreetly regretted coarse commercialism and had reproached the agencies behind it, had even discussed remedies, yet none of them had caused a stir of any magnitude in the public mind.

Muckraking, then, had its precedents. But why, the muckraker could reflect, had these magazine protests—and anti-monopolist feeling in general—been ineffectual?

That answer was that it had been impossible to unite the anti-monopolists. If Americans were still divided on the tariff issue, not yet realizing that the high tariff favored the greatest capitalist; if they were still confused as to the difference between a "good" capitalist and a "bad" one—a point of discussion highly amusing to Vanderbilt, Morgan, and the others—how could they unite in effective action against doubtful industrial practices? In the oil industry those who denounced Rockefeller for his bullying conquests knew nothing, cared nothing about similar troubles in the coal industry, and dissatisfied coal operators were indifferent to what was happening in the oil fields and refineries. The public was similarly divided. One issue had brought some general agreement: railroad carriers should not discriminate against individuals. But that was hardly the basis of a philosophy! And so, even though a victory had been won in the Cullom Act of 1887—an act intended to restrain the railroads—it was soon clear that the Act was even weaker than it had seemed and represented only a Pyrrhic victory. More divided than united, the distraught middle-class had muddled on, hoping for some fairer industrial era in a changing world.

The rages and hopes of those who found themselves thrust back and ruined by corrupt legislatures and "bought" railroad companies were spent in futile appeals to the courts. They banded against the enemy in trade associations and unions—which dissolved as their best leaders and legal talent deserted them. The deserters were called "traitors," but they were well able to ask, "Traitors to what?" For by this time it was palpable that centralization was not to be prevented.

How much bitterness went into the jeers and imprecations of the beleaguered worker and small businessman as they watched the trusts organizing to crush them! Their anger at last produced the Sherman Anti-Trust Act. But the legal profession, finding its kinship with the powerful in industry, quickly developed its legions of equivocating interpreters—Chauncey Depew and John G. Johnson among them—and rendered the Act practically useless. And as the legal battles increased in complexity and number, the general public, so intimately a part of the entire process, so blindly chained to jobs and simple prejudices, looked on in bewilderment.

The American press continued to print, along with its garbled and conflicting accounts of trust litigation, reassurances that America was the land of opportunity. They pointed to the floods of immigrants, the rapid development of the West, the leaping figures for production, export, and import, the multiplying factories —to all the evidence of American vigor and wealth. Visiting foreigners like James Bryce acknowledged their amazement at the unbounded energy and material riches they saw on every hand, and so, in a fashion, confirmed the panegyrics of the newspapers. But such visitors concluded, too, that America was a barbarous land of mounting crime waves, corrupt municipal governments, contempt or indifference toward law and order, *nouveaux riches,* and infertility in literature and the arts. Many Americans could point to immigration as their proof of America's superiority to the Old World; others, in the minority, helplessly deplored the vices of their homeland, not because they loved her less but because they wanted to see her better than she was.

It was the discerning minority that, after the turn of the century, produced the muckrakers—men and women in whom the accumulated indignation and conscience of the preceding decades were finally brought to something of a focus. Reviewing in perspective the failures of the earlier critics, and with a more experienced public to hear what they had to say, they could point their criticisms as never before. If they were long overdue, now at last the times were ripe for them, and ripe with a vengeance.

JAMES FISK, JR.

II. MINORITY OPINION

ALTHOUGH when the muckrakers appeared a strong industrialism ruled, it did not rule unchallenged. Those who complained that muckraking was the result of imported radical theory, stemming from anarchism and socialism, were not acquainted with the facts. America had always known bold opposition to the worse aspects of industrialism, and the most powerful opposition had been the most native. Precedents for protest had been set long before the Revolutionary War in Bacon's Rebellion in Virginia, and after the War in Shays's uprising which threatened the government in New England. In those days, too, a man was free to hold property, as much of it as he could acquire, and to the extent of his holdings, he was free to disregard the rights of his neighbor. Periodic disturbances had been the consequence. As the nation grew and new sources of wealth—markets, concessions, land—were tapped, the lion's share had been quickly seized by the most diligent, the most ruthless, the man with the best "connections," while the ordinary citizen had remained poor. Long before the muckrakers, moreover, had appeared that most ominous of all business phenomena, that breeder of misery and agitation, the periodic crisis.

In the national scramble for wealth the farmers clung to individualism, but the landless, voteless workers in the early days saw the need for unity. The manhood-suffrage movement spread quickly; radical pamphlets and exhortatory journals carried on the bitter and many sided fight. After such disturbances as the popular uprising in Rhode Island, led by lawyer-politician Thomas Dorr, state after state was forced to extend the right of the vote to the underprivileged. With such periodicals as *The Mechanic's Free Press* to speak for it, labor also asked the abolition of debtor's prisons, agitated for free education and for free land in the West; it demanded laws which would protect it in the factories and mills

It made sporadic attempts to found a labor party, and in several cities labor candidates even won elections. In 1834 there was an actual effort to federate all the trades, but quarrels wrecked the enterprise.

In those days agitators for women's rights were vociferous, too, but it was the abolitionists who were the arch-radicals. Others avowed more revolutionary economic aims, but those for whom *The Liberator* spoke focused upon the crucial national issue, thus more popularly representing discontented and contradictory America. Men like Garrison, Wendell Phillips, and Parker Pillsbury not only were violently opposed to slavery but extended their propaganda in behalf of women's rights and the freedom of the press, which badly needed defenders. Abolition also meant sympathy with the Irish in their struggles at home, and the condemnation of liquor-drinking. In Wendell Phillips's case it meant going on, after slavery had been abolished and Garrison had laid down his pen, to see that the emancipated Negroes were not crushed by economic and political discrimination, and to urge general reforms which were sometimes strikingly suggestive of the credo of the First International.[1]

If industry leaped ahead with seven-league boots during the post-Civil War years, labor was no less heroic in its efforts to unite. Many of its programs were worded like manifestoes of rebellion. After several attempts at organization on a radical basis, the Knights of Labor in 1869 won over thousands of workers. It demanded the eight-hour day, equal pay for men and women, workingmen's compensation, a Labor Department, and other "radical" measures. Growing by the panics which continued to strike with significant regularity—in 1866 and 1867, then in 1873, and again in 1882—by 1886 it was able to boast of its 700,000 members.

Meanwhile, in the lawless anthracite regions of Pennsylvania desperate miners took to secret organization and what corresponded to Nihilist tactics in order to preserve their rights. (Here was European ideology with a vengeance!) The "Molly Maguires" were finally broken up by the Pinkerton detectives and

[1] Louis Filler, ed., *Wendell Phillips on Civil Rights and Freedom*, Hill and Wang, New York, 1965.

their leaders were sent to the gallows, but the desperation which the affair revealed made a deep impression upon the public.

Calumny and misrepresentation were the consequence for workers who had been driven to extremes.[2] Nevertheless, strike movements and riots did not abate. The great panic of 1873 brought on many of them, and the breathing spell that followed it only made more furious the railroad strikes which swept up and down the East four years after. In 1886 the Haymarket bomb exploded in Chicago. Public opinion, of course, condemned the anarchists and approved the sentences of death and imprisonment for those who were charged with "moral" responsibility for the crime. But it is important that these tragedies were not forgotten: they continued to serve as centers about which dissenting opinion was able to form itself.

The Knights of Labor in time was torn with dissension and finally dissolved. In its place grew the powerful American Federation of Labor, which was deliberately guided by Samuel Gompers into the path of capitalist-labor conciliation. Gompers wanted nothing to do with radicalism; union meant to him a better means of bargaining. He wanted the union to be exclusive rather than inclusive; hence members paid high rates for the privilege of belonging, and the Federation made little effort to ameliorate the condition of workers outside the fold. It expanded despite its leaders, since in courting respectability it tried to avoid the bitterest issues of the labor question.

The unions were a factor in politics, making deals with Democrats and Republicans alike; but various third-party movements reminded the country that there were crucial questions which could not be settled behind doors. The Prohibitionist Party, begun in 1872, represented the cause of those who thought that "the trouble with America" was rum. The Greenbackers, believing that currency reform would stabilize the national economy permanently, publicized their theories sensationally between 1876 and 1884, and the Nineties inherited these movements of political revolt. The People's Party, running a hardy third in the 1892 elec-

[2] An example of this is Allan Pinkerton's *The Molly Maguires and the Detectives*, G. W. Carleton & Co., New York, 1877. A scholarly survey of the same subject is Wayne G. Broehl, Jr., *The Molly Maguires*, Harvard University Press, Cambridge, Mass., 1965.

tions, electing Congressman and state officials and threatening to establish itself solidly, all but frightened the conservatives out of their wits. Populism sank roots in the West and the distraught South, and sounded more intrinsically radical than it really was. Nevertheless it incorporated radical legislation in its programs. It was highly socialistic and might well be considered as one of the

I SIMPLY DEMAND JUSTICE! WHERE IS SHE ?

AMERICA IN THE NINETIES—A POPULIST VIEW

important forerunners of muckraking as it later manifested itself.

Among the dispossessed there were a few who looked at society with something more than the will to find work. Particularly in the East, and among those immigrants on whose shoulders the oppression of industry had fallen most heavily, anarchistic and Socialistic ideas were sprouting. These workers were not philosophic rebels like Thoreau and Emerson; they were more akin to Johann Most and Emma Goldman, who looked to action. Unlike the Molly Maguires, however, their ideas came from the mature European roots. They gathered support from the immigrant masses who were struggling for a position in their adopted country. But while anarchism must be considered in any serious study of protest, it did not dictate any of the larger social relationships of the time. So far as deeper currents were concerned, it tended to be rather a bogeyman to conservatives than an effective force.

"In my youth," wrote Charlotte Perkins Gilman, the author of the pioneer *Women and Economics*,[3]

the world was full of 'movements,' of an eager massing together to work for 'causes.' There was the Labor Movement, the Temperance Movement, the Woman's Suffrage Movement, the Dress Reform Movement, a general movement toward better methods in education, from the kindergarten to University Extension, and a broad, deep liberalizing of religion. There was the Society for the Prevention of Cruelty to Animals, and another to protect children—the state reaching out at last to recognize the child as a citizen, not the property of his parents. There was the Organization of Charities, steps in Prison Reform and in the Care of the Insane; a demand for right teaching of children as to sex, and for an equal standard of chastity, equalizing up, not down; there was that wide-spread educator, the Woman's Club. . . ."

Yet why was there so little to show for all that liberal and reformist activity? Why did muckraking later succeed it so sensationally?

To one who scans this era of movements it is clear that where a movement had public attention, it was not serious; where it was serious, it was not respectable and could get no public hearing. Among the "respectable reformers" there were too many incompetents, too many well-meaning amateurs, wandering among vague theories and unable or unwilling to see the connection between the deep social problems and the work they did. There were, for example, the Woman's Clubs. The subjects discussed there were so insignificant and the discussions were so inferior that the clubs in time became the object of a withering attack by none other than *The Ladies' Home Journal*, certainly no radical publication. Dress reform was talked about, but even this was not put into practice. "Labor betterment" among the societies was likely to be the merest condescension. Charity itself was so conducted

³ *The Living of Charlotte Perkins Gilman: An Autobiography*, D. Appleton-Century Co., New York, 1935.

that, later, it was a special target for the hatred of the muckrakers, who despised it as a corrupting class-biased agency.

Serious students of American life found little nourishment in the official movements, of which eccentrics and fanatics became the most vigorous and prominent representatives. Those were the days when "spiritualism" became a fashion and when a public that was able and willing to support the sisters Fox was able also to condone such fanatics as Carry A. Nation and Anthony Comstock.[4] Woe to the man or woman who talked realistically about business, politics, labor, or prison reform, or who had the boldness to study the realities at first hand. Like Henry George he might find himself basically at odds with fellow-Americans and suffer intellectual loneliness; or he might be destined for martyrdom like John Peter Altgeld, the great Illinois governor, who was castigated from New York to California because he freed those who had been imprisoned for the Haymarket riot.

America at the advent of the muckrakers already had a full tradition of revolt; yet it had not produced any writer of the genius of Emerson and Thoreau, Whitman and Mark Twain, who could come to grips with the political and economic forces which had engendered that tradition. So few literary reports of industrial conditions were there that Rebecca Harding Davis's "Life in the Iron Mills," printed in the *Atlantic Monthly* in 1861, was still remembered. No books or articles after *Uncle Tom's Cabin* had been sufficiently vigorous and competent to influence political and economic thought and action profoundly. The muckrakers themselves viewed this work as a predecessor of their own. They spoke of "industrial emancipation" as the new rallying cry for all right-thinking citizens, and referred to one or another controversial book by a fellow-muckraker as "the new *Uncle Tom's Cabin.*"

Harriet Beecher Stowe's novel had roused the entire country because the issue it raised, slavery, was national. Other issues, as we have seen, were usually buried in newspapers and periodicals which had few or partisan readers. There was no *popular* literature, and literature of high merit could make little out of the new issues in a civilization more complex than the Abolitionists had thought possible, less easily understood, and hardly controllable. The post-

---

[4] See Gilbert Seldes's *The Stammering Century* (John Day Co., New York, 1928) which treats these and other such figures in detail.

Civil War days did not lack writers eager to attempt serious sociological literature, but truth was not easily snared, nor was it certain to find a hearing when it was captured. Furthermore a writer jeopardized his livelihood when he wrote unconventional accounts of American life.

It was an event, therefore, when Edward Bellamy scored roundly with *Looking Backward*. Socialism had been talked for years, but never had it attracted as many readers as did Bellamy. The reason for this was clear: Bellamy's mechanistic Socialism seemed less dangerous than a Socialism evolved out of labor struggle and revolution; it was also quite an intellectual adventure. *Equality*, the sequel to this book, was less popular because it added thoughtful details to the Utopia already mapped out. What was perhaps Bellamy's most interesting story made no public impression at all: *The Duke of Stockbridge*. This excellent account of Shays's Rebellion offered cogent reasons for its occurrence, but critics who were willing to argue the possibility of a planned state in the twenty-first century were less willing to review the real history of the country. Published posthumously in 1900, *The Duke of Stockbridge* was a contribution to American literature which ended fittingly the work Bellamy had done. Bellamy was a Socialist, but more than that he was a writer with clerical New England ancestors and a journalistic training. As a journalist, and novelist, as a Socialist editor, he foretold the new time, and yet so fast and furious was the age that followed his that it brought forth no account of his life, no analysis of his work. The muckrakers were then too busy making history.[4a]

More important than *Looking Backward* was Henry Demarest Lloyd's *Wealth against Commonwealth*, published in 1894. Lloyd, unlike Bellamy, was no Socialist, although his strong logic and integrity guided him to a thorough understanding of that ideology. After taking his law degree at Columbia and joining the "free trade" movement, Lloyd had gone to Chicago to work for the Chicago *Tribune* as literary editor and, later, as financial editor. As early as 1881, he had written on Standard Oil, condemning it as a public enemy: it was an instance of Howells's courage that

[4a] The best case for Bellamy is in Joseph Schiffman, introduction to *The Duke of Stockbridge*, Belknap Press of Harvard University, Cambridge, Mass., 1962.

he had dared print "The Story of a Great Monopoly" in the *Atlantic Monthly*. Now, after thirteen years, during which he had gathered and digested an enormous amount of material concerning Standard Oil, Lloyd produced his *Wealth against Commonwealth*. In this gripping book was for the first time revealed the intimate details about that giant corporation which had been twenty years a-growing but which, despite its countless lawsuits and conquests, was almost unknown to the general public. In carefully documented pages Lloyd presented his description of Rockefeller's creation and enumerated the crimes by which it had grown—graft, treachery, bombs, corruption—as well as business acumen.

Although eight years were still to pass before muckraking became a movement, *Wealth against Commonwealth* can be regarded as the first muckraking book. It struck no such blow as *Uncle Tom's Cabin;* it was bitterly arraigned, was buried where possible, and was quite forgotten by the time Ida Tarbell's more voluminous history appeared. It was premature. But it did expose the vices of a great corporation, laying the foundation upon which Tarbell was later to build her more famous study. It is, moreover, one of the few books that gave permanent expression to the strong feeling unleashed by the Populists in the Nineties.

Worried middle-class Americans accorded Lloyd all honor, but they were too busy trying to elect Bryan to learn much from Lloyd's book. The times were desperate; there was another unnerving depression, and all the disturbances it produced held their attention. Messiahs were appearing; Coxey marched his army to Washington; "Bloody Bridles" Waite of Colorado made loud and angry appearance at the Democratic Convention; Populists, Free Silverites, and labor leaders filled the political atmosphere with their slogans. But in the end there was little to show for all the protest and enthusiasm. The Populists disintegrated, Bryan lost his election, strikes were broken everywhere. With the middle-class thrust back, with labor pinned down, the great capitalists were now in the mood and able to push forward their enterprises with more aggressiveness than ever.

One of the consequences of their victory was the Spanish-American War, to which millions of Americans were opposed. But

Harper's Weekly was able to report disdainfully [5] that nothing could stop the issuance of war bonds, and that

any attempt of the Democrats and Populists to prevent this action will fail. . . . Now that we are in a war, the people are in favor of finishing it, and of taking all the steps necessary to the speedy accomplishment of that end. Any man or any party that stands in the way is likely to be crushed.

The opposition was crushed all along the line. Not only was the war pushed with vigor, but the trusts, which had been shiftily fighting the defenders of the Sherman Anti-Trust Act, now boldly multiplied; every industry was seized and consolidated. A climax was reached with the incorporation in 1901 of the billion-dollar United States Steel Corporation, which a thousand magazine articles were unable to make understandable to the public. A veritable flood of books about trusts appeared, but unlike *Wealth against Commonwealth* these books were designed merely to acquaint the public with the fact that there was a new king in business, which must be accorded the respect due to companies legally incorporated under the laws of the land. These companies were not "trusts"; they were "holding companies"; and one was challenged to prove that there was no essential difference between the two.

The time had come, then, for a showdown. The issue was clear; the questions that needed answers were clear. What control had the ordinary citizen over the power of the trusts? What rights had the laborer? What position did the government take on these matters? Whither, in short, the American System?

But a forum was necessary for the airing, and established magazines with their established editorial policies were inadequate. *The Independent,* for instance, under Henry Ward Beecher, had taken a virtuous stand on *Crédit Mobilier* government, and *The Nation* under E. L. Godkin had been even more principled, more intellectual in its approach to political and economic problems. Under analysis, however, it was clear that neither periodical would tolerate any question of things as they were: they would discuss effects, not causes. During reform years, they would demand a "clean-up" of crime, but "business" was not to be questioned, "government" must neither interfere nor be interfered with. Gov-

[5] May 14, 1898.

ernment ownership, the sources of wealth, the private lives of public corporations—these things were not to be discussed. The labor leader, strikes, radical panaceas—sardonic quips and contempt sufficed for them. But such questions were just what the public wanted to discuss. And, with a suddenness that startled the "established" editors, the public was offered its opportunity.

A SURPRISING RESULT.

HENRY GEORGE CHALLENGES THE NEW YORK POLITICOS

III. VOX POPULI

IF one wanted to read bold articles on business and politics during the pre-muckraking era, one read the popular press. One of the developments of the Eighties and Nineties, in fact, the rise of newspapers which studied the art of plain speech, and sought deliberately to rouse the public on social questions, was one of the most significant. Those years saw an unending struggle between the independent press on the one side and the Associated Press plus the conservative press on the other.

E. W. Scripps, whom Lincoln Steffens came to regard as one of the two or three great men of his day, built a string of newspapers not out of advertising but out of the pennies of workingmen. His newspapers were openly pro-labor. Scripps himself was a strange, complex man who frankly thought that labor was entitled to all it could get. Although he became very wealthy, he remained democratic in an almost superstitious, American sense. He made his money by fighting the policies of stand-pat journalism. He founded the United Press, which competed with the Associated and transmitted a more liberal type of news than the older service. His papers often lent themselves to campaigns in the interest of good government, and their best targets were, of course, the municipal gangs. In Cincinnati, for example, the local Scripps paper was so inflammatory in its battle to discredit the corrupt Campbell ring that in 1884 the well-known Berner riots broke out and the city hall was burned by an infuriated mob of citizens.

Joseph Pulitzer, another newspaper publisher who made a career by enlisting in the public cause, was the one man able to beat Scripps at his own game. He declared open war on the "idle rich" and the "government of the trusts"; he turned his St. Louis *Post-Dispatch* and New York *World* upon both. By the use of cartoons and violent headlines and startling news stories, he gained a large following among the laboring classes. He was the real creator of

"yellow journalism," and at that time provided the most outstanding example of it. Today we need to remind ourselves that "yellow journalism," now associated with the morbid and sensational,
was once the means by which the general population was educated
to new conditions of life.

In the Nineties Pulitzer and Scripps were left far behind in
the contest for masses of readers by William Randolph Hearst, the
son of a California railroad and mining millionaire. Hearst was a
volatile, erratic young man who had ostensibly made up his mind
to lose money in journalistic ventures. He began with the San
Francisco *Examiner* and then, in 1895, took up the New York
Journal. It was soon clear that he was less foolhardy than he
seemed. Assisted by Arthur Brisbane, whom he had taken away
from Pulitzer, and using every possible trick of demagogy, he
proceeded to fight for a wide circle of readers. His artists made
simple drawings that expressed ideas a child could grasp; the news
pages were made vivid with italics and boldface. The platform of
the Hearst papers—for this newcomer soon had a chain of them—
was the crudest possible attack on "vested interests" and, in fact,
was very much like the conservative's idea of wild-eyed Socialist
propaganda, except that Hearst also played up scandals and other
nonpolitical sensations. Hearst was no Socialist; he more or less
made the Spanish-American War, which no Socialist wanted. Yet
unlike Pulitzer and Scripps he was not obscured by the muckrakers; he became one of them—even if a doubtful one—and
flourished more than ever.

But muckraking was not merely an extension of the work the
popular newspapers had done; the newspapers, in fact, played
second fiddle to the great muckraking magazines. "Journalism"
evidently lacked something that the magazines possessed. Yellow
journalism was able only to stimulate local protest, since it depended for effect on quick reading and looked to quick results. It
was for that reason a good school for the muckrakers, who were
confronted with the task of describing and explaining the nation
to its inhabitants, and who therefore had to know how to present
facts pungently to the popular mind. Nor did training in yellow
journalism produce mere sensationalists for the muckraking corps.
The new reform movement attracted fully informed, fully

rounded men capable of expressing and interpreting large sectors of the national life as they had found it.

Muckraking was literary rather than "yellow." Critics who were bemused by Shakespeare and Thackeray were quick to deny its literary character, and men who opposed muckraking as detrimental to their business interests spent much of their time proving that the muckrakers were mere journalists. Sometimes the liberal crusader, stung, would point to Dickens, who also had been attacked as being no "artist," or he would set up for discussion the whole question of literature and journalism, which question had previously received little attention in American thought. The truth was, at any rate, that muckraking inherited the spirit of the great journalists.

The magazines that provided the forum for the reformer-journalists after the turn of the century stemmed from the enterprise of such publishers as Frank Leslie, who began his work as far back as the Sixties. That decade and those following demanded popular education as nothing else, but media for public enlightenment were hard to establish. Reading matter was then a luxury; the workingman was unable to spare money for magazines, and the magazines themselves offered little of interest to him. As for the middle-class home, *Vickery's Fireside Visitor* and *Frank Leslie's Boys' and Girls' Weekly*, *The People's Literary Companion*, or the ubiquitous *St. Nicholas Magazine* were the representative publications on the parlor table. *Puck*, a truly popular humorous magazine, was born in 1877. *Judge*, established in 1881, and *Life*, first issued in 1883, represented further advances into the domain of the ordinary reader. *Life* in particular took a vigorous course, and it gathered sufficient strength to join the muckrakers during the first years of the new century.

It was into this experimental and uncertain field of journalism that John Brisben Walker, Samuel S. McClure and Frank A. Munsey—men with destinies—groped their way. Three more different individuals would have been hard to find; each achieved his own particular success. Walker, born in Pittsburgh in 1847, was a robust and many-sided man. He attended West Point, and shortly after graduation accompanied the American Minister to China as military adviser, but at the age of 23 he was back in

America manufacturing iron. He made a fortune, lost it in the great panic of 1873 and turned to journalism for a living. After making a start with Murat Halstead, the famous Cincinnati editor, for whom he wrote a series of articles on the mineral industries, he worked his way quickly up to the managing editorship of the Washington *Chronicle*. When that newspaper was discontinued in 1879, he turned to raising alfalfa in Colorado: here he showed the same natural energy he had manifested in all his enterprises and finally sold the ranch for a profit. In 1889 he bought *Cosmopolitan Magazine*, and made it pay.

S. S. McClure, an Irish boy whose family had early emigrated to America, was a contrast to Walker in personality and purpose. After a poverty-shadowed boyhood, which as he later described it resembled nothing so much as a long, slow, hopeless struggle through quicksand, he managed to begin a career. His benefactor was Colonel Albert A. Pope, the founder of the Pope Manufacturing Company and the Columbia bicycle, who made him editor of his new magazine *The Wheelman*, which was later incorporated with *Outing*. Later McClure left the magazine to work in New York at the DeVinne Press, then one of the best in the world, but although he was always fascinated by typography and was one day to make his magazine a model of excellent printing, he had no liking for printer's work. Leaving DeVinne, he took a position with the Century Company. Meanwhile, however, he had conceived his syndicate idea, and it became such an obsession with him that he could not remain employed happily even with excellent employers. He wanted to organize a syndicate to reprint stories and articles in a number of papers at the same time. Without capital or connections, he set it painfully on course.[1]

As an editor and agent McClure was not subtle or aloof; probably this was why he was able to make the syndicate work. But it was not only his literary astuteness that made him a pioneer; it was his democratic method of handling material. He aimed for the large public which Olympian-minded editors had hitherto avoided; he was bringing literature to the masses. Soon he was

---

[1] For McClure's *Autobiography*, a folk-classic which Willa Cather helped him prepare, see 1963 ed., Frederick Ungar Publishing Co., New York.

offering markets to such writers as Octave Thanet, Elizabeth Stuart Phelps, Conan Doyle, Mrs. Burton Harrison, and Brander Matthews. His own tastes in literature ran to Kipling and Stevenson, whom he esteemed much above the *Yellow Book* writers, and he still revered these two when he was later handling the work of a new set of writers, all of them Americans and many of them muckrakers.

While McClure was struggling with his syndicate, a third man pushed into the field. Frank A. Munsey had none of John Brisben Walker's zest for life, none of McClure's "urge," as he put it, to edit the best material possible. A cold, humorless man, he had little purpose other than to make money. He was a New England native who had been born poor, had lived poor, and had nourished the gaudy desires of those post-Civil War days.

At twenty-eight Munsey was a local manager in Augusta, Maine, for Western Union. Although he had never been in New York, he had already made the curious resolution to edit a magazine there. And evidently he had the ability to convince other men of his abilities, for he soon managed to extract several promises of backing from hardheaded businessmen and some hard cash with which to go to New York. It was sheer ignorance of what he was up against that enabled him to move so boldly upon the metropolis. But there he began his magazine on credit. Several of his backers now decided not to risk money on his schemes, and apparently wisely, for *Golden Argosy*, when it appeared, "Freighted with Treasures for Boys and Girls," seemed to have less chance of surviving than any other magazine in the city. Munsey, however, fought for it with every weapon of desperation; he borrowed; he worked incessantly; he himself contributed stories like those of Horatio Alger, Jr., which won juvenile attention. Struggling with debts constantly, he established *The Puritan*, a magazine for women, which later absorbed the old *Godey's Lady's Book*, and also launched *Munsey's Illustrated Weekly*, which in time became *Munsey's Magazine*.

Munsey had no particular intellectual principles; he simply wanted to secure his magazines, and he wanted very much to make money out of them. In 1884, his *Weekly* supported Blaine rather than Cleveland for President for reasons of pure opportunism.

Such tactics, with his tireless efforts, brought results he desired. Although *The Puritan* went under, *Munsey's* continued to hold its own, and by 1887 *Argosy* could report a circulation of 150,000. Then began a decline in his fortunes that kept him against the wall until 1893. It was during this year that he made the coup which secured him above all danger of failure.

Magazines were now all priced at twenty-five and thirty-five cents. McClure, who had in his youth wondered that anyone would pay such a price for a magazine, was ready by 1893 to join Munsey and Walker in the magazine field and to undersell them both. He made up his mind to create something new: the popular periodical, the magazine that would be within the price range of everybody. The year of the crisis might have seemed inauspicious for such a venture, but to McClure it seemed that the time was ripe. He had built a famous syndicate upon nothing but his conviction, and now he was financially stronger and had such friends and associates as John S. Phillips to temper his enthusiasms and look to his budget. With high hopes, therefore, he launched *McClure's Magazine* into the magazine world.

Not only was there a public need for such a periodical, but the time had come when it was financially feasible. The older magazines had been unchallenged because, for one reason, of the costliness of wood and steel engraving. *Century* had been accustomed to spend $5,000 a month on engraving alone, and other magazines had met similar high costs. The development of photo-engraving enabled the publisher to make pictures from photographs, which were cheap, rather than from drawings, which came high, with the result that cheap magazines were practical.

McClure charged fifteen cents for his new publication. Walker promptly retaliated by cutting *Cosmopolitan* to twelve and a half cents; and in the *Sun* of October 2, 1893, Munsey made the announcement that established the popular magazine in America: he reduced *Munsey's* from twenty-five to ten cents.

Munsey's Magazine, [the advertisement continued.] Beginning with the October issue—*now* ready. Why can we do it? BECAUSE we deal direct with news dealers and save two profits you pay on other magazines Yearly subscriptions reduced from $3. down to $1.

This meant simply that the American News Company, which monopolized magazine distribution, had refused to tolerate Munsey's extreme cut in price and that Munsey was prepared to fight the great concern to the finish. His brief and bitter battle was the most important of his life. He fought with a cold persistence and courage that caused some bystanders to admire him and even feel a certain affection for him; for he had been known as a lonely

MUNSEY'S AT TEN CENTS.

MUNSEY'S MAGAZINE at ten cents a copy and one dollar a year inaugurates a new era in magazine publishing. It has come down to healthy, reasonable, rational prices. It has found the substratum—the solid rock foundation. No first rate magazine can ever go lower In England, where labor and material are cheap and where no McKinley tariff worries and wearies the soul—even there no magazine of good grade has ever sold at so low a price as that at which MUNSEY'S now sells. This tremendous reduction foreshadows the end of the old war prices so far as pertains to publications of large circulation.

THE POPULAR MAGAZINE IS LAUNCHED

man of limited qualities. He now exhibited that courage which inspired his general manager Erman J. Ridgway, whose own magazine was soon to tower among the muckraking organs, to write feelingly of him after his death.[1a]

Munsey's Magazine never rose above mediocrity in content. Although Munsey had, as his biographer George Britt wrote,[2] "fitful prejudices against monopolies which occasionally led him into unorthodox paths," he avoided muckraking conscientiously and was among the first to rush out with the premature news that it was dead. *McClure's* and *Cosmopolitan* went on to become magazines of the muckrakers; Munsey only went on to become very, very rich. But he did break the domination of the American News Company, strengthen the common news-carrier, and so open the sluices for popular literature.

[1a] *This for Remembrance,* an appreciation by his associate and friend, privately published, Chula Vista, California, 1926.

[2] In *Forty Years—Forty Millions,* Farrar & Rinehart, New York, 1935.

The aim of these new magazines was to entertain. Although they looked deliberately to large strata of readers for support, they had no sharp editorial differences with magazines like *Century* and *The North American Review*. They aimed only to popularize their ideas. But each of them reflected in some degree the personality of its publisher.

Few editors had the democratic impulses of John Brisben Walker, who was anxious to educate his readers to the new and better things. Like all the pioneers in the field, Walker edited as well as published his own magazine and at times was aided by men of the caliber of Howells. In 1896, as a demonstration of his enterprise, he offered a prize for the automobile showing the best all-around superiority on a run from City Hall Park, New York, to suburban Irvington, where *Cosmopolitan* was published. This was the kind of initiative that individualized *Cosmopolitan*; an initiative, incidentally, that was in the end to draw Walker away from the magazine field entirely.

Walker was a vigorous liberal but, although he was anxious to speak to the people on crucial questions, he did not secularize his magazine; it was for its reflection of live, current thought and events that *Cosmopolitan* had its place. McClure's mind ran along different lines in those years of magazine spadework. He lacked Walker's dynamic identification with life; he was also more desperate. *McClure's* began as the syndicate had—on nothing at all— and the syndicate, in fact, had to support the magazine until it was on its feet. But McClure had that genius, necessary in editors, of finding people who were able to help him advance his plans, and he early found a person whom the magazine seriously needed —one who was in great part responsible for its success.

One day McClure noticed on Phillips's desk a proof of an article signed "Ida M. Tarbell." The article, "The Paving of the Streets of Paris by M. Alphand," impressed McClure so much that later, when in London buying material, he went over to Paris to see its author. Ida Tarbell, he found, was a Pennsylvanian, born in the oil regions of that state. She had been the associate editor of *The Chautauquan*, which was at that time one of the important educational magazines in the country. She had also studied at the Sorbonne and was now planning biographies. Highly impressed by her judgment and ability, McClure saw how much she had bene-

fited from the French historians, who were then far in advance
of the Americans. He invited her to contribute to *McClure's,* and
she later sent him several important articles. Finally, despite the
fact that the magazine was undergoing stormy weather financially,
McClure advanced her money to return to America and join his
staff on a salary basis.

He reaped quick benefit from his new employee. *Century* having begun in November its *Life of Napoleon,* which had been
in preparation for years, and considerable interest having been
aroused in the subject, McClure set Tarbell to work on a short
life that would be profusely illustrated. McClure, a pioneer in the
new use of illustrations, realizing that the public was likely to find
original pictures more fascinating than the most highly priced
"art" illustrations, made the best of the available illustrative material. *The Short Life of Napoleon Bonaparte* was a success, and
it encouraged the editors of the magazine to believe that they
would soon be out of financial dangers.

But it was Ida Tarbell's *Early Life of Abraham Lincoln* that
established *McClure's.* And this was striking, for no series of
articles seemed less likely to succeed. *Century* had been for two
years running an imposing *Life* by Nicolay and Hay, who had
served under Lincoln, had vast quantities of original material, and
were personally famous. McClure had been urged to abandon his
idea of another life of Lincoln. Richard Watson Gilder himself,
Century's editor, was amused by the announcement that another
Lincoln biography was to appear in *McClure's:* "I hear," he said,
"that *McClure's* has a girl doing another book on Lincoln." Under
such auspices Tarbell's story, made vivid with innumerable illustrations, many of them hitherto unpublished, was given to the
public. The results for *McClure's* were told in circulation figures:
in August 1895 the circulation was 120,000, in November it had
risen to 175,000, by December it was 250,000 and still growing.
Uncertainty and dread departed from the offices of *McClure's:*
that publication was now solidly established among the most important magazines in the country.

Home periodicals, too, were experiencing a transformation. The
old-style magazine for women had been made up partly of piety
and partly of misinformation. Modern women, in order to cope

with the complicated problems of the home, needed more concrete and reliable information concerning reality. In the Eighties and Nineties their new needs were beginning to be reflected in new and altered home-magazine policies. The most prominent of the publications that responded to the contemporary desires of the women was *The Ladies' Home Journal.* Begun in 1883, under the shrewd management of Mrs. Cyrus Curtis, the *Journal* opened its real career six years later under the guiding hand of Edward Bok. Periodicals like this might seem at first glance to have been as distant from the profound problems of the country as they could be. On the contrary they were concerned with one of the most serious problems of all: consciously or unconsciously they were instrumental in breaking down the high walls that had been erected by society around women. The radical feminists, in fact, could have made no headway without the help of the women's magazines. *The Ladies' Home Journal* of the Nineties and the first decade of the twentieth century, far from being the same magazine that it is today, was then a power in the process of liberalization.

Edward Bok may have been a simple soul, easy prey for the iconoclast, but the most fanatical anti-Babbitt critic could not have said that he was insincere or unintelligent. The boy who was able to visit Emerson and not forget that it was Emerson's autograph he wanted, despite the pathetic picture the sage made of failed powers, knew what he wanted and would not be moved from attaining it. He had come to America a poor little Dutch boy, and America was very good to him, rewarding his persistence and diligence according to his merit. Where others wasted, he saved; and he held that in America the road to success was easy, that anyone who would leash his appetites and drive ahead was bound to succeed. As editor of the *Journal* he sometimes despaired of finding the writer who could fulfill some editorial need, for although there was plenty of work to do, there weren't enough capable writers. Bok never asked himself the meaning of "capable," but the work his magazine did was good work; and he galvanized the publication with a vitality that women's magazines had never before known. If cartoonists made fun of his department "Side Talks with Girls," surely there were millions of girls who had never before received even such recognition as "Ruth

Ashmore" accorded them. Before Bok's work was done the *Journal,* commenting and advising on every phase of home life, was selling a million copies. Bok was not only gratified but proud that his reproductions of masterpieces of art sold almost two million copies of each issue of the magazine. He was proud of having had Theodore Roosevelt say,

Bok is the only man I ever heard of who changed, for the better, the architecture of an entire nation, and he did it so quickly and yet so effectively that we didn't know it was begun before it was finished. That was a mighty big job for one man to have done.[3]

The Ladies' Home Journal, then, was lively and healthy, and it printed articles by writers of the first importance. Although it later avoided the drive and fury of the most ardent propagandists of the muckraking period, it challenged its readers with several of the most important issues of that time. Its greatest significance for our history, however, lies in the fact that it was once of those publications that, by broadening the circle of popular-magazine readers, prepared the way for the muckrakers.

At the other extreme of these new magazines was *The Arena.* Its editor, Benjamin Orange Flower, was uninterested in modernizing the tastes of the middle-class woman, nor was he intent, like McClure and Munsey and Walker, on being an entertainer. About McClure's age, he had been born in 1859 in Illinois, the son of a minister, had been educated in the public schools and in Kentucky University, and had stayed for a time in the West, drinking in its radical sentiments. He edited *The American Sentinel,* a social and literary weekly, until 1880, and then he went to Philadelphia and afterwards to Boston. There he established *The American Spectator,* subsequently merged into *The Arena,* which he founded in 1889.

B. O. Flower was a scholarly writer who felt that America needed reconstruction; he felt a very personal interest in the fate of the nation and never forgot that his grandfather had founded his home town. He also felt a certain evangelical urge which had once all but caused him to follow his father and brother into the

---

[3] Quoted in *The Americanization of Edward Bok,* Charles Scribner's Sons, New York, 1920.

ministry of the Disciples of Christ. During his editorship of *The Arena* he was a Unitarian and ardently desired a Church that could lead as Christ had led.

Distinctly he was no Socialist: he believed that the very ideas of Socialism were utopian and that revolution could result only in chaos. What was wrong with America, so far as he could see, was degeneration of character: too much wealth had brought about greed and inequality. Americans needed, according to his views, to re-evaluate their ideals and reform their practices, and to understand their heritage of freedom and opportunity. He made no effort to overlook the harsher realities of social life, but for him they did not warrant rebellion; they demanded discussion and education. Flower himself wrote a number of books which were models of this type of thinking and which make moderately dull reading today, with their moral exhortations and battle cries. *Civilization's Inferno, or, Studies in the Social Cellar*, for example, was more arresting in title than in content, even though Flower had not failed to recognize "deplorable conditions existing at our very door which are a crying reproach to the Republic." In this book he thundered against monopoly, modern Fagins, and the saloon as the causes of the poverty he saw in the cities, and thus he unwittingly symbolized the dilemma of the reformer who groped for causes and found nothing but effects.

Flower was less significant for his books than for his editorial work. He edited *The Arena* from 1889 to 1896, when John Clark Ridpath, the historian, and Helen H. Gardener, the novelist, succeeded him, continuing the magazine on the way its founder had set it. Meanwhile he turned to editing *The New Time*, "a magazine of social progress" in Chicago, with the talented Frederick Upham Adams, who invented among other things the electric lamp post and who made remarkable contributions to the radical literature of the time before he finally, in the muckraking period, accepted the trusts as inevitable and became one of their most ardent defenders. Flower was also co-editor with Anna C. E. Reifsnider of *The Coming Age* until it was merged with *The Arena* in 1900. In that year he rejoined the editorial staff of *The Arena* and, in 1904, resumed full editorship.

Throughout these years *The Arena* remained the most influential of all radical journals and yet it is, perhaps, as thoroughly dull in retrospect as it has seemed to latter-day reviewers. "The Woes of the New York Working Girl" by Edgar Fawcett, a typical *Arena* article, compares badly with articles on the same subject which the muckrakers later wrote. There is little to glean from such "controversial articles" as Dr. Eliot's "The Gap Between the Common Schools and the Colleges." The "literary" articles, the discussions of "psychic" phenomena—Flower's special phobia—and the verse are all unreadable today. But *The Arena* was thoroughly dull precisely because it was trying to grasp the "general problems" of the country: this aim was revolutionary enough to place it in the first ranks of radicalism. There was no other magazine capable of attempting the same task. *The Arena* reflects no vivid picture of the Populist Revolt (in which it was highly interested) because it only reflected what was considered significant in the most educated and intelligent circles. Those were the days when Tolstoi's *Kreutzer Sonata* was barred from the mails by the United States Post Office.

But even then there were many articles in Flower's magazine that repay reading. Henry George, Hamlin Garland, Eugene V. Debs, George D. Herron—the Socialist reverend who was later so cruelly immolated upon the spits of newspaper sensationalism—Frances E. Willard, and others wrote substantial articles on subjects that ranged from the single tax to women's suffrage and strikes. These subjects needed airing. Had workers a right to strike? Didn't the strike threaten democracy? Debs's article and others on the subject helped establish the justice of the strike in open intellectual forum.

Professor Frank Parsons, too, who wrote a series of articles in the very best tradition of the coming muckraking movement,[4] was not afraid to advocate public ownership of one of the most powerful of the trusts. It is to be noticed that Parsons's series was later forgotten by those who should have best remembered it. Parsons's work generally caused no national sensation, perhaps because in *The Arena* it was surrounded by too much less effectual work; and so lacked the supportive quality structure of *McClure's*.

[4] *The Telegraph Monopoly* (C.F. Taylor, Philadelphia, 1899) is one of the best productions of this outstanding liberal, who deserves to be known better than as the "founder of vocational guidance"; see Howard V. Davis, Frank Parsons, *Prophet, Innovator, Counselor*, Southern Illinois University Press, Carbondale, 1969.

In *The Arena's* pioneer days the times were not yet ripe for a hard-hitting muckraking content. *The Arena* itself reported with approval that municipal organizations were springing up everywhere in opposition to local corruption. It too hastily commended the "civic awakening" of San Francisco, unaware that San Francisco was very soon to provide an illustration of extreme corruption. And this premature enthusiasm demonstrated the essential fault of the magazine: it believed too much in words—it was too ready to approve the manifestoes of this or that civic federation. Nevertheless *The Arena* was ahead of the times. The word *civics* had only just been coined by Henry Randall Waite, who derived it from the adjective *civic*.

The Arena stands the direct forerunner of the muckraking magazines, and in fact when the time came for genuine muckraking the magazine awoke. It did not become the greatest of the exposers but it ceased being thoroughly dull and became thoroughly readable: it became concrete. Flower's moral fervor was quite as effective as McClure's resolution to be interesting and instructive in plowing the ground for the sowing that was to follow.

IV. T. R.

THE profound truth about triumphant Republicanism toward the turn of the century is that it could not produce statesmen able to control the industrialization of the country. Its Presidents were inadequate and its governors and Congressmen were either pawns or, at best, upright men who were tolerated in the Party because they were ineffectual. The real political rulers of the country were of the stamp of Roscoe Conkling, Tom Platt, Marcus A. Hanna, Boies Penrose—men of personality and strength, "boss" prototypes of the rude industrial conquistadors whom they represented. Praiseworthy men of the quality of Samuel J. Tilden and Grover Cleveland, who were possessed of character and honesty, were in the minority among the "sound" citizens, and they had little understanding of the forces of evil they desired to fight. Tilden led the prosecution of Tweed, but he was not to be found among the opponents of monopoly. Love of honesty and fairness did not prevent Cleveland from breaking the Pullman strike, when it came; and his other decisions were no less colored by class bias: reverence for private property under all conditions was to him a first principle—and Cleveland was a Democrat.

Yet the common man's dissatisfaction during the past years had not been fruitless. Victories in Civil Service reform, the propaganda of third parties, the organizing campaigns of labor, the mounting power of the Socialist Party and other radical groups, these had operated along with other social processes to leash ruthless individualism. So far had opposition to the predatory capitalist progressed that, by the time of the muckrakers, any President of the United States who dared to order troops to fire on strikers would have had revolutionary disturbances on his hands. Times had indeed changed. It was well for industrial peace that Theodore Roosevelt now appeared to dull the edge of labor's bitter feeling.

Calumny followed every President, no matter how drab or mediocre, but in the case of Theodore Roosevelt it reached unprecedented proportions. He was charged with every conceivable crime by gossip-mongers and the extreme reactionary press. He was so openly accused of being a drunkard that he felt constrained to fight the allegations in the open himself. Throughout his campaigns against "the malefactors of great wealth," as he called them, it was generally whispered, among the highest circles of righteousness, that he was insane. To certain influential persons he was an incendiary who was ruining America, and every weapon that might be used to discredit him was justifiable. For conservatives sensed revolution, or at least genuine reform—which was just as bad—and Roosevelt, far from applying force to it, was trying to conciliate it. When contrasted with McKinley, in particular, Roosevelt appeared a prophet of doom to those who clung to the old economic traditions.

Roosevelt was generally held responsible for the appearance of the muckrakers and identified with them, despite the fact that he himself in anger gave them their opprobrious name. A hundred apologists for him have been unable to disentangle him from apparent kinship with the exposers he despised. How incongruous is the notion of his muckraking connections appears from the evidence. Still, it had its logic. It assumed that he had indicted only the "sensational fringe" of the reformers; but that the best of them were literary equivalents of the Roosevelt who wielded the "big stick."

Roosevelt lost stature with the years, but it yet remains to be seen if with time he will resume the stature he enjoyed in his days of triumph. If Roosevelt dominated his era, it was only in the sense that he formed the most outstanding figure for attack and defense. The great social developments of the time made less sensational news. The growth of organizations which represented the diverse needs of a new and complex social order—consumers' leagues and associations for furthering child-labor legislation, social research, housing improvement, and the like—these were not widely publicized. Before anyone was aware of it they were functioning and mature. Labor groups of the modern variety were organized and energized without any assistance from Roosevelt. As for the muckrakers, who formed the very pivot upon which all this social activity swung, they were consistently described in derogatory terms by Roosevelt and those whom he particularly represented.

To show that in these years popular victories—municipal reform, pure-food and social legislation, the exposure of infamy in business and finance, the triumphs of labor, and the rest—involved Roosevelt only incidentally is not to explain the role he actually played. That role is best suggested by a review of the opinions of Roosevelt that were then current.

Roosevelt was seen in three characters. The partisan, purely political opinion of Republicanism and Democracy, both party-bound, was to praise or blame him according to one's political affiliation. The more thoughtful dissident party members, Socialists, muckrakers, and political independents saw a man of mixed qualities. The Roosevelt Cult, to whom the Master's every word was sacrosanct, said "God bless him" whenever they thought of him. These three schools of opinion have passed into history; nothing remains of the passion which marked their differences. It has been the task of Mark Sullivan, who in his day was part muckraker and part cultist, and who subscribed to men of both parties, to weave tenderly the best tribute [1] that all the factions together could have prepared for T. R.—a more substantial tribute, at any rate, than the cultists could have prepared by themselves.

Of all the cultists none was more sincere than Jacob Riis, whose voice of praise was not to be at all embarrassed by the good-natured or vicious fun which the cynics made of him. Roosevelt was to him true Americanism incarnate. For Riis was a naïve sentimentalist who had brought with him from Denmark something of the simplicity and idealism of the Scandanavian fairy tale. At the same time he was a journalist and a man of action who abhorred the dirt and grime of New York City, and was not afraid of confronting the Mauve Decade, which he was otherwise incapable of judging, with it. He lectured and wrote persistently of the dark corners of life in the East Side, and accomplished certain reforms. "The most useful citizen of New York," Roosevelt

[1] In the first several volumes of *Our Times*, Charles Scribner's Sons, New York, 1927-35.

called him, and there was much truth in that descriptive phrase. For Riis, unprofound and unsophisticated, was the typical successful reformer of that time, thoroughly of New York, with no understanding of the nation as a whole and no conception of national policy. The West was still the Far West to him; Populism was not so much a political credo as a violent aberration of Western ignorance; for him social maturity lay in the direction of New York civilization. He had no respect for the "yellow" press, no understanding of such individuals as Henry George, whom he considered beneath discussion. On the other hand, he could not help seeing that despite the best efforts of conservative reformers, social inequalities continued to produce unrest and to rouse the sections of the country against one another. Something, Riis concluded, had to be done.

And here was Theodore Roosevelt to do it, a shining young knight in the habiliments of chivalry, emerged from among the machine politicians! It was enough for Riis, who hated politics and did not care to acquaint himself with its realities, that Roosevelt spoke vigorous words and got things done. For him, Roosevelt was little less than perfect and he followed the man's career with frank delight. As the 1904 election approached, Riis was set to writing an informal biography of his friend and idol. Never was a political tract written with greater sincerity than *Theodore Roosevelt, the Citizen*. It was full of loyalty and conviction that could not have been bought at any price: the biographer, although older than his subject, was never able to discuss him in any other terms than those of reverence.

It was significant that Roosevelt should have had so selfless an admirer as Riis: the very fact described the radicalism which Roosevelt professed better than a hundred essays. Riis innocently gave the game away, for he was out of the running, old-fashioned, of secondary importance, when the muckraking era came; his work was done. The plain truth was that Roosevelt typified the new young man who was succeeding the old in politics. The new young man understood that labor could no longer be ignored, and that the West had to be conciliated, and that the inequalities among farmers and workingmen and capitalists required a new approach, concrete proposals, action. The new young men made no windy appeals to abstractions: that had been the failure of their fathers, who had merely talked while the country was carved up according to the practical plans of industrialists and promoters. Among the newcomers Beveridge, from Indiana, had a quasi-Lincolnian dream of equal justice and imperial glory. La Follette of Wisconsin was gathering forces behind him for a revolution in state politics. In Oregon, U'Ren was building a reform machine that could fight the lumber and railroad interests on major issues; Hiram Johnson was doing the same in California. The senate and the House of Representatives, with these men up and coming, had a day of wrath ahead.

Roosevelt, too, had his principles, and they included first and foremost a strong desire for law and order. Law and order meant two parties, not three. And so, although Roosevelt knew that Blaine, "the plumed knight," was no chief to follow, because of his known traffic with corruptionists, he went along with "the party," that is, the Republican Party, on the candidacy of Blaine in 1884. He went along not with the cold, financial calculations of a Munsey but with sound and fury. Did this compromise make any difference to Riis? It simply proved to him that Roosevelt was not only a man of ideals but a practical man, a man who knew how to compromise at the proper time:

When Mr. Roosevelt's term [that is, in the legislature] was out [wrote Riis], he had earned a seat in the National Council of his party. He went to Chicago in 1884 as a delegate to the convention which nominated Blaine. He was strongly in opposition, and fought hard to prevent the nomination. The outcome was a sore thrust to him. Some of his associates never forgave him that he did not bolt with them and stay out. Roosevelt came back from the far West, where he had gone to wear off his disappointment, and went into the fight with his party. His training was bearing fruit. . . . He did not join in the revolution; the time had not come, in his judgment, to take the isolated peak.[2]

The time never did come—a fact that was more apparent to those who did face the need for doing so squarely than to those who did not. Men took isolated peaks because of bold and personal analyses which they dared to make of social situations. There

[2] From *Theodore Roosevelt, The Citizen.* By permission of The Macmillan Company, publishers.

was never any danger that the Roosevelt who, in his history of New York, could write thus of the tragic draft riots, would ever feel called upon to stand alone:

The troops and the police were thoroughly armed, and attacked the rioters with the most wholesome desire to do them harm; . . . a lesson was inflicted on the lawless and disorderly which they never entirely forgot. Two millions of property had been destroyed and many valuable lives lost. But over 1200 rioters were slain—an admirable object lesson to the remainder.[3]

Riis approved every word of these remarks. He himself had witnessed the riots of 1877 and remembered the deeds of the striking workers with abhorrence. The question never crossed his mind whether there might have been provocation on both sides, provocation of which he had no inkling.

Roosevelt was absolutely honest in his passion for law and order; and that passion masked his political opportunism. Behind his hearty enthusiasm and earnest argumentativeness there was a shrewd political climber whom Riis was incapable of seeing. Roosevelt made a principle of party loyalty to the extent of holding on to Republicanism in its worst phases—its Hanna and Morgan phases. Riis himself quit the Democrats in order to support Roosevelt, and loudly voiced his "dream" that after Roosevelt had finished his "labors" in Washington he should sit "in the City Hall in New York as Mayor of his own city. . . . That year I would write the last chapter of my 'battle with the slum,' and in truth it would be over." Roosevelt, he was certain, would crush Tammany and eradicate the slums of New York. . . . Roosevelt a Mayor, after having tasted kingship! Riis was indeed naïve.

How principled Roosevelt was in the alliances which dictated his policies we can see from his break with the Taft he had been unable to control. Taft, too, was Republicanism as Roosevelt had known it; a little less glamorous, a bit more pompous, but Republicanism. When Taft was renominated for the Presidency, Roosevelt did not go along, as he had gone along with Blaine. This time he bolted to the Progressives who, coincidentally, nominated him for a third term in the White House.

[3] Quoted, *Theodore Roosevelt, The Citizen*. By permission of The Macmillan Company, publishers.

Roosevelt, then, was never the violent radical his enemies called him; he was still less the father of muckrakers and sponsor of Socialists. He was certainly less soundly based intellectually than others of his own time and place and general ideals. Still, he represented an enormous change from the Eastern politician who had so long ruled American government. He was, at least, someone to make a hero of, if hero there must be: a correct and acceptable hero. Roosevelt hunting big game, Roosevelt charging San Juan Hill, Roosevelt denouncing and exhorting, was a forceful and arresting personality. His career in the New York Legislature, as Civil Service Commissioner, as reform Commissioner of Police of New York, and as reform Governor of the State compared well with the histories of the more venal and unscrupulous politicians to which the East was accustomed. And this reformer really reformed. He made principled concessions, it was true; but he would never have risen if he had not done so. As it was, party bosses sought to bury him in the Vice-Presidency. Hanna, going to Washington to witness McKinley's second inauguration, remarked that he was hurrying to see Roosevelt take the veil. T. R. was potent political material.

And once T. R. was President, he presaged trouble. He talked too much; he had too much joy in life. He destroyed all the rubber-stamp dignity that financial America had labored to build up in its figureheads. He had opinions of his own which, to say the least, threatened to interfere with the smooth and usual movement of the politics of state. There was, for example, the affair concerning Booker T. Washington. The Negro leader—no revolutionary figure—had been invited to the White House for luncheon. The occasion had no significance, yet a veritable scream of rage went up with charges that Roosevelt had insulted the entire South. Roosevelt stuck to his guns, realizing perhaps that liberalism was here very much in order. He was, in fact, extraordinarily acute in those matters and rarely made decisions that might really weaken his conservative support. Only three years after, when Maxim Gorki's American visit had been turned into a tragic ordeal by the barrage of lies laid upon him, Roosevelt refused to see the Russian novelist.

Roosevelt was talkative, open, independent, with a gift for vigorous phraseology that was startling and real and as the times gathered momentum these characteristics stood him in good stead. McKinley would never have been heard amid the clamor of the muckrakers; or, perhaps, he would have been heard as Herbert Hoover was heard when crisis came again to America. T. R. *was* heard. He invited the confidence of the journalists, he fraternized with them, and he won in this way the entire forum of the press.

Roosevelt enjoyed one of his great opportunities when the great anthracite strike broke out in Pennsylvania, and he stepped forward to act as mediator. It was a long time since the story of the Molly Maguires had come out of the mines, darkly, as from another and fiercer world. Labor had multiplied, and learned how to behave. The miners had struck in 1900, but Hanna had at that time run to the mine owners and forced a truce so that the disturbance would not interfere with McKinley's re-election. Conditions, however, had grown worse, and in May of 1902 the miners had struck again. Their plight could have been appreciated by less than passionate liberals. So certain was it that they could hold public sympathy that John Mitchell, who was no radical and who looked more like clergyman than labor leader, offered to arbitrate the case. The operators, however, wanted nothing to do with him or his union. They would not recognize the union and they had no intention of raising wages, reducing hours, or providing for the honest checking of coal mined. So the strike dragged on, and winter suffering seemed imminent not only for the strikers but for the city folk who needed coal. The miners having won the sympathy of the public with their excellent organization and discipline, an aroused public now demanded that the strike be settled and justice administered. As the situation stood, the strikers were in position to win; their opponents could win only with the help of strike-breaking government troops—if the public would stand for such intervention.

It was at this moment that Roosevelt stepped in. The operators were outraged and horrified, declaring that this was proof positive that the man was a radical. Riis and others like him spread the word far and wide that the country at last had a great President who could do things. Yet Roosevelt's actual achievement in the affair reveals facts that look neither like the charges of the mine owners nor the praises of Riis. Roosevelt first sent Hanna to George F. Baer, the leader of the operators, with a plea for conciliation. Baer was adamant: he would not give an inch to the union. There was a time-wasting and futile conference in Washington on October 3. Roosevelt then sent Secretary of State Root to New York to plead with Morgan for arbitration. What followed is not too clear. It is said that Roosevelt was determined to send troops to the mines and see that coal was sent out under government supervision, and that he had in preparation an order for the sending of such troops. It has been said that Morgan, under this threat, gave in to Root's pleas. It is possible that Roosevelt convinced Morgan of the senselessness of standing out against public opinion. In any event, the strike ended. There was arbitration and the award included several concessions to the miners but no union recognition.

Whatever labor thought of Roosevelt—and he was called a demagogue from many sides—there was no question as to what the conservatives would now make of him. The country rang with the sensation he had created. But today it is quite impossible to make startling and absorbing his role in the great strike. The sensation can only be "recaptured" as Mark Sullivan "recaptured" it by a furious concentration upon Roosevelt, upon what Roosevelt said, and said he said. Our retrospective interest is in the strike itself, in its demonstration of a power and maturity in labor organization which would, in due course, create its own enigmas.

Much more original was T. R.'s unexpected prosecution of the Northern Securities Company. The Company had come into the world heralded like the United States Steel Corporation a little while before. It was the fruit of a sudden battle in which Hill and Harriman, the great railroad magnates, had become embroiled. These two, backed by Kuhn and Loeb on the one hand and by Morgan on the other, suddenly began to struggle for monopoly of the Western railroads. The violence of the struggle threatened to precipitate a national crisis. To save themselves the combatants finally called the battle off, and a compromise was agreed upon. The Northern Securities Company was organized, representing a division of shares which kept Harriman and Hill still strong and still enemies.

The Company was a gigantic trust, one of the most ambitious of the Morgan projects. When Roosevelt, through his Attorney-

General, struck at it and demanded its dissolution, it seemed as though the trusts, which had been multiplying so quickly since the beginning of the new century, had met a David at last. Roosevelt was actually doing what Bryan and the Populists had promised to do; Roosevelt was a sort of Populist! Again the country echoed with his name, and arguments concerning him waxed hot. Roosevelt was evidently no bluffer: he had the prosecution pushed to a conclusion, and the Northern Securities Company was dissolved. What more could any radical ask?

And yet, seen in perspective, the suit dwindles in significance. Roosevelt never carried out the promise it implied: of the several thousand trusts in the land only the merest fraction received the Rooseveltian rebuff. Several of the most important suits, as we shall see, did not originate with Roosevelt; on the contrary, he served, with full consciousness of what he was doing, as a brake upon the activities of more militant antitrust fighters.

Of the Northern Securities case a number of pointed remarks can be made. Before the suit the Company was in the public consciousness as a vivid reminder of the nerve-shaking duel between Hill and Harriman; it foretold future trouble in the railroad councils; it was known to be seriously overcapitalized; its formation impressed people as a truculent gesture on the part of the big financial interests involved. The prosecution of the case was therefore an obvious necessity and did not require particularly radical motives. Morgan himself was less outraged by the government's action than were some of the smaller fry in the business. Morgan was said to have remarked mildly that abrupt counteraction had not been needed; if he had known that the President was against the combine, he would have been glad to talk things over. At best the suit against the Northern Securities Company was a pledge of further action, further prosecutions under the Sherman antitrust laws: a pledge Roosevelt did not keep.

One could view Roosevelt as a product of social forces. One could show that he had been reared amid wealth and was both cultured and virile; that he was likely, therefore, to dislike brutality and coarseness either from labor or from capital. His ideal would be a kind of benign but firm capitalism that would strive to render justice and make sure, at the same time, to keep all classes in correct order. But Roosevelt was also very much an individual, with a mind of his own, with personal ideals concerning national welfare. He sponsored the Reclamation Act with real enthusiasm. The Newlands Act of 1902 set aside the proceeds of the sale of public lands in sixteen states for use in the development of irrigation. Such measures were due, were demanded, for the bitter competition among the lumber barons and mine operators was laying waste expanses of territory which it had seemed would require hundreds of years to develop, let alone exploit. The nation's soils, too, were being impoverished and eroded away. The long, sad story is being told only now of how the national resources were being squandered.[4] Government intervention was necessary if physical debilitation of the nation was to be checked.

And so again Roosevelt was a radical and a leader of radicalism. The Newlands Act, it was true, took only a step in the direction of control; it left loopholes for recalcitrant capitalists. Roosevelt took not one step toward reclaiming for America any of the numberless acres of which the nation had been brazenly robbed. The muckrakers, not Roosevelt and his followers, were those who told the American people about those facts.

There was a Rooseveltian Era; there was, at the same time, a Muckraking Era, and this was more solidly based in social conscience. From it stemmed the reforming zeal that was to leaven future American politics. The crux of muckraking was the realistic analysis of the deeper maladjustments of society. Future crusaders for pure-food laws would turn for guidance to the muckrakers rather than to the Roosevelt caucus which passed the compromise measures which we shall soon examine. Labor experts, too, turned to the muckrakers for their information, rather than to Roosevelt's National Civic Federation which was a poor substitute for a Labor Department. Foreign-policy experts were not likely to turn to the hero of San Juan for light on peace, nor to the man who sent the American fleet about the world as the emblem of American power, nor even to the arbiter of the Russo-Japanese War.

Roosevelt's mark was, however, inevitably upon all the agita-

---

[4] *Holy Old Mackinaw*, by Stewart H. Holbrook (Macmillan, New York, 1938), one such story, tells vividly how the great trees fell, a billion feet a year. With the donkey engine, the highball, and the double-cut bandsaw the lumberjacks did work that had been better left undone.

tion and reform that attended muckraking and Progressivism. He balanced himself upon that movement; he even managed to represent it at Armageddon. He was, in fine, the Average Man: ambitious, well-to-do (as the Average Man hoped to be), enthusiastic, wordy. Whether the Average Man was poor or rich, Roosevelt's illusions were his. Roosevelt was therefore bound to influence the ideas and achievements of men who were more bold than he, more sincere and principled, who dared to see and think what he could not.

Roosevelt was a promise as well as a fulfillment. The excitement that attended him was mainly the excitement of anticipation. But there was never any danger that T. R. would do more than he promised: he was settled and complete; he did no more than he meant to do. Detached observers who have looked back on the Rooseveltian Era for light to cast on the present and future wonder at the storm and controversy that attended so much of T. R.'s career. But when they examine the records carefully, they are likely to become aware of a gleam of teeth and a flash of glasses symbolizing something intensely dynamic and explaining in part the hold that T. R. had on the citizenry. If he warranted no more than Riis was able to make of him, he warranted, surely, no less. Even those muckrakers who anticipated least from him, who had fewest reasons to accord him wholehearted admiration recognized this.

V. "THE FIRST MUCKRAKER"

THE honor of having been the first muckraker—of having written the first muckraking article—was given by default to Lincoln Steffens, evidently because his *Shame of the Cities* began in *McClure's* one month before Ida Tarbell's series on the history of the Standard Oil Company. In his *Autobiography* Steffens printed a facsimile of the first page of his October 1902 article "Tweed Days in St. Louis," and entitled it "The First Muckraking Article." Steffens was never averse to accepting honor, even though he had his own methods of satisfying a rich and fascinating ego.

But the chronological method of assigning precedence among the muckrakers has not been very successful. Ida Tarbell had been working on her version of the building of the oil trust long before Steffens hit on the idea of his municipal-government stories. And the issue of *McClure's* which contained Steffens's article also contained a long editorial announcement concerning the forthcoming Tarbell series, with a *précis* of its contents that, to all intents and purposes, promised the equivalent of a muckraking article.

This line of thought leads to quibbling: it does not exhaust the question, but only opens it to further inspection. Quoted below is an opinion regarding muckraking priority which takes issue with the most deeply rooted of all the legends that surround the muckraking era; it deserves respect because it comes from one of the most thoughtful of the muckrakers, Charles Edward Russell, and so merits thought. It denies that Steffens was a muckraker in any sense—hardly a tenable point of view, as we shall see, but surely provocative:

The ascription to Lincoln Steffens of the first muckraking article is all wrong. Steffens never was a muckraker at all. He was classed thus only by the University Brahmins that hailed him as one of themselves and distorted the meaning of the term to suit the occasion. Muckraking meant originally the exposure of the rascality of corporations and trusts. The first muckraking article of the muckraking period . . . was written by Henry George, Jr., and published in the *National Magazine*. But [Henry Demarest] Lloyd had long preceded him. How Lloyd's exposé of the Standard Oil Company came to be completely forgotten when Ida Tarbell got the limelight, I never understood. . . .

Exposure of corporation and trust rascality was undoubtedly an important aspect of muckraking, but just as certainly it was not the *sole* function of the movement. Muckraking—and this point must be reiterated—was concerned with the criticism and revaluation of *every* aspect of national life. The crusaders denounced rascality in government just as bitterly as they denounced it in corporations. They produced, moreover, books and articles which were less destructive than constructive in purpose, and which were vital elements of their achievement. If we take this as our understanding of the meaning of "muckraking," Steffens was surely a muckraker and an early one for all that, as the above remarks indicate, he was accorded more honor by "respectable" intellectuals than other muckrakers whose work was equally honest and of comparable literary merit.

The question of priority in the muckraking field constantly raises the question of definition and the attempts of individuals to limit the movement according to their own purposes. Just a short time ago readers rubbed their eyes to see Mark Sullivan assert [1] that he, and not Steffens, had written the first muckraking article. Mark Sullivan a muckraker! Sullivan referred to the article he wrote for the *Atlantic Monthly* in 1901, "The Ills of Pennsylvania," a general diatribe against morals and methods in the Keystone State. In those days Sullivan was actually much less interested in emphasizing his connections with those at whom the term "muckraker" was directed than he was in disassociating himself from them.

Although they often worked together the muckrakers were not organized; they were personal spokesmen for a common impulse. Some were very distinctly muckrakers; others were borderline adherents to the movement. And the muckrakers themselves were not always the best authorities on the subject of membership.

[1] In *The Education of an American*, Doubleday, Doran & Co., New York, 1938.

Here is the suggestive opinion of Ray Stannard Baker,[2] one of the most authentic of the reform writers:

I note that you quote Steffens to the effect that the first muckraking article was in October 2, 1902. But look up two articles of mine, one in *Collier's Weekly*, November 30, 1901, on "The Northern Pacific Deal," the other in *McClure's Magazine*, November 1901, the leading article, entitled "What the United States Steel Corporation Really Is and How It Works." . . .

Reading the two articles, however, only emphasizes the question: What was a muckraking article? For Baker's writings impress one as being even less frank and less "new" than were the generality of muckraking articles in that year. His articles did not attack the two trusts in question; on the contrary, they were respectful and even partial toward them. Baker's opinion as quoted here throws light on his attitude toward his work as a whole.

Baker, certainly, was less the muckraker, at least at first, than Steffens. Steffens was the outstanding example of the "acceptable" reformer—a leader and innovator. But there were still others who might legitimately have laid claim to having preceded Steffens in the muckraking field with contributions motivated by reform ideals.

There was, for instance, Edwin Markham, whose poem "The Man with the Hoe" was one of the literary sensations of 1899. Bailey Millard, editor of the San Francisco *Examiner*, heard the Oakland school teacher recite it at a private party. He was so impressed by the few lines that he was able to make out above the din that he asked to hear it at another time, and alone. In the end he gave it such appreciative hospitality in his newspaper that it was picked up by the other Hearst publications and flashed to world fame.[3]

The almost savage success of this single poem, which called forth innumerable commentaries from preachers, statesmen, and men of letters in every part of the globe, showed the true temper

[2] From a letter to the author.
[3] This poem takes on new perspectives in my *The Unknown Edwin Markham*, Antioch Press, Yellow Springs, O., 1966.

of the people who were supposed satisfied with good times and imperialist conquest. "The Man with the Hoe" was praised and quoted and reprinted. It was hailed by educators and critics as the greatest poem of the century, and one of the noblest poems ever written. Today we are free to comment that this major poem of Markham's was of lesser stature than the highest praise accorded it. It is no less true that it is a good poem, drawing its strength from social considerations of the first importance. Markham was a muckraker not only in poetry but in his eloquent reports concerning social evils that needed attention. Because of the fate that overcame those of his generation, in reputation he lived on to become, not a teacher and inspirer to the young, but the man who had written a single poem.

Another early muckraker of the first importance was Finley Peter Dunne. A native of the Midwest, he was a Chicago newspaper man and one of the "White-chapelers"—a group of brilliant young journalists who were to go far in the next years. They included George Ade and Opie Reed, Alfred Henry Lewis and Frederick Upham Adams, and Brand Whitlock—talented men who were learning life at first hand and had things to say concerning it. By 1900 Finley Dunne was already famous for his "Mr. Dooley" articles. He wrote about trusts and government with an impudence that few writers would have dared to attempt; his own "Mr. Dooley" was of a social class—that of bartender—that only a bold journalist would have introduced to the American public. Dunne succeeded with his disreputable philosopher because he was able to make his readers laugh—as Beaumarchais had made the royal court of France laugh with his *Marriage of Figaro*. Such a comparison would have seemed far-fetched in the days when Dunne was making his reputation, but he too was a genius, and his articles too were firecrackers that turned out to be cannonballs.

Here is what he wrote about the crushing of the Philippine insurrection by American troops in 1899:

"Whin we plant what Hogan calls th' starry banner iv Freedom in th' Ph'lippeens," said Mr. Dooley, "an' give th' sacred blessin' iv liberty to the poor, downtrodden people iv thim unfortunate isles,—dam thim! —we'll larn thim a lesson."

People laughed. When Bryan and Senator Hoar and other anti-imperialists were bitterly attacked for denouncing America's colonial methods, Dunne found a welcome in every home for his comprehensive comments on American policy, foreign and domestic. Since it was not possible to tell people to stop laughing, the fiction spread that he was innocuous. Mr. Dooley, however, continued to make his observations and voice his opinions, and it became more and more clear that he was not on the side of the "angels." He appeared with Steffens and Baker and John S. Phillips when they left *McClure's*, finally, and took over the *American Magazine*, for reasons which will appear. By that time "Mr. Dooley" was an unshakable institution; there was nothing to do but accept him.

Finley Dunne helped to relieve some of the strain attending the hard years that preceded muckraking. When that avalanche began, he was with it, was part of it, and served to temper some of its intense if fascinating seriousness. Dunne was all things to all people, but the man who could suggest a book entitled *Alone in Cubia*, to be written by Roosevelt, and who could write so deadly a sketch on poisoned meat, was more worrisome in certain quarters than the most conscientious reformer.

Dunne suggests a characteristic of the magazine reformers generally: despite the violence and thunder of many of their works, they were simple and hopeful men. They planned no diabolical revolutions. They had no super-theories concerning the world situation: they were likely to think of the French as irrational and the English as dull, and of the Germans as over-regimented. They liked America, considered her the greatest of all the nations; they felt that we could settle our problems, with a little patience. They discerned no good reason for our participation in a war, since America appeared to be self-sufficient. The only real difficulty they saw was that of keeping "our capitalists" in line and making sure that they avoided foreign entanglements. Their naïveté accounted for the height of their indignation when they discovered evil; it also accounted for their certain and devout faith in the remedies they offered, remedies which they were convinced would bring peace and plenty to all.

This characteristic is illustrated in the remarks of John Spargo,[4]

[4] In a letter to the author.

then an outstanding Socialist educator who disliked sensationalism and was angered by the idea of being labeled a muckraker:

> The things we were advocating were not advocated with a view to overturning the capitalist system. All that we wrote might as well have been written by an earnest Christian trying to apply Christian principles to a very definite and serious human problem.

Religious earnestness did not endear Spargo—who was a muckraker, whether he thought so or not—to those who insisted that the principles of free competition and individualism were not to be tampered with by insolent writers. Fanatical conservatives condemned everything that interfered with traditions. No matter what the motives of the writer were, the fact that he dealt with revelations was enough to damn him. And the public was less interested in whether a writer was a Socialist, and in his theories, than in the story he had to tell.

Another early liberal crusader of proportions was Frank Norris, who, in his article "The Frontier Gone at Last" helped to popularize [5] the fact which the historian Turner had demonstrated ten years before. Norris, more an artist than a publicist, portrayed in *The Octopus* the great dilemma of the West, the irreconcilable conflict between the railroads and the farmers. *The Pit*, which he published in 1902, contained stirring pictures of the Chicago Exchange and represented one of the sources of the purely literary activity of the muckraking movement. Frank Norris died young, in 1903, a forerunner of the new time—in the spirit of it, but not actually part of it.

The case of Mary E. Wilkins showed how quickly sociological literature matured in those days. In 1900 she attempted a "labor" novel [6] set in New England, with lamentable results. It was hard to recognize the conscientious artist that she was in the worthless story she wove.

Marie Van Vorst, who was vastly less talented, did better a few years later in her *Amanda of the Mill*. Unlike Mary E. Wilkins, she had acquainted herself personally with some of the elements of manual work. During 1902 she and her sister, Mrs. John Van

---

[5] In *The World's Work*, February, 1902.
[6] *The Portion of Labor*, Harper & Bros., New York, 1900.

Vorst, ran in Wanamaker's *Everybody's Magazine* a series of articles entitled *The Woman Who Toils, Being the Experiences of Two Ladies as Factory Girls*. These articles, published the next year in book form, excited controversy at a time when new and arresting books were appearing day after day. Although it is now completely outmoded, the book remains a landmark of importance: it was pioneering. For these two "ladies" had really worked: in a pickle factory in Pittsburgh, in a clothing mill in New York State, in a shoe factory in Lynn, Massachusetts, and in a Southern cotton mill. They showed, not unforgettably but clearly, that workers who were women if not "ladies" were subjected to treatment that would have been shameful even if they had been men. The facts were known in some social circles but they had not before seen print; and what was not in print, no one had to imagine or trouble himself about.

The Woman Who Toils contained all the characteristics which stamped the genuine muckraking book: personal experience, a moral concern with underlying social factors, and a sympathy with labor. These appeared in a somewhat under-developed form, but they represented muckraking. Some other, deeper work did not. When Jane Addams, for example, penned an article in *The Annals of the American Academy* on Chicago's housing problem, she was not muckraking: her article was simply a wise and practical report by the guiding genius of Hull House, and one of the products of the new sociology, which such pioneers as Mary Richmond, Edith Abbott and Jane Addams herself were creating. The stamp of muckraking is clearer on the work of Ernest Poole who, when he wrote on the rent protests then taking place on the East Side of New York, and who suggested municipal ownership of tenements, wrote because as a resident of University Settlement he was in close touch with the poor and their problems, and because he was a writer who wanted to express himself. His work was muckraking—and a kind, incidentally, that was somewhat stronger than that of the Van Vorsts. Poole later visited Russia and assimilated a radicalism which fulfilled itself in *The Harbor*, a story of strikes along the New York river front that was one of the best to come directly out of muckraking. Like many others, Poole, though he continued to write, was finally lost in the changing currents of time.

Among the poets, novelists, critics, journalists, and professional reformers who helped to span the years from Populism to muckraking, and who foretold the emergence of the latter, was Ernest Crosby. He was a typical figure of the transition and one of the most gifted. His life has a special significance because it might so easily have become something other than it was. Crosby might have become a "goo-goo" like the early Roosevelt—that is, a defender of the existing order who skirted the more serious implications of liberalism. Crosby chose a more difficult way.

Like Roosevelt, he was born in New York, in 1858, the son of a wealthy and well-known divine. He graduated from New York University and the Columbia Law School, and was presently admitted to the bar. He interested himself in Republican politics, served eight years in the National Guard, and in 1887 succeeded Roosevelt to the New York Legislature. During President Harrison's administration he was named a judge of the International Court in Egypt.

So far his life had taken standard shape; and since he was distinguished-looking, impressive with his beard and mustaches, quick-witted and brilliant, there was no reason why he should not have gone far in conventional success. He might have become a governor, or a Supreme Court justice, or the author of a dozen seemly books about the future of America, or the past of America, or the legal interpretation of justice. He was, in a word, the kind of man whom success seeks out.

But during his stay at Egypt, Crosby happened to read a little book by Tolstoi called *Life*. What happened to Crosby after that experience was something that happened to many people during those crucial years: Tolstoi's words changed his life in a day; the old career and ambitions ended immediately. Crosby read other works of the master, and these carried him to other seminal literature. He visited Tolstoi at the writer's home, and the two men liked each other and became fast friends.

When Crosby returned to America, he was a changed man whom his friends could hardly recognize. He threw himself into a multitude of activities. He helped to establish the Social Reform Club and became its first president. He interested himself in settlement work, aid to immigrants, neighborhood development; he devoted time and effort to the furtherance of international peace, industrial conciliation, vegetarianism, and free speech. Following Tolstoi, he was a "non-resister"; following Henry George, he propagandized for the Single Tax. All the while he was quite good-humored about his long list of causes, laughingly declaring that his aim in life was to reconcile all of them. But he was sincere, and his efforts led him like the links in a chain into countless centers of progressive activity. He knew fierce and determined Socialists, who were prone to criticize him for having so wide a circle of interests. There were conservatives who, resenting his apostasy from respectability, dismissed him as a man who had not kept his wits about him. But Crosby was manifestly generous and capable, and he won thousands of valuable and co-operative friends.

His lasting work, however, was his writing. He began hesitantly but soon, finding his stride, was producing essays and books notable for their clarity of style and their pungency. Militarism was his particular *bête noire*, and his writings on this subject were among the best that the time produced. *Garrison the Non-Resister* was an arresting reminder to those who had begun to apotheosize the abolitionist, forgetting that he had also been a radical. *A Precedent for Disarmament* shrewdly reminded the public of the pact—a model for friendly relations between nations—which had been agreed upon by the United States and Canada after the War of 1812. His best book on this subject was *Captain Jinks, Hero* which he produced early in 1902 as his antidote for the rising American imperialism. This novel precipitated considerable deserved comment. A long, witty satire on war in the "Cubapines," it showed delightfully that the best soldier was inevitably the robot. Captain Jinks himself, aspiring to be the perfect soldier, suffered mental collapse because he could not convince himself that, on command, he would readily shoot his own wife. Crosby left Jinks in the insane asylum, perfectly happy with lead soldiers to maneuver and, as the doctor said, perfectly harmless.

In the same year Crosby published a truly original work, his essay on Shakespeare.[7] This established a principle of dynamic

[7] *Shakespeare's Attitude Toward the Working Classes.* The Mason Press, Syracuse, N. Y. It has been generally thought that the germ of Crosby's idea came from Tolstoi's famous criticism of *King Lear.* The fact is that Tolstoi was inspired to his work by Crosby's essay.

literary criticism that was to increase in importance as the old, stultified writing was pushed aside and fresh, significant work took its place. Shakespeare's "universal sympathy" had encouraged the notion that "impartial calm" was necessary to the Highest Genius. Crosby showed irrefutably that Shakespeare had been anything but impartial and that, on the contrary, he had been very much a man of his time and had ridiculed the lower classes mercilessly. So unconventional was this thesis that it never became popular, exercising its influence only at second hand. It did inspire a thoughtful essay by George Orwell on Tolstoi.

Crosby also wrote poetry, and here followed after Whitman, as his friend Horace Traubel was doing, although several of his most successful poems were written in more conventional meter. It was fortunate for Crosby that he was well-to-do and able to dispense money to organizations instead of calling on them for aid. Whitman's ideas were winning ground slowly, and Crosby was destined to pioneer for them rather than to fulfill them. As he wrote,[8]

> This is the kingdom of God,
> As if one should cast seed in the ground,
> And should sleep and arise, night and day,
> And the seed should spring and grow up,
> He knoweth not how, for the earth,
> Bringeth forth fruit of herself.
>
> Thus would I sow to the winds
> Broadcast the seed that may bear
> Fruit in the harvest to be.
> Others may raze and destroy—
> Tear down, demolish and waste;—
> Others may frame and construct,
> Fitting together the stones,
> As they think, of the city of God.
> Mine be the lowlier task,—
> Mine be the dropping of seed
> In the long, silent furrows of earth,
> Where she bringeth forth fruit of herself.

His articles and poems were scattered through countless periodicals. For several years he edited his own journal, *The Whim.*

[8] In *Broadcast*, Funk and Wagnalls Co., New York, 1905.

He wrote for Michael Monahan's "pure art" *Papyrus,* for Louis F. Post's Single Tax weekly, *The Public,* for *The Arena, The Comrade,* and many other publications.

Beside the books already mentioned Crosby wrote a number of others, all richly suggestive and educational. His several books on Tolstoi gave first-hand versions of the master's educational work and ideas, and he acquainted the American public with the ideas of Edward Carpenter. He also wrote one of the few accounts we have of the life and work of the great Toledo mayor, "Golden Rule" Jones, whom he himself had introduced to Whitman's writings. Crosby associated himself with good men, influenced them, was influenced by them, and then wrote articles and poems spreading his happy and stimulating message of a good time coming. He willingly admitted that he was a dreamer, but thought himself one of a new kind of dreamers who were appearing on every side: the kind whose dreams come true:

> You may choose to fight if you like
> To skirmish and strike—

he said. Some people wanted action, and nothing but action; poems and essays were just "talk" to such people—"talk" that got nowhere. That writing, too, is action was a new idea, one that never quite got itself understood, by a generation which was producing a great deal of writing-as-action, but too little of it in genuine poetry.

Crosby meant well, but in poetry he was too much like "Petit, the Poet" as later limned by Edgar Lee Masters, himself unfulfilled in the Progressive era:

> Seeds in a dry pod, tick, tick, tick,
> Tick, tick, tick, like mites in a quarrel—

Crosby's message was better than Petit's but less well expressed than that of a true poet-Progressive, Vachel Lindsay, as in his unforgettable tribute to the dead Altgeld as "The Eagle that Is Forgotten." The era gave Lindsay a choice of poetry or Progressivism, and he rightly chose poetry. Crosby had less of a choice to make. Adjuring tragedy, he filled his eyes with visions of "fighters and workers," marching with banners and streamers to a promised land.

As he said:

So I choose to be a dreamer—
A dreamer whose dreams come true.[9]

This writer was obviously a poet and will be counted as such when open-eyed reviewers re-examine the muckraking period.

Crosby was not a poet in the sense of Edwin Arlington Robinson, then just emerging out of darkness and obscurity. But he shared a spirit without which no movement can subsist. Muckraking had, among its genuinely literary personalities, such disparate figures as Finley Peter Dunne and Crosby.

Crosby died suddenly in 1907, leaving a host of friends and admirers who felt keenly their loss. At the Cooper Union memorial meeting a galaxy of tributes was paid to him. Howells, Tolstoi, and William Lloyd Garrison, Jr., wrote feelingly of him. Hamlin Garland and Abraham Cahan, among many others, spoke highly of him. Edwin Markham read an original poem of his own composition, "Crosby Called Back." Labor unionists, muckrakers, and social workers praised him.

There were others writing "before Steffens" who made reform contributions to the magazines of the time. David Graham Phillips, for example, wrote unusually bold articles; later he was to be responsible for one of the great muckraking achievements of the entire period. Phillips was more interested in developing his creative powers, and it was only reluctantly and for duty's sake that he stole time from his novels to do his magazine work. But he developed the muckraking novel—the novel whose theme was the reconsideration of American mores and ideals—to its highest level. There was also Brand Whitlock who, in his *The Thirteenth District*, gave such a frank picture of American politics as had not been known before. *The Honorable Peter Stirling*, by Paul Leicester Ford, which had been sensational in the decade before—being based on the career of Grover Cleveland—was faint and shapeless in comparison with Whitlock's study.

Still others there were—reformers and near-reformers—who helped to shout down the walls of reaction. In the pre-muckraking days not all of them were hard at work, however, in demolition. Samuel Hopkins Adams was well content to write miscellaneous articles with no particular purpose; Charles Edward Russell was doing likewise, except that he had left journalism and was settling

[9] From *Swords and Ploughshares*, Funk and Wagnalls Co., New York, 1902.

comfortably into a literary career. And similarly with others. Some were "before Steffens"; some were after him.

But if muckraking was a national movement which roused public opinion and concentrated it, and was modern in the sense that it explained public error and prescribed for that error, then yet one other writer, one of the strangest of them all, one of the most extraordinary, must be mentioned. Josiah Flynt might be considered more than any other man as legitimately the first muckraker or magazine reformer. He was, in fact, so considered when he first came over the literary horizon. Once the movement was stabilized, much of his glory was taken from him; he was set down with those who were not to be considered as performing a public service but were rather setting themselves outside the pale of respectability. The frankness of his autobiography, coupled with the details of his death, completed his fall from critical grace. The word about Flynt became Hands Off. Flynt's books are today read respectfully by scholars who are unaware that their author was ever anything but a scholar himself—a sociologist, perhaps, or a criminologist. Flynt was neither of those: he was just barely a muckraker—the first of the modern muckrakers.

VI. "CIGARETTE"

JOSIAH FLYNT WILLARD came of a family and station which from the beginning guaranteed him opportunity and place in the world. He was born in 1869 in Chicago, where his father was the cultured and wealthy editor of a liberal newspaper. Frances Willard, temperance leader and feminist, was his aunt. The general future of an ordinary boy with such antecedents might not have been difficult to predict.

This boy, however, turned out to be anything but ordinary. He was small, but handsome and intelligent, and also extremely individual and self-willed. While still a child, he took to going off on excursions by himself: he simply went away as any boy might dream of doing. "Running away" was not an uncommon phenomenon among boys, but the realities of "the road" were usually disillusioning and terrifying. Not so for Josiah. He took naturally to such adventures, returning home only because he was not yet weaned from it. It was never long before he was off once more for another experience into the surrounding country.

His tramping was not all idling under trees on well-kept farms, nor did Josiah find a lack of fellow-wanderers. Those were days in which the homeless and the vagrants were multiplying: between 1870 and 1880 economic changes had doubled the number of workless and lawless on the open highway. There was no known method of dealing with these uprooted individuals except to throw them into the infamous police "lodging rooms" or to keep them on the move. Types of hobo and habits of hobo life were developing faster than observation could record them. Child tramps, occasional workers, and degenerates were all growing in strange permutations, and being falsely or inadequately reported. The trains swarmed with tramps; alarming legends and stories were told of their number and ferocity. Cases there were in which trainmen who challenged them—or failed to challenge them—were fallen upon and literally torn to pieces.

The roads were not safe, as this growing and well-favored Josiah soon learned. But they held a fascination for him and he returned to them again and again. Each time he was wiser than he had been before, and bolder in his dealings with the criminals and tramps who were his companions. Fortunately for him he was a born actor and mimic and was able to conform to the ways of the hobo society. As it was, being small and slight, he was always in danger among people for whom brute force was a ready resort. Several times, Josiah narrowly escaped injury at the hands of vicious tramps who suspected him of not "belonging" or simply did not like him.

Josiah's personality was soon marked by these escapades. Neighbors, aware of his predilection for running away, shook their heads when they saw him going off to school, clean and impenitent; they distrusted him and prophesied that he would come to no good. His own family tried to prevent this trait of vagrancy from taking root; they tried to understand him, to win his confidence. His father was impatient, but his home life was otherwise happy, and his environment was much above average. Why then was he so set on interrupting the normal course of his schooling and associations? His parents could not understand: something simply drew the boy away. Josiah later tried to formularize that "something": he called it an insatiable longing for The Beyond. He loved to see new places, to meet people as they really were when stripped of conventions.

The Willards tried to "settle" the boy in many ways. They sent him to the country to experience farm life with friendly and congenial relatives; they tried to get him to pledge his obedience; they kept watch on him. And all in vain. He was always slipping away—a small, not strong, but agile and clever boy who could not so much be called headstrong as persistently self-willed. Early pictures show his luminous eyes, humorous yet somehow shy for all their aggressive intelligence. He later wrote lucidly of these years, but the man no more truly understood himself than the boy had. There was more to his lust for tramping than the apparent need for novelty.

Josiah at any rate had no liking for academic life: it impressed him as unreal and gave him no satisfaction. He managed nevertheless to finish secondary school and enter an Illinois college. Then he was off again on the road. This time he was arrested and put into a reform school for having expropriated a gig, and in that "school" he first experienced the bestial stupidity of the penal system as it was before reform broke upon it. The experience was sobering, and for a time after his release he applied himself to regular living.

He went next to Europe to attend the University of Berlin, for at that time one thought of German universities when one thought of education. Josiah, however, never took his degree. Instead he was off again first on jaunts, then on serious enterprises, acquainting himself with Europe as he had already done with America— that is, without money or clothes, and in company with tramps. He became intimately acquainted with the dregs of German society and French society, of Russian and Italian and Swiss. His ability to adapt himself to strange situations was amazing. Friends later told how he could take them with him to the slums of a city, then change completely before their eyes merely by shifting his gait, altering the movements of his hands and eyes, and talking rapidly in a strange, unfamiliar language. It was, in fact, at such times that he became creatively alive; he was otherwise a quiet young man, unassuming and attentive to others, who never thought any thoughts but his own.

Wandering over Europe, Flynt did not fail to pay visits to various famous men—among others, to Sala, the journalist, and to Kuropatkin, whose revelations concerning the Russo-Japanese War were later a great sensation in *McClure's*. He talked with Ibsen and Tolstoi, then sacred to serious young men all over the world. Many of these young men later wrote reverent accounts of their visits to the masters, but Flynt's memories of them were unique: more than the other youthful visitors he appreciated the giants, esteemed them, honored them; and yet he was remarkably impersonal about them. They were not so much great men, great thinkers to him, as they were extraordinary people; and he was always interested in seeing extraordinary people.

In London he became acquainted with Arthur Symons, who was already famous. Two more opposed types than Symons and Flynt would have been difficult to imagine: one was a lover of words, an intellectual; the younger man was all realist, caring nothing at all for books, loving life and particularly the seamy side of it. The circles in which Flynt's personality and talents flourished were such as Symons could not have cared to see. Tramp life was raw and grim; poverty and vagabondage in Montparnasse was a very different sort of thing. Yet Symons and Flynt enjoyed one another's company and became friends.

By this time Josiah Flynt (when he began to write he dropped his surname) was recognizably the man who was soon to make his place. Small and gnomelike, with independent ways, he was very much a man of the world. He was known in two circles: that which accepted him as the son of distinguished parents, and another which thought of him as shiftless and as socially lost as itself. The latter knew him as "Cigarette," a brilliant young man who would sometimes appear with strangers from the respectable world, out for excitement, whom he evidently meant to fleece. Flynt seemed to live easily the dual existence which Dr. Jekyll and others had found impracticable, and it enriched his mind with a wide variety of experiences.

Through Symons, Flynt was in contact for a time with the leaders of the English literary and artistic movements: men like Dowson and Wilde and Aubrey Beardsley, heading cliques which were to be highly esteemed by Americans of the next generation. These men were Stylists, and America had no Stylists; yet Flynt was not particularly impressed. He respected them perhaps even more intelligently than some of his countrymen could, but he was also an intimate of the underworld, and he knew some things of which these intellectuals had no inkling. A great figure of the English decadence meant no more to him than did some living, breathing thief with whom he drank and talked in some out-of-the-way dive.

After Flynt became famous it was hard for people to understand that he had not merely gone slumming in those early days. "Cigarette" was actually part and parcel of the men and women who formed the separate category of the homeless and outcast. He was one of them; as hard and cynical as they were, able to drop his culture and habits of respectability as though they were masks. When he went among them he became no more than an outcast himself, whether in England or on the Continent or back home in America.

But Flynt was as intellectually alive as was "Cigarette." As early as 1894 he was writing and publishing sketches of tramp life in *Century*, *Forum*, the *Atlantic* and other such magazines. Arthur Symons, in the characteristically thoughtful introduction he wrote for Flynt's autobiography, told how he struggled with his friend to get him to write naturally. In Symons's opinion Flynt never really developed a literary style; his work would live only as supreme documentation of a strange and significant career. But neither Symons nor American critics were then aware that the future of "English" prose was as much with the Americans as the English, and that the subtlety which the English were then cultivating was not so portentous as they imagined.

Flynt may have written, and learned to write, the hard way; if so, almost nothing he wrote betrayed the effort. His clarity and economy are remarkable. When he issued his first book in 1899,[1] he was already writing with a firm, sure hand, even in the earlier essays. That book made him famous overnight. It introduced a new type of writing and experience with which criticism hardly knew how to cope. The introductory studies of tramp life were followed in a second section with sketches of personal travel which were literally infused with experience. Flynt pointed out a fact important to American writers—that academic studies, such as there were, had failed because they recorded the tramp under false conditions, portraying him merely as he sat behind bars and in the workhouse. The tramp at ease in his sordid surroundings really was not different from other human beings: he was good, bad, intelligent, unintelligent. Tramping, in fact, *was just another way of living*. This fact about the knights of the road had implications which left most critics entirely at a loss.

Having become a recognized writer, Flynt was now in position, had he chosen, to be feted and praised. Instead he continued to go off upon extraordinary adventures which he hardly made record of and which came to the public ear as rumor rather than narrative. Flynt was no exhibitionist; writing was writing, and his life

[1] *Tramping with Tramps.* Studies and Sketches of Vagabond Life, Century Company, New York.

was his own. He seems, however, to have worked with the police at one time, tracking down criminals by means of inside information which he alone could get. He also worked as a railroad policeman—this had become a profession since he was a boy—and in this capacity he covered a "beat" two thousand miles long.

By 1900, however, Flynt was ready to change his way of life. He had lived fast and unusually since early childhood, and tramping as such had no future. It was up to him to preserve his powers against ruin, to put them to regular use. He therefore turned to S. S. McClure with a proposition which McClure heard with interest and on which the publisher told him to go ahead.

Flynt had been convening with some free souls at a bohemian center in Washington Square in New York. There he had met an interesting young man, slightly older than himself, Alfred Hodder by name. Hodder was a brilliant university man who had given up academic work in order to try literature and who was also concerning himself with problems of practical reform, as were many alert young *littérateurs* of the time. Hodder was soon to formulate his experiences as an aide to William Travers Jerome, the reform district attorney, in an excellent volume which epitomized the facts of any reform movement, its meaning and its value.[2] At this time, however, he and the famous little Flynt who stood out among them all, came together and wrote a series of articles for *McClure's*.

The series began to appear in August 1900 under the title *True Stories from the Underworld*. Whether it can or cannot be taken as a muckraking series, the announcement in *McClure's* remains of interest:

The following story is the first of a series by Josiah Flynt and Francis Walton,[3] men who have spent many years among the criminals and are known amongst the "profession" as men of their own class. It is needless to say that their life amongst them is not to break the laws, but to understand as thoroughly as possible the motives and methods of that great part of the community which they describe as "The Under-World." These stories are not fiction in the ordinary sense; they are entertaining stories, but more than this, they are philosophical studies, about a class concerning which the great mass of people know nothing,

[2] *The Fight for the City*, Macmillan Company, New York, 1903.
[3] Hodder's pseudonym.

except that they are law-breakers. All the names in these stories are fictitious, but the characters are real and the incidents have all occurred in various times and places. The stories are intended to point a moral as well as to adorn a tale.

The announcement acknowledged what those who were to constitute a muckraking movement were up against: a public that knew nothing about crime except that it was committed. Flynt, with Hodder's collaboration, was breaking hitherto untouched ground, and their spades revealing swarming life where there had apparently been nothing. It was no wonder that the series aroused great interest. It "pointed a moral," even as McClure had promised; but it did more than that: it made very clear that police and criminals were by no means violently opposed. The Lexow investigations, a few years back—a "lid-off" inquiry into New York police corruption—had demonstrated the same fact, but not so clearly and not nearly so systematically. The series as finally printed in book form under the title *The Powers That Prey* gave vivid and enduring pictures of the underworld, not as it existed in fancy but as it really was. "Degradingly veracious," opined the liberal *Nation*, in an ungrateful review of the book.

That year, also, Flynt published his *Notes of an Itinerant Policeman*, in which he continued to develop the momentous point toward which he was steadily driving. He made the flat assertion that

Until the general public takes an interest in making police life cleaner and in eliminating the professional offender and the dishonest public servant from the problems which crime in this country brings up for solution, very little can be accomplished by the police reformer or the penologist.

Why was this so? Because, as he showed, the policing of a city was a far more difficult matter than the reader thought. The police must *of necessity* have deep connections with the criminal class. Otherwise the policeman was of little aid to society; he was merely a watchdog who might or might not be useful at the scene of a crime; he could be of no service in a *systematic battle with crime*. It was lightheaded, in other words, to talk about "wiping out" crime. The business of public-spirited citizens was to develop a potent police system, clean and subject to public control.

This was a shrewd and thoughtful opinion for a man who was no theoretician, who in fact disliked theory and loved life—life in its brutal phases. But Flynt had not written himself dry; he was able to go still further in this difficult task of understanding social processes. In 1901 he scored the success of his career with another series for *McClure's*. This series, which he wrote alone, began in February and was introduced with the following note:

Just one year ago, through an arrangement made with *McClure's Magazine*, Mr. Josiah Flynt undertook an investigation of the criminal classes in several of the leading cities of the United States. These studies were not made to gratify an idle curiosity, but in the hope that they will aid in the movement now in progress to better the government of our cities. For fifteen years, Mr. Flynt has spent much of his time among the vagrant and criminal classes of this country and Europe, living with them under their own conditions. *It is a mere coincidence* [4] that these articles are published just as Chicago and New York are arousing to the need of reform. It should be remembered that Mr. Flynt writes of what he saw in the Spring of 1900, but practically the same conditions exist today.

It was indeed a coincidence, but the need for such work was in the air, just as the idea of a newspaper syndicate had been in the air years before, when McClure had started out to make his career. McClure was an editorial genius; the "coincidence" was only an indication of his ability to scent the needs of the reading public. One short year later he was to announce still another and more epochal "coincidence."

The present series by Flynt was unusual in form as well as in subject: it consisted of interviews with criminals concerning the state of crime. The criminals, under Flynt's expert questioning, and with the aid of his explanations and translations of criminal phrases, appeared to prove that the police were more to blame for flagrant crime in the country than were the criminals themselves. They, indeed, did not believe that the public desired change; otherwise the public would not tolerate, as it was tolerating, corruption among the police.

The World of Graft Flynt called his new book. Most readers had to go deeply into the book before they understood what

[4] Our italics.

"graft" meant. Flynt had taken the word out of the argot of the criminal and with it had enriched the language. His appendix of criminal words and phrases which were expressive of the smooth-running system of crime that operated according to set patterns in

JOSIAH FLYNT

Drawn by Louis Fleming for *Success*, March 1907

all the cities, was as educational as any treatise on municipal government since James Bryce's *American Commonwealth*.

Flynt drew a picture of city grafting as a phenomenon of modern life. He then presented "Chi" (Chicago) as an honest city—that is, frankly corrupt, contrasting it with "York" (New York), which was a dishonest city, the creature of Tammany and hypocrisy. These two metropolises were juxtaposed with Boston, which was a "plainclothes man's town." Flynt interviewed "one who had squared it"—that is, gone "straight." He described the "mouthpiece" system, examined the known thief's expense account and the taxpayer's bill. Finally he made recommendations which looked to a mitigation of the evils he described.

The World of Graft was a choice plum for a book reader at any time, but the time was 1901, and the book really made news. Its material was so novel that it was difficult to believe. It made Flynt nationally famous, and famous to people who were not normally interested in writers or literary sensations. It was read by reformers of every stamp; police were condemned by its evidence, and civic movements were goaded by it to more vigorous action. The outraged New York police were even reported to be hunting for Flynt; the head of the detective division loudly told newspapermen that he was out to "get" the little writer, and threatened what *McClure's* reported with a sense of shock as "the infamous Third Degree." But if they looked for Flynt they did not find him; he was not to be overtaken by any police, for he lived no regular life like that of most New York authors. He was not seen again until the matter had blown over—until, in fact, Jerome had become reform District Attorney.

The World of Graft may safely be taken to be the first genuine muckraking book. It analyzed the police-vice-criminal setup scientifically; it did it nationally, by way of key cities; it incited to reform. This was muckraking and it broke the ground for Steffens and the others who were quickly to follow. Although it was sensational, unlike Steffens's work it did not become a direct force in actual municipal reform as practiced, outstandingly, in Toledo, Cleveland, and Detroit. Steffens was more immediately effectual because he was more civilized than Flynt. Steffens had learned corruption not as one of the corruptors—Flynt was often hard put to extricate himself from the criminal plans of his associates—but as a journalist; his articles therefore represented virtue much better than Flynt's. Where Steffens argued and thought and discussed municipal reform, Flynt remained himself to the end, a waif, strangely objective and apart. Altogether he was less a champion of righteousness than he was an informer. The criminals who spoke out so clearly concerning their class did so in response to the sympathy and friendliness of one who was very much like themselves.

Many who read Flynt's books later, and who accepted him as a pioneer sociologist and a writer of great power, were startled to read how he died. His books, woven of the details discovered by a born investigator, are very plainly the work of a gifted writer. It was not easy to accept the fact that Flynt not merely had associated with tramps and criminals but had actually lived their life, even seen life, to some extent, as they did. But this was the secret of Flynt's genius, and a secret that few realized. Stuart P. Sherman, who was then a young literary man, did see it; although he had no sympathy for Flynt, he understood: Flynt had little hold on life. That accounted for the unique hardness of his personality. For him there were neither sunsets nor flowers, nor thrilling and uplifting thought. When he was in the Orient, for example, he wrote Symons that he had just seen the tomb of Tamerlane: he did not mention it because the sight had inspired him but because he knew Symons would be interested to hear of it. He himself got joy only from the stir of life, the intimacy of people and, particularly, his own people. For all his wide acquaintance, for all his peculiarly wide reading, for all his background and intelligence, Flynt was at heart flotsam.

That was why he was so shy when confronted by the significant things of civilization: they were not for him. And that was why this man, who had dared so very much among the violent and the degenerate that he had been able to paint enduring pictures of them, was abashed completely by love as other men knew it. For years, as his friend Hodder said, Flynt loved a girl of his own "set" and station[5] and never dared to tell her. Once he made up his mind to see her and traveled across the Atlantic to do so—and, in the end, didn't.

Flynt drank; he took cocaine. These habits, his other excesses, and his lack of true psychological integration destroyed him. He made money and fame easily, yet had no principle or purpose in his life that could keep him in sound moral and physical health. He paid heavily for having been "Cigarette": he wasted away. Drink particularly spelled doom for him despite his several attempts to break free from it.

[5] The woman was Clara Clemens, according to his friend Hutchins Hapgood (see *A Victorian in the Modern World*, Harcourt, Brace & Co., New York, 1939).

Flynt wrote several books after *The World of Graft*—stories unavoidably, as it seemed, with the feeling and method of the investigator. In 1906, when muckraking was in full swing and Flynt had competitors in the field, he was commissioned to write exposés of the poolroom rackets. But his powers were failing. It was no longer easy for him to go down into the underworld, mix with the racketeers, play with them, talk with them, and dig out the hidden facts of corruption. Friends, who undoubtedly included the loyal Hodder, himself destined to die soon, helped him to carry through his investigations. His articles were good; they showed the ramifications of the wireless monopoly, its connections with the poolrooms, the betting swindles and the characters who perpetrated them. But the articles were not outstanding.

At the age of thirty-nine Flynt wrote his autobiography [6]—*My Life—Till Now* he called it in its magazine form. He evidently thought at this time that he was about to put away the old life forever: he was writing it up, once and for all. He told of his youth, his travels, the great men he had met, the books he had written: the gist of his life. He planned to go on from there, for when he died in 1907 he was writing a chapter about honor among thieves, in which he aimed to show that it was highly exaggerated in the popular legend.

One friend wrote regretfully that much had been irretrievably lost with Flynt: memories, adventures, observations. The probability is that little was lost. Although the last chapter of his autobiography remained unfinished, he had told it all; he was not moving toward any system of thought. He had cared only for people, not for things or ideas.

[6] *My Life*, Century Company, New York, 1908. Flynt's problems troubled his aunt Frances Willard for years before her death in 1898; see Mary Earhart, *Frances Willard, from Prayer to Politics*, University of Chicago Press, Chicago, 1944, 315, 317, 385.

VII. THE McCLURE IDEA

McCLURE was always enthusiastic about the articles and stories that made up his magazine. Enthusism was his major characteristic. He evolved many more ideas and projects than ultimately found their way into the magazine, and he was always ardently explaining them and following them up. The calm-tempered Ida Tarbell and his businesslike associates, John S. Phillips and Albert Brady—old school friends—were often hard put to keep McClure and his ideas within bounds. The magazine was always first in his heart; writers were only grist for its mills. Even before an issue of it came from the press, McClure was far away looking for new material.

McClure's had everything, so far as its publisher was concerned, and it would continue to have everything. At the same time that McClure was running Flynt's series he was featuring *The Life of the Master,* by Rev. John Watson. He was printing articles by Gladstone, John Hay, Theodore Roosevelt, Edwin LeFèvre, Clara Morris—articles on life in India and England, on the stage, the Klondike, politics, the Civil War, the new world-shaking Marconi invention, and so on forever.

To McClure the new century was only a continuation of the old. He nevertheless sensed change and responded to it. He printed O. Henry's stories when O. Henry was still in prison. His publication of *Monsieur Beaucaire* was a venture that turned out to be a sensational success. He took Jack London in hand and kept him there until the Western Socialist's vigor and independence became too strong. (McClure liked to have people work with him rather than for themselves.) Bruno Lessing, David Graham Phillips, Dreiser, and others appeared in *McClure's* at least once. Yet McClure put a solid foundation under his experiments; these merely emphasized his flexibility of mind, his willingness to try something new. Though he was restless, ever hurrying off across country or to Europe looking for new writers and material, he was the substance of the magazine as well as its reigning genius, and he was shrewd, knowing very well what he was after.

One thing McClure wanted was the facts: these were his obsession. He insisted that his articles must be written by experts in the various fields—experts who could give scholarship to their subjects as well as life. This meant, in actual practice, and particularly in a movement that dealt with material never before developed, that he had to build up writers, to subsidize them while they learned what they were to write about, to hunt for precisely the writer for a particular job. McClure often invested an inordinate sum on the ground of his conviction that one writer rather than another could fill a given assignment—and he rarely lost by these ventures. As it was, he could never find enough writers to satisfy his needs.

All this was true of McClure and his magazine at the turn of the century. Tarbell had become indispensable to him, as much a part of *McClure's* as the editor himself. Now in 1902 he took Steffens from his post as city editor of the New York *Commercial Advertiser* and set him up in the *McClure* offices. That same year he published *The Taskmaster*, by George Kibbe Turner, a book that showed how puzzled and disturbed was the New England journalist by the dilemma of employer-employee relations. Subsequently McClure called Turner to New York and made him editor and staff writer. He made the sturdy, *Sun*-trained Samuel Hopkins Adams managing editor of McClure's Syndicate, and then added him to his small, superb group of special writers for *McClure's*. He commissioned William Allen White to produce for the magazine such vigorous articles as the one on Tom Platt, which caused that New York boss so much discomfort that he threatened to sue the Kansan for his disclosures.

Even earlier, in 1899, McClure had recognized in Ray Stannard Baker just what he was looking for. Baker, a reporter and sub-editor on the Chicago *Record*, had contributed to *McClure's* and *Century* articles which impressed McClure mightily. They gave off an irresistible aura of fact, roundly and unmistakably presented. McClure had impetuously sent off a telegram to Baker, as he had to Tarbell, telling him to come to New York. And Baker, like Tarbell, had recognized the summons and come.

By 1902, then, these writers—from Baker and Tarbell to Turner and White—were producing a new *McClure's*, a twentieth-century *McClure's*, up-to-the-minute and ahead of it. These writers, though scarcely aware of it, were ready to become the spearhead for that movement which was now in the making.

With legend regarding *McClure's* in mind, the reader is likely to be disappointed on seeing a copy of the magazine—particularly if he has had a special "muckraking" legend in mind. Is this the famous periodical—this magazine with its old-fashioned cover illustrations, its worthless verse, its reams of stories and articles having little if anything to do with muckraking? Is this the great trust-busting, reaction-smashing tribune of the people?

One's disappointment can be blamed on the fact that the magazine was never soberly evaluated, was never what some legends have made it. Yet when some final accounting has been made, if the magazine does not loom as the giant of its editor's imagination, it is no less certain to take almost as high a price as the public accorded it. For it expressed the times as few other magazines did. The verse *was* bad—as bad as most of the other "magazine" verse of the day; the fiction and the scientific, historical, and other articles were, on the other hand, productions of quality, and they have been and are a rich source of reference for specialists in history and literature.

Credit for the sponsorship of muckraking does undoubtedly belong to McClure and *McClure's*. Steffens printed his famous *Tweed Days in St. Louis*, already mentioned, in the October 1902 issue of *McClure's*. In the November issue Tarbell began her serialization of *The History of the Standard Oil Company*. For December, Steffens had an article on the world-championship bronco-busting contest at Denver—a subject on which he was an authority, as readers of his *Autobiography* know. That month Tarbell continued her history, and John Mitchell gave the miners' side of the anthracite coal strike.

In January 1903 Steffens contributed *The Shame of Minneapolis*, Tarbell had still another chapter on Standard Oil, and Baker wrote on *The Right to Work*. Three articles—long, detailed, highly intelligent and informed articles—all dealing with labor, capital, and government! No wonder McClure and his colleagues awoke to the possibilities even before the public had a chance to be stirred. An editorial—one of the most important in American magazine history—was printed, calling the articles to the readers' special attention. *Concerning Three Articles in This Number of McClure's,* it was captioned, *and a Coincidence That May Set Us Thinking.* It pointed out that the three articles in question by chance combined to show one and the same thing: the glaring American contempt for law. This was a coincidence, McClure insisted. Yet here was Steffens demonstrating the disgrace of boss rule in the cities; here was Tarbell showing "our capitalists conspiring among themselves, deliberately, shrewdly, upon legal advice, to break the law so far as it restrains them, and to insure it to restrain others who are in their way." And what awful thing did Baker's article reveal? *The Right to Work,* the article was called, and it showed—how unions deliberately and planfully kept non-union men from working!

McClure, at least was aroused: the editorial continued its indictment. Capitalists, workers, politicians, citizens, were all conspiring to break the laws. The courts were for sale to the highest bidder; the churches were asleep or worse, and one of them, it was hinted (Trinity Church), had been compelled to put its tenements in sanitary condition. The colleges? They did not understand. "There is no one else; none but all of us," the editorial eloquently continued. It was for "all of us" to decide whether disrespect for law was to continue; if it did, our liberty was bound to be the forfeit.

With this issue of *McClure's* muckraking was thus created, defined, and set on its historical way. It was not yet called muckraking, and it was to be interpreted differently by different magazines and citizens. But it existed beyond the possibility of dispute: a moral, concerned writing up—or rather writing down—of American ways and institutions and leaders. The people, the middle-class and working-class people, particularly in the big cities and in the West, liked it immediately. They cleaned the newsstands of *McClure's* and clamored for more. And the other magazines, startled, hastened to try to understand and follow this new path which McClure had blazed.

The popular magazines had already been in a state of thorough readjustment and needed only this hint to find a direction in which to develop. *Current Literature* served as one indication of the change which came quickly over them. Formerly a dull periodical

EDITORIAL

Concerning Three Articles in this Number of McClure's, and a Coincidence that May Set Us Thinking

HOW many of those who have read through this number of the magazine noticed that it contains three articles on one subject? We did not plan it so; it is a coincidence that the January McClure's is such an arraignment of American character as should make every one of us stop and think. How many noticed that?

The leading article, "The Shame of Minneapolis," might have been called "The American Contempt of Law." That title could well have served for the current chapter of Miss Tarbell's History of Standard Oil. And it would have fitted perfectly Mr. Baker's "The Right to Work." All together, these articles come pretty near showing how universal is this dangerous trait of ours. Miss Tarbell has our capitalists conspiring among themselves, deliberately, shrewdly, upon legal advice, to break the law so far as it restrained them, and to misuse it to restrain others who were in their way. Mr. Baker shows labor, the ancient enemy of capital, and the chief complainant of the trusts' unlawful acts, itself committing and excusing crimes. And in "The Shame of Minneapolis" we see the administration of a city employing criminals to commit crimes for the profit of the elected officials, while the citizens—Americans of good stock and more than average culture, and honest, healthy Scandinavians—stood by complacent and not alarmed.

Capitalists, workingmen, politicians, citizens—all breaking the law, or letting it be broken. Who is left to uphold it? The lawyers? Some of the best lawyers in this country are hired, not to go into court to defend cases, but to advise corporations and business firms how they can get around the law without too great a risk of punishment. The judges? Too many of them so respect the laws that for some "error" or quibble they restore to office and liberty men convicted on evidence overwhelmingly convincing to common sense. The churches? We know of one, an ancient and wealthy establishment, which had to be compelled by a Tammany hold-over health officer to put its tenements in sanitary condition. The colleges? They do not understand.

There is no one left; none but all of us. Capital is learning (with indignation at labor's unlawful acts) that its rival's contempt of law is a menace to property. Labor has shrieked the belief that the illegal power of capital is a menace to the worker. These two are drawing together. Last November when a strike was threatened by the yard-men on all the railroads centering in Chicago, the men got together and settled by raising wages, and raising freight rates too. They made the public pay. We all are doing our worst and making the public pay. The public is the people. We forget that we all are the people; that while each of us in his group can shove off on the rest the bill of to-day, the debt is only postponed; the rest are passing it on back to us. We have to pay in the end, every one of us. And in the end the sum total of the debt will be our liberty.

MUCKRAKING IS "DISCOVERED"

in content and format, *Current Literature* now brightened up; a little later it absorbed *Current History*, began to have pith and dimensions. It never became a muckraking magazine, but it reflected an excited era of activity, and if it ignored or minimized the portentous doings of the muckrakers in its review of the news, it could not but carry news of the effects of those doings. *Collier's*, hitherto a medium for old Peter F. Collier's subscription-book business, had acquired the scholarly Norman Hapgood, who had made a name for himself on Steffens's *Commercial Advertiser* as an outstanding dramatic critic, and with young Robert Collier, Hapgood had set out to remake the magazine. *Success*, founded in 1897 by Orison Swett Marden, a Dale Carnegie of the time who distributed messages of hope and inspiration, once had printed anything and everything that would catch the eye: quotations, cheer-up poems, success stories of such divergent figures as Lincoln and J. P. Morgan. (Even so it had quickly won several hundred thousand readers.) Now, in 1903, it began to discriminate material, to curb the loose nature of its articles, to carry more weight and substance. *Leslie's*, under Ellery Sedgwick, having celebrated its twenty-fifth anniversary in 1901, set itself to cleaning out the old-fashioned remains of Mrs. Frank Leslie's editorship, with its eye on *McClure's*. And *Everybody's*, which had been merely another of Wanamaker's departments, was taken over by Erman J. Ridgway, the former associate of Munsey, who proceeded to follow suit.

Not all the young, popular magazines in the field seized upon muckraking as a guide to policy, but McClure's discovery was something that could not be ignored, and it became a focal point for the approval or disapproval of the various editors. The January 1903 issue of *McClure's* changed the magazine world entirely in plan and purpose, with McClure and his writers as its recognized leaders.

Since outstanding men abounded on the magazines of McClure's rivals, since most of the great muckraking sensations were produced by those rivals, it remains a question why *McClure's* rather than any of the others should have held its ascendancy in the public consciousness throughout the entire period and why it should have been preserved to memory when the others were no longer familiar names even to the scholar. There was no question so far as McClure himself was concerned: *McClure's* was simply the best of all the magazines. No other magazine spent nearly so much money as he did getting the very best talent and material. *McClure's* articles were above all authoritative, and could be read as the last words on the subjects they discussed. As McClure wrote, in an editorial [1] summing up two feverish years of the new journalism,

> During the past two years, since Mr. Baker began work upon the labor question, he has prepared for the magazine eight articles. Mr. Steffens in a longer period has prepared ten. Miss Tarbell's eighteen articles on the Standard Oil Company have required over four years' time in preparation. Some of these articles have demanded as much time and labor as the compilation of an ordinary book. The writers, indeed, usually gather enough material to make a book, and condense it into the space of a magazine article. None of the contributions of these staff writers has cost *McClure's Magazine* much less than one thousand dollars, and fully half of them have cost as high as two thousand five hundred dollars each. . . . The editors know of no other way of securing for *McClure's Magazine* that high degree of truthfulness, accuracy, and interest which is required for this magazine.

Again the facts. But it was not merely because it gave the facts that *McClure's* was read with approval by conservatives, used as a text by Harvard professors, and became the standard organ of exposure in popular esteem. McClure, whether or not he admitted it, did have a point of view, and his point of view was more acceptable to the respectable than that of other muckraking organs which were no less earnest and no less careful to print the truth. It was the point of view which made *McClure's*, and the most consistent exponent of that point of view was, not Steffens, not Tarbell—though they loomed largest in the popular mind—but Ray Stannard Baker.

Baker, born in Lansing, Michigan, in 1870, studied at Michigan State College and then took courses in law and literature at the University of Michigan. After that he entered upon a career in journalism. When he came to New York he was already practiced and mature. He was a quizzical, studious-looking man with

[1] November 1904.

a high earnestness regarding the meaning and purpose of his work. If he lacked something, it was on the side of humor, but he tried seriously to understand the motives and ideas of the men and events which he reported. He had, for example, traveled with Coxey's army on its march to Washington, and though he considered it a harum-scarum adventure from every point of view, he gave as honestly as he could the composition and purpose of the marchers. Surely he was infinitely fairer than Harry Thurston Peck, who in his *Twenty Years of the Republic* labeled them a band of criminals and marauders.

Baker had the gift of absorbing himself in his subject. For this reason he was able to give fascinating accounts of a wide variety of events, people, institutions and places: the casting of a great lens, Joel Chandler Harris, salmon fisheries, Mormonism, Yellowstone Park. His articles had character. During his best years as a journalist he was known as the greatest reporter in America.

He was very much like McClure himself, in the way he kept traveling about this country and going to Germany, Turkey, and other lands, sending back his excellent reports of men and things. Muckraking, however, asked more of a writer than deftness; it asked a philosophy, and Baker was not without one. He was perfectly aware of the economic and political problems that troubled the land. When he was yet in college, he had read Henry George and been stimulated to further study. He was acquainted with radical ideas of every kind.

In 1899 Baker published *Our New Prosperity*, a book that summed up the boom days which followed the Spanish-American War and the Klondike gold rush. It was written with a disarming simplicity that hardly revealed the vast amount of data and personal investigation that had gone into it. It was a book to warm his editor's heart. It expounded the conviction that "hard times" were but passing phases of the American way and that they were due to human greed and recklessness. The book contained facts in profusion. Yet it showed that Baker had his blind spot. Where was any mention of the labor unions, the excesses of the trusts, and the shame of Southern Negro policy, subjects with which Baker was soon to deal? These were facts, too; but Baker was not anxious to have his faith in American institutions troubled. Masking unpleasant facts with generalizations, he busied himself with a survey that could not but win the approval of respectable folk.

The labor question caught up with him, not he with it; it caught up with McClure, who sent Baker off to report it. And in the eight articles which Baker contributed to *McClure's* on the question, he gave the first authentic picture of labor racketeering that had appeared in print. He composed the picture confidently, with a wealth of detail and personal observation. He made sure not to make it appear the entire fault of labor: capital, he averred, was as much to blame as labor for the damage inflicted upon the "citizen" and the "consumer." He drew the picture of Chicago, caught between the racketeers of the Coal Teamsters' Union and the Owners' Association; of anarchy in Colorado as fostered by the Western Federation of Miners; of San Francisco, ruled by the "labor boss" Schmitz. Invariably both sides of the issue were presented, for Baker was by no means anti-labor. Yet he did betray that he was more deeply worried by the rise of the unions than by the ever-tightening grip of the monopolies.

Labor racketeering was undoubtedly a growing phenomenon. It troubled labor as much as it troubled Baker. Baker, however, dared not consider the efforts labor itself was making to keep its ranks clean. That way lay Socialism! Baker was, in a word, desperately holding on to the middle ground of that Americanism which suited him; and in his first really serious effort to state his position he complained of the menace of labor.

This was a difficult position for an honest man to be in. Leroy Scott's novel *The Walking Delegate*, published in 1905, exhibited more peace of mind regarding labor and labor racketeering than did Baker's articles. But Scott was a radical in politics, a Socialist. Baker was constrained to follow a difficult course of logic until he developed that strange fantasy which enabled him at last to escape from what was apparently an inescapable dilemma.

McClure was less troubled than Baker by that dilemma. He was highly pleased with Baker's work. The old formula sufficed for him: Baker had the facts—all of them, both sides of them, and he had a wholesome fear of a too powerful, too belligerent labor movement. McClure cherished Theodore Roosevelt's remark: "Yes! The White House door, while I am here, shall swing open as easily for the labor man as for the capitalist, *and no easier.*"

Why were Roosevelt and Baker so emphatic? Had labor hitherto had such easy access to the White House? What is certain is that they feared labor, encouraged, might clamor for more attention than they cared to give it. Here was the central reason for *McClure's* success: it was the unofficial organ of the Square Deal— the middle-of-the-road policy. If McClure himself was not like the President, intellectually Baker was: less hearty, more earnest, but no less like him. *McClure's* printed John Mitchell's account of the coal strike, it printed Grover Cleveland's account of the Pullman strike, but it did not print Debs's account of the Pullman strike. Debs was biased.

Myopic conservatives lumped *McClure's* with the more deadly of the muckraking magazines, refusing to study the differences between them. Shrewder politicians and business men, aware that the public desire for reform was not to be ended by a policy of silence or contempt, saw the difference, saw that by and large *McClure's* constituted no serious threat to the established order. If the magazine was virile, it was because corruption was so deeply imbedded in the body politic that even partial investigations into its ramifications brought up startling evidence of disorder. Roosevelt too, as we have seen, was a reformer who could not or would not probe to the bottom of unrest and yet won a reputation for uncompromising radicalism.

Baker's vehement articles did not sound so extreme to reformers as Steffens's municipal series. McClure, however, for a very cogent reason, was quite willing to give Steffens his head in his revelation of the cesspools of corruption existing in the centers of American communities.

VIII. THE SHAME OF THE CITIES

FREDERIC HOWE met Steffens after the muckraker's first municipal-graft articles had made their appearance. In his reminiscences he later told of his astonishment on meeting Steffens. He had expected to see a tall, imposing, worldly type of reformer, the kind who could be expected to make himself at home among thieves and hard-mannered financiers and politicians. Here was, instead, a little keen-faced gentleman with a string tie—an artist, not a reformer at all. This man was, in fact, an artist of sorts. Although during the ten active years of his life that preceded muckraking he was a newspaperman and editor, he always believed that his ultimate work would be novel writing or social philosophy. Throughout these ten years, he debated with himself just what to do when and if he put journalism aside.

Steffens was, after all, no ordinary city boy who had gone to work, no ordinary reformer. The son of well-to-do people, he had spent his youth in Sacramento, or rather, around it; for his remarkable parents had given him a horse to ride and the freedom to do as he pleased. This freedom had been the making of him; it had made him rich in experience and strength, with a wealth that he was to pour out in sunny profusion when he came to tell the full story of his early days.

Steffens was not brought up; he grew—and, growing, drank in the free, varied life about him. He couldn't understand the political corruption to which he was casually introduced at the Capitol, but he remembered it; knowledge of it entered into his personality. He attended a military academy and then the University of California. When he left for Germany to complete his education, he was interested in history, philosophy, and science, in the active, questioning manner that characterized him. Germany was to be a training ground for him, not an end in itself: Steffens meant to bring back something with him to the America he had such good reason to love. And so, though he absorbed himself in art and ethics and studied seriously the methods of Wundt, and though he traveled to Heidelberg and Munich and Leipzig, on his return to America he was perfectly willing to discuss with his father the possibility of entering business.[1] Business, he recognized, was America in a special way, and he wanted to understand America: such understanding would fill out his equipment for literature. But he remained in Europe long enough to marry, to study at the Sorbonne and in the British Museum, and only then returned to conquer his native country.

At quarantine Steffens was met by a stunning letter from his father. The letter informed him that he had received everything in the way of preparation for which he had asked; enclosed was one hundred dollars, which should keep him till he could find a job and support himself. Steffens at once began his search for work, which he finally found with the help of introductions: he became in 1892 a reporter for Godkin's *Evening Post*. Ethics and philosophy and fiction went overboard as he labored to make a place for himself in the esteem of the editors.

Being a reporter meant meeting everybody—business men, the clergy, professionals, politicians, and the common people of the city. Steffens won them all with his personality. He had an air that gave them confidence and, very significantly, encouraged them to tell him what he wanted to know. He was "the gentleman reporter"; it was a pleasure to talk with him. But there was another quality in his makeup that enabled him to succeed with these people and finally brought him to the attention of the nation at large: imagination.

Steffens had a fascinated interest in men and motives that completely individualized him. If the study of ethics had done nothing else for him, it had emancipated him from the conventional habit of dividing people into the good ones and the bad, friends and enemies. His courtesy was more than deference or form: it was his tribute to the essential humanity and importance he saw in everyone. Trying to understand people, he made them feel important. All the while he thought he was storing up knowledge

[1] See *The Letters of Lincoln Steffens*, Harcourt, Brace & Co., New York, 1938.

that would help him in future literary works. Yet he was no scavenger. The attention and sympathy he gave to people was free and sincere; and these people—from "Clubber" Williams of the New York police to J. P. Morgan—appreciated it.

After a period of general reporting Steffens was assigned to Wall Street, where he picked up basic information and put it to good use. He then became a police reporter, and this job revealed to him the police-criminal tie-up. That tie-up was disillusioning, but whereas it would have made the ordinary reporter a cynic, it turned Steffens toward men with a will to fight the rank social evils. He learned to despise the ordinary reformer; the resolution-passer, the club-paper reader, the charity matron who had nothing to offer but vanity and leisure. He became the friend of men like Jacob Riis and reform Police Commissioner Roosevelt and vice-crusader Rev. Charles H. Parkhurst—people capable of causing a genuine stir.

Steffens did not theorize or generalize about what he saw: he was much too busy. But he followed a logic of inquiry that enlightened him beyond many of his associates. The sight of wounded strikers brought in regularly by the police sent him out to the sweatshops to find the reason for the trouble. The experience of talking to Richard Croker, New York's boss politician, humanized the Tammany-ogre for him, made him see that Croker was no isolated corruptionist but an agent of respectable men—men who considered themselves the boss's moral and social superiors. This discovery did not cause Steffens to look suspiciously at the financially successful men whom he was always meeting, for he understood them, too. He himself took a legacy he had received from a German friend, invested it in Wall Street, and so provided himself with a competency that freed him for life from money worries. Again, Steffens was still as ignorant as anyone else of the deeper economic issues—more ignorant than labor leaders or radical intellectuals, more ignorant than advocates of the trust who knew how inevitable were the current industrial consolidations. But Steffens learned from everyone, and forgot nothing.

In 1897 a group of newspaper editors which included Steffens seceded from the *Evening Post* and took over the broken-down *Commercial Advertiser*. Steffens became its city editor, and with his associates he made it an extraordinary newspaper. It rejected the usual methods and journalists. It called frankly for men who were fresh and ambitious, individuals who were or wanted to be writers. Steffens surrounded himself with unorthodox young men who were to go far in the following years: Abraham Cahan, Harvey O'Higgins, Hutchins Hapgood and his brother Norman, Eugene Walter, and others.[2] This circle turned out a newspaper which was the delight not only of literary folk but of a much larger public.

This work carried Steffens through the Spanish-American War and the succeeding prosperity into the new century. By 1901 he was well-known, counting among his friends and co-workers many of the most able people in New York. He had sold a number of stories and articles, some of them to McClure, and had written a large section of a novel which dealt with Schmittberger, one of the police officials who had figured in the Lexow investigation. But in 1901 he was tired, worn out, uncertain of his next move. Newspaper life had no more to give him, and, as his fellow editors were beginning to observe, he had no more to give it. It was at this opportune time that one of McClure's editors approached him with the proposition that he join them as managing editor. Steffens accepted. He always described himself as managing editor; his letters reveal the same notion. McClure himself seems to have considered Steffens merely a "desk editor"; Steffens was surely not Tarbell's superior. At any rate, he was given a desk, wrote articles and stories which drew richly from his knowledge of politics and police, and otherwise made himself part of the magazine.

Whatever his official position, Steffens was no editor; he was a writer. It was because he was a writer that he had done so well with the effervescent staff of the *Commercial Advertiser*. *McClure's* was different: there were no writers to direct; contributions came from the outside; staff writers brought in material that demanded editorial discussion and arrangement; articles had to be planned and public interest sounded. Steffens quickly became aware that he knew nothing of all this, and although McClure believed in him and was pleased with his work, he found no use for him in the office. Steffens, he felt, would have to learn how a

[2] See his *Autobiography* (Harcourt, Brace & Co., New York, 1931), Chapter XVIII, "A Happy Newspaper Staff."

94 CRUSADERS FOR AMERICAN LIBERALISM

magazine was made, how the staff writers did their work, and he could not learn it in New York.

McClure therefore decided to send him out on a roving commission to look for material. Apparently Tarbell suggested that there would be the makings of a good article in the Cleveland city administration, which Tom Johnson had made front-page news. Steffens did not heed the suggestion, for Johnson was a "reformer" and Steffens knew "reformers"—there was nothing to them. At all events, *McClure's* had a bill against the Lackawanna Railroad for advertising. So Steffens boarded a Westbound train and settled back to enjoy the ride.

New York, Philadelphia, Pittsburgh, Chicago. St. Louis, Butte, San Francisco. . . . No wonder the average American did not know what to make of his country or government! If so practiced a journalist as Steffens did not know the bare facts of corruption in any city but his own, what was the ordinary reader of party newspapers to make of even his own city?

Dr. Albert Shaw, the scholarly editor of *The Review of Reviews*, had written careful and detailed studies of municipal government in England and on the Continent, and these seemed to indict the American way, at least by inference. They taught method (but only method, and only by inference) to Frederic Howe when he came to write his own standard studies of American municipalities. Again, E. L. Godkin had turned a direct gaze on America,[3] but only to show that "democracy" had not done so well as its founders had hoped it would: "the people" had not shown a desire or competence to employ leading men to manage the growing cities. "Politicians" were corrupt, not at all like the "business men" who were the real support of the country. Godkin had not gone into the dirty details corruption involved: he had sustained a kind of polite faith in the ultimate good sense of the people and for the edification of his countrymen had reported democracy as it was being practiced in Australia and New Zealand. If *The Boss*, by Henry Champernowne,[4] had been a less seemly

[3] In *Unforeseen Tendencies of Democracy*, Houghton Mifflin & Co., Boston, 1898.
[4] *An Essay upon the Art of Governing American Cities*, G. H. Richmond & Co., New York, 1894.

production, it had, at least, the virtue of feeling. This writer had lost faith in democracy; he expected nothing of the people. Blindly, misanthropically, he had modeled his book after Machiavelli, advising "the boss" on how best to extend and preserve his control.

There had been other such productions revealing an awareness of the change that had come over government—the awareness of bewildered men unable to grasp or explain that change, much less to give battle to it. When Steffens entrained for Chicago, Hazen Smith Pingree was already dead—Pingree, who for ten years, and apparently without advice or encouragement, had waged a single-handed war against gas, electric, and street-railway corporations in the interest of the people of Detroit. Pingree had exercised an alarming influence on the public imagination. Mayor (then Governor) Pingree's "peculiar economic notions" had been a public scandal for years, but not so public that details were easily available. Now he was dead, but one heard disturbing rumors of a certain Samuel Minton Jones, who had, in a moment of aberration on the part of the local political machine, been made mayor of Toledo. Welsh-born, he had been brought to America as a child and after youthful hardships had gone to work in the oil fields. His rise had been rapid: inventions had made him wealthy, and he had finally founded in Toledo the Acme Sucker Rod Company, which he made famous as the "Golden Rule Factory"—a factory which treated its employees with unprecedented humaneness. Just the man for a reform administration! But to the general dismay, Jones had gone ahead as though he owed nothing to party or politicians. He was revealed in all his awful belief in the practicality of Christianity; he issued to his employees *Letters of Love and Labor* [5] (which must be read to be believed), gathered inspired young men about him, turned the police department on its head with his humane and unorthodox treatment of criminals, fought the public utilities corporations. Naturally he was denounced in the churches and boycotted in the newspapers, and both parties disclaimed him. "Golden Rule" Jones had run on a non-party platform and had been triumphantly re-elected. He was

[5] Privately printed (uncopyrighted), Toledo, 1900; expanded, with an introduction by Brand Whitlock, Bobbs-Merrill Company, Indianapolis, 1905.

about to be re-elected again in 1903: nobody wanted him but the common people.

Tom L. Johnson, Mayor of Cleveland, had publicly asserted, rather than confessed, that he had made his fortune from unfair monopoly holdings. Johnson was now a Single-Taxer—had been for years. He had been Henry George's campaign manager in the New York mayoralty elections. As a Congressman he had banded with several others to read into the *Congressional Record* the entire text of George's *Protection or Free Trade,* a million copies of which had been distributed free to the citizens of America. Opinion was that he was a dangerous demagogue and ought to be curbed. Meanwhile he was creating fearful battles in Cleveland, where he was fighting his former colleagues on franchise issues.

Such were the forces for protest in the land when Steffens went forth to find articles for McClure. Steffens could have been no voice crying in the wilderness. Had there been no one but Steffens, *The Shame of the Cities* would never have been written, let alone printed. Steffens was a son of his times.

He went as far as Chicago and there looked up William Boyden, a lawyer, who suggested that there should be an article in Weyerhauser, of St. Paul, who had become, in a quiet way, the timber king of America. Steffens did see Weyerhauser and had a heart-to-heart talk with him concerning the cost of becoming a rich man. He was, he said, sworn to secrecy and therefore had no article. He returned to Chicago, and from Boyden now learned for the first time of Joseph Wingate Folk, who was raising so violent a row in St. Louis. Steffens now boarded a train for that city to investigate the suggestion.

Samuel Merwin, of whom we shall hear again, later declared that it was Folk, not Steffens, who began political muckraking, and in more than one sense this is true. Folk forced the issue of exposure upon Steffens. Having started desperate events moving in St. Louis, Folk was looking for help at the same time that Steffens was looking for material. Steffens had no plan when he went West —only the conviction that articles could be written to synopsize some event that had been spreading its interesting details over many days: "to take confused, local, serial news of the newspapers and report it all together in one long short story for the whole country." [6] Here was an aim as revolutionary as it was simple; and here was Folk who needed that synopsis as he needed nothing else.

Folk, a native of Tennessee, had come to St. Louis to practice law. A pleasant young man who was "regular" in politics, he worked hard and patiently expected that it would be long before he became a success. He quietly assumed that the St. Louis regime was a government of, by, and for the people, and therefore said nothing about it. He was more surprised than overjoyed by the offer he received to run as attorney for the circuit. The local bosses had come to an impasse in finding a man for the office, and the harmless, popular Folk seemed just the man. "I'll have to do my duty," Folk warned. And nobody, of course, expected him to do anything else. But to their consternation he went ahead and did it! He prosecuted men who had been caught repeating at the polls, not only Republicans but the very Democrats who had elected him. He refused to accept men into his office merely because they were party men. He followed up the cases that came to his attention with such persistence that he was threatened with political ruin. He held to his course, however, with the stubborn determination to make his official position mean something at any cost.

Late in January 1902 Folk's attention was called to a brief newspaper item stating that promoters had just banked a large sum of money to pay for the bribing of assemblymen in a street-railway grab. With daring and imagination, Folk went ahead to uncover the truth about the proposed bribery. He indicted hundreds of witnesses, made deals with them, discovered the higher-ups hiding in the background. With horror he found the latter to be not criminals but the most revered and respected of all the citizens in St. Louis—and elsewhere. The newspapers which had at first approved his work now deserted him entirely, and Folk saw himself in danger of losing all public support.

This was the story that Folk poured out to Steffens in a hotel lobby in St. Louis. Steffens listened eagerly. He wrote McClure that he had a story for him, and, as an editor, he looked about for the man who could write it. Folk suggested Claude Wetmore,

[6] See Steffens's *Autobiography*, page 368.

who had been writing actively on the subject. Steffens assigned the job to Wetmore, but when he read Wetmore's manuscript he saw that it was not what he wanted: Wetmore had toned down many details that Steffens had wanted brought out. Wetmore remonstrated; he had to go on living in St. Louis, and he couldn't do it if he told the whole truth. (Later, when muckraking was se-

JOSEPH W. FOLK
Ohio *State Journal*

curely established, Wetmore was emboldened to write a more elaborate version in *The Battle Against Bribery*.) Steffens compromised by dividing responsibility with him for the exposé sections that were forthwith added.

When it appeared in *McClure's*, "Tweed Days in St. Louis" had the character of an S O S to the American people. Folk became at once nationally known, as convictions were brought in against outstanding millionaires. Steffens's name, too, was on every tongue. McClure recognized that he had discovered a public vein of interest that needed only mining. And Steffens did not look for any more subjects: he had them.

During the next several years Steffens visited many cities and wrote them up for his magazine. Each article made its separate

sensation and placed him higher in public estimation. Many were
the reasons why his reputation grew enormously despite the fact
that other writers soon joined him in producing exposés. Wetmore,
for instance, never again rose to the opportunity Steffens had given
him. He knew nothing except St. Louis, and he could not get at
such first-hand material as Steffens found—material such as the
famous "big mitt ledger" of Minneapolis, which showed the daily
accounts kept between the police and the criminals whom they
directed. Wetmore also lacked Steffens's knowledge of human nature, his artist's ability to draw vivid and rousing pictures of the
politicians and characters whom the stories presented. This gift of
Steffens's was enough to make him the outstanding writer on the
themes which he had introduced in their most dramatic form, but
it was not the reason that the reader kept turning to him instead
of other writers. Steffens was accounted political muckraking's
greatest authority because he gave more than sensations, more than
corruption: he gave the *formula* for municipal corruption as it was
to be found not only in St. Louis, or Minneapolis, or elsewhere,
but *anywhere*. With the laboratory scientist's eye for fundamentals
he traced out the American city structure with the party machine
acting between organized business, the official city government,
graft circles and plain criminals.

The picture was damning. Heretofore the East had blamed the
West for the disgraceful state of government; the "old stock"
families had blamed the immigrants; the old cities had blamed
the new. Here was St. Louis, Western and German, indeed, but
what of Philadelphia? "Corrupt and content," Steffens labeled it.
And Rhode Island—with the very best of the old stock—was being
sold by its voters for small change.

The old apologists were not silenced by Steffens, but they lost
their influence upon the thought of the nation. People turned
eagerly to Steffens for remedies. But Steffens vigorously disclaimed
having any to give: he himself was learning just as fast as he
could, and was still only one step ahead of his audience. His own
uncertainty was what gave a certain air of tense expectancy to his
articles; no one knew where they would lead. So far as he could
see, the trouble lay in the lack of representative government.
There were plenty of laws, but what remedy could help a people
that would not insist on having the laws enforced? At that very

moment Folk in St. Louis was seeing his convictions set aside by
the State Superior Court; the people of St. Louis were not supporting him. Folk was forced to run for Governor of Missouri to
support his work—and he was elected Governor at a time when
he could not have been re-elected to his attorneyship! In Philadelphia, Steffens observed an attempted gas-franchise grab that

A PICTURE POST CARD

Thousands like it were mailed to Philadelphia Councilmen by
irate citizens.

Collier's, June 17, 1905

brought out a citizens' vigilance committee which threatened the
councilmen with lynching if they gave the city's gasworks away.
Civic rage stopped the grab, but the political machine went on as
before. In Chicago, too, Steffens observed a strong reform movement literally being killed by the leading citizens: it seemed they
wanted "good government," not representative government.

What *was* the solution? McClure thought he knew, and he was
willing to have Steffens go as far as he liked in exposure: Steffens's
work provided him with added proof for his own theories. The
trouble with America *was* democracy. And here McClure was willing to push ahead from where Godkin had halted: what the cities

needed was strong men, dictators if necessary. Steffens was at liberty to puzzle over the failure of government so long as his puzzlement produced good articles. It would be clear in the end that the cities' difficulty was that they were not run according to a business plan like cities in Germany and England.

McClure seemed unable to notice that business men had been found at the bottom of bribery and public robbery in the great exposures. Seemly business names, it is true, occurred in Steffens's articles; all business men were not robbers. Yet even the most virtuous did not contribute to campaign funds, for example, out of pure party loyalty. If there was any conclusion to be drawn from such analysis, McClure failed to reach it. His was an ironical blindness, for even then Ida Tarbell was telling *McClure's* readers of curious facts about business—in fact, about the biggest business in the country: the Standard Oil Company.

IX. THE MOTHER OF TRUSTS

BACK in the days of the World's Fair of 1892 and 1893 Armour and Company had founded an Institute of Technology to explain stockyard methods to the public and, in general, to advertise the firm. McClure had sent a staff writer to Chicago to write an article on old P. D. Armour and his Institute; not an article of exposure, of course—nothing was farther from McClure's mind. The article that he wanted and that everybody expected materialized: it accorded due respect to the remarkable organization and economy prevailing in the greatest corporations. Big business was good, the article pointed out—the product of our best native inventiveness and enterprise.

The memory of this article suggested to McClure that the public would like to hear more of the great American business achievements—and what greater achievement was there than the Standard Oil Company? The idea of preparing an article on that company was carefully discussed in McClure's offices, and it was decided that such a subject would make more than one article—perhaps as many as three or four.

In about 1897 the subject of trusts, and particularly of Standard Oil, had begun to assume proportions. The State of New Jersey had opened the door wide to companies interested in getting around the law, and its easy payment plans were making a laughing stock of the Sherman Anti-Trust Act. The reading public wanted to know the meaning of the strange legal activities which made everything right, and yet not right. McClure's policy, however, had not been to answer his readers' questions about such matters; he aimed only to cater to their interest in business as such. Now, however, he hit upon the idea of abandoning the general trust and business articles. He assigned Ida Tarbell to study the Standard Oil Company exhaustively, to write its story in full, showing its history, effects, tendencies. He believed that in such a long, concrete illustration the reader would learn more about big business than he could from discussions and sketches of a hundred firms.

Had McClure combed the literary circles of the nation he could have found no better writer for his purposes than his own associate editor. This tall, matter-of-fact woman, who looked much more a schoolmistress than an editor, had every attribute he might have asked. To begin with, she had been born and bred in the oil regions, in Erie County, Pennsylvania. Her birth date, 1857, approximated the date of the discovery of oil there. Her father had been one of the oil men whom Rockefeller and the oil refiners had found in the path of their monopoly. She had graduated from Titusville High School, and later yet from Allegheny College. At twenty-six she had become associate editor of *The Chautauquan*, holding that position until 1889. Because she had wanted to be a writer of biographies, and because American biography was still primitive, in 1891 she had sailed for Paris and there entered the Sorbonne and the Collège de France, where she took courses and practiced writing. It was here that McClure had discovered her.

The oil regions had apparently left no deep impression in her life. She had diligently pursued a career which led definitely away from them—toward Napoleon and Madame Roland. But the point of view of Rockefeller's enemies, the oil producers, was, as she has said, instinctive with her, and she had by no means forgotten that point of view when she sat down to write for McClure. If she harbored so much as a grain of resentment against the interests that had taken over the oil fields from their original owners, however, it did not appear on the surface. Ida Tarbell was objectivity itself.

Tarbell had two great qualities for her work: patience and the ability to simplify artlessly. Both were imperative for anyone who planned to write a history of the Standard Oil Company. For well over thirty years it had been engaged in business and litigation in a hundred parts of this country and beyond. Literally thousands of people had been intimately involved in its rise. But Rockefeller and his associates, having no eye on posterity when they undertook to consolidate the oil industry, made no effort to lighten the task of the future historian; on the contrary, they were extremely careful to hide the evidence of their business dealings from public inspection. Their record was a maze of contradictions and denials. To get to the heart of their countless activities and then to present it so that it could be understood, was a job to test the resources of any writer.

Tarbell set out to master the subject. She traveled extensively, read long and detailed records, examined libraries of information —including part of that which Henry Demarest Lloyd had collected for his own work—and interviewed individuals who had been concerned in separate controversies. When H. H. Rogers, one of the leading figures of Standard Oil, heard what she was about, he sent word through his friend Mark Twain that he would be glad to help her in any phase of her work. Tarbell accepted his offer with alacrity: she would be delighted to get every point of view; she wanted her story to be impartial, complete, definitive. Such were the standards she set for herself that it was five years before her study was complete, and by that time she had become the outstanding authority on the subject.

The story, as it began to shape up, presented an aspect somewhat different from that which McClure had originally expected. Standard Oil was to have emerged as the very symbol of efficiency and organization. It did. But it was so heavily laden with questionable business maneuvers, so bound up with bribery, fraud, coercion, double-dealing and outright violence, that the fact of efficiency and organization inevitably gave place to the question of whether such a concern had the right to exist. Tarbell did not invent the serious charges. They were a matter of record: she merely gave the evidence as it appeared.

Was she secretly content to let the record speak for itself? McClure, at any rate, was deeply satisfied with the material his writer was evolving. It was just and complete in its proportions. Tarbell took the evidence of the anti-Standard men and submitted it to Standard officials for comment; she took Standard's explanations to Standard's enemies. She approached the enigmatic character of Rockefeller himself with an open-minded willingness to get at the facts.

Tarbell's style was herself: calm, analytical, factual. It is well to remember this, for after her book began to appear in serial form, the notion was quickly established that drama and excitement were its major characteristics. That notion, unfortunately, it was impossible to eradicate. *The History of the Standard Oil Company* was not really the work of an agitated investigator. Nor was it so "monumental" a study as reputation had it, for its two volumes, as they appeared in 1904, totaled only some 550 pages, with several hundred more of appendix. The agitation existed in the minds of the readers who were compelled to face the truth that Standard Oil was tangible, corrupt and inescapable; the monumental nature of the exposure lay in the fact that Tarbell had telescoped into a relatively few pages a history which had involved the nation as a whole and still involved it at the time of reading. No wonder the series was news; no wonder the history of a business house was followed month after month as though it had been a romance!

Tarbell was already famous when her series began to run in *McClure's;* her Lincoln books had established her among the most popular writers of non-fiction. *The History of Standard Oil* skyrocketed her to a place among the most eminent people in the land. Discussion of trusts was going on everywhere, and that meant that discussion of Tarbell could not be avoided. In the West, where *McClure's*—and all the other popular magazines— sold best, her name became a household word, a slogan against the trusts. Standard Oil, which had always carefully avoided engaging in public debate with its enemies, was compelled to exert itself against the influence of her work; not directly, of course, but through loyal journalists and agreeable newspapers.

A bitter review of Tarbell's history appeared in *The Nation,* which indicted her on the grounds of sensationalism, misrepresentation, and ignorance: Tarbell was an outsider, and naturally could not know as much about Standard Oil as its officials. All the muckrakers in turn were accused of being writers and not business people. *The Nation* reviewer (anonymous) declared that it was only because Miss Tarbell's so-called history was an outstanding example of a type of current writing that so much space had been allotted it in *The Nation.* Interestingly enough, this review was reprinted "by permission" of *The Nation* and scattered by the hundreds of thousands throughout the country. Other pamphlets defending Standard Oil were distributed widely. As late as 1910 Elbert Hubbard wrote a brochure of praise for the Company which was, in the main, a studied attack on Tarbell's scholarship and presentation.

No denigration or abuse could veil the fact that Tarbell's story was not sensational, but a sensation. And it is worth discovering why it should have been a sensation at all. She had not attempted to discredit Standard; she had rather taken pains to explain its "real greatness." She had noted with approval the method and devotion of its founder to his company, his long, regular work, his religious point of view, his perfect family life. She showed in great detail the savings that had accrued from the elimination of competition, the minimum of waste that consolidation had entailed, the sending of Standard products throughout the world. She described the very beginnings of the oil industry, from the first wild days when gushers had sprung up in the Pennsylvania fields and fortunes had been made and lost in minutes. Since then the pipeline system had been put into operation which had done away with the rough and ready methods of transportation. Problems presented by the crude oil had since been mastered; inventions had made it possible to use every bit of it; products of important use to the country had been evolved.

Standard had achieved its position only through illegal contracts with the railroad carriers, contracts which had meant the ruin of competitors. Tarbell told about these contracts because they were a part of the history. There was no muckraking tone to her story. If compared with that which Henry Demarest Lloyd had written, the story seemed actually complimentary to Standard. For Lloyd had made no effort to be impartial. He had written with a brilliant and burning pen. With his conviction that the trusts had captured government and were doing as they pleased, he had as much as called the public to revolt. He had frightened away the reader with the inexorable logic of his indictment, as Populism had finally frightened away the voters.

Tarbell called her readers to no action whatsoever; she simply stated what had happened. The reader was put into a position in which he had to furnish his own answers. Having admired and appreciated the business genius of Rockefeller, his regular working hours, his complete concentration on work, the reader was compelled to ask what manner of man this was who had nothing in his life but money, who had already corralled a good proportion of all that was in sight. Rockefeller's religious convictions only angered or annoyed him the more. The poor took him to be a hypocrite; the more sophisticated summed him up as a simpleton and a fool. And having understood and respected the perfection of the Standard system, the reader was compelled to face the fact that it was one of the major rulers of the country; he had to ask what the end would be when Standard had completed its quest for power and had allied itself with other industrial titans to keep the ordinary worker and small business man in its power.

Tarbell's plain facts and the thoughts they inspired, generated revolt faster than Lloyd could ever have done. No wonder Standard Oil feared Tarbell's book as it never had feared Lloyd's, and read into it a cunning and purpose which did not exist. Rogers of Standard would have done well to leave Tarbell to her own devices during her research. His advice and collaboration, with her obvious honesty and willingness to learn from everyone, made him party to the final version of the history, and so impressed the reading public with Tarbell's painstaking efforts to tell the whole truth and damned Standard Oil as no other account of its iniquities had done.

The country was overrun with trusts, and all the important ones were exposed to the public eye before the muckraking era was over. Yet no other trust ever caught the imagination of the public like Standard. This was Tarbell's consummate achievement. It was because she gave a careful, detailed account of its rise, because she described minutely the manner in which it actually functioned, because she portrayed its leaders, its departments, its daily routine, and its products, that she succeeded above all other competing writers. As in the case of Steffens and Baker, it was ultimately her point of view which determined the value of her work. Her clear, dispassionate manner enabled her to produce what became a source book of information, a book that could be consulted no matter what mood the reader was in. She had focused steadily upon description; no other writing element was allowed to take precedence over it. No expression of bias interfered with the public's chance to understand a trust as a separate entity with a separate significance independent of individuals and motives.

This truth about Tarbell's book is apparent when one compares it with another history of a great corporation which was written with a like intent and purpose and which appeared in a popular edition at precisely the time when her history began in *McClure's*. *The Inside History of the Carnegie Steel Company*, written by James Howard Bridge, made as great a stir as Tarbell's book. Bridge, who was anything but a radical, had gathered material much as Tarbell collected it: he had read long records of court negotiations, interviewed the great men who had been associated with the company, and otherwise steeped himself in the subject. His book purported to give the clear, unbiased history of the great company. If he had any thesis, it was to prove the usual estimate of Carnegie to be a myth. He dedicated his book to those whom he conceived to be the real founders of the Company—and they did not include Carnegie. He also denied that Carnegie had worked well with his partners, that he had introduced the Bessemer process into steel making, that he had been on the alert for new inventions, that he had been the main force behind the growth of the company, and that he had carried on the best possible relations with labor. Otherwise, he told the story of the development of the corporation from its beginnings with a small forge at Girty's Run, in 1858, at what became the city of Allegheny, Pennsylvania, from a $5,000 plant to a $500,000,000 one.

Here was no revolutionary production, yet it stirred the country and called forth diatribes and insults. Even John Brisben Walker, in a pamphlet reprinted from articles in *Cosmopolitan*, protested against Bridge's unfair treatment of Carnegie. Bridge, in his reply, rightly pointed out that although Walker was not seeking to rehabilitate Carnegie, he was too obviously influenced by the Carnegie myth to be able to judge his book reasonably. It was interesting to have Walker, indeed, defend Carnegie from personal attack. The defense defined Walker's "radicalism" better than a hundred editorials: there were "good" trusts and "bad" ones—and the Carnegie trust was a "good one."

Bridge gave the facts of his subject with a satisfying willingness to apprise the public rather than to please the conservative. But his book did not have that special quality which enabled the reader to understand beyond the subject. It lacked, too, the central figure of Rockefeller, who so completely symbolized all the ideals and products of the trusts. Although it was and has re-

mained required reading for those interested in serious study of
the subject of steel, or even business generally, Tarbell's history
more successfully transcended the special matter on hand; it became an enlightening source for any study of any trust. In the
succeeding years that were to be so crucial for Standard Oil and
its fellow-corporations, a flood of literature on trusts was poured
out, and for the most part it drew from Tarbell's work.

The History of the Standard Oil Company marked an epoch.
Once it had appeared, there could never be any further question
about the existence or significance of trusts. Even the books which
Tarbell wrote after muckraking had ended—books which were, for
the most part, focused conservatively—were unable to modify the
knowledge she had given to the public. Through newspapers and
magazines the intrinsic message of her masterpiece filtered down
into the very consciousness of the average American citizen.

With what result? Some Americans, even a number who had
entertained radical notions, scrutinized the trust and decided that
the future was inevitably with it. They abjured their radicalism
and jumped upon the *laissez-faire* bandwagon: evolution would
take care of everything. The majority of people stood neutral,
repeating the old clichés about law enforcement, undecided but
yet undefeated.

A little vanguard, however, decided to do battle with the trust
and stepped boldly out to demand its dissolution. More or less
openly, more or less radically, they took up arms and fought, as
lawyers, as reformer business men, as politicians, or as developers
of the work Tarbell had begun—that is, as muckrakers.

X. MUCKRAKERS

THEY came from everywhere, these journalists, sociologists, *littérateurs*, and it was often difficult to tell just what they were and whom they represented. Rheta Childe Dorr, a newspaper woman and feminist, was resentfully called a Socialist so often that she finally joined the Socialist Party. And Robert Hunter, who *was* a Socialist, could never understand why anyone should call him a muckraker. His book *Poverty* was the product of ten years of brilliant investigation and social work begun under the aegis of Jane Addams and her colleagues. It had been written in the spirit of the scientist and fact-finder. Why should it be dubbed "muckraking"?

Those who felt threatened or insulted by the investigations and exposés which appeared on every side had no time to choose words. So Hunter, William Hard, Florence Kelley, Dorr—they were all muckrakers, or no better than muckrakers; in a word, trouble-seekers. In these writers, muckrakers and near-muckrakers, worried men could find few easily distinguishing marks. Each writer borrowed from the other; yet a careful weighing of any one would have shown individual patterns of development that were not superficially apparent. Actually the rude attempts of disturbed critics of the time to pigeon-hole writers according to the "scientific," "literary," or "exposure" content of their work were uniformly inadequate and absurd. When journalists produced novels and novelists took to making investigations, when poets produced histories and politicians took to writing poetry, and when such things went on at an unheard-of tempo, the average critic was likely to lose his head and begin to strike out in all directions.

That was what happened. In certain quarters it was impossible to make clear that America was not England, that strange things were likely to happen in a land in which everything was yet to

be done, that the hunt for "immortal values" in literature and life
had best be humanized and extended. The most virile writers of
the generation were too busy creating to have time for criticism;
those who did develop the critical faculties ran abroad to find
light at the shrines of unadulterated Genius; and those critics who
remained behind preserved a grim and forbidding watch over the
sacred achievements of Emerson and Bret Harte (so recently de-
ceased) and . . . Longfellow.

What, then, made the muckrakers what they were? It is safe
to say that hardly one of those who made his name in that history-
packed decade had any more intention than Steffens, Tarbell, or
Baker of challenging the *status quo* in the way that he did. The
muckrakers originally meant to be merely novelists, merely scholars, merely politicians, according to the tradition they had inherited. They wanted merely to make careers. And they became
muckrakers, most of them, by popular demand.

This does not mean that muckraking was, as its enemies charged,
a pandering to corrupt taste. The public's lust for information,
for understanding, was enormous. It charged the air with vitality.
It called into being a veritable army of writers to interpret and
describe the accumulated history of thirty and more years. Naturally, mistakes happened. Cleveland Moffett was a mistake: his
series, *The Shameful Misuse of Wealth*, was futility itself—a
sermon in the key of moral indignation concerning the "excesses"
of the rich. And there were such ridiculous articles as the one by
Frederic Thompson, written in all seriousness, called *After the
Salome Dance—What?* [1] But there were surprisingly few such
mistakes.

Most of the writers meant only to write, not to muckrake, as
their biographies testify. Will Irwin, for example, who had been
a classmate of Herbert Hoover at Stanford University, began his
career on the San Francisco newspapers and then moved to New
York to work with the *Sun* and then for McClure. He loved to
write, and he wrote movingly of his own San Francisco. Otherwise he was as willing to report baseball as Chinatown. It was the
drift of the times, as well as the palpable corruption of newspaper

[1] *Success*, March 1909.

methods, that called forth the series which capped his work of the period.

His brother Wallace was even less concerned with contemporary affairs in their more profound aspects. He was a wit, a jingler, a satirist in light verse. Ten years before, he would have been capable of not much more than excelling Gelett Burgess at his frivolous rhyming game. But this was the muckraking period. He made his literary start in poetry with a book of irresistible fun, *The Love Sonnets of a Hoodlum*. Then, not without qualms, he followed his brother, Will, East, to make his living as a magazine poet; and soon all the periodicals carried his clever verses on immediate events. He made poetry pay. *At the Sign of the Dollar, Random Rhymes and Odd Numbers,* and other of his volumes took the age in their stride, from the trusts to the muckrakers themselves; and finally came "Mr. Togo" to make his Oriental observations regarding American modes and ideas.

Among the fiction writers of the period, Samuel Merwin and Henry Kitchell Webster had together written the first of the "business novels": *The Short Line War,* published in 1899, described the struggle for control of a Midwestern railroad. *Calumet K,* also written in collaboration, told of the contest that marked the building of a grain elevator. Such subjects had been new; but the books lacked the disturbing quality which Frank Norris's detailed treatment and superior craftsmanship were soon to provide for the reader. For Merwin and Webster were primarily romancers, not social historians: as Arnold Bennett showed, they had simply applied the method of Dumas to American conditions. *The Road to Frontenac,* which Merwin wrote alone, was actually a romance, with all the trappings of swords and chivalry.

But again the times directed its writers. After the turn of the century Webster began writing such books as *The Banker and the Bear,* dealing with a corner in lard, and his friend wrote *The Whip Hand,* which dealt with a corner in lumber. Contemporary pressure forced Webster to adopt the shallow philosophy he finally evolved in *The Duke of Cameron Avenue,* a novelette of New York ward politics that touched on "practical" reform. But the times did better for Merwin. As contributing editor to *Success,* he made first-hand surveys of business and politics; as associate editor, he became a co-worker with the most virile of the muckrakers; finally he became editor of *Success,* and it was while he held this position that the magazine became a powerful organ of exposure—and was stamped out by interests which could no longer tolerate its existence.

Better than all the fiction produced by Will Irwin, Webster, and Merwin, among the best novels that the era produced, was Isaac Kahn Friedman's *By Bread Alone,* which McClure's publishing house issued in 1901. It was a novel of Steel, an intense, fervid, moving story that handled capital-labor, man-woman relations with revolutionary sincerity. The story was written at white-heat and, since it stayed within limits and was distinctly middle-class in feeling, it called forth instant appreciation from all except the most sluggish readers. The author, a second-generation German Jew and a Chicagoan, was one of the many who had learned about labor through study in the settlement houses, who had visited the steel mills, had felt the insufferable heat of the blast furnaces, had been taught by such friends of the working-man as Clarence Darrow, the brilliant novelist Will Payne, Ernest Poole, Joseph Medill Patterson, and of course Jane Addams.

By Bread Alone was a most notable work. In 1901 the social novel attracted no more promising writer than I. K. Friedman. His skill and sophistication were matched by many, but no other man was able so to immerse himself in his theme, to give so much of himself to the crucial characters and problems of American life. Friedman understood the laborer, understood the capitalist, not just objectively and not for the sake of argument, but with emotional entirety. He forced his protagonist, Blair Carrhart, to leave wealth and position, to go down among the helots and become one of them. This was a situation that became stagey, foolish, in the hands of a dozen novelists, but it did not fail with Friedman. Face forward and with exhaustive honesty he met the crises and contradictions that inevitably confronted him as he worked out his story.

The middle-class dilemma was sustained without any faltering. The great strike (which Friedman borrowed from Homestead) revealed Carrhart's anomalous position with the working and capitalist classes, neither of which would accept anything but his entire support. Yet Friedman did not degrade his tale with dogmatism or lectures. His hero was at last retired into personal happiness—and, perhaps, to attack the social problem anew from the political end. Such a conclusion was hardly magnificent, but it was honest, and understandable in the light of the strained, clouded life—one which a Dreiser could not attempt to handle.

Friedman wrote nothing of comparable dignity after *By Bread Alone*. This had been a vast improvement over his sentimental *Poor People; The Autobiography of a Beggar*, which followed *By Bread Alone*, was a book of rather pointless sketches. *The Radical* (1907) was the sequel which *By Bread Alone* implied: it presented Blair Carrhart in politics, and it was a complete failure. It was also Friedman's last book, though he lived twenty years longer.

Perhaps disillusionment had already enervated this talented writer's mind; perhaps he lacked the equipment for the work which an adequate sequel would have demanded. At any rate, his fate was the fate of every writer who tried to produce without taking sides. The attitude of impartiality could not naturally be sustained. The best that could come of it was the McClure type of writing, which, as we have seen, had its own hidden partiality. Other muckraking was more direct: recognizing evil, it turned upon the evildoers frankly and with avowed partisanship; it spent its energies not in a search for "understanding" but directly in exposure. *By Bread Alone* was unique in that it recognized the middle-class dilemma and portrayed it fully. As an artist, Friedman should have gone on to muckraking or Socialism (for obviously, on his premises, something had to be done); instead, he attempted the cant and the conventional gestures of *The Radical*. Then he stopped trying.

Charles Edward Russell, who began the century innocently enough, was one more of the group who had no intention of becoming muckrakers. He was an Iowan, born in 1860, the son of a newspaper editor who had been one of the founders of the Republican Party. The last fact alone practically committed him to early entry into the political differences of the Eighties. As early as 1881 he spoke out boldly in defense of free trade.[2] That

[2] *The Reason Why.* "A Republican Free Trader Gives His Reasons for Opposing What Is Falsely Called a Protective Tariff." (Davenport, Iowa, 1881.)

same year he founded with Henry J. Philpott a free trade journal and the first of the free trade leagues; and it was not long before the gospel was being preached vigorously throughout the West. Russell supported, in turn, Populism, Henry George, and miscellaneous reform movements. Early in his career, however, sturdy Republicanism practiced in the Lincoln tradition reduced the fortunes of the Russell family, and this youngest Russell was forced to earn his living. He went to New York, where he began with the *Commercial Advertiser* and then joined the staff of the *World* which sent him to Chicago in time to be present when the Haymarket riot occurred. With time Russell ran the gamut of newspaper experience, eventually becoming city editor of the *World* over an impressive corps of reporters and helping Hearst to found the Chicago *American*.

By 1902 Russell had saved enough money to ensure his freedom from want, and, after the hectic experiences of a score of years, issued his first book: *Such Stuff as Dreams*. Poems! It was amazing how such productions were passed over by those who pretended to interpret the age. Actually there was a poet burning in many a fierce muckraker—and Russell was one of the fiercest of them all: a proud, sensitive man who yearned romantically to accomplish worth-while things. The truth about Russell was that he had been hurt by the successive political and financial failures of old-time Republicanism, and he was anxious to keep away from it all; besides, he wanted more than a journalistic career. Yet he was no mere escapist; his purely literary ability and interest were genuine. Even at the height of muckraking, he was to issue studies and articles having nothing directly to do with exposure.[3]

Russell, however, had not lost by any means his passionate belief in the necessity for democracy. His bitterness toward those who had stripped the Western middle-class of its former strength was soon to start him upon what was to be his real career. He became, in the following years, one of the most sincere, most partisan of the reform writers.

Russell's friend David Graham Phillips was less reluctant to

[3] See, for example, *Thomas Chatterton, The Marvelous Boy* (Moffat, Yard & Co., New York, 1908), the first of his biographies, and a pioneer work on Chatterton.

do battle with his times. He had been anticipating a national up-heaval for years. A Hoosier, bred somewhat like Russell, Phillips had been matured by Princeton and Park Row. An outstanding newspaperman, he might have gone on to high editorial honors. But he had cherished the determination since college days to paint America whole, to tell the truth and avoid the sentimentali-ties that had defined and limited the work of Howells and Twain and Bret Harte; so he had held on to the career of journalism deliberately, in order to learn his country thoroughly.

In 1901 Phillips broke away from the newspapers and set him-self to writing with a resolution and regularity and capacity that, in the end, made him a legend. He wrote articles, stories, and novels, sounding his audience and experimenting with his ma-terial. Until about 1906 his articles were, in the main, more im-portant than his fiction. He wrote on every subject: housing, charity (which he abhorred), the steel trust, travel; but he gravi-tated naturally toward pen portraits of outstanding men and events. These were the stuff of his fiction. And once muckraking was in full swing, Phillips's straightforward evaluations were being featured in *Cosmopolitan*, *The Arena*, *Everybody's*, and other magazines. Such an article as "The Real Boss of the United States" (dealing with Senator Aldrich) precipitated wide discus-sion and carried more than a suggestion of the great muckraking scoop that was brewing.

It cannot be too much emphasized that the reading public in those years was just beginning to understand that home things—ways of living, ideas, government—in a word, *Americana*—were as interesting, as worth knowing, as foreign things. "Confession" and other personal-experience stories, whatever their merit or lack of it, were being read eagerly and widely for their realistic ac-counts of everyday American life. They were a valuable supple-ment to muckraking because they created a background for the muckrakers' themes. Such work as Owen Kildare's,[4] for instance, was extremely popular. Kildare had been a Bowery tough who, at the age of thirty, became respectable. By study and application

[4] *My Mamie Rose: The Story of My Regeneration*, The Baker & Taylor Co., New York, 1903.

he made himself an educated man, and he finally wrote the story of his life, the frontispiece of the book being a map of Manhattan with the Bowery indicated as though it were in a foreign country. Kildare became merely respectable, but his story was good, and it became a pattern for similar works.

Will Irwin reported *The Confessions of a Con Man*, Frederic Howe wrote *The Confessions of a Monopolist* (fiction, but based on fact), *World's Work* ran *The Confessions of a Commercial Senator*. Confessions were elicited from thieves and salesgirls and other men and women in every walk of life. Not all of these unburdenings of the soul were breath-taking. *Everybody's*, for example, printed among others the "confessions" of a life-insurance agent: this was standard writing and might just as well have come from the life-insurance companies themselves, for all the revelation it contained. It appeared before scandal in the life-insurance field broke loose. But even the most pedestrian "confession" was eagerly read for light on the country and the experiences of its people.

Among the writers who made a career of such work was Hutchins Hapgood, who never, in fact, considered himself a muckraker. Hapgood's newspaper training had given him a taste for loitering in the parks and among the colorful East Side people. Unlike his brother, Norman, who was pure intellectual, he looked for human interest and the East Side was particularly the place for it: the waves of immigration had crowded it with vivid and lively people, such as the Russian Jews who had fled from the Czar and his bureaucrats, bringing with them the finest of a gifted intelligentsia. Using this human material Hapgood wrote *The Spirit of the Ghetto* (1902). It was a remarkable production for a non-Jew, for it revealed an extraordinary effort to understand his subject and the people it involved. Hapgood was deeply interested in the actors who held court at the splendid Second Avenue and Bowery theatres. He profoundly respected the mature poets and artists who argued and debated in the cafés. He was eager to report the achievements of his friend Abraham Cahan, who had already written masterly English prose, and was now forswearing active Socialism in order to build the mighty Jewish *Forward*.

Hapgood was, in fact, one of the foremost exemplars of a fashion, for the muckrakers were deeply infatuated with the Jews. Lincoln Steffens nailed a mazuza on his office door and attended synagogue religiously. David Graham Phillips later made a Jewess a heroine of one of his novels, and planned an epic of Jewish progress through the ages. There was, too, a vast ghetto literature, of which Bruno Lessing's stories were representative. This interest in the Jews was much more vital than that which Charles G. Leland had felt, a generation before, for the gypsies.

Hapgood's *The Autobiography of a Thief* was made of somewhat different stuff. Hapgood had met a reformed criminal and had conceived with him the idea of writing a case study of the criminal as a type. For five months they had met together, and Hapgood had amassed data for his book. The book was quite unlike Flynt's work; it was written frankly from an outside viewpoint. But so carefully was it executed, so fully was it documented, that it constituted an important social record.

During the muckraking period Hapgood issued, in turn, *The Spirit of Labor, An Anarchist Woman,* and *Types from the City Streets*—all case studies and observations set down with extreme care. No one could complain that Hapgood was not eager to give the truth as he saw it among all kinds of people, from intellectual Socialist to street gamin.

If Hapgood was the sociologist of the muckraking movement, then Gustavus Myers, more than any other—certainly more than either Tarbell or Steffens or Baker—was its historian. He, too, never quite considered himself part of the movement; probably he resented the difficulties he encountered in the way to fame and influence, and coveted the prestige and national attention won by men like Steffens and Russell and Phillips. But he also harbored something of the scholar's feeling of superiority to the man of action. Writers like Russell and Phillips used their material to drive home points and call readers directly to reform; Myers was completely—too completely—the student.

As a young man Myers specialized in original historical research. In 1900 he wrote for the Reform Club Committee on City Affairs *A History of Public Franchises in New York City,* which was immediately recognized as required reading for any serious student of the franchise. Cold fact and history though it was, it constituted a sensational indictment of franchise practices. The next year Myers completed *The History of Tammany Hall*, which publishers refused to accept and which finally had to be issued on a subscription basis. Speaking of the book, Myers explained that he had begun his study in no partisan spirit; it was not he, but the evidence, that showed every prominent leader of Tammany to have been involved in some theft or swindle, public or private. But Myers's detachment—lack of guile—went unappreciated: seventeen years were to pass before a second edition of the book was published.

Myers's researches turned up staggering amounts of material on the great financiers of America—startling evidence which shook down all his preconceptions regarding them. While the other muckrakers captured popular attention with articles on trusts, insurance, labor trouble, impure food, and other national scandals, Myers patiently turned pages of old books, magazines, and newspapers to learn the true history of capitalism in America. Nine years passed before his book was ready for publication, and he was justified in considering it his masterpiece. But *The History of the Great American Fortunes* was not greater than all the other books produced by other investigators; it was merely different—it was history: tendentious, narrow-gauged, but history.

Alfred Henry Lewis was called a muckraker. It would have surprised the common critics to learn that he would be remembered—not if at all, but unquestionably—as a creator of substantial literature. They had already forgotten the excitement his first book, *Wolfville*, had caused in 1897, and the praise they themselves had accorded it. Criticism was, in fact, unequal to the task of weighing the numerous and varied books that Lewis had written by the middle years of the muckraking period. When Lewis died in 1914, he was buried as a muckraker, as a Hearst man, without honor.

Lewis was born in Cleveland in 1857. He became a lawyer, but when his health broke down he gave up law and went West, where he spent more than five years as a cattleman on the plains of Texas, New Mexico, and especially Arizona. There Lewis's rough, lawless kind of temperament—three-fifths of it pure individualism, the remainder a compound of learning and forensic aptitude—found itself. He was precisely the character who could understand the men who lived on the plains, played cards and drank and held life cheap, hated Indians and Mexicans, despised Negroes, had a placid irony and talked little. In this society Lewis's *Wolfville* was conceived, although it was not written until later. The central character of the book, which dated Bret Harte as no criticism could have done, was the Old Cattleman, now in the twilight of life, who sat by the hour telling tales of Wolfville, Arizona, where his best years had been spent. In Doc Peets, Texas Thompson, Dave Tutt, Cherokee Hall, and all the others of that permanent company, the Old Cattleman conjured up a pageant of the entire Far West.[4a]

After leaving Arizona Lewis spent a number of years practicing law in Kansas City, where he was subsequently attracted to newspaper work on the Kansas City *Star.* He began sending Western sketches to newspapers, including Hearst's *Examiner,* under the pseudonym "Dan Quin." These were gathered into *Wolfville,* dedicated to Hearst, and quickly found readers.

When Lewis returned East as Washington correspondent for the Chicago *Times* and other papers, he had the individualistic and comparatively lawless traits of a Westerner. Yet he was not naïve, for he had been born and raised in a large Midwestern city. Half-sophisticated, half-primitive, he took a peculiar role among the Eastern scribes. He had no faith in reform; he despised Socialism. Trying to reconcile the ethics of the West with those of the East, he wrote *Richard Croker,* a book that purported to be a history of the Tammany chieftain and his demesne. It was a fantastic production, a weird attempt to mix philosophy, history, and appraisal in the manner of Sterne—or, rather, in the manner of the Old Cattleman. Lewis was unable to make up his mind whether Croker was to be praised or condemned; he confused personality with principles; he alternately attacked and discussed his man without balance or sequence.

The Boss (And How He Came to Rule New York), which Lewis published in 1903, was supposedly a muckraking book but was actually a mere fictionalization of the Croker material. By this time Lewis had a grip on the Eastern method and was able

[4a] See Filler, ed., *Old Wolfville: Chapters from the Fiction of Alfred Henry Lewis,* Antioch Press, Yellow Springs, O., 1968.

to control his impulsive amorality. But the material wasn't his material; the story lacked life and depth. *The President* likewise was a failure, and so were the several other books and many articles which represented Lewis as a political thinker and observer.

Meanwhile Lewis produced a constant flow of stories about his beloved West. *Wolfville Days, Nights, Folks,* and others joined the original book as the garrulous Old Cattleman filled out the huge canvas of his memories. Lewis himself became large and imposing, the Dr. Johnson of a group of men who met in the back room of Considine's saloon on Broadway near Forty-Second Street. The group included, among others, Charley White, the prize fight referee; Bat Masterson, the famous Dodge City sheriff of the "bad man" period, whose life Lewis told fictionally in *The Sunset Trail;* Kid McCoy, the fighter; Eddie Foy, the actor; a famous crook; and Val O'Farrell, a detective sergeant, some of whose cases were told in Lewis's *Confessions of a Detective.* As they sat about the table with Charles Edward Russell, whom they accepted despite his radical point of view,[5] they told marvelous stories of personal adventure. Here the real Lewis sat and warmed himself among his kind of men.

The other Lewis felt himself bound to attack despoilers of national wealth and honor. This was the "muckraking" Lewis who wrote voluminously on railroads, corrupt politicians, and trusts, and who, in the way of a Westerner, applied names prolifically. But muckraking was the least of Lewis. His unbridled violence little more than indicated how much the times could stand; it was nothing more than pyrotechnics, and only the historian or acolyte will ever interest himself in it. It was his Wolfville stories that found their way into the American heritage.

These muckrakers with whom we have just become acquainted were, for the most part, men: they looked at life maturely and sought to find their place in it as mature minds.

Upton Beall Sinclair was a boy—a desperately earnest one, with a head filled with dreams and fancies. His father and mother had stemmed from Southern "quality," and their decline had made

[5] See Russell's *Bare Hands and Stone Walls: Some Recollections of a Side-Line Reformer,* Charles Scribner's Sons, New York, 1933.

its mark upon their son. He was proud and Puritan. At sixteen he thought it time that he lived alone and independent.

Joke writing, and then dime novels for Street and Smith, supported Sinclair while he made his way through the City College of New York and Columbia University. This sort of writing gave him the glib, easy style which later characterized his work. But even now Sinclair was profoundly unhappy, for he burned to do great writing. He had discovered poetry, and felt that nothing was more worth-while than to join the immortal company of Shelley and Heine. The verse in his first several volumes, however, showed less poetic ability than a frenzied need for self-expression. Sinclair felt weighed down by an intolerable injustice in human affairs, an injustice which allowed people with no sympathy or consideration for his ambitions to deprive him of the hearing his efforts deserved.

So Sinclair, "discovering" Socialism, went about lonely with the knowledge that only brotherhood and honesty could solve the world's ills. His first book, *Springtime and Harvest*, a passionately undirected and immature novel, was published by himself in 1901 and was stillborn. Hopelessly he haunted the publishing houses, living meanwhile so straitly that he destroyed his health. Despite the indifference he attributed to the publishers, he did find one for *King Midas* (as he titled *Springtime and Harvest*), and in 1903 for *Prince Hagen*, which was not markedly superior.

These books made no popular impression, and there can be no doubt that Sinclair contemplated suicide. Death self-inflicted, the inevitable end for the uncompromising idealist, was the *leitmotif* of *The Journal of Arthur Stirling*. It occurred to Sinclair that the book would carry greater power if the poet Stirling appeared really to have died because of the failure of publishers to accept his masterpiece, *The Captive*. The book, published as authentic, in the spring of 1903 was a sensation. Revelations of the hoax brought down insults and contempt upon Sinclair's head, but nothing could prevent its success. Sinclair had broken through.

He announced his victory in a cosmic snarl [6] which reads as bitter and as startling today as it did then. Excitement over *The Journal of Arthur Stirling* called Sinclair to the attention of

[6] "My Cause," *The Independent*, May 14, 1903.

George D. Herron, who acquainted him with the existence of the great Socialist movement and showed him the path ahead. Sinclair enlisted as a soldier in what he visualized as a long, arduous campaign that would yet free the world and make it habitable for poets. Having beaten at the doors of the publishing houses, he now turned to beating at the walls of organized society.

Of all the Socialists, Sinclair was throughout the decade most thoroughly the muckraker. The Socialism within which he worked was to the muckraking period almost what Populism had been to the period preceding. Socialist newspapers and magazines sold to wide strata of the middle-class and working-class. They were the last refuge for muckraking articles which could not find print elsewhere, but they worked on a premise different from that of the muckraking magazines proper. Having given up capitalism, intellectually at least, they felt more constrained to discuss fundamental social change than to make the wide-eyed and amazed announcements of the muckrakers. The muckrakers had not given up capitalism; it was still practicable to them, by no means damned.

The Socialist movement, however, in many of its phases only supplemented the muckraking movement. Some of the muckrakers, like Sinclair, were Socialists, and many of the muckrakers who did not become militant defenders of capitalism, and even capitalists, after the movement had been destroyed, became Socialists. "Can't you see it?" Sinclair urged Steffens, while *The Shame of the Cities* was devolving upon the public. "Can't you see it?" For Steffens was painting a picture such as no Socialist could have achieved. And it was precisely because Steffens could not "see it" that he was able to see so many things other than Socialism; and it was precisely because the public desired to "see" these many things that he was encouraged to do his work.

Sinclair was by no means certain that muckraking was by itself enough; others were certain. That was why David Graham Phillips pleaded with Russell not to join the Socialists when, in 1908, Russell so decided. It would destroy his influence, Phillips insisted. It did not, of course; but Phillips could no more foresee that than Sinclair could understand Steffens's position, than Sinclair could foresee thirty years ahead to his own principled break with the ideas which had guided him so far. Decisions regarding party support and alliances were made in the heat of daily work, and with the dogmatism of men who perforce must act with full conviction. It might be added that insincerity and intolerance of other men's decisions were not qualities which began or ended with the muckraking movement.

Almost unique among the Socialist comrades, therefore, was Jack London. Fatherless and declassed, he had become a rebel among the San Francisco wharf-rats and by self-education. He had marched with Coxey's army and had joined the Argonauts in the Klondike gold rush. Then in the desperate ways which he described in his greatest novel, *Martin Eden,* he set himself to getting a foothold in literature.

Socialist, muckraker, romancer, London loved freedom as much as he hated injustice. Love of freedom complicated his personal life, making him a lawless pessimist while he preached the good time coming. He varied his adventure stories of the Yukon and Hawaii with *The War of the Classes* and *Revolution,* traveled about the world in search of personal certainty and understanding. In *The People of the Abyss* he told the somber story of those who lived in the slums of London, but he could offer America no more than *The Iron Heel*—a forevision of fascism.

London ultimately had no hope for muckraking, and Socialism was only something which beckoned beyond. He more than any other writer of the time was a proletarian; success only declassed him further. That was what killed him—not drink, as his friend Sinclair thought: drink was an effect, not a cause. But Jack London was exceptional among the Socialist intelligentsia—an intelligentsia that became, as David Graham Phillips recognized (for all his opposition to Socialism as the best vehicle for reform), the outstanding educational force in the country, and one that was to be found in every field where reform was in progress.

Socialism's outstanding educator was John Spargo, a Fabian who came to America at twenty-six, in time to join the new party which Debs had created. Fabianism suited the principles of the party very well. Even the elections were considered an instrument of education, although Socialists were polling sufficient votes to suggest to the most sanguine that the millennium was near. It was only a few years before Victor Berger, using Fabian methods, captured Milwaukee. Spargo, sympathetic with this brand of radicalism, threw himself into the work and soon had a commanding position in the party. His fine logic, grasp of history, and literary ability enabled him to compose what became standard expositions of Socialist principles.

William James Ghent was among the leaders of Socialism on the educational front. Born a Hoosier, he worked as compositor and proofreader in many cities, and in 1899 aided "Golden Rule" Jones in his mayoralty and gubernatorial campaigns. In 1902 he issued *Our Benevolent Feudalism*—predicting fascism—and two years later he published the important *Mass and Class*. In 1906 he became the first secretary of the Rand School of Social Science, which was a target for the concerted abuse of the conservative press, but with the Intercollegiate Socialist Society became the outstanding center for developing Socialist propaganda among the middle-class.

The Socialist press poured forth an endless stream of books, pamphlets, and newspapers. In New York *The Call* sent out broadsides of denunciation and protest. The Charles H. Kerr Publishing Company in Chicago, a co-operative, issued a distinguished list of foreign Socialist classics which included the standard translation of *Das Kapital*. The same company published major works such as Louis H. Morgan's *Ancient Society*, and productions by Myers, Russell, and Spargo. The Chicago *Socialist* and the *International Socialist Review*, edited by A. M. Simons, and the famous *Appeal to Reason*, distributed from Girard, Kansas, disseminated Socialism. And among the most remarkable of all these organs was *Wilshire's*, the organ of Gaylord Wilshire, brilliant "millionaire Socialist," who followed events closely with his battle cry of "government ownership." *Wilshire's*, like the muckraking magazines, was ultimately put to the wall by recalcitrant advertisers, but not before it, too, had made its mark upon America.

These radical papers enjoyed a vast circulation and, if they made no startling changes in social conditions, they made indelible impressions upon the public. Yet all of them together caused less excitement and perturbation than one contemporary chain of newspapers. William Randolph Hearst's publications were intrinsically popular. They were condemned in every corner of the land as Socialistic and anarchistic, as being directly responsible for the unrest that appeared everywhere. Nor was Hearst scorned by the doctrinaire radical. Wilshire himself took time and space to prove that Hearst was not a Socialist, even while Socialists were in Hearst's employ—and preaching Socialism. The bitterest attacks upon Hearst came, not from Socialists, but from conservatives and others directly interested in privilege.

What, actually, was Hearst's connection with the muckraking movement?

LINCOLN STEFFENS   R. S. BAKER

"THESE, LADIES AND GENTLEMEN, ARE MAGA-
ZINE REFORMERS . . ."

The World, December 3, 1905

XI. HEARST

TO begin with, did Hearst exist? Steffens submitted that he did; Finley Dunne vehemently denied it. Hearst, declared Dunne, was a figment of Arthur Brisbane's imagination, a vain mountebank with money to burn. What should be said of him, therefore, was, first, that he was a myth and, second, that he was an obscene, slanderous demagogue. Steffens protested that Hearst had been very much in the world long before he acquired Brisbane; also, there must be someone behind the newspapers that bore his name. Hearst papers were recognizable anywhere: in New York, in San Francisco, in Chicago, in Boston—

But it was no use—it was impossible to conduct a calm discussion about Hearst. From 1887, when he entered journalism, not controversy but biting calumny and accusation dogged him. From 1900 on through the muckraking period he was a topic for public discussion second only to T. R. This was particularly true in 1905, when he was elected Mayor of New York City but was cheated of that honor; through 1906, when he failed to win the New York governorship by 60,000 votes; and from 1908 on, when he released the famous Archbold letters. Yet during that time only one studied, disinterested article was written about him, and that was done by Steffens.[1] This article succeeded beyond all the others because it had an air of impartiality which was utterly lacking in all other writings about the man. Steffens, personally, was not really impartial. He was convinced that Hearst was a great man and that his methods were justified; it was Steffens's editorial associates who saw to it that both sides of the publisher were presented.

One was either pro or con—never neutral—regarding Hearst. The man therefore remained a myth, adorned by all the inspired Hearstiana which appeared in his own newspaper columns. A book

[1] "Hearst, the Man of Mystery," *The American Magazine*, November 1906.

purporting to give merely the bare facts of his life was inconceivable during the muckraking era. It was forty-one years after Hearst's journalistic debut before such a work appeared. *William Randolph Hearst, an American Phenomenon*, by John K. Winkler, was interesting to read simply because its author had no ax to grind but a journalistic one, and so allowed the reader to learn the elementary facts of Hearst's life. Eight years later, unexpectedly, not one but three long, detailed biographies appeared. Immediately apparent was it that not one of these books involved Brisbane appreciably. Hearst, if nothing else, did exist.

The innocent reader of *William Randolph Hearst, American*, by Mrs. Fremont Older, would have been justified in feeling that Hearst was incomparably the greatest American of his time. The list of his accomplishments, of the battles he had fought in the public interest, of his innovations, was staggeringly long. The same reader would have been bewildered on turning then to *Imperial Hearst, a Social Biography*, by Ferdinand Lundberg. He might have wondered whether Lundberg were dealing with the same man. From the book's mordant preface by Dr. Charles A. Beard, which compared Hearst to Caligula and Nero, to its highly documented, concentrated indictment, it gave the picture of a monster of moral and mental iniquity. Hearst was obscene, Hearst was a demagogue, Hearst was a profit-seeking rabble-rouser who besmirched whatever he touched. Nothing relieved the vitriol in the portrait. If Hearst had his virtues, according to Lundberg, they were not relevant to the subject. Whoever had a good word for the condemned man was himself either condemned or explained away.

Hearst—Lord of San Simeon, written by Oliver Carlson and E. S. Bates, was another attack which supplemented and affirmed that of Lundberg. Hearst in the year 1936 had no standing with the intellectuals at all, except for those intellectuals who were employed by him.

But in 1936 Hearst was seventy-three years old, and much water had passed under many bridges.

Hearst never did enjoy much prestige. "Everybody" despised him. "Everybody" considered his papers the dregs of journalism.

Hearst in journalism [wrote Steffens[2]] was like a reformer in politics; he was an innovator who was crashing into the business, upsetting the settled order of things, and he was not doing it as we would have had it done. He was doing it his way. Journalists and all newspaper readers who were dissatisfied with newspapers as they were, thought, like good citizens in cities, that they wanted a change, something new, but they did not want what Hearst was giving them. It was an old story. The Jews of old were looking for a Messiah, but they pictured him as a king coming on a throne to do what they wanted done. The good citizens of Jersey City had been looking for a leader, but they did not expect him to be an Irish Catholic undertaker like Mark Fagan; and the best people of Cleveland hoped to be saved, but not by a jolly captain of industry such as Tom Johnson. Well, it was so with my fellow-craftsmen; they wished that someone would come along with money and brains enough to make a newspaper which they could all read, and perhaps write for happily. But Hearst—he with his millions was making a paper that nobody liked. . . . We forbade it in our clubs; we wouldn't be seen with it, except here and there one of us would "fall for the money" and write for it. And some of these "hirelings" had the decency to be ashamed and to betray the Hearst papers. It was true that his papers began to win a circulation. Of course. He had discovered that there was room at the bottom, and with sensational news sensationally written and pictured, he did reach for and get the people. He was a demagogue; he was pro-labor. I cannot describe the hate of those days for Hearst except to say that it was worse than it is now. . . .

Hearst, then, far from being a myth, existed too much for anyone's satisfaction. The papers were his; he was personally responsible for whatever went into them, and whatever was left out. Who was this man who spoke to millions of people daily, in a way peculiar to himself, and influenced opinion as no other man, barring the President, could do?

He was the son of George Hearst, a Forty-Niner who had made millions in gold and silver strikes. When the old man died in 1901, he had served four years in the United States Senate. He left an inheritance of $17,000,000 in mines and ranches located in California, Nevada, Montana, Mexico, and elsewhere. Hearst's mother, Phoebe Apperson Hearst, had been a school teacher before marriage and wealth came her way.

[2] *Autobiography*, pages 539-540.

Hearst, raised in California, was an unprepossessing boy given to pranks and not deeply touched by the culture and idealism with which his mother attempted to saturate him. Both Lundberg and Bates have made much of his youthful characteristics which, they insist, showed a definite feeling of inferiority. Perhaps they did. In any event, Hearst declared that he revered his parents and that they inspired him to carry on the Jeffersonian Democracy which they personified. Whatever the principles that guided the parents, there can be little question that George Hearst was a "robber baron" of his day and that his wife was the genteel female companion of whom practical Westerners dreamed.

William Randolph Hearst was never at any time a student, and his motives were generated by experience, not from the bookish transmission of ideas, Jeffersonian or otherwise. Disliking the East, but following his mother's wishes, he attended Harvard. His one achievement there, besides lavish spending and Piccadilly clothes, was to become the successful business manager of the *Lampoon*. It was while he was there, also, that he became interested in Pulitzer's newspaper methods and studied the *World* diligently to discover what made it go. In his junior year he was expelled from Harvard for mischief, and, unabashed, he returned home to his father with a business proposition.

George Hearst had taken over the San Francisco *Examiner* for bad debts and been running it as an adjunct to his political and financial interests. If it was not then the broken-down wreck described by Mrs. Older, its 30,000 circulation certainly placed it low among Western journals. William now suggested that the paper be turned over to him. Having studied the *World* to advantage, he felt confident that he could make the *Examiner* a success. The old man attempted to dissuade him: journalism was no business for his son; there weren't many businesses in which money could be lost more quickly. Evidently George Hearst did not think much of his son's ability, but in the end he gave the youth what he wanted. In 1887 the *Examiner* came out with a new format, under a new proprietor, and with a changed staff.

Hearst, wrote Steffens, was born amoral. Steffens was complimentary. He meant that Hearst saw—and saw correctly—that the end justified the means, that idealism unsupported by practical sense would come to nothing. Practicality, at least, was in Hearst's lexicon. Every day, from the moment he took over the *Examiner*, he acted from impulse and for expediency. Those who were passionately for and against him, were reacting to his personality, not his "philosophy." Hearst was a boss; he ruled his property as he saw fit; and what he saw fit to do influenced American life all along the line.

From the start he took the path by which we know him: it was Pulitzer's path—with a vengeance. Lurid stories, bold headlines, truculent interference in all public affairs, soon informed the Pacific Coast of this new meteor in the newspaper game. Hearst meanwhile paid liberally to get the best talent available. He hired Samuel Chamberlain, an outstanding "yellow" journalist, and Ambrose Bierce. Edward W. Townsend, of "Chimmie Fadden" fame, conducted the business of the organization. Homer Davenport's cartoons became one of Hearst's most popular assets. Writers like Mark Twain, Gertrude Atherton, Joaquin Miller, and Rudyard Kipling contributed special articles and features for velvety fees. Hearst, in a word, threw real talent into the arena of public controversy, and carried on battles concerning franchises and labor issues with effect.

Hearst fought for his career—that career which the careful researches of Lundberg and Bates reveal as having had many curious deviations and dark shadows. He was capable of the most lucid and proletarian approaches to matters of public interest. But he was also fighting for himself. Within several years he had raised the circulation of the *Examiner* to 800,000 and had acquired hosts of enemies.

He opened fire on the Southern Pacific Railroad, the octopus of the Pacific Coast and beyond, the villain of Frank Norris's masterpiece which at that time carried the affairs of the State of California around in its pockets. His critics have shown that his campaign never had the firm ring of selflessness. But there can be little question that it was chiefly because of this campaign that the Southern Pacific was clearly established in the common mind as the outstanding enemy of democracy in the Far West. If Hearst the rabble-rouser earned the inexpressible hatred of the monopolists, the "rabble" itself read his headlines, looked at his pictures, and moved slowly in the direction of reform.

"Willie" Hearst was very much the playboy. Stories of the

personal life of this tall, ungainly man, with the weak voice and flaccid handshake, contrasted strangely with accounts of other newspapermen, including Scripps, who despised public opinion. Scripps was a student, a philosopher; Hearst became indistinguishable from his newspaper and the issues it propounded.

Preaching nationalism, public ownership, and democracy, in 1895 Hearst made up his mind to carry the fight to New York, to come to grips with Pulitzer himself. The New York *Journal* was for sale, and Hearst, still dapper, still the playboy, put down the money for it and, to the accompaniment of bad wishes and jeers, came East to conquer.

The story of his great fight with Pulitzer is history: how the prices of the *World* and the *Journal* dropped to one cent; how Hearst stole Morrill Goddard, Pulitzer's "yellow" genius away from the *World*, and how Pulitzer bought him back within twenty-four hours, and how Hearst rebought him. The story of his "yellow kid" cartoon, which introduced colored comic strips and revolutionized newspaper methods, and the account of his alliance with Brisbane, have been many times repeated. But what should be made clear is that the great New York campaign was not a sudden development of Hearst: it was merely Hearst on the up-grade. He was already a famous—or infamous—newspaperman when he bought the *Journal*. His strong and victorious battle simply made him nationally more prominent.

Hearst's stand for Bryan in 1896, a stand which brought him more opprobrium than ever, made him the outstanding Democratic publisher in the country. True, the "robber barons" of the silver mines, of whom his own father was an eminent member, were heartily for Bryan. Machiavellian Hearst! Yet the sum of the crusades for which he stood; the court battles he fought, first with San Francisco and New York combines, then with trust and party organizations in other cities—these make it plain that he was more than a threat, that he was a positive enemy, to the established order which the muckrakers were trying to destroy. The worker and farmer could read—if he was willing to read at all—more decorous editorials and news items in Godkin's *Post*, but in the end he was no nearer security or political power than he had been before. *Hearst, more than any other man, was the absolute expression of all the blind need and ignorance and resentment which troubled the worker and farmer.* He dived to the bottom of the reader's mind and stirred up the filth and despair that had lain so quiet before. He, not the writers of exposures, was the "muckraker" whom Roosevelt should have had in mind when the latter quoted Bunyan on the man "who could look no way but downward with the muckrake in his hand, who was offered a celestial crown for his muckrake but who would neither look up nor regard the crown he was offered, but continued to rake to himself the filth of the floor."

Hearst was steeped in mire. His long campaign against McKinley was virulent to the degree of insanity. But did McKinley really deserve much better treatment? It would have been splendid if another, more upright, more principled man than Hearst had been present to carry on the quasi-Socialist battle. But no such man existed. The question about Hearst was and is now: What good lived after him, and what evils, after the outraged sensibilities and personal resentments of individuals ceased to matter? Lundberg has insisted that Hearst wrested the banners of revolt from sincere and capable reformers, and dragged them in the dust. Carefully Lundberg collated the criticisms and insults of all Hearst's enemies and sometime friends to prove that the fights the man waged might have been better waged, that the man himself was insincere, autocratic, narrow.

How easily are inter-reformist disagreements forty and more years old touched to life! Indeed, Hearst lied, distorted, sensationalized. But throughout the later years of the Nineties, and particularly during the muckraking period, there was hardly a reformer or revolutionist of note whose thoughts were not at one time or another woven into the skein of newspapers and magazines which carried the stamp of Hearst's personality: Tarbell, A. H. Lewis, Henry George, Crosby, Russell, Jack London, Upton Sinclair, Gustavus Myers—the list could be extended indefinitely. There were, of course, muckrakers and reformers who loathed Hearst. *Collier's* in particular showered a burning contempt on him. Norman Hapgood, Mark Sullivan, and others of that magazine lost no opportunity to expose him as a liar and a charlatan and, as we shall see, a forger. Very healthy and worth reading, a corrective influence, were the *Collier's* broadsides. Norman Hapgood, the purest of pure intellectuals, regarded the Hearst papers as a nightmare in the American Dream. But Hapgood's heart's desire was to instruct his fellow citizens, not to bring them to *Collier's* door shouting for action. *Collier's* had its own type of "sensationalism."

Hearstism, then, meant stirring the prevailing muck. It meant fighting privilege with the weapons of privilege. It premised the expansion of Hearst and his tribe on the theory that more Hearst meant less privilege. And so Hearst grew. What the end would be when Hearst had so much expanded that he himself would require wholesale correction no one knew. But meanwhile a larger and larger percentage of the population ran and read, and there was worry and venom in the citadels of conservatism.

What shall one say of Hearst and the Cuban War? There can be no doubt that the Spanish rule was reactionary. The Spanish government was fundamentally incapable of doing anything with its possessions. America, or American capitalism, was certainly more alive than Spain to the possibilities of those possessions. But how was the chasm to be bridged between Spanish ownership and Cuban liberation?

Was it right for America to seize another nation's lands? That question has been delicately avoided for two generations. If it was right, if it was a step in the direction of progress, then Hearst must be given all credit. For American politicians were entirely inept in the tense pre-War situation. Hanna, arch-spokesman for reaction, was against war; Roosevelt, the very symbol of reform, was for it. Right or wrong, however, Roosevelt and Hearst were invariably at one on the issue of imperialism, for all their difference in method, and America went to war.

Those were glorious days for Hearstism. The Hearst correspondents swarmed over the land fanning the flames of war. In the matter of the blowing up of the *Maine*, Lundberg boldly presents a case of circumstantial evidence that does no less than point to Hearst. To Hearst's journalism of action were called such eminent men as Stephen Crane, Frederic Remington, and particularly James Creelman, who was Hearst's most faithful servant.[3] Hearst himself was the hero of a farce-adventure which

[3] See Creelman's *On the Great Highway*, Lothrop, Boston, 1901.

his papers trumpeted to all the country. Whatever the cost of the War, it made the *Journal*, and Hearst entered the new century as one of the lords of the press.

In 1901, when McKinley was shot, Hearst's name was again written black in every household and every center of public gathering. He was burned in effigy. He took to working with a revolver beside him. Already he had been accused of deliberately intending the disintegration of the American system, with his attacks on great business and central government; now he was accused of nothing less than the murder of McKinley. For years he had singled out that President as a puppet of monopoly.

What could this verse mean, which Ambrose Bierce printed shortly before the tragedy?

> The bullet which pierced Goebel's [4] breast
> Can not be found in all the west;
> Good reason, it is speeding here
> To stretch McKinley on his bier.

Was Bierce, was his employer Hearst hinting that McKinley deserved to be assassinated? Or was its author trying to say that monopoly and contempt for the common people bred anarchy? No one who believed the latter could be heard in those days of unbridled emotionalism. Hearst was branded a murderer, and in the new President's speech was a passage that could not be interpreted except as signifying agreement with that accusation.

No decent man read Hearst; and yet his circulations leaped higher and higher. In 1901 Hearst founded the Chicago *American* with the approval of Bryan, who saw it as important to the Democratic Party. Hearst was rewarded with the presidency of the National Association of Democratic Clubs, and he needed no more: he straightway set himself to turning them into an instrument for his own advancement. In 1901 he looked already to 1904, which was the Presidential year. In 1902, as a regular Democrat, he made an alliance with Charles F. Murphy, the Tammany leader, and was sent to Congress as a Representative from the Eleventh District.

But Representative was hardly a position of influence for the powerful Hearst; he was looking farther ahead. He made 1902,

---

[4] Governor of Kentucky, earlier assassinated during an inter-party feud.

therefore, the year which inaugurated muckraking, the turning point of his life. He ceased being "Willie" Hearst. He took to wearing the traditional clothes of a statesman: black string tie, black felt hat, long coat. Since it was not becoming for a Hearst to be unmarried at the age of forty, he took to himself a wife and set about founding a family.

Hearst was hardly a sterling Congressman. Carlson and Bates have established that, in sessions packed with issues and events, he answered to the roll-call only nine times. Lundberg has gone further to show that the "Socialistic" bills which he submitted were designed to frighten his enemies or win popular favor or gain personal profit. Self-interest—nothing but self-interest!

But what campaigns were the *Journal* and *Examiner* and *American* waging in the meantime? In all the cities Hearst was fighting the water and gas and street-railway franchise monopolies. In New York he held on in his battle to dissolve the ice trust, and ultimately he placed Charles W. Morse, its president, in prison for tampering with company books. He was active in the great coal strike and saw to the nominal dissolution of the coal trust. In Chicago he joined with Darrow, Altgeld, and others to fight for the five-cent fare, municipal ownership of public utilities, and fair taxation. Still further, he publicized the rebate practices of the sugar trust, which after years of litigation resulted in the trust's payment of a fine of $108,000.

In 1899 Hearst began his attacks on the beef trust, exposing the "embalmed beef" scandal and forcing a Senatorial investigation. In 1901 he employed Ella Reeve Bloor to investigate the stockyards. For his own reasons he avoided the issue of conditions in the stockyards and concentrated on the rebate practices of the packers. His articles and suits forced an injunction upon the packers to stop their criminal terrorization of competitors. The suits continued until 1905, when the great corporations and their owners, including Swift, Armour, Cudahy, Morris, and others, were convicted of conspiracy, fined, and sentenced to a year's imprisonment. Of course these men never served their terms—Judge Humphrey ruled that under the law, corporations were immune from conviction—but the Hearst suits were instrumental in the great pure-food and railroad-control campaigns, and were of considerable aid to the muckrakers.

And all the while *Hearst was running more poisonous patent-medicine advertising than any other publisher*. This is the undebatable evidence from Lundberg's investigations. Again, Hearst ran the advertisements of houses of assignation (Hearst, who had forced Bennett's *Herald* to pay a government fine for the same offense!) and fraudulent stock advertisements.

Hearst was, then, made in black and white. Inconsistency in good and evil was his manner of working. This was why men, generally, with the exception of the Socialists, were not party men but pro-Hearst or anti-Hearst men.

Clarence Darrow, who was at this time in the pro-Hearst camp, seconded his man's nomination for Democratic Presidential candidate in 1904. The Democratic Clubs were pro-Hearst. The Hearst papers, too, cried Hearst's slogans of municipal and government ownership, death to the criminal trusts, and so forth, to the four corners of the country. But Hearst failed to capture the nomination. In the sullied elections of 1905, however, he broke with Tammany and ran for Mayor of New York City as candidate of the Municipal Ownership League—which was again Hearst. In 1906 excitement over his political exploits once more focused national attention on him. For if Hearst captured the Governorship of New York, there was no power on earth that could keep him from the Presidential nomination in 1908. And if he got that—

This time it was the Independence League that represented him. The campaign took twenty days: twenty days that were cyclonic in their frenzy. Charles Evans Hughes, newly famous because of his work during the insurance investigations of the preceding year, was hurled into the breach to stem the tide of Hearstism. Roosevelt instructed Elihu Root to speak out publicly and in his name against Hearst. Still the tide rose. The Hearst papers printed solemn pictures of Hearst and his family, and the context of sex and scandal was temporarily toned down. Brisbane found something good to say about Anthony Comstock. When election night arrived, the nation held its breath; but then the returns came in, and Hearst had lost.

Yet even while the campaign raged, Hearst held trump cards in his pocket. He bided his time, meanwhile announcing that both parties were no longer capable of resurrection. In his high-pitched, quavering voice, he declared that the Republican Party was sold to the trusts, and the Democratic Party likewise. Nor did he fail to follow up this beginning. In 1908, when his puppets ran for the Presidency on the platform of the Independence League, he proclaimed that the American who wished to preserve his liberties

"WILLIAM ALSO-RAN-DOLPH HEARST"

Drawn for Wallace Irwin's *Random Rhymes and Odd Numbers*

must vote the Independence ticket. He hinted and warned that he would prove it. And on September 17, 1908, while speaking for his League at Columbus, Ohio, he presented his evidence. He took from his pocket and quoted from letters which he asserted had been written by John D. Archbold, Vice-President of the Standard Oil Company, to various Senators and Representatives in Washington. The meaning of these letters to Senator Bailey, Senator Foraker, and others was unmistakable: Standard Oil had paid for desirable legislation in Washington and in the states.

If this was not news, surely never before had such *evidence*

been available. Quickly the significance of the letters sank into
the consciousness of the public. The next day, when Hearst made
his next stop on tour, he was rushed by an army of reporters demanding further information about those letters. Could he prove
they were genuine? How many did he have? Would he make
them all public? What other public figures did they involve?

Meanwhile Bailey had admitted the authenticity of the letter
to him from the Standard chieftain and had given a clever explanation of the money matters it involved. But Bailey was not
aware that Hearst had other letters that contradicted his explanations. Hearst made a triumphal march East, reading new letters
at every stop and promising more. High finance was thrown into
a panic. Roosevelt himself summoned Hearst to Washington to
make sure that none of the missives contained "gossip" that might
be interpreted to Presidential discredit.

For four years at intervals Hearst continued to publish fresh
Standard letters, and they continued to harass the nerves and
shake the reputations of prominent men. But they helped the
Independence League not a bit. As to the origin of the letters,
on the platform, in the press, and on the witness stand, Hearst
told contradictory stories. The truth, however, came out. Late in
1904 lowly employees with access to the Standard Oil files, in its
headquarters at No. 26 Broadway, had conceived the idea of selling letters of the Company to the newspapers. Hearst had come
to terms with them. During the following years, letters were
secretely removed at night, photostated, and returned to the files
during the day. Hearst had kept the letters in his safe for three
years.

Why hadn't he released them at once? Had those letters been
given to the public in 1905, their effect might have been nation-
shaking. For in 1905 the muckraking movement was nearly at
its height. The public was reading the exposures with wild excitement; reform was advancing boldly and the most desperate
insults and calumny were being showered on the muckrakers. Had
Hearst's evidence been given to the public at that time reform
might have moved with the tread of revolt against monopoly.
Why, then, did Hearst withhold the letters until their powder
was wet? The answer is that he feared they might redound to
Roosevelt's benefit. Why, too, did he abridge and retype original

letters, and then present them as the originals? The answer here is that he was playing politics with individuals whom the letters involved, some of whom he was not ready to expose. It was for the same reason that he released the letters at intervals.

And why, why, groaned liberals, did Hearst, having masses of authentic letters—real, incontrovertible evidence of the highest importance to the American people—go out of his way, as *Collier's* proved, to forge five futile letters which were played up so exaggeratedly as to discredit the entire exposure of Standard methods? The only plain reason was that Hearst was Hearst. He wanted to serve the people, as Steffens pointed out, but he insisted on serving them in his own way, insisted on giving them democracy under his own irrational, personal, temperamental dictatorship.

The murky glory of Hearst's muckraking years was followed by wild campaigns in the pre-War days and his complete degeneration of character and purpose after the War was over. When in the post-muckraking days new line-ups of pro- and anti-labor fighters were created, Hearst never cared to submit himself to the moral discipline the new pro-labor tasks involved. As for "Jeffersonian democracy"—that old Hearstian shibboleth—it sounded more and more fatuous.

Intelligent, honorable people—many of them—once believed in Hearst. Upton Sinclair predicted that he would be the first Socialist President, and that he would be elected in 1912. Writes Sinclair today: [5]

> There is nothing I am more ashamed of in my whole life than having believed in Hearst, which is the reason I have never reprinted *The Industrial Republic*, which otherwise is a very good book. . . .

Sinclair was not alone in this early conviction. Hearst was capable of the most vividly correct analyses and action. The painful truth is that he was himself.

Had Hearst been able to curb his ambition, to work with the muckrakers wholeheartedly and consistently, the muckraking movement might have gone on even to a more tangible success than it achieved. The Archbold letters, had they been publicized

---

[5] In a letter to the author.

at the right moment, might have taken the matter out of Hearst's irresponsible hands. Handled as they were, they merely drove Foraker out of politics: a slight victory; and they ensured the nominal dissolution of the Standard Oil Trust, which, in 1908, was already certain to happen.

Hearst was destined to be the soil, or the subsoil, of the muck-raking movement. As such he is enitled to credit on many scores. But he was not the greatest American at any hour, nor was he ever particularly imperial. He was surely a power in the land, and it is likely that in his prime he wrought better than his enemies believed. It is certain only that in his old age the evil predominated, and there was none to stand up for him.[6]

[6] See for example, W. A. Swanberg, *Citizen Hearst*, Charles Scribner's Sons, New York, 1961.

XII. THE POISON TRUST

THROUGH 1903 muckraking was dominated by Steffens, Tarbell, and Baker. By 1904 the work of these writers in particular had made the existence of a definite vogue of exposure apparent to the least alert citizen. It was obvious, too, that more than an expansion of magazine influence had occurred. The magazines were dealing with hard facts, indeed, but they and the newspapers also reflected an unprecedented amount of public agitation. On the debit side of the national life they were revealing scandal, not only in industry but in the Post Office, the Bureau of Statistics, the Land Office, and other agencies. On the credit side they were reporting remedial action—action which the citizen had reason to believe involved real changes in business and politics. The enormous land frauds in Oregon, for instance, one of the worst examples of a practice that had been going on for years, were now aired by the splendid work of government prosecutor Francis J. Heney, and three United States Senators and a horde of lesser men were indicted. Suits against Standard Oil, the American Tobacco Company, the sugar trust, and practically all the other trusts were going strong. T. R. himself was re-elected on a wholesale-reform program, and the citizenry with their mouthpiece, the muckrakers, were looking for still more of this heart-warming action.

The year 1905 was reform year. Insurance trials opened wide the entire question of business ethics and practices. The machines which had ruled the cities for a quarter of a century were overthrown. A flood of revolt swept from New Jersey to California, submerging political bosses and their cohorts. This was no mere "wave" such as had earned "Boss" Croker's sardonic contempt, for statutes were written into the books which changed the rules of the old political game and put a legal finish to industry's fiction of rugged individualism. *America's Awakening*,[1] Philip Loring Allen called this national zeal for reform, and that was how it looked to all thinking and unthinking minds alike. Even the Socialists, who most volubly considered reform not enough, thought of the events of those years as victories to be extended until Socialism was established nationally.

But during these tumultuous days one issue stood out above the rest as needing certain solution. It was bad enough to pay tribute to the railroads and tolerate their accident rate—the worst in the world. It was bad enough to be mulcted by trusts and politicians. But the food and drug question touched everyone more immediately; it involved not only health and happiness but life itself. And it was inseparable from the general ignorance that had allowed political bosses and trusts to wax so strong. Medicine was open to quacks and patent medicines—many of them poison—had become a $59,000,000-a-year business in a country with only 80,000,000 inhabitants.

"Medicines" there were which contained as high as eighty per cent of alcohol, "soothing syrups" which had morphine and cocaine as basic constituents. No wonder children cried for it! Not only the newspapers but the magazines themselves contained pages and pages of advertisements of "cures" which preyed—and preyed with enormous success—on hope and ignorance. Yet the only criticism of advertising that the periodicals printed repeatedly was that it was an eyesore in the city and "defaced nature" in the country.

What was anyone to do about it? (The same question had been posed by Tweed.) Action began, as usual, among conscientious workers rather than revolutionaries who were so far "in advance" that immediate problems were scorned by them. Actual war against impure food was begun by Dr. Harvey Washington Wiley, who carried on a lone fight for twenty-five years before he saw his struggle bear fruit. Dr. Wiley, not the muckrakers, was the solid force behind pure-food and patent-medicine reform; contrariwise, the muckrakers, not Dr. Wiley, were responsible for its success.

[1] *The Triumph of Righteousness in High Places*, F. H. Revell Co., New York, 1906.

The agitation for the Pure Food and Drug Act was a micro-cosm of the entire period. It showed how dependent upon each other were politics, science, literature. Not only that: it also made clear just what the old American economic life had involved, and how different the new was destined to be. The conditions under which Americans ate and medicated themselves before 1906 are inconceivable to us today; more likely than not, we are apt to wonder how they managed to survive them.

Dr. Wiley was anything but a revolutionary; in fact his politics as such were never of moment. He was a chemist—the brilliant, persistent type of scientist who has made America noted for its practical inventions and discoveries. Like Edison and Luther Burbank, Wiley experimented and deduced, experimented and de-duced, accomplishing by sheer labor vast amounts of work. Wiley was, moreover, a man of substantial culture and understanding: he had a fine literary background, and he had taught Latin and Greek in his native Indiana, and had been the first chemist of the newly founded Purdue University, before he became, in 1883, Chief Chemist of the Department of Agriculture.

Dr. Wiley was aware of social implications of development in the food industry—that industry that had begun to demand at-tention in the Seventies and had quickly become a national prob-lem. The food industry, like all the others, had been centralized by ambitious men. No longer did one buy meat that had been freshly killed in the vicinity, or fruit that had been picked on near-by farms. The refrigerator car, newly developed, sped ani-mal and plant products hundreds of miles. Since ice was not ef-fective to preserve all products, preservatives were introduced: boric acid and borax, benzoic acid and benzoates—all of which came to Dr. Wiley's attention and received his analyses. Whisky was now manufactured in gigantic quantities, and almost none of it was pure. For most of the products fantastic claims were made and advertised.

The patent-medicine business was a swindle almost from its inception. Folk experience had originally gone into the making of such medicines, but innocent nostrums were soon succeeded by useless or harmful money-making preparations. People believed vaguely that these were "cheaper" than the doctor, that educated physicians in the big cities had prepared pills and syrups to which common people in need could turn safely. And so, with such doubtful beginnings, patent-medicine companies became the public's doctor and confidant. Campaigns were waged to win large followings; personal correspondence regarding symptoms and complaints was solicited; billboards screamed assurances that colds, headaches, consumption, deafness—anything and everything—could be cured by the advertised remedies. Some advertised products were supposed to end cancer and the tobacco and morphine habits, to enlarge female "busts," and to bring on abortions.

Fantastic formulas which at best were ineffectual and at worst destroyed health brought the patent-medicine practitioners millions of dollars. Quacks and swindlers, they became outstanding members of their communities. They donated money to churches and political campaigns. They took a firm grip on the newspapers. And since they were respectable, typical examples of American enterprise and success, it became nothing less than Socialism to challenge them.

Dr. Wiley cared nothing about Socialism nor, for that matter, about money. His absorbing interest was chemistry. In 1892 he published *Songs of Agricultural Chemists*—a title that described the man as well as the book—and between 1894 and 1897 he issued a series of volumes on agricultural chemistry. Loving his work, he felt constrained to tell the truth about it, and part of the truth was that Americans were daily consuming poison—and had no choice in the matter, since there was no power or authority to compel the manufacturers and nostrum venders to reveal how they prepared their products or what was in them.

Being a persuasive writer and speaker, Dr. Wiley drew attention. His explanations as to why there must be a food and drug law involved the naming of specific corporations, and he therefore stood out as an "enemy" of the capitalist system. His name was put on the black books of respectable people; his ruin was sought; time and again he was insulted and pilloried as a sensation-monger.[2] Being resolute, however, and having a sense of humor, he managed to weather the storms that broke over him through the Nineties.

[2] See Wiley's *An Autobiography*, The Bobbs-Merrill Co., Indianapolis, 1930.

During those years, moreover, his work was getting results. The National Association of State Dairy and Food Departments was formed in 1898, and men of enterprise and ideas rose to its head. They turned the eye of science on food in their own states; they called for government control of the food and drug industries. They were forced to see beyond the limits of their work, and to perceive (although vaguely, of course) that it was no accident that products Americans consumed were unfit for human consumption. To understand was, for them, not to pardon but to be aroused to action.

Exponents of food administration joined Dr. Wiley in his crusade. Edward Fremont Ladd, who was to write his name deep into North Dakota history and Sheppard of South Dakota, Emery of Wisconsin, Bird of Michigan, Abbott of Texas, Frear of Pennsylvania, Allen of Kentucky, and others added their experience and ingenuity to the fight. Alice Lakey, of the Consumers' League, was inspired by Dr. Wiley to devote herself to propaganda for a national food law. The Federated Women's Clubs and labor organizations banded together to struggle for the law. Even the American Medical Association, although already a conservative body of physicians, bestirred itself, but unfortunately its interest was in directly discrediting patent medicines—its great competitor—rather than in pushing radical legislation that would protect the health of the citizenry.

Little enough of this crusade came to popular attention. In books, magazines, and newspapers references to it were few, so that even Dr. S. Weir Mitchell's long-short story, *The Autobiography of a Quack*, rough and casual though it was, deserves mention. To write on food and medicine, to write critically and *effectively*, required both literary and medical training, and these were not common together. On the other hand, there were plenty of laudatory articles being written about the great Armour organization; and the truth was not told about its food products even when nostrum advertisements were being virtuously barred from many of the magazines.

Dr. Wiley himself carried much of the burden of informing the public about the food problem, and he did it in his stride. He swept past unessentials and fastened attention on the fundamental questions: What was contained in the food that America took into its stomach? What effects did the food have on people?

In 1902 he began those experiments on men which became world-famous as the "poison-squad" experiments. They were purely scientific. Controlling his factors as best he could, Dr. Wiley fed his human guinea-pigs and made records of the results different combinations of food had upon them. The subject was, specifically, the effects (bad) of common preservatives, but the interest of the public went beyond even the important conclusions which he obtained, and clamor for a pure-food law increased. That very same year Senator Weldon B. Heyburn of Idaho, who was to carry the brunt of the legislative fight of 1906, reported in Congress on pure food and demanded the labeling of all products in interstate commerce. His bill was actually carried through the House but was stopped dead in the rigidly reactionary Senate.

Dr. Wiley continued to lecture and write. Pushing his "poison-squad" experiments, he published in government pamphlets as many of his results as he was able to get past the alert guardians of special interests who held Federal positions. In 1904 a dramatic situation developed when the State Dairy and Food men at the St. Louis Exposition managed to obtain a display booth adjoining the exhibit prepared by manufacturers of preserved foods. For the edification of Fair visitors, the food crusaders extracted dyes from well-known preserves and with them stained pieces of wool and silk: animal products. It did not take much imagination on the part of the visitors to realize that what happened to the wool and silk was happening to the lining of the stomach and intestines of those who were eating preserved foods. Such spectacular triumphs increased the optimism of those who felt that victory was inevitable and that food would finally be brought under public control.

And yet it was impossible for the reformers to batter past the iron doors of the Senate. The Senate was the direct representative of the trusts, and these included the beef trust—which, it was true, had not yet been embarrassed by exposures—and what amounted to a patent-medicine trust. Legally, there was no actual quack trust, but the National Wholesale Liquor Dealers Association and the Proprietary Medicine Association were sufficiently organized

to have powerful representatives in Congress and to trip up legislation inimical to them.

It seemed as though Dr. Wiley and his followers were destined
to spend their energies in vain on a matter of more immediate
importance to the people than any other question. From the
presses of the quacks poured vast amounts of printed matter explaining that the pure-food agitation was only a plot by physicians
to extract more and higher fees from the people. The argument
was broadcast that a national law would infringe states' rights.
Pressure was applied to the newspapers, which were warned to
take a positive stand against pure-food legislation: silence was not
enough, since their advertising interests were at stake.

Only the magazines—the popular ones—were free to criticize.
Yet though they were anxious to interest the common reader, they
did not take readily to the pure-food campaign. The average editor did not know what its consequences would be on his magazine's
circulation; besides, that campaign was uncomfortably "radical."
It was therefore remarkable that the battle for pure food was
begun, not by *McClure's*, not by *Everybody's*, not by any other
of the magazines that had tuned themselves to the general public,
but by the magazine of Edward Bok, the women's magazine, *The
Ladies' Home Journal*.

How did it happen that Bok of all people, with absolutely no
idea of promoting circulation, should have alone pushed pure-
food reform? As far back as 1892 the *Journal* had set itself against
patent medicines and thus been an example of righteousness soon
to be followed, at least in some degree, by other magazines. Pure
food had not been a matter of prime consideration, and the
Journal had still carried advertisements of canned foods and beef
products. It was specifically patent medicines that had aroused
Bok's ire, and from time to time he had made outraged protest
against their existence.

Bok, as editor and guiding genius of the *Journal*, represented
the middle-class home, and what was more reactionary than that?
Bok's audience, larger than any other magazine's, was composed
of the vast, anomalous mass of women whose personalities were
no longer satisfied by the outmoded ideals about womanhood. Bok
could, then, afford to do without the patent-medicine advertisers.

So long as he could stir a little life into the problems women were forced to take seriously, to suggest the deeply serious problems of sex, marriage, and feminine hygiene (which decent women were supposed to be ignorant of), he was assured of more circulation than any other periodical. Modernity, in other words, was enough to make his magazine successful.

Food, on the other hand, could be talked about endlessly, and it involved politics and economics: it meant becoming truly alive and vital. Bok had no intention of anticipating history. But the patent-medicine game was distinct in itself, and exasperating. Denunciations of it committed Bok to no theories of economics and politics; they merely dovetailed with his other editorial opinions, which deplored women's incapable handling of the duties of wife and mother.

In 1904, then, Bok began his series of editorials calling upon all decent people to boycott patent medicines. The style was the man: he appealed to the Woman's Christian Temperance Union to campaign against preparations which were nothing less than cocktails. He sternly announced that he knew, personally, people who allowed patent-medicine advertisements to be painted on their barns. He deplored the fact that the religious papers accepted and even solicited nostrum advertisements. How, asked Bok, could people be expected to honor the churches when such practices were allowed?

Now Bok did not have too much information about his subject, and the result was that he made a serious mistake. He obtained from the Massachusetts State Board food analyst (a progressive) a chart which gave the percentages of alcohol in a number of preparations, and he printed the chart in the *Journal*. The facts about one of the preparations, "Dr. Pierce's Favorite Prescription," happened to be out of date and entirely wrong. Bok and the *Journal* were sued, and he was forced to print a retraction of his charges.

Bok saw that if he wanted to continue his crusade he would have to do better. He therefore sought an investigator who could prepare the background of information he required. McClure suggested Mark Sullivan, whom he had kept in mind for himself ever since Sullivan's "The Ills of Pennsylvania" had succeeded in the *Atlantic*. Sullivan had just come to New York from Boston, and was beginning a law practice. Bok wrote to him, asking him to come in for a talk.

Sullivan, it seemed, was just the man he was looking for. Sullivan was a natural-born journalist and research expert, a healthy, self-confident young man, born and bred in rural Pennsylvania, who had been part proprietor of a newspaper and had influenced local politics before he could vote. He had worked his way through Harvard, writing pieces for the Boston *Transcript* and other papers. He had a remarkable sense for news and never failed to make more than enough for his needs.

A good illustration of his ability was the article he wrote for the *Transcript* concerning buffaloes. It was known that the buffalo had been practically exterminated from the plains, but how many were actually left? Sullivan set out to learn for himself. He carried on a voluminous correspondence with zoo keepers and conservation experts, and in short order made himself the world's leading authority on the buffalo situation. The article which he finally wrote was incredibly thorough and caused widespread interest in the fate of the few surviving buffalo.[3]

Bok urged Sullivan to give up law and work for the *Journal*, and the young man was not hard to persuade, for he had no real interest in law. He was therefore sent out to collect data on the patent-medicine concerns for use in the campaign, and he at once applied himself in his characteristic way. He visited various cities —all the while trailed by patent-medicine detectives—and by means of shrewd stratagems ferreted out secrets of the patent-medicine trade. He advertised for "experienced patent-medicine men" and learned a good deal in "interviews" with them. He bought and photographed "exchange lists" of letters which had been written by sick, trustful men and women to the quacks— letters which were laughed at and passed around, and, after the unfortunates had been thoroughly cheated, sold in bulk to other fake concerns.

The Lydia Pinkham Company was urging women to write to Mrs. Pinkham herself for expert advice. Sullivan visited Pine Grove Cemetery, in Lynn, Massachusetts, and photographed

[3] See *The Education of an American*, Doubleday, Doran & Co., New York, 1938.

Lydia's tombstone, which plainly told that she had died in 1883! He also obtained the minutes of a meeting of the Proprietary Medicine Association, during which its president, F. J. Cheney, explained how clauses in his newspaper contracts bound the press to fight on his side against hostile legislation. Sullivan showed the influence of these advertising methods upon the Massachusetts legislative debate on patent medicines—a debate which had been boycotted by the newspapers.

Well supplied with facts, Bok was now able to go on with more confidence. He wrote "Why Patent Medicines Are Dangerous" and "The Diabolical Patent Medicine Story"—articles which made public impressions. Meanwhile Sullivan had prepared "The Patent Medicine Conspiracy against the Press." Just why it was not printed in the *Journal* is not certain: Sullivan writes that it was too long for the *Journal;* Bok himself wrote that it was too "legalistic" for his audience. However, Bok did want to see it printed, and therefore took it to Norman Hapgood and Robert Collier, who were duly impressed with Sullivan's information and style and bought the article for *Collier's.*

Bok, it appears, caught *Collier's* at an auspicious moment, for the magazine was in the process of change. Norman Hapgood, thin, ascetic-looking, scholarly, was determined to be popular and yet fair—absolutely fair. For that reason he had allowed Brisbane to print an encomium of Hearst—whom he detested—and had accepted an article on "Our Bourgeois Literature" by Upton Sinclair, whose Socialism was anathema to him. In 1904 Hapgood had begun the first of the distinguished *Collier's* campaigns: the discrediting of *Town Topics* as an organ of filth and blackmail. Capable writers had helped Hapgood to balance *Collier's* on the prescribed tightrope of honesty and progressivism. Samuel E. Moffatt, Mark Twain's nephew, contributed addenda to Steffens's "Shame of the City" articles, and Arthur Ruhl, Broughton Brandenburg, and others had written on social questions and current events.

On March 25, 1905, Hapgood had expressed himself at length on "The Epidemic of Exposures": Steffens and Tarbell were doing worth-while work, it seemed, but Lawson, Hearst, and Russell—commentators never agreed on which names should be bracketed together—did not give their work sufficient dignity, earnestness, scholarship. But it was clear that *Collier's* could not avoid the movement which Lawson, Hearst, and Russell (as well as Steffens and Tarbell) were leading. The issue of April 22, 1905, was a turning point in the magazine's history and an index of what was going on in Hapgood's mind. It literally bristled with muckraking—but, as it happened, mostly on the wrong side! The most important item in the entire issue was an editorial note regarding a letter of protest from William Jennings Bryan: Bryan's *Commoner* was printing patent-medicine ads, and Hapgood had commented on so virtuous an editor as Bryan accepting ads for "Liquozone"—a flagrantly fraudulent patent medicine. Bryan protested that, as *Collier's* well knew, every magazine printed advertisements which were not known to be false, and he challenged Hapgood to prove that "Liquozone" was not all that it claimed to be. *Collier's* editorial answer was that they were throwing frauds out as fast as possible and that they would have more to say on the subject.

It was at this point that Bok approached Hapgood and Collier with Sullivan's article, and they saw their way clear to a venture in muckraking that would have all the virtues and none of the vices of muckraking as they conceived it. Hapgood and Collier were less inflexibly honest than they thought themselves to be—and persuaded others that they were—but for the patent-medicine campaign, among others which they now began, they deserve all honor.

The opportunity to conduct the campaign was just waiting and begging for Samuel Hopkins Adams, who during his editorial work for McClure had been making a public reputation. Besides articles he had written many stories and was supposed to have literary talents.[4] But beside his literary competence he had a feeling for medical problems: during 1905 he had written a number of articles for *McClure's* on health and surgery. These articles had called Adams to the attention of Hapgood and Collier, and the latter now set him to work on the patent-medicine problem.

It is quite impossible to give too much praise to Adams and

---

[4] *Samuel Hopkins Adams, '91*—a biographical pamphlet, reprinted from the *Hamilton Alumni Review*, January 1937—contains a valuable bibliography of his work.

Hapgood for their campaign. To them undoubtedly belongs credit for the revival of the pure food and drugs issue, which inspired new bills in Congress and roused—or rather forced—Roosevelt to make his too well-publicized one-line recommendation [5] for Congressional legislation.

On June 3, 1905, *Collier's* printed the great full-page Kemble cartoon, "Death's Laboratory": a death's-head with teeth consisting of patent-medicine bottles. On June 24 Wallace Irwin contributed a poem: "To the Pure All Food Is Pure." Meanwhile Adams was out in the field gathering material. Detectives trailed him, and he had to take the usual precautions against being decoyed into scandal. Among the several quacks who did not take him so seriously, one of the richest laughed in his face—but within a year that manufacturer's profits were to be cut in half.

On July 8, 1905, Hapgood printed the long editorial "Criminal Alliances with Fraud and Poison," and several weeks later Irwin waxed clever again on the value of "A Testimonial." Editorial followed editorial, whetting the public's impatience. All the while Bok persisted with his agitation in *The Ladies' Home Journal*. By the time Adams was ready to begin publishing his momentous articles, the atmosphere was charged with expectation. At last, on October 7, 1905, *Collier's* appeared with the streamer "The Great American Fraud"—Adams's opening gun. With logic and wit, with documents and illustrations, he went deep into his subject, and people read his facts avidly. The very title of his article became one of the great slogans of the time, and Adams was quoted everywhere.

Immediately the cry arose that *Collier's* had joined the scandalmongers. Hapgood found himself pilloried along with the writers with whom he had chosen not to associate himself! But he knew he was right, and that his method was right—did any of the muckrakers consider themselves wrong?—and, furthermore, *Collier's* rose to a new crest of success on the wave of the campaign. Accordingly Hapgood pushed his advantage.

Adams himself established his name among the great names of muckraking as his introductory article was succeeded by others. His second article dealt with the patent medicines which were

[5] *Special Message to Congress,* December 5, 1905.

nothing but liquor drinks and upon which many women were genteelly keeping themselves in a constant stupor. On November 4, Sullivan's sensational article appeared (without his name). In the same issue *Collier's* boldly printed a notice to advertisers that

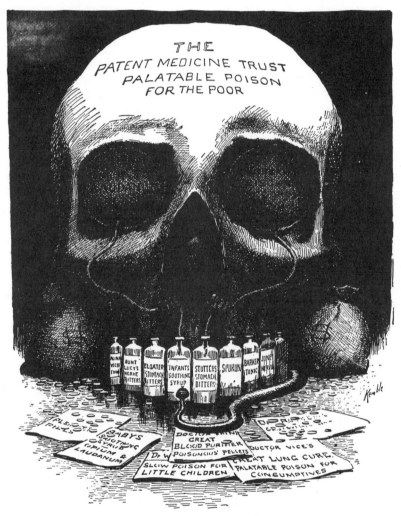

"DEATH'S LABORATORY"

Collier's, June 3, 1905

it would accept no further patent-medicine advertisements of any kind.

By November 18, *Collier's,* whose daily mail was becoming enormous, was able to report that beneficial results of the campaign were multiplying daily. "Peruna," for instance, had been outlawed in South Carolina, and similar action was developing in other states. If the medical societies had taken little action, they had at least passed resolutions.

Adams now took up "Liquozone" (which had started the entire fight) and revealed its chemical formula: nine-tenths of one per cent sulphuric acid (a vitriol), three-tenths of one per cent sulphurous acid (also corrosive), and, finally, ninety-nine per cent water. From that he passed on, in another article, to the wild claims that were made for "Liquozone," and the fake endorsements that served to decoy the public. Then followed articles on "The Subtle Poisons"—catarrh powders that made cocaine fiends, the death record of acetanilid, the irresponsible sale of other drugs. Still later Adams described the preyings of the manufacturer-vampires on incurables, and the advertising disgrace, and in each case he called to the carpet millionaires and millionaire concerns.

On December 5 the pure food and drug bill was reintroduced into the Senate by Heyburn. Aldrich (whom both David Graham Phillips and Steffens were denouncing as the boss of the United States), backed by a cordon of reactionary followers, fought the bill in the name of popular as against "bureaucratic" government. Public indignation against this treachery seethed. The American Medical Association, recognizing that the tide toward the law was irresistible, brought pressure upon Aldrich. The Association at last saw the need for a law that would do no real damage to "business." Yet with Adams's vivid exposures going on—a first edition of *The Great American Fraud* was already on the market and selling furiously—it was a question how such a law could be passed.

The January *Ladies' Home Journal* contained forceful articles by Mark Sullivan and Bok which made it certain that the longer Congress delayed, the more difficult it would be to pass harmless laws. Dr. Wiley and his cohorts worked without pause. Revolt boiled in the A.M.A. The February issue of the *Journal* made a dramatic appeal for action, and printed a copy of the bill which its readers in all the states were urged to send to their representatives. Roosevelt made a personal plea to Aldrich not to oppose the bill. Finally, having stripped it of its most important provision— the forbidding of false advertisements—the Senate opposition, on February 15, 1906, gave way, and the bill went to the House.

The patent-medicine lobbyists were unhappy. Even though the advertising clause, which would have killed outright the entire business of fraud, had been defeated, the bill was still revolutionary enough to place any and all of the quacks in jeopardy. It provided for the analysis of drugs by Dr. Wiley and his Bureau of Chemistry and protected the retailer against responsibility for the manufacturers' swindling schemes. Its most drastic provision was one that ordered the manufacturer to print a record of his product's ingredients on the label. As Adams wisely observed,[6] the law emphasized not the poisoning, which would be difficult to prove, but the *fraud*, which could more easily be ascertained.

Political machinery was therefore set into motion to side-track the bill entirely and, once popular agitation had been successfully smothered, to weaken it further. The bill was referred to the appropriate committee in the House, and obstructions were at once placed in its way. It was certain to pass if put to a vote; the aim of the reactionaries was to see that it did not come to a vote. So the matter stood in March 1906 when a new factor was suddenly introduced and the entire aspect of the crusade changed.

[6] "Food or Fraud? A Question for Congress," *Collier's*, March 17, 1906.

XIII. THE JUNGLE

HOW, during all this agitation, did meat escape the searching criticism that overtook patent medicines and preservatives? Dr. Wiley was well aware of the "embalmed meat" scandal which had disgusted the nation in 1899. Roosevelt had testified at the Senate investigation of the time that he would just as soon have eaten his old hat as the canned food that, under a government contract, had been shipped to the soldiers in Cuba. It was certainly known in some influential quarters that the meat being served to the American public was very far from being above criticism.

One reason why the meat industry for a time remained immune was that the beef trust had conducted a counter-campaign to remove the stigma with which the revelations had marked it. And the public had forgotten. The very magazines which were leading the pure-food fight carried the advertisements of Swift, Armour, Morris, and the others of the beef trust. These were powerful and respected companies. Dr. Wiley, working in his laboratory, was not in position to know under what conditions meat was being prepared in Chicago for the open market. His pure-food law that was before Congress made no mention of government inspection of prepared meats. The public, on the other hand, assumed vaguely that government inspection of meat was somehow provided for, and that the "embalmed meat" incident had merely been an isolated case of underhanded and unscrupulous business. Americans were not aware that meat being shipped to foreign ports was subject to regulations that domestic products did not have to respect!

The propaganda of the packers was indeed carefully planned and widely spread. So successful was it that only a few were not fooled by it. When the beef trust—the National Packing Company—was formally launched, *Success*, which became one of the most persistent of the muckraking organs, printed an article by

John Gilmer Speed which argued that the recent high price of beef was justified by economic conditions and that the packers were giving good service and would continue to do so. *Leslie's,* in October 1902, printed "Beef," by Earl Mayo, which gave substantially the same story. *Cosmopolitan* later ran an article dilating upon the "marvels" of meat preparation. Some such praiseful articles were no doubt diplomatically arranged by interested parties, but, by and large, the majority of the writers did not know any better. The packers were alert; they made sure that visitors were given planned tours through the plants and saw only what it was "safe" for them to see. Even Charles Edward Russell who as city editor of the Chicago *American* had had ample opportunity to hear the worst that could be said of the packers, had harbored at that period only the most indefinite idea of the evils existing in the plants.

As the editor of a popular newspaper—even a Hearst paper— Russell had not been in position to see labor horrors from the point of view of the workers; likewise he had been blind to horrors from the viewpoint of the consumers. A. M. Simons therefore had an advantage over him in receiving, as a Socialist editor in Chicago, direct reports about meat-packing conditions. He gathered his information into his pamphlet *Packingtown* (first written in 1899, then altered with rapidly changing conditions), which contained in its too brief pages facts concerning the beef alliance not only as a trust but as an oppressor of labor and also as a wholesale jobber in spoiled and filthy meat. Russell was also to find that following up a campaign of exposure demanded so much energy that one had no time to go off into bypaths; moreover, a muckraker found himself obliged to work fast before all sources of information were shut to him.

This was his dilemma when he later began exposing the beef trust. He did not so much as hint that the products of the trust deserved condemnation from the sanitary as well as the economic point of view. To him the economic point of view seemed more important. Upton Sinclair himself, when he went to Packingtown, did not have the pure-food question especially in mind, and he did not have it in mind while he was describing the methods of food preparation in *The Jungle.* It was the public, not the muckrakers, which first chose to emphasize the unsanitary conditions in the plants.

Hearst, as we know, had begun a fight with the packers in 1901 because of their terrorization of competitors. The Hearst campaign continued for some time; but, being journalistic and therefore diffuse, it remained purely a Chicago issue. Late in 1904, however, the Interstate Commerce Commission investigated the private-car evil, which had become the packers' scheme for receiving rebates and crushing competition. The refrigerator cars belonged to the packers: the cars were "borrowed" by the railroads, which paid the packers for their "use" of them, and, naturally, charged the packers' competitors for *their* use of them! So there were thousands of the famous yellow cars running in all directions from Chicago. By means of the cars the packers were able to monopolize not only the meat industry but the fruit industry likewise. Wherever the cars came they kept the prices of meat and produce high, and the packers triumphant.

The railroads, of course, would have made much more money from free and unrestricted competition than they were able to make from the packers. They tolerated what amounted to a blackmailing system of tribute for the same reason that they tolerated the similar system which Standard Oil had developed. The railroads feared the loss of the trust's traffic: they preferred easy profits from the trust to the hard-won profits that could be obtained through competition.

Those were the facts brought out before the Interstate Commerce Commission by M. J. W. Midgeley, who had been studying the subject for thirty years—ever since the refrigerator cars had come into use. He was the most famous expert on railroad rates in the country and his testimony was news.

Erman J. Ridgway of *Everybody's*, which had already taken up muckraking and had already presented Thomas W. Lawson to the public, saw an article in that news. Ridgway wired his friend Charles Edward Russell (who had since left the Chicago *American*) to approach Midgeley regarding a possible article for *Everybody's*. As Russell later told in an appendix to his book *Lawless*

Wealth (1908),[1] nothing was then farther from his mind than muckraking. Steffens, Tarbell, his friend David Graham Phillips, Hearst—they could take care of that. But he *was* interested in the beef trust. He remembered how, at one time, when Chicago's water supply was running short, it had been discovered that the packers had been systematically stealing from the city's water supply by secret pipes. Russell therefore delivered Ridgway's proposition to Midgeley and then strolled over to the Interstate Commerce hearings to look over the testimony. The Commission was in session, and Russell heard a few of the stories told by farmers who had been roughly treated by the packers. He was so outraged that, when Midgeley finally declined to write the article (he was too busy), he accepted Ridgway's offer to do it himself. Russell now put away his poetry and piano, to which he had devoted himself since his Chicago *American* days. He divided his time between Packingtown and South Water Street, where the produce commission houses were. He discovered so much information that obviously no one article could hold it all. He therefore decided to study his subject thoroughly before publishing a single article, particularly because he realized that, once his series had begun, he would find it difficult to get any further material. As it was, within ten days his explorations made him an object of suspicion in the stockyards.

Luck ran with Russell. A friend who had access to the stockyards was able to get him valuable details which he needed. Disagreements among the packers enabled him to profit from information meant to discredit one of them. When, early in 1905, his series "The Greatest Trust in the World" began to appear in *Everybody's*, it attracted immediate attention and was not overshadowed even by the tremendous Lawson series that was running beside it. Immediately after the series began, Russell—like most muckrakers in a similar stage of activity—was threatened by mail, and attempts were made to involve him in personal scandal. His motives were assailed by conservatives. The packing trust bought editorial space in the Western newspapers to refute his charges that suicides, banking failures, and the paradox of abundant crops and high prices could be laid at their door.

---

[1] "Confessions of a Muckraker: How I Came to Write an Exposé of the Beef Trust, Instead of an Essay on the Amphibrach Foot."

Russell was backed in his work by *Success*, which had traveled far since its naïve review of the beef question. Control of *Success* had slipped from the hearty, inspirational hands of Orison Swett Marden, and the confused editorial policy which had resulted in issues containing at one time advice by Edwin Markham, stories and articles by Theodore Dreiser, thoughts on insurance by James W. Alexander (who was at that very moment busily mishandling the Equitable Life Assurance funds!), muckraking stories by Phillips and Samuel Merwin, and success stories about anybody and everybody—this editorial policy had given way to a clear advocacy of not only successful but upright Americanism. In May 1904 *Success* announced that it was taking greater care with its advertisements than *McClure's, Leslie's, Cosmopolitan, Scribner's,* and *The Review of Reviews*. In the same issue David Graham Phillips spoke some harsh words concerning trust manipulation of prices in his "The Advance in the Cost of Living." It was, then, only a step further to send Merwin out to Chicago to review the packing situation. The articles Merwin wrote supplemented the more definitive ones by Russell in that Merwin had less information and more indignation to offer his readers. Merwin, too, emphasized the pure-food angle, asking whether it was true that the packers were, as was so often charged, deliberately selling diseased meat, and telling how dead hogs were removed from the stockyards and "rendered" into lard.

If Merwin's charges were true, why were no reports of unsanitary packing conditions brought in by government inspectors? The answer was the practically unknown fact that *government inspection was the merest fiction*. The empty shell of so-called government inspection of beef had been deliberately arranged by the packers to leave them free to do as they pleased. The "inspectors" —all of them political pawns—saw the livestock; they did not see, or did not bother to see, the meat in the process of being prepared, nor did they inspect it afterwards. In the newspapers and magazines those advertisements that spoke of trust products as "government inspected" were fraudulent.

As the excitement about packing conditions mounted, pressure was exerted upon Roosevelt to investigate them. Roosevelt was quite aware of what was going on in Chicago, but he made certain not to involve himself personally in the situation. He happened, at that time, to be on excellent terms with William Lorimer, the Republican boss of Cook County and a beef-trust champion. He therefore sent as his representative his Commissioner of Corporations, James Rudolph Garfield, the son of the former President. Garfield made a formal inquiry into the charges of Russell and Merwin—and he whitewashed the trust. Roosevelt, affecting to believe Lorimer's added assurances that all was well in Chicago, straightway forgot the entire matter.

The public had serious misgivings. Even the more conservative magazines admitted that Garfield's report was a "disappointment." But the entire influence of the Administration was thrown against Russell's book when it appeared in 1905: adroit use was made of the Garfield whitewash to establish that Russell's charges were either untrue or grossly exaggerated. Subsequently his book was used as the basis for the action of the Interstate Commerce Commission against the trust. This use of Russell's book, incidentally, never became widely known, for it was the mode to bury muckraking books and then, as quietly as possible, to look to reform.

This was the state of affairs when Upton Sinclair appeared with the most sensational book of his career. As the papers said, he awoke one morning and, like Byron, found himself famous.

Sinclair had become one of the most fiery of the Socialist followers. He had also established himself with the popular press as a capable although dogmatic writer. In 1904, too, he had published *Manassas,* his Civil War novel, which his new friend Jack London called the best Civil War story he had ever read. (Few other substantial Civil War stories had appeared, and London evidently had not seen Stephen Crane's *The Red Badge of Courage.*) Thus, Sinclair had standing, and he had the daily and weekly Socialist organs at his disposal.

In September 1904, when the Packingtown workers struck, he wrote for *The Appeal to Reason* a broadside addressed to them, and this was distributed widely in the working-class districts. *The Appeal to Reason* now offered Sinclair five hundred dollars to live on while he wrote a novel dealing with the lives of the Packingtown workers. Sinclair went to them, lived for seven weeks among them, and then returned to his home in New Jersey to write about what he had seen.

Sinclair returned from Chicago a sick man—sick at heart and rebellious. The smells and tragedies of Packingtown filled his mind; they stood out in horrid contrast to the Socialist utopia which he cherished. He therefore wrote as he was able to write fiction only three or four times in his life—with the fire of a poet, with the passion of a man who had been hurt. He had a seething story to tell; there was no space, no time, for contemplation of self or glib characterization. And the result was *The Jungle*.

In that generation were written greater stories than *The Jungle*, more profound stories, but there was no novel with more lyrical emotion, or a nearer approximation of what was generally thought of as "genius." *The Jungle*, from the moment it began to appear serially in *The Appeal*, was recognizably the literary sensation of the time.

Was this muckraking? The question may seem irrelevant. Yet it was raised by Mark Sullivan when, many years later, he reviewed this book and the pure-food fight in *Our Times*. It was not muckraking, Sullivan decided, for muckraking referred to documented exposures of current ills, and *The Jungle* not only was fiction but it was "overdrawn." Sullivan's conclusion is in line with the charges that Sinclair was merely an amateur—and an "emotional" one at that—who had set himself up against "experts." It calls to mind the charges that were made against Tarbell for not having been in the business of selling oil, and suggests the general charges against the muckrakers—including Mark Sullivan himself—for mixing into business which was no concern of theirs.

But Sinclair had been in Packingtown seven weeks. He had taken his impressions at first hand, against the will and designs of the packers; he had studied the meat-inspection laws; he had talked to the workers. This was enough. Sinclair, in Packingtown, was the consumer and citizen—only more resolute and acute—who was horrified to see what was being done to him. Sinclair was a writer who had given his subject feeling and attention. Seven times seven weeks would not have given him more—not while America continued to pay toll to the trust and eat its products.

The novel had been accepted in advance, but when the publisher saw it in full he insisted on cuts in the manuscript. Sinclair refused to make them. *The Jungle* was then offered to four other publishers, who likewise rejected it as it stood. Now Sinclair prepared to publish it himself. Jack London responded to the call with his usual generosity, and, in a few months, four thousand dollars was collected. The book was set up and plates of it were made.

Sinclair meanwhile approached *Collier's* with the story. He had met the editors, Norman Hapgood and Robert Collier, while Steffens's *The Shame of the Cities* was still appearing in *McClure's*. At that time Hapgood and Collier had accepted and then declined to publish a letter which Sinclair had written to Steffens asking what was to be done about the municipal conditions which Steffens had described so vividly.[2] But times had since changed. Sinclair was now on the way to becoming well-known, for *The Jungle* was being avidly read in *The Appeal to Reason*. Collier and Hapgood therefore studied the book carefully and also read with interest an article which Sinclair submitted regarding the foul methods of food preparation in Packingtown.

Sinclair was not alone in advancing his charges regarding food preparation, for he had met in Chicago a remarkable man who was internationally famous as a student of meat packing and, under another name, as a Socialist. This was Adolph Smith of the London *Lancet*, England's great medical journal, who had written for that journal four papers which condemned the Chicago meat-packing methods. Now Hapgood was well aware of the charges these papers contained, but he also violently disliked Sinclair's approach. He abhorred his constant clamor for Socialism and his insistence that the packers were a band of murderers. Collier, being a full-blooded man who was not averse to a fight, was for accepting *The Jungle*. Hapgood therefore sent to Chicago a "special investigator," Major L. L. Seaman, who spent—so Sinclair later charged—only twenty-four hours in Packingtown and returned with an article which gave the packers a clean bill of health. On April 22, 1905, then, in the issue which signalized Hapgood's left-handed entrance into muckraking, *Collier's* printed the article "Is Chicago Meat Clean?" which gave three paragraphs of Sinclair's article, torn from context, and a number of quotations from the *Lancet* articles and Seaman's worthless article.

[2] The story is bitterly detailed by Sinclair in his *The Brass Check*.

Hapgood's move was manifestly unfair, and Sinclair was justified in feeling that he had been badly treated. Hapgood's dignified refusal to answer Sinclair's charges directly in his own autobiographical story [3] scarcely supported his pretension to impartial honesty. In justice to Hapgood, however, it should be noted that he later accepted and printed a long letter from Sinclair which reviewed the entire matter, printed an article by Sinclair which repeated and expanded his charges against the packers, and enlisted *Collier's* itself in the crusade for clean meat, as well as wholesome medicines. But this happened after Sinclair had managed to push *The Jungle* past the boycott of fear and special interest.

The book was finally published by Doubleday, Page and Company through the decision of Walter H. Page, the editor of *World's Work*, which was honest, sincere, and always one step behind the muckrakers. And *The Jungle's* success was instantaneous. But ironically enough it was successful for reasons which Sinclair had hardly considered. He had visualized a public reaction against the oppression of the Packingtown workers: that was the theme and substance of *The Jungle*. The public, however, fastened its attention upon some dozen pages which gave gruesome details about meat production: the casual grinding of rats, refuse and even employees into beef products—the generally foul conditions under which the meat was prepared. An immediate clamor began for reform. The Pure Food Bill was swept out of the Congressional committee meetings, where it had been languishing, and the entire pure-food issue was raised to a new and more hopeful level.

The public had no interest in the manner of legislation; it did not care whether beef inspection was incorporated in Dr. Wiley's bill or was separately provided for. But it wanted protection. Letters poured in upon Theodore Roosevelt demanding action. He proceeded to act with his usual force and ambiguity; that is, he made public statements showing concern, and conferred with the Secretary of Agriculture, who sent another of the endless commissions to Packingtown. When, however, Roosevelt received

[3] In *The Changing Years*, Farrar & Rinehart, New York, 1930.

proofs of three articles which were to appear in *World's Work*, he was roused to more positive action. With his sanction Senator Beveridge prepared an amendment to the Agricultural Appropriation Bill which called for meat inspection that would really protect, and this was submitted to the mercies of the House and Senate. Meanwhile Sinclair, having got into touch with Roosevelt, had pointed out to him what was sufficiently obvious—that nothing could be expected from the commission sent by the Secretary of Agriculture because the Department of Agriculture was itself implicated in the charges. Roosevelt was finally persuaded to send to Chicago another commission composed of two New York social workers, Neill and Reynolds.

Sinclair was now working frantically. He engaged an extra secretary to help him in his enormous correspondence. He wrote articles. He engaged in innumerable conferences regarding the Beef Inspection Amendment which was being tossed about in Congress. And the packers were likewise furiously engaged. Protests and demands were pouring in upon them. England and Germany sent sharp notes regarding the export of condemned meat. Cargoes of the meat were being returned from foreign ports.

In *The Saturday Evening Post* presently appeared a series of articles, purportedly written by J. Ogden Armour, actually written by Forrest Crissey of the magazine's staff, which calmly denied all the exposés by Russell, Merwin, and Sinclair. Needless to say, the magazine refused to print any refutation by Sinclair. Yet, interestingly enough, it had just finished serializing *The Memoirs of an American Citizen*, by Robert Herrick, then a professor at the University of Chicago: Herrick's work was nothing less than a fictionalized account of the rise of a packing-house king and the unsavory methods he had employed in rising. Such a seeming turnabout was, however, not surprising in *The Saturday Evening Post* and its editor George Horace Lorimer, who could print David Graham Phillips's cogent articles on American customs and ideals and at the same time print such fatuous comment as the Crissey articles. Lorimer's magazine was virile and healthy on the side of literature and Americana; it was deathly weak, even then, on the side of factual accounts of American institutions. Herrick's book passed editorial inspection because Herrick was an "artist," and tolerant, and because he "understood character" and gave his meat packer full sympathy.

Sinclair was outraged by the treatment he received from Lorimer. Full of his subject, he dashed off in a few hours an article called "The Condemned Meat Industry" and took it directly to Ridgway of *Everybody's*. Ridgway read it then and there. He stopped his presses, took out a short story, and set the Sinclair article in its place. When the article appeared, it was devoured by a public which had been highly sensitized to the entire subject of meat packing.

Meanwhile the Neill-Reynolds Commission had returned from Chicago with a report that embodied the main charges of *The Jungle* and added the personal observations of the investigators. It was a report worded to excite the deepest indignation. Roosevelt withheld it from the public, for, by this time, he saw that the Meat Inspection Bill was less dangerous than the report—a fact which the packers were unable to realize. Roosevelt urged the opposition in Congress to allow the bill to pass, since the uproar which Sinclair and the pure-food advocates were raising was keeping the public feverish with anxiety. *Success, Collier's,* and other magazines in issue after issue were clamoring that the Pure Food Bill and the meat inspection amendment must under no circumstances be permitted to wait. But Roosevelt still could not obtain co-operation. Unable to hold back any longer, he sent a message to the House demanding the passage of the Beveridge amendment, and with it he released the first part of the Neill-Reynolds report.

A storm of amazed indignation swept over the country. The packers, violently denying the charges, made frantic efforts to clean up the packing plants. To save themselves, they became earnest advocates of an amendment—thoroughly emasculated—and, in the Committee of Agriculture, which was working entirely in their interests, they played their final cards. The amendment that was needed was squelched. A substitute amendment was brazenly offered instead, and the farce of legislative action was then rapidly accomplished: toward the end of June both the Pure Food Bill and the Beef Inspection Act were passed and became laws of the land.

Sinclair was bitterly disappointed. The workers of Packingtown had been completely forgotten in the general confusion; the bill that had been passed was no more than a step toward necessary laws. Samuel Hopkins Adams, for his part, was more sanguine. Foods and drugs would henceforth bear labels, and the cocaine purveyors had been wiped entirely out by the Post Office and the Department of Agriculture. The states, moreover, were hurrying to back up the interstate laws with state legislation. Adams accordingly continued to add to his story of *The Great American Fraud,* and he was now backed by the American Medical Association, which was glad to lend a hand in the exposure of patent-medicine frauds (though not of meat packers) now that exposure had the stamp of respectability.

But the patent-medicine quacks and the meat packers had only begun to fight. Down to the end of the muckraking period battles were constantly fought in the press and in Congress for pure food and drug amendments, on the one side for strengthening the laws and on the other for weakening them still further. A gigantic conspiracy, involving the heads of the Department of Agriculture, lobbyists, and President Roosevelt himself, was devised to rob the Bureau of Chemistry—that is to say, Dr. Wiley—of the power to do further damage to the food industries through propaganda and chemical analysis of the manufacturers' products. The struggle went on until the Bureau of Chemistry had been reduced to a shadow of itself and Dr. Wiley had been practically forced out of the Department.[4]

This was a tragic defeat, and it hurt Sinclair as much as anyone else. Reviewing the entire battle, he asked himself what he had accomplished. He had taken a few millions away from the packers and given them to the Junkers of East Prussia and to Paris bankers who were backing meat-packing enterprises in the Argentine. He had given Doubleday, Page a fortune and a reputation. Old Nelson Morris had died from a broken conscience.

This was a dark picture indeed. Adams, had he chosen to do so, might have painted an even darker picture. In 1912, in one of the editions of his masterpiece *The Great American Fraud,* he

---

[4] The full story is told in Dr. Wiley's *The History of a Crime Against the Food Law,* privately printed, Washington, D. C., 1929.

was already able to note the Supreme Court's cabalistic decision regarding the Pure Food and Drugs Law: that although quacks must, under the law, print on the label a record of the ingredients

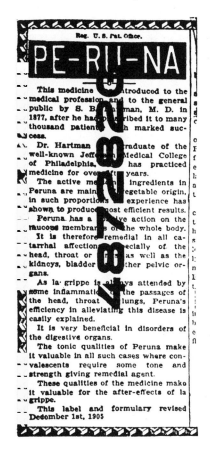
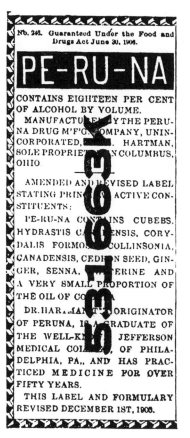

ONE EFFECT OF THE PURE FOOD LAWS

which had gone into the preparation, they were at liberty to claim for the product whatever cures or virtues they pleased! But after 1912 Adams, full of honors and prestige, faded into the background, a respected but not outstanding member of various societies permanently organized to encourage progressive activity. The articles he wrote for the New York *Tribune* in 1915 and

1916 were quite undistinguished. They were, more than anything else, an advertisement for the *Tribune*.

But what would Sinclair have said had he known that pernicious advertising and general negligence in the handling of food and drugs were to prevail far into the 1930's? His pessimism at the time was quite unwarranted. If from the Utopian point of view the Pure Food Law and the meat-inspection amendment were inadequate even with various amendments to provide for changing conditions, the achievements of the muckrakers were nonetheless substantial. The important figures in the struggle made the best of their opportunities. They exposed the reactionary character of the Congress and thus prepared its day of reckoning, and at the same time by their example they encouraged other campaigns in other fields. It was proof of the inadequacy and outwornness of the legal and social machinery of the time that men of such stature were required to accomplish reform. These crusaders did not transform the nation; they *modernized* it. No other band of social workers in any other country or time ever accomplished more.

The tragedy of the campaign, if tragedy there was, was due to the uneven tempo of events, which exhausted men before their time. Like muckraking generally, agitation for pure food and drug laws ended all too soon; the functionaries were scattered and deprived of their proper tasks. Sinclair in particular had less to complain about than other men who were blighted and rendered useless to further reform.

XIV. FRENZIED FINANCE

MANY people of wealth—though perhaps not of his wealth—professed more "radical" ideas than Thomas W. Lawson, and lent their names and gave money to causes sponsored by Socialists and even anarchists. Lawson never professed to be anything but what he was: a multi-millionaire who had made his money in the legitimate, amoral ways which the common people condoned because of their ignorance and impotence. Lawson was distinctive among rich radicals because he stood ready to fight the very cliques and individuals by and with whom he had made his fortune.

And fight them he did—he fought against them as he had once fought with them. Having once crossed the Rubicon, he applied to his social purpose the same tremendous energy, courage, and enterprise that he had heretofore used for personal gain.

It is not surprising that Lawson has been almost forgotten. That he should have lived at all seems, in the light of post-War thought and events, unbelievable. But those who read David Graham Phillips's *The Deluge,* which novelized Lawson's personality and exploits, should remember that, whatever other impression they may have of the book, the incidents described, the characters portrayed, the psychology explained, *were essentially true.* The critics who have been pained by the "melodrama," the "unreality," of *The Deluge* have not been acquainted with the period it expressed; they have judged it, or tried to judge it, by inappropriate standards.

The people had dreamed of such a man as Lawson: a man who knew the heart of corruption, and had turned against it; one experienced in intrigue, who had repudiated his past. The country had dreamed of such a politician—and had received Theodore Roosevelt. It had dreamed of such a journalist—and had had to content itself with Hearst. Tom Lawson was nearer in every way to fulfilling the dream. Being bold and decisive, he went to work without fear of consequences, and what came of his work was of historical significance.

Lawson's beginnings were significant. He was born in Charleston, Massachusetts, in 1857, the son of a carpenter. His education was brief, and at the age of twelve he decided that he was tired of school and wanted a job. He found work in State Street—Boston's Wall Street—and rapidly learned the intricacies of finance. Having a natural instinct for speculation, by the time he was sixteen years old, even while he still held humble positions, he had managed to amass some $60,000 through gambling in stocks. This money he subsequently lost in a "pool" that was to have made him several hundred thousand dollars. He and his associates celebrated this event with a magnificent dinner at Young's Hotel, which they capped by leaving the waiters all their spare money.

During the next fifteen years Lawson made and lost a number of fortunes, and all the while extended his experience and otherwise enjoyed life to the full. Nothing could interfere with his inordinate self-confidence and enthusiasm: he saw quite early that success required only courage and imagination. That was the American system, and Lawson found it good. He had no patience with scruples and excuses. On the other hand, he disliked the cold, brutal maneuvers of human strength preying on human weakness. He was, in other words, a good sport, a gambler enriched by speculation, singularly clean in his personal life, wholly frank in his delight with the financial system which gave him his endless opportunities for profit.

Lawson was hearty, handsome, and magnetic. He brought the methods of a Barnum into State Street. He was a born advertiser who always kept his affairs public—some of them, at least. His traits made him unpopular with the more decorous business houses, the "sane" business men who preferred to work with piety—and in the dark—but Lawson rather despised them and made few efforts to climb socially. He recognized that his strength was in the public, in his ability to catch their interest and win their support. A generous, emotional fighter, he cultivated personal qualities that enabled him to develop an entirely original and independent approach to finance.

Before he was thirty he took charge of the Rand-Avery Publishing House, of Boston, and proceeded to make it very lively. He invented a pack of baseball playing cards which for a time had a vogue and he issued sensational books. One of the books, *Why Priests Should Wed*, which cast slurs on the Catholic Church, provided an occasion for a story illustrating how Lawson's reputation was made. One day, according to the story, a man gathered a crowd before the Rand-Avery book store, where the offending item was prominently displayed; he denounced the publishers and then suddenly threw a brick through the window. He was arrested, then released on Lawson's plea and payment of a fine. The entire incident was later branded a fraud, a bit of publicity which Lawson had staged himself. It may well have been a fraud but it should be emphasized that Lawson was sincerely kindhearted and open-handed and might well have befriended an irate window-smasher. The many charges brought against Lawson when he had attracted national attention were part of a vast and deliberate conspiracy to destroy him.

This man who was to advertise his opinions and business like no other promoter did not pass up the opportunity to use his own printing presses. Interesting on many counts were the several publications of his own issued by the Rand-Avery press. One was *The Krank*—a pungent bit of Americana glorifying the now firmly established national pastime of baseball: Lawson was alive to the fun of the world. Another of his works was *Our Bandanna*, also issued in 1888, an elephant-sized, succinct history of the Republican Party, telling why General Harrison should be elected rather than Cleveland. Three hundred copies were issued at twenty-five dollars each. A sumptuous, special "Presidential" edition of five copies was also printed, one of which was sold to the public in typical Lawson fashion. Readers were invited to send one dollar and their guess as to the number of votes by which Harrison would defeat Cleveland. The one who guessed nearest received the beautiful book after the election; the others, of course, received nothing.

In 1888, then, Lawson was still a firm believer in capitalism, an eager victor in business. But his career had only begun.

He made his first major public appearance in his battle with the Rand-Avery Supply Company, which was a parasite on the publishing house. Lawson attempted to dispossess its directors, but in the succeeding battle was himself ordered to wind up his business in three weeks and deliver it to the supply company. Lawson made the three weeks memorable. He printed an enormous catalogue, itemizing every bit of property belonging to the house, and flooded the city with announcements of a great sale. When the crowds came they heard him declare his wrongs personally and assert that he would leave his successors nothing to put their hands on. And he did what he promised. Tireless, talking incessantly, he stood day after day on the stand (while one auctioneer after another succumbed to weariness), hammering down bids on the machinery, the furniture, the plate glass, the very pipes in the wall. Within three weeks he had sold Rand-Avery down to the ground; there was nothing left of it.

An incident of this feat was that Rand-Avery stockholders were ruined. Lawson himself claimed to have lost money, but in any event the ethics of the game ruled only that one take care of himself, and from that point of view he had acquitted himself well.

In 1889 and 1890 Lawson engaged in a major fight of a somewhat different kind. The Lamson Consolidated Store Service Company was at that time exploiting patents relating to the overhead-carrier system in department stores. The Lamson Company was a monopoly which, by means of many underhanded methods, had bullied and ruined competitors and otherwise mismanaged its privileges. In its course it encountered the Lawson Manufacturing Company, a rival concern run by Lawson, and in typical buccaneering fashion it attempted to put Lawson out of business. Lawson took up the challenge. He issued circulars calling upon the stockholders of the Lamson Company to demand an investigation into its affairs. He then went to Pulitzer, who was at that time conducting a powerful campaign against the Louisiana lottery, and presented the great journalist with documentary proof regarding the misdeeds of the store-service trust. In short order Pulitzer's *World* was running "The Remarkable History of a Notorious Monopoly."

Lawson went into this fight for personal reasons, and the trouble he stirred up made only a local sensation, affecting the Lamson Company only. Yet he was very plainly muckraking! Inter-company battles were usually carried on by means of innuendo and back-stage assassination. Lawson was fighting differently: he carried his troubles to the public and apprised it of facts which concerned it theoretically as well as directly. From any standpoint the battle which Lawson, through Pulitzer, conducted in 1890 was a dress-rehearsal for the work that was being prepared for him in national life and by his own business course.

The immediate results of the struggle were twofold. Three and a half millions were cut from the value of Lamson Company stock, and Lawson was thus enabled to make three-quarters of a million for himself. A later gambit in the business enabled him to make still another "killing"—which, by the way, he lost speculating in sugar. But the second result of Lawson's attack on the monopoly was more interesting: it resulted in marked improvement in the management of the Lamson Company. Lawson had been operating as a "bear"—that is, he had tried to depreciate the value of Lamson stock in order to put the company into difficulties. Although he had made money by his maneuvers, they were actually a public service. It is true that the public was likely to be fleeced whether the stock market went up or down. An analysis of Lawson's methods shows, however, that his "bear" play was usually in the line of reform.

As a "bull" Lawson was, of course, a different person—a promoter, a grandiloquent creator of magic pictures of prosperity, a confidant of a public which he served much less than he served himself. That was his role in the famous Grand Rivers project in which he appeared as a land promoter, town builder, and iron extractor. Promises of wealth and success poured from him as he talked to stock buyers and settlers. Within a year Grand Rivers City, Kentucky, had been incorporated and Lawson himself had been elected mayor. But iron was not discovered and the entire real estate project collapsed.

In justice to Lawson it should be said that his enthusiasm was genuine. Had it been within his power, he would have extracted ore from the sadly inadequate mines by sheer will; he would have put up Grand Rivers City with his own two hands. The public which read his high-pressure advertisements knew this; they felt it in his style and presentation. Trying to be more than middle-class, or at least more securely middle-class, they were putting out the money for the thousand and one mining and real-estate schemes that were constantly flooding the newspapers—money which did less to secure them than to add to the power and wealth of an increasingly exclusive clique of promoters. But the public—blind, confused, hopeful—were aware that Lawson was one of them to a degree other promoters were not, and they accordingly followed when he called.

From a lone guerrilla fighter Lawson was thus gradually transformed into an outstanding general of finance who kept the Street in an uproar for years. The Street did not like him, for he smacked too much of the people, and he talked too possessively of his "public"—the public which had allowed him to conduct his many battles and campaigns and had taken, he hoped, its losses as cheerfully as it had taken its profits. The "inside men" of Standard Oil and its affiliates, the "inside men" in the wars for control of gas franchises, particularly in and around Boston—these financiers, too, disliked Lawson. But needing him, they tolerated his contempt for conventionalities, his colorful personality, his bold bids for popular attention. They tolerated his lavish display of money at the races, his payment of $30,000 for the naming of a carnation after his wife, his campaign for an important opera box. And Lawson knew that he was only tolerated. He protested to the end that he despised society, but one may surmise with David Graham Phillips that he resented being snubbed by the respectable financial and society circles which kept him off the Boston Stock Exchange, ridiculed his gaudy, picturesque art collections, and otherwise prevented him from "conquering" society as he had conquered elsewhere.

In the late Nineties, Lawson engaged in many momentous financial battles which fattened his personal fortune and drew him ever closer to the Standard Oil forces. His relation to Standard was unique. Standard rarely made deals with outsiders whom it was unable to control: rather, men became pawns of Standard Oil and remained pawns until their usefulness was ended. Lawson, well aware of this, knew it was only because of the big following he commanded that he was tolerated. And so, much though they disliked it, the Standard Oil chieftains dealt with him as an independent.

In that capacity Lawson enthusiastically developed the great scheme of his life: the creation of a gigantic copper trust. It was a staggering project, one that demanded the consolidation of vast interests, principally in Montana, in the teeth of the bandit labor and financial wars that were being waged there. But Lawson finally won H. H. Rogers, his friend and the real master of Standard Oil, to its support, and in 1899 the Amalgamated Copper Company was formally launched under the direction of Lawson, who stood behind its tremendous promises to the public. Within five years Lawson had been thoroughly double-crossed by his colleagues, and the public had lost in the trust about $100,-000,000. But meanwhile several other incidents had brought to a crisis his relationship with the great financiers. For one thing, he had been sharply insulted by the New York Yacht Club. He had built a great racing yacht, *The Independence*, at the cost of $200,-000, in order to compete for the right to defend the America's Cup against Sir Thomas Lipton. The New York Yacht Club submitted that only its members could enter into the competition. The ensuing controversy between Lawson and the Club attracted international attention. Lawson put the matter on a high, democratic basis, loudly insisting on his right, as a free American, to represent his country for the trophy. (Actually, cf course, all that was involved was Lawson's position in society.) After a disastrous preliminary race, Lawson destroyed his boat. Capping the matter in his usual fashion, he then wrote with Winfield M. Thompson *The Lawson History of the America's Cup*, which gave him ample opportunity to express himself regarding the New York Yacht Club.

Following the launching of Amalgamated Copper, Lawson returned to speculation in Boston gas. His relations with the financiers grew more and more strained. A climax was reached when, early in 1904, various gas chieftains combined and attempted to throttle him financially. At this point Lawson broke with Standard Oil, with Rogers in particular, and began to issue his famous newspaper broadsides denouncing the machinations of his enemies.

The brilliant idea of a series of articles by Lawson now occurred to the editors of *Everybody's*, and they approached him regarding it. As muckraking had caught up with them, so it had caught up with Lawson and presented him with the opportunity of his life. Lawson recognized it and took it, and began on a new career. Had there been no muckraking period, he would have remained one of the most enterprising, one of the most interesting, of the great speculators. But muckraking soon took him out of that category entirely.

In one of the many of his public confidences which help the reader reconstruct the full picture of his later career, Lawson admitted that one reason for his revelations concerning the crimes committed by the sponsors of Amalgamated was that he wanted to divert the fire of his enemies from his Boston gas interests and cause them to look to their own defenses.[1] This was exactly the same tactic that he had employed in the Lamson affair. But, in addition, he had by now become inflamed by the spirit of reform. Like the other great muckrakers he had imagination, and, knowing as he did the enormities committed by his friends the trust manipulators, he saw that nothing short of radical reform of finance could prevent either a destruction of democracy or revolution. Lawson was truly a man of the people. He loathed weakness, but he was deeply distressed by those who took advantage of it. He was horrified to receive—as he sometimes did—bitter letters from men who, having followed his confidential, friendly advice, had been drawn into embezzlement, into financial ruin or prison. All this, Lawson thought, was wrong. He knew that he could take care of himself—at the height of the Amalgamated bubble and his gas negotiations he could have laid hands on some $50,000,000—but to him it was unfair, as well as dangerous, to tax the entire people for their ineptness in the stock market.

Exposure of the financial realm promised not only revenge but the new, fascinating game of reform. Yet as Lawson listened to the proposition offered by *Everybody's* editor and publisher, he hesitated. He knew that if he began to fight his erstwhile associates there would be no turning back. Finally, however, he decided for reform.

[1] *"National Stock"* of *Thomas W. Lawson* (pamphlet), Boston, August 15, 1908.

Lawson now made ready for a campaign that would be as carefully planned as a flotation of stock. He wanted no money for his work, of course; he only stipulated that *Everybody's* was to spend $50,000 to advertise the series (he himself spent many times that amount before the series was terminated). He did not want his attack to miss fire.

John O'Hara Cosgrave, *Everybody's* editor, was sent up to Boston. It was arranged that he should live near Lawson, see to it that he wrote his monthly article, help him in the preparation of his manuscript, and otherwise direct its production. Lawson was a great advertising man with a powerful and original gift for expressive language. His *Frenzied Finance* was to be more than an appeal or an explanation: it was to be a history, vividly and artistically told. Cosgrave, a practiced newspaperman and writer, an editor, a friend of Frank Norris and other literary men of the first order, made him an excellent partner.

In the July 1904 issue of *Everybody's*, announcement was made in bold type that *The Story of Amalgamated*, by Thomas W. Lawson, of Boston, was to appear in future issues. Full-page pictures of Lawson, H. H. Rogers, and William Rockefeller were printed. Lawson, in his foreword, submitted that he was not aiming his story at individuals. These men in their private lives were exemplary parents, husbands, friends. It was only when they were doing business, when they operated under the compulsions of "The System" which bound them, that they acted with the inhumanity of fiends.

With similar forthrightness the foreword went on to state that Lawson had been betrayed, in the Amalgamated Copper deal, by his associates who comprised the System—this was the arresting name Lawson coined for the group of Standard Oil leaders who constituted a separate clique the sole purpose of which was to combine personal power for the furtherance of personal interest. The public had lost money, men had committed suicide, property had been despoiled. How this had been done, how Lawson had been made a criminal in his own eyes, it was the purpose of the story to explain. Lawson meant to paint a full picture so that it would be completely understood. He planned to spare no one—not even himself. However, he meant to deal concretely with his relationship to John Edward O'Sullivan Addicks, of Delaware; H. H.

Rogers and William Rockefeller, of Standard Oil; the National City Bank of New York and its president James Stillman; the United Metals Selling Company; the "notorious" F. Augustus Heinze, of Montana; and James Keene—all of whom had contributed, in one fashion or another, to the crimes of Amalgamated. When his story was finished, Lawson promised, he would demand the overturn of the System.

The foreword was reprinted completely or in part in most of the daily papers of the United States and Canada, and was commented upon all over the world. But it was only a prelude to more excitement. When the August *Everybody's* appeared with the first article of *Frenzied Finance,* the issues were snatched from the stands, and the same happened to the September issue. The next month *Everybody's* announced that its circulation had risen to 400,000, and in November half a million copies were sold with more being ordered. Within three months *Everybody's* had overtopped *McClure's, Munsey's,* and every other popular magazine in the field.

Lawson went into all the details. He explained that he would have to take his own time telling the story: it was complex, difficult to understand, so unbelievable that, unless it was simplified and made tangible, it could have no effect on the public. Lawson made clear what he had in mind: *nothing less than to set the people in motion.* How? He stated that he had a remedy for existing conditions, and when he felt convinced that the public could understand it, he would explain it fully. But these remarks were only incidental to the body of facts from which an excited and impatient nation learned how its finances were conducted by its authorized and unauthorized representatives.

The System, Lawson asserted, was able to *make* money. He meant that literally. He showed how, through manipulations, through the strategic and illegal use of credit, through the deliberate falsification of books, the combine was able to increase its already kingly powers and possessions. And who paid for its victories? The public—tempted by false promises of gain, or simply cheated, by men who were responsible to nobody, who were entirely free to plan new manners of legitimate fraud upon a helpless people.

Lawson went on to explain how interlocking directorates

THE STORY OF
Amalgamated Copper

A PERSONAL WORD BY THOMAS W. LAWSON AND A
STATEMENT BY THE PUBLISHERS OF

The Personal Word by Mr. Lawson

Personally I know that one hundred millions of dollars were lost, thirty men committed suicide, and twenty previously reputable citizens went to the penitentiary, directly because of Amalgamated.

It was largely because of my efforts that the foundation of Amalgamated was successfully laid. It was created because of my work. It was because of what I stood for, because I had the public's confidence, and because my promises had been kept that the plain people invested two hundred million dollars of their savings, and it was because of trickery and broken promises that the public lost the enormous sums they did.

My motives for writing the Story of Amalgamated are manifold: I have unwittingly been made the instrument by which thousands upon thousands of investors in America and Europe have been plundered. I wish them to know my position as to the past, that they may acquit me of intentional wrong-doing; as to the present, that they may know that I am doing all in my power to right the wrongs that have been committed: and as to the future, that they may see how I propose to compel restitution.   THOMAS W. LAWSON.

A Statement by the Publishers of Everybody's Magazine

In the articles by Mr. Lawson, beginning in the July number, under the caption of "Frenzied Finance, The Story of Amalgamated," we have a narrative from Mr. Lawson's own lips, how, in the last few years, he has seen millions of dollars won without right, and thousands of men ruined. It is a story of financial tragedy of to-day.

In the great financial happenings of recent years story tellers have given their version; political economists their theories; reformers their pictures; and historians their tablets. For the first time in the history of High Finance we have the High Priest tell it as it happened, and it is for *Everybody's Magazine* to publish "the cold-blooded facts," for Mr. Lawson has pledged himself to tell the truth, the whole truth, and nothing but the truth.
                                        THE RIDGWAY-THAYER COMPANY.

Frenzied Finance IS ANNOUNCED

New York Evening Post, June 21, 1904

worked: how one man, acting in many capacities, through dummy and real agents, was able to utilize untold sums of money to which he had no right. Casually, and by way of mere illustration, Lawson mentioned (in his September 1904 chapter) that the New York Life Assurance Company was fully controlled by the System, and that its funds were considered part of the "resources" of the National City Bank. This was sensational news, since life insurance, dimly comprehended though it was, was understood to be protected from speculation; the funds of the insurance companies were supposed to be "in trust." Yet Lawson went on to show the "links" in the System which made the two-billion-dollar assets of the Big Three—Equitable, Mutual, New York Life—a happy reserve for ambitious financiers, and particularly for those of the System.

Not four chapters of *Frenzied Finance* were out before Lawson was forced to requisition space in the advertising sections of *Everybody's* in order to deal with new matters which kept cropping up. His story had become a *cause célèbre*. Although deathly quiet reigned at Standard Oil headquarters, defense of the trust was offered in a multitude of centers. Lawson was reviled and insulted. His past was brought up and distorted; he was accused of turning "state's evidence"; he was jeeringly challenged to produce his Remedy; his entire project was branded a fraud, a brazen advertising dodge. Lawson had, of course, gained a highly valuable forum for himself, and it was up to the public to judge whether this was being used for his personal benefit or in the public interest. The most secret of the Standard Oil group's machinations were soon being discussed as familiarly as though the entire public had been present when they were plotted. Were these secrets the truth? When such questions were asked, only profound silence issued from the Standard chieftains—despite charges which, if false, were unspeakably libelous. The public was hardly to be blamed if it concluded that Lawson was telling the facts.

Even national issues were drawn into the caldron Lawson had set to boiling. In November 1904 Lawson warned the public that the Standard Oil crowd, in order to defeat Roosevelt, was plotting to buy a group of doubtful states for Judge Parker, the Democratic candidate. The warning at once became a factor in the election campaign. Lawson then reported that John D. Rockefeller, fearing public anger, had called a special meeting to put a stop to those plans.

In 1905 Lawson had made further revelations regarding life insurance—revelations which caused panicky disturbances in the entire insurance field. In that same year occurred the "Lawson panic," precipitated by Lawson's warning that an artificial "bull" market was being rigged up to catch the public. He himself was accused of making money by his warning, but he persisted in his campaign, and the market finally collapsed.

Lawson had by now established himself firmly in his new work. Naturally he was at odds with all his associates who set him down as a traitor who was perpetrating the basest crimes against economic order. With his entire family he was forced to endure endless abuse and threats. But he was enjoying status as a national figure of the first magnitude with an untold number of devout and convinced readers.

Convinced readers—why not followers? For followers were what Lawson aimed finally to create: an army of them. In 1905, when his burning exposés of insurance conditions brought about the epochal Armstrong insurance investigations and caused the reorganization of the major companies, Lawson warned that the furore was being used to consolidate the System's control of insurance funds. He urged the policy-holders to send him their proxies, to commission him to lead the fight for democracy in the insurance companies in their behalf. He was answered with a flood of letters and appeals, and by enough—but no more than enough —proxies to alarm the financiers and hasten reform.

Lawson on another occasion told of a bogus subscription, framed by the National City Bank, through which the public paid two-thirds of the purchase price of Amalgamated, while the conspirators retained two-thirds of the property. Yet the government did not act on this direct charge of fraud and misrepresentation, and Lawson was unable to stimulate popular demand for such action. In 1907, again, he announced that panic had been deliberately inspired by the Morgan interests. As crowds clamored in Wall Street, he urged Ridgway of *Everybody's* to make a fighting campaign for extreme reform, while he himself went down to Wall Street to muster the investors for a financial revolution. Ridgway, knowing that Lawson was capable of doing just that, was fright-ened and declined to join in such a move. As for the stockholders —they tossed their hats for Roosevelt and Morgan, the "heroes" who had stopped the panic at its height.

The public, in short, was willing to give its ear to Lawson, but it was not willing to give its hand. Why, then, thought Lawson,

LIFE'S SUNDAY SCHOOL

Present: Johnny Rockefeller, Johnny Gates, Tommy Lawson, Hen. Rogers, Little Pierpont Morgan, Andy Carnegie.

Life, March 23, 1905. Courtesy of Harry Newman.

should he reveal his Remedy—a Remedy which would only be still-born in such an atmosphere? Lawson had said that the hand-writing was on the wall, that frenzied finance would soon be a thing of the past. But such were his disappointments after he called for popular support that he began to grow impatient of the role of reformer. In 1906 he gave notice that he was going to discontinue his story; the volume of his revelations issued in 1905 [2] was not to be succeeded by further sections, at least for the time being.

[2] *The Crime of Amalgamated,* Vol. I [*sic*], The Ridgway-Thayer Co., New York, 1905.

Lawson did not give up the fight entirely; he changed his tactics. He put away his Remedy temporarily, convinced that events would soon make it more timely. In the interim he wrote miscellaneous articles on insurance and finance, one of which articles startlingly prophesied the Congressional investigation into the existence of a "money trust" in 1912.

In November 1906 Lawson announced that he was about to take a rest from the exigencies of history and exercise his fancy: he was going to write a story! The following month the story began to appear. Perhaps Lawson had been jealous because of the industrious collaboration of John O'Hara Cosgrave on his articles; at any rate, this story was done by Lawson alone. Curiously enough, it attracted attention just as though it had the same significance as *Frenzied Finance*. As a matter of fact, it was quite valueless.[3]

It soon became clear, however, that fiction was not to a transitional project preceding a return to further fighting on the old lines. On December 7, 1907, the newspapers appeared with the following sensational notice:

Boston. Dec. 6.—I have perfected certain arrangements whereby it is proper for me to say that I shall probably take the next election of Amalgamated, electing a new Board of Directors, with myself as President. But, on asking the Presidency, I shall place in the hands of a committee my resignation in favor of a certain internationally known Boston man of corporation affairs, to take effect three months after my election, and after a thorough investigation of the company's affairs since the inception of the enterprise up to the annual election.

Also:

Barring accidents, the property of the Trinity, Nevada, Utah, Balaklala, and Arizona Smelters will be merged, and these merged into another property.

Also:

I have devoted three and a half years of my time and some millions of my fortune to reform work in the interests of the public. Beginning January 1st, I shall allow the public to do their own reforming, and I shall devote my time and capital exclusively to my own business of stock

---

[3] *Friday the Thirteenth*, Doubleday, Page & Co., New York, 1907. A succinct criticism of it appeared in the April 1907 issue of *The Bookman*.

"gambling" [4] in Wall and State Streets—particularly Wall Street—for the purpose of recouping the millions I have donated to my public work.

P.S.—One of the oldest of human laws and as immutable is "the devil take the hindmost."

THOMAS W. LAWSON

Lawson had quit.

The famous muckraker's decision stirred up great excitement. Ridgway of *Everybody's*, "deeply grieved," wrote him asking whether it was true that he had given up the fight. Lawson answered in a series of remarkable letters which explained his disappointment with the public. Lawson, of course, was not whining. No one had asked him to begin his campaign; he had begun because he had wanted to. But it had developed in ways other than he had anticipated. Apparently he had been regarded as a mere "informer" rather than as a competent and earnest leader. Lawson, as "Mr. Dooley" put it, had used a burglar as an alarm clock. But to what purpose? He had endured insults and money losses merely to see the System more firmly entrenched (above a vast net of reforms) than ever before.

"Forgive me, my dear Ridgway," he wrote, "but the people, particularly the American people, are a joke—a System joke."

And yet, he promised, he was not returning to his old ways in the old spirit. He had his Remedy in order, and when the people were ready to hear him—really to hear him—he would release it. Until then he was saying farewell.

The responses to the letters were interesting. *Everybody's* readers poured quantities of mail into the offices. For the most part they admitted that Lawson was justified, and they thanked him gratefully for all he had done. On the other hand, they protested feelingly that a man like Lawson could not simply leave his work; it would call him back, and he would have to return to it.

Meanwhile *Success* was running a series which amounted to a climax for this, the major phase of Lawson's campaign. Frank Fayant, a brilliant young financial expert, who had been doing

[4] Lawson meant, by this, that an "insider" like himself was not really taking chances like the ordinary investor.

amazingly thorough work on fake stocks, had set out to make the first full-length, impartial analysis of Lawson and his career, in *The Real Lawson*. *Success* had been honest with its fellow-muckraker—much more so than *Collier's*—and now through Frank Fayant printed the most useful record of the phenomenon of Lawson which the period produced. *Success* differentiated between Lawson the writer and Lawson the speculator—which was only just. While the series was running, Lawson, who had been commissioned by the Guggenheims to promote their "coppers," became involved in a situation suggestive of the old Amalgamated deal. Fayant interrupted his chronological story of Lawson's doings to discuss whether Lawson's predictions were *ever* right, rather than whether they were *always* right. Fayant, quite justified in his analysis, treated Lawson's exploits in the market with consummate fairness. He was open-minded enough to record that Lawson himself had given him free access to private archives and had commented on Fayant's promise to "muckrake" him with "Go it!"

In short order Lawson began promoting many schemes. Not with the old success, however; he could not quite regain his old stride. Muckraking had deprived him of something of the magic touch, the old enthusiasm for promotion; also, he had antagonized certain financial circles permanently. Still, how brilliant were his new prospectuses!—how perfectly did he anticipate the investor's objections!—how ádroitly did he lead up to the contract, the purchase of stocks, the delegation to him of power!

So the muckraking era continued to hear from him, but not as before, nor with similar consequences.

What was the Remedy of which Lawson had so often talked and which he could not divulge because the public was not in position to understand? Fayant in his study considered the question closely. He asked what it could be, this Remedy that no man was able to understand but Lawson himself. He collected and reviewed the scattered hints which Lawson had released, telling how the great idea had come to him in Paris in 1894, how he had submitted it to internationally known economists who had declared it sound, and how $100,000,000 would be needed to put it into operation. On the ground of these statements Denis Donohoe, a

Standard Oil defender, had, during the height of *Frenzied Finance*, tried to prove Lawson crazy. Lawson, however, was not mad. Fayant had not grasped his meaning. Lawson had said, not that no one could understand him, but (what he had repeated many times before) that the public *was not yet ready to follow him* in his plan.

By 1913, when the country was still seething from revelations of the money power by the famous Pujo Investigation Committee, Lawson felt that the time had come to tell. *Everybody's*, which was just then closing its muckraking career, published his new series, *The Remedy*. This series was bound to be less gripping than *Frenzied Finance*, for since the days when that series was news, the public had been well educated regarding the stock market. But Lawson could still point out that the financiers continued to ply their trade, and that the middle-class still required succor. Aware that reform's center of gravity had slipped from the muckrakers, Lawson appealed to the middle-class desire for melioration and to the working-class desire for lower living costs. And he appealed, summarily, for government regulation of the stock exchange.

Fayant had surmised that the Remedy involved government regulation. He had laughed at the idea of distinguishing between "good" stocks and "bad" stocks. But now Lawson demanded the end of stock gambling and, in doing so, threw out his arresting condemnation of "counterfeit capital." He demanded the exposure of the "trick" machinery of the "Money Trust" and submitted a plan for legislation which had been tested and retested by lawyers and which could render effective control over the stock market.

The Remedy was logical, brave, reformistic; yet it brought on no crusade. It might have given Lawson some satisfaction to know that it was twenty years ahead of its time, and that the Securities and Exchange Commission, operating under the Securities Act of 1933, would provide many of the safeguards which he had demanded. Even so, what difference did the Remedy make to a nation that was prepared to embark upon a fantastic adventure in speculation during the Twenties?—which was to be so thin and unpluckable as it became in the Thirties?

The Remedy, in a word, was beside the point; it was a heavy

underlining of effects rather than causes. No wonder it made only a casual appeal to *Everybody's* readers—who had had ample time to learn the difference between effects and causes. In *The Remedy* Lawson unconsciously recognized this weakness of his plan in his affectionate references to *Frenzied Finance*, the real high point in his career. *Frenzied Finance*, "mere exposure," had moved people to action; *The Remedy* could not.

Frenzied Finance had intrinsic merits which insured its permanence after the peculiarities of the period had been entirely buried. For, considered by itself, it was the one authentic picture of high finance which had been written from the "inside." It was as though Lawson had torn down the walls of the most seemly houses in New York and Boston and exposed their inhabitants as they really were. The finest novelists, the most conscientious students of the "robber barons," were not able to do more. [5]

[5] This does not mean that Lawson's account is not open to challenge. It has been disappointing that further work has not been contributed by others to help put the matter in complete perspective. Additional materials on the Lawson phenomenon appear in Filler, *Appointment at Armageddon*, Greenwood Press, Westport, Conn., 1976. See also my introduction to David Graham Phillips, *The Deluge*, Johnson Reprint Corporation, New York, 1969.

XV. INSURANCE ON TRIAL

I am going to cause a life insurance blaze that will make the life insurance policy-holders' world so bright that every scoundrel with a mask, dark-lantern, and suspicious-looking bag will stand out so clear that he cannot escape the consequences of his past deeds, nor commit future ones.

SO announced Tom Lawson in the December 1904 installment of *Frenzied Finance,* in the editorial section [1] he had created for his immediate controversies.

His original plans for exposure and reform had not included an attack on the life-insurance business. It was a token of the sincerity of his crusade that he stepped out against foes whose power to crush him he could only vaguely measure. But what prompted him to the article?

The amazing phenomenon that had occurred was like that which soon after rocketed Upton Sinclair to fame: the people, rather than the muckrakers, discovered an issue which mortally concerned them—a situation they wanted cleared up immediately. Lawson, by showing in *Frenzied Finance* the uses which were made of "sacred" life-insurance funds, had merely meant to illustrate the methods of the System—no more. But he had been quickly inundated with a flood of letters demanding to know how and since when life-insurance money had become subject to such illegal manipulation as he described. He had retorted that there was nothing to be surprised about: insurance companies other than that one he had mentioned were all similarly tools of the great financiers. He had cited examples to prove it.

And so insurance became a distinct feature of the Lawson campaign. As the doubt and excitement grew, John W. Ryckman, of *The Era Magazine,* who had been diffidently observing the activities of the muckraking organs, suddenly saw a golden opportunity

[1] "Lawson and His Critics."

and, before anyone else, began a life-insurance exposé entitled *The Despotism of Combined Millions.* The series greatly expanded his magazine's circulation and carried him up to editorial heights on the tide of the succeeding scandal.

The series was pure inspiration on Ryckman's part, since no one had supposed that life insurance was subject to the regular laws of business or that it could be effectively proved to be so. Life insurance was not supposed to be a business. It was, rather, a service; it was assumed to be a democracy—much like the United States—which operated in the interest of the policy-holding community. On this theory the life-insurance companies demanded and received special privileges from the state and national governments. Respected names adorned their directorates. Positions with life-insurance companies were considered positions of trust to be honored as one honors the highest public service.

Before Lawson's revelations, magazine articles were uniformly deferential toward insurance. They were regularly written with the patient air of one who has to explain what the common person could hardly be expected to understand. *Everybody's* itself had been preparing the usual kind of insurance articles for publication when Lawson made his first charges against the great companies. His statements had upset all the calculations of Ridgway and Cosgrave. They had conferred with him and, being assured of the truth of his claims, had given him free rein.

With Lawson printing inside details regarding life-insurance management, and *The Era* printing fiery demands for an investigation, and the newspapers echoing the concern of the public, the life-insurance companies unbent sufficiently to deny the possibility of mismanagement in their affairs. As for Lawson, they merely reported that he was seeking revenge because no company would grant him insurance [2]—an absurd charge that was repeated with

---

[2] Lawson had just published a chapter of *Frenzied Finance* which had captured the imagination of the public. It told how his work was interrupted by an attack of appendicitis, requiring an operation; how his associates in the gas-franchise war had attempted to assassinate him financially while he lay sick; how he had had himself carried on a stretcher to their meeting place and warned them that he would expose their plans and send them to the penitentiary if they tried to victimize him.

astonishing success by the companies' hired agents. The majoi magazines continued to accept those large advertisements which insisted that it was the duty of every husband and father to protect his own against unforeseen calamity.

Suddenly, in January 1905, there were rumors of trouble in the Equitable Life Assurance Society. James W. Alexander, its distinguished president, had had a falling out with James Hazen Hyde, son of the founder of Equitable, and his successor. The two men were trying to oust each other from control. Lawson himself had been giving more attention to the New York Life, whose president, John A. McCall, he denounced as a representative of the System; but now charges of mismanagement in Equitable assumed first place in the news.

During the month premonitions of disaster became more numerous. To relieve public anxiety the New York State Department of Insurance ordered an investigation of Equitable—an investigation which, of course, made little progress. Meanwhile Lawson continued his systematic indictment of insurance management, showing how public funds were jeopardized in securities disguised as bonds, and demonstrating also how nonexistent was democracy in the insurance companies—how completely they were controlled by their officers. He singled out for indictment John F. Dryden, New Jersey Senator and president of Prudential, exposing his methods and policies and quoting a long extract from the annual report of the Massachusetts Insurance Commissioner— a critical report which the insurance companies had been able to suppress. Yet Lawson's powerful exposure apparently had no more effect on public imagination than the newspaper campaign which acquainted the public with details of the famous French ball given by young Hyde, of Equitable, on January 31.

Hyde was not the insurance man his father had been. Old Henry Hyde had lived and breathed insurance. His offspring was a dandy who fancied himself a scholar and exquisite. He had been left a gigantic inheritance—the scepter of Equitable, which his father had ruled completely. Young Hyde was willing and determined to rule after him, but he could not realize that times had changed; that, following the fabulous development of insurance in the last thirty years, there would have to be an accounting; that, if he really wished to rule, he would have to face the financiers—who were aching to take Equitable away from him—and conquer them. Hyde understood only that Equitable was his inheritance; it belonged to him. When he gave his ball, therefore, as a matter of course he charged it to company expenses. This was

"HIGH LIFE INSURANCE"

James Hazen Hyde seen by the New York *World*, April 1, 1905.

a common procedure; all the "insiders" did the same with the company's resources. No wonder the growth of the life-insurance business had not been accompanied by a corresponding growth in the dividends it paid!

The Morgan interests, acting with consummate skill through President Alexander, used this instance of graft to discredit Hyde's

entire system of control. They drew a picture of aristocratic abandon which suggested Versailles before the revolution. Hyde,
backed by E. H. Harriman, answered in kind. Charges and counter-charges were cast back and forth.

The magazines now began to show a strong interest in the situation. *World's Work*, which had just been printing extremely
complimentary, extremely "sensible," articles on insurance, re-
examined its position. *Collier's* fixed an anxious eye on the proceedings and, ignoring Lawson's deadlier charges, agitated for an
extension of voting privileges to the stockholders. It informed the
public that insurance had become the world's greatest single
money trust, and the alarming thought was suggested that such
a concentration of power might be used for evil as well as good.
Collier's hastened, however, to assure its readers that the scan-
dalous facts that were coming out should not be permitted to cause
panic. Dividends would continue to be paid; insurance claims
would be met. There was need for reform, not revolution.

In the succeeding months the picture became clearer. The fight
in Equitable was seen to be nothing better than a struggle for control. The rumors and accusations concerning the conduct of New
York Life and the Mutual emphasized the fact that insurance
had been too long neglected by the public. Despite the best efforts
of the insurance companies to erase the impressions the war in
Equitable was making, month after month the insurance question
continued to hold the public's attention.

By September the state investigating committee had been thoroughly reorganized and was ready for work. Its chairman, William W. Armstrong, under the concerted abuse of insurance magazines and reactionary journals, went ahead to gather the best talent
possible for his investigation.

When Equitable went on trial in Albany, during September, it
was before a memorable body of state officials who had given a
legal opportunity to a man whose power and potentialities even
they did not realize. Charles Evans Hughes was not unknown
nor untried. By the time the insurance scandals had reached the
stage demanding legislative action, he was one of the most highly
esteemed of the younger New York lawyers. He had practiced
law, had taught it, had given special lectures on the subject at Cor-

nell and the New York Law School. Hughes was in no sense a radical; on the contrary, he was highly respectable and a joiner of respectable groups. But if he lacked the dramatic qualities which several years earlier had enabled District Attorney Jerome of New York City to become nationally known, he had what was more useful to the citizens of the muckraking era: the capacity for work, a strong, common-sense logic, and—ambition.

Early in 1905 he had acted as counsel for the Stevens Gas Commission and acquitted himself honorably in the interests of the people. The insurance investigation was infinitely more momentous. It was several decades since a serious investigation of insurance had been last conducted, and that investigation had been successfully gutted. With the eyes of the nation upon him, therefore, Hughes set himself to giving his job all he had.

The unrest in Equitable was something which had to be resolved, because the factional troubles were giving Lawson's revelations more and more authority with the public—which was growing angrier. Hughes accordingly concentrated upon getting the facts quickly, and it was soon evident that he meant to spare no one. Early witnesses were terrified to find that he could not be put off with platitudes and generalities, and that it was dangerous to lie to him. Hughes carefully collated the charges which the directors hurled at each other, widened the dissensions between them, followed up clues, and in short order had involved New York Life and Mutual as well as Equitable in a series of charges and confessions that shocked the nation.

Hughes disclosed that life-insurance funds had been used for political campaigns; that they had been used for speculation, for influencing legislation, for bribing the newspapers, for personal profit. He revealed company methods by which small policyholders were confused, cheated, bullied; by which the widows and orphans left with no other support than supposed insurance were defrauded. Finally, he exposed the system of interlocking directorates—as Lawson had already done—and laid on them official condemnation.

The company heads had made the bad mistake of attempting to overwhelm Hughes. When he called for data, they sent him, literally, carloads of matter relating to their companies and affairs. Hughes promptly put a corps of investigators to work on it; they went through all the papers, organized them, and mastered them. When Hughes faced the insurance leaders, therefore, he did it with complete confidence, and he dominated them.

The exposé was complete—of life insurance. But what of fire and marine insurance? What of business in general? Hughes followed the trail as far as he deemed advisable, and then stopped.

There could be no doubt of Hughes's honesty. During the investigations he refused the nomination for Mayor of New York City—having become famous he might well have won that office—in order to complete his work. Hughes had principles.

The Armstrong investigation rocked the country. Not only Equitable stood condemned, but all insurance; and all business, in fact, was directly affected by the Albany revelations. Observing the shady ramifications of a business which was, more than any other business, of direct public concern, seeing how it had become a corrupt system which disregarded the best interests of the policyholders, thousands of citizens began to believe that no business could be trusted to take care of itself. The consequence was, throughout the entire country, a wave of legislation that made many objectionable business procedures illegal and no longer practicable.

Through the winter of 1905 the investigations continued. Hyde and Alexander were both retired from Equitable. Chauncey Depew, of the United States Senate—he was a man of thin repute, but eminently respectable—now stood pilloried as a shameless grafter and thief. Housecleaning committees began to function in Mutual and the New York Life. As the high-swelling facts came out, the public was increasingly shocked and disgusted. Only the remarks of the irrepressible "Mr. Dooley" brightened the sad picture.

In March 1906 the Armstrong Committee delivered to the New York Legislature its historic report calling for sweeping reforms in every department of insurance. The backwardness and inadequacy of the laws that had governed insurance previously could be fully realized only as one read the long list of rudimentary, obviously indispensable measures which the Committee recommended. Through March and April various bills were submitted to the Legislature and were passed.

Those were triumphant days in business reform—triumphant days, too, for such men as Louis Brandeis, the "people's attorney," who was now acting as counsel for the Protection Committee of Policy-Holders in Equitable. Men like Brandeis wrote frank opinions concerning specific insurance companies and were given a forum. They even advocated and urged state insurance, and were not for that reason barred from the magazines as Socialists.

World's Work accepted the evidence of the Armstrong Committee, approved the Committee's recommendations, and indicated that the old days were well done with. Mark Sullivan, going further, wrote for *Collier's* a stirring article muckraking Prudential, which had successfully avoided the troubles that had overtaken the New York firms. And all the while the public became more alive to insurance. When, in December 1906, elections were held for directors of New York Life and Mutual, public interest in the elections was as great as if they were being held for public offices.

Norman Hapgood was glad to announce that the reform laws were safe and indestructible.

Not only Lawson, but the muckrakers generally, could have been justly proud of the role they played in insurance reform. *The Era* had served excellently, B. O. Flower and *The Arena* had been active, and *Collier's* had done its part. *World's Work*, once it had elected to recognize the realities of the situation, had printed worth-while articles on it.

Yet it remained for McClure to publish the series of articles that would be most likely to attract a future reader looking not for historical documents but for work which was immediately interesting and useful. The need for a good history of insurance was generally realized, although a history would not seem so radical and exciting as direct agitation for reform. Actually, when "The Story of Life Insurance," by Burton J. Hendrick, began to run in *McClure's* of May 1906, it was immediately accepted as a muckraking work—and principally because it gave a true account of insurance's past.

Hendrick, a Yale man and a journalist, had been working for the New York *Evening Post* and venturing out into the magazines when McClure asked him to submit work about insurance. Hendrick had done so, and McClure had recognized immediately that Hendrick had the qualities he wanted. Hendrick had then joined *McClure's* staff and set to work on his story.

As the story developed, it shamed and made ridiculous the bland accounts of insurance that had previously been featured in the magazines. Hendrick showed how the enormous surpluses which the companies collected were the basis for the corruption and degradation of the insurance principle. Then he painted a full-length portrait of Elizur Wright, the father of life insurance, whose dramatic and inspiring fight to establish a secure reserve for the policy-holders confounded the vague notions that business was dull—Wright, whose earnest labors were the principal reason that scandal had not destroyed Equitable, the New York Life, and Mutual. Hendrick then drew the founder of Equitable, Henry B. Hyde, who started insurance on its long way down, developing the modern type of life-insurance agent, building up his company by forcing the wholesale forfeiture of policies, and otherwise, audaciously and persistently, taking insurance through the gilded age to its days of disgrace. Also described by Hendrick was the great Tontine scheme of insurance, Hyde's masterpiece of corruption, an incredible lottery masquerading as "insurance" through which Hyde amassed his fortune. So shameless a gamble was this, so fraudulent in practice, that it was finally banned by law—only to be succeeded by the so-called "semi-Tontine" which continued Hyde's career of evil.

All this Hendrick told in round, popular prose with a wealth of illustration and explanation. The series made him famous; it was one of the great muckraking books, and Hendrick might well have taken pride in it. His succeeding stories of the great American fortunes nourished the expectation that he might become the historian of the muckraking era. For Hendrick had a strong and powerful grasp of trends and motives. No one could make more human and comprehensible a Vanderbilt or Gould, who, in the hands of other muckrakers, was likely to appear wholly fiendish and contemptible.

It soon appeared, however, that Hendrick's ability to paint the "robber barons" so humanly was due to his secret admiration for them. He waxed less radical rather than more. He soon became a staunch admirer of the work of the Carnegie Foundation and the Rockefeller Institute—noble organizations, whose existence justified the methods by which Carnegie and Rockefeller had made their fortunes—and ceased to have anything to do with muckraking. Far from becoming the historian of the muckraking era, he became the historian of those whom the muckrakers had fought. Though strong and vivid, his *The Age of Big Business* [3] was, in comparison with his book on insurance, half a story and certainly not impartial. The same is true of his biography of Carnegie. Despite Hendrick's change of heart, however—a change that reminds us of Herbert N. Casson, who blazed more brilliantly and then turned colder—not many of the lesser muckrakers left so substantial a memento of youthful enthusiasm as *The Story of Insurance*.

Wrote Upton Sinclair in *The Brass Check:*

"When thieves fall out, honest men come into their own." If, for example, you had studied the press of New York City at the time of the life insurance exposures, you would certainly have concluded that the press was serving the public interest. As it happens, I followed the drama of life insurance with the one man in America who had most to do with it, the late James B. Dill. Judge Dill ran a publicity bureau for several months, and handed out the greater part of the scandal to the newspaper reporters. He told me precisely how he was doing it, and precisely why he was doing it, and I knew that this whole affair, which shook the nation to its depths, was simply the Morgan and Ryan interests taking away the control of life insurance money from irresponsible people like "Jimmy" Hyde, and bringing it under the control of people who were responsible—that is, responsible to Morgan and Ryan. The whole campaign was conducted for that purpose; the newspapers of New York knew that it was conducted for that purpose, and when that purpose was accomplished, the legislative investigations and the newspaper clamor stopped almost overnight.

Sinclair went on to notice a "curious" thing; namely, that no one made any effort to advocate the "one intelligent solution to the problem—that is, government insurance."

It was even more curious, how Upton Sinclair was able to vary a deep pessimism concerning the victories of the muckraking era with a solid understanding of the fact that the reforms were per-

---

[3] Chronicles of America, Vol. 18, pt. 2, Yale University Press, New Haven, 1919-21.

manent and fast-multiplying. The reason for his half-blindness was that he was filled with the urgency of Socialism, that he expected and willed a quick evolution to Socialism, and that the reforms stimulated by muckraking could not be fitted into his schema. He could not realize that the purpose of muckraking was not expressly to achieve Socialism but to strengthen the middle-class and the working-class. Both were fated to be plunged into war, it is true, and later still to be tried by economic depression and spiritual crisis; but neither, when aware of their situation, could fail to be grateful for what they had inherited through the muckrakers.

The muckrakers themselves might well have been optimists as they watched great reforms develop on every side. Because he was heartened by those reforms David Graham Phillips, who was as deeply concerned as Sinclair about his country, could sustain a more logical position. In his "insurance novel," *Light-Fingered Gentry*—actually, insurance was less the theme of the book than its vehicle—Phillips represented the insurance reforms as products of democracy and necessity (which they were), and indicated that further democracy and more necessity would make for more reform.

Lawson could logically have been angrier than Sinclair at the conclusion of the insurance scandals. He, not Judge Dill, publicized them. And whereas Hughes went up to Albany as Governor and became less and less the reformer until there was little left of his earlier zeal [4]—until he was a fit candidate for President and could lose to Wilson in 1916 by only twenty-three electoral votes—Lawson himself was allowed to return unthanked to private life. Lawson knew very well that Morgan and Ryan had drawn the insurance companies into their orbits. He was outraged to see how his efforts to further reforms in the companies had been frustrated: frustrated principally by a public which heard what it wanted to hear, which refused to credit his assertions that the System was more firmly than ever in control of life insurance.

But neither Sinclair nor Phillips nor Lawson was in position to be aware of the most important fact of all: in securing complete

---

[4] The story of Hughes's transformation is told in Oswald Garrison Villard's *Prophets True and False*, Knopf, New York, 1928.

control the System had cut itself off entirely from the rank and file of policy-holders. The December 1906 popular election of directors for New York Life and Mutual was the first and last serious effort to introduce democracy into insurance. After that, high finance assumed full and undisputed sway. Popular interests were now represented no longer in the insurance companies, but outside, in the legislatures, in private organizations, and through pressure groups called into being by the special needs and demands of the middle-class and working-class.

In a word, insurance had been made efficient and entirely capitalistic—how efficient and how capitalistic it was difficult to realize until in 1939, thirty-three years after the Armstrong investigation, another insurance inquiry was held—this time not in Albany but in Washington. Conditions had changed markedly. The colossal sums which the insurance companies had controlled in the days of 1906 were small change beside the fabulous funds which the modern companies possessed. Insurance had ceased being a giant; it had become a cosmos. But now the investigations had not been undertaken in answer to popular demand; they had been dictated from above. Why? Had rumors of trouble in the business reached the government? On the contrary: the purpose of the investigation was merely to review the business, and assurances were given that the government did not intend to harass the companies.

How meager were the results of the new investigations! With what remarkable frequency did the old Armstrong report—thirty-three years old; centuries old in point of events—crop up. Had insurance been stocked with so much virtue in 1906 that it required no radical reconsideration in 1939? This was, in a sense, the truth. Life insurance was no longer a people's institution; it was entirely a capitalist institution; it was as inextricable from capitalist government—its faults and virtues—as Congress itself. Business was politics, and politics was business.

The participants in the fight of 1905 and 1906 had been thorough in the extreme. Where other issues—the railroad issue, for example—were destined to stagger along, to furnish a topic of public contention for years, insurance was settled out of hand; it was so completely modernized that it was transposed beyond the age of muckraking into an age that thought in terms of labor and capital almost exclusively. The final achievement of the muck-rakers in this field, then, was that they had prepared immense archives of history and experiment for a new generation to consider when it should feel impelled once again to concern itself seriously with the question of insurance. [5]

[5] Louis D. Brandeis gathered distinction in the battle for a positive insurance policy. For his savings bank life insurance program and approach, see Melvin I. Urofsky and David W. Levy, eds., *Letters of Louis D. Brandeis*, State University of New York Press, Albany, 1971, vol. 1, 362–590 *passim*.

XVI. THE FIGHT FOR THE
HEPBURN BILL

IN 1903 no one needed to be told that there was a railroad problem. Most Americans had been reared amid discussion of it. The immigrants and other settlers in the Midwest and Far West, especially, were very painfully aware of it. The railroad had absolute control over their lives: it told them how much they were to receive for their grain and cattle, dictated land values, settled the destiny of towns by passing through them or outside them, and otherwise showed its hand in nearly every phase, political, social, and economic, of national life.

In *The Octopus* Frank Norris could afford to write with equal appreciation of the railroad builder Collis P. Huntington and the farmers and workers whom Huntington oppressed. The farmers and workers themselves could not afford the luxury of broad-mindedness. As far back as the Seventies, and particularly in the Midwestern states, the practices of the railroads had driven them to physical resistance as well as to innumerable legal suits. The result had been the Granger state laws, which were immediately taken to the carpet by the courts. The Grangers had sought to establish that the railroads were subject to state authority; litigation proved to them that the railroads—interstate carriers, for the most part—would have to be controlled by the federal government if they were to be controlled at all.

Attention now shifted to Congress, which was importuned to pass laws forbidding railroad iniquities. The result of the campaign was the famous Interstate Commerce Act of 1887, which was deliberately phrased to be vulnerable to railroad lawyers—and was. Within ten years the Act's provisions had been reduced to utter debility and the railroads were evading them with serene immunity. The courts consistently ruled against the people. Capping the irony of the situation was the fact that the decisions of the Interstate Commerce Commission were not compulsory; they had to be fought out in the courts, just as though there was no Commission at all! The hearty fanfare which accompanied the passage of the Act was, therefore, soon succeeded by resentment and disillusionment.

But the worst is not yet told. Since 1887 the railroads had come of age. They were now no longer speculative investments at most a few thousand miles long; the systems had grown enormously, and giant consolidations had made them as strong as government —and much more menacing. They were ruled over by masters of doubtful integrity. Freight services had grown five times faster than railroad mileage, so that the country was more dependent upon them than ever. On the other hand, the railroad magnates— James J. Hill, the "empire builder"; Harriman, the "organizer"; Morgan, the versatile financial genius—had destroyed competition. And who was profiting from the big consolidations? The answer was plainly to be read in the rates schedules. For a generation, competition—selfish and anarchistic though it was—had steadily forced down the freight rates; in 1900 the average railroad revenue per ton mile had been reduced to three-fourths of a cent. Now, in 1903, it had risen to two and even three cents.[1]

The rise of rates, moreover, was unfairly distributed among all classes of goods and throughout the country. That the railroads' schemes for fattening upon the public were practically endless was discovered by muckrakers and their allies who made patient efforts to summarize the many means of discrimination.[2] "Classifications" of goods (requiring different rates) were arbitrarily changed, minimum carload ratings were arbitrarily increased, free storing privileges were prohibited, return transportation for cattlemen was suddenly withdrawn, goods of favored shippers were not billed. . . . There was, in brief, very little limit to opportunities for favoritism in the railroads' dealings with its customers.

Finally, of course, the railroads were not working only for themselves. They operated in the interests of all the trusts—sometimes against their own will. We have seen to what uses Armour

---

[1] "Changes in Railroad Conditions Since 1887," by Wm. Z. Ripley, reprinted from *World's Work*, October 1905.

[2] See, for example, *The Heart of the Railroad Problem*, by Frank Parsons (Little, Brown & Co., Boston, 1906), which dealt solely with discrimination.

put his private yellow cars. The Standard Oil Company still habitually practiced the rebate system by which it had grown gigantic.

The New York, New Haven & Hartford Railroad had corrupted politics so long that it could afford to leave the routine work of corruption to others. The Southern Pacific, which operated in newly exploited territory, preferred to control actively the affairs of California, Oregon, and adjoining states. E. H. Harriman, the meteor of modern railroad history, in effecting merger after merger of railroad properties, left a wake of degraded businesses and political functionaries. Worth perhaps $10,000,000 in the late Nineties, when he died in 1909 he left an estate of some $150,000,000, which did not by any means represent the extent of the influence he had wielded or tell how he had wielded it.

The railroads, then, were the Octopus. Turn where he might, the citizen could not but see the evidence of their power and ruthlessness. Who could foresee a time when, undersold by the motorbus and snubbed by the automobile owner, the railroads themselves would agitate for "fair play" and a "square deal"? In 1903 they were strategically placed among the industries; they were the front-line representatives of the trusts; they were indomitable. Who or what could move them—short of an economic revolution?

Toward the close of the century a man had arisen who was as strong a personality as the transportation kings and was grimly determined to fight them to the finish. Robert Marion La Follette was not the first to fix upon the railroad system as his mortal enemy, but the railroads had absorbed most of the earlier talented dissenters and left the others exhausted and embittered. La Follette was not absorbable; nor did he become embittered, because he had the extraordinary faculty of combining rigid principle with necessary compromise. He was, as Steffens saw with deep insight, the kind of leader the people needed. He was a boss, but a boss who demanded and ordered democracy—the one kind of democrat who could cope with the Octopus.

La Follette discovered his true strength and career slowly. The son of a Wisconsin pioneer, born in the conventional log cabin of the settler, he grew up in the afterglow of the Lincoln tradition.

He was a Republican, naturally, and who was not?—for the Republican Party held the Midwest in the palm of its hand. Although La Follette in his youth read Henry George and was thrilled by Ingersoll, it was long before he weighed all the elements of political faith and made his choice among them.

He distinguished himself at the University of Wisconsin as a militant "plebeian" and orator, served a brief apprenticeship in a lawyer's office, and then, in 1880, at the age of 25, announced himself as candidate for district attorney of Dane County on the platform of efficiency and willingness to work. He did not bother to apprise the Republican boss of his decision, for he was not aware that politics were not now a matter of the people's will.

The people, indeed! La Follette was summoned before the local boss and told that he was wasting his time in traveling about and introducing himself to the farmers of the vicinity. La Follette needed, however, no more than this to convince him that a principle was involved. He increased his exertions, worked night and day despite the machine, and won unexpected victory.[2a]

In the four years of his service as district attorney, during which he built up a remarkable record of convictions, he demonstrated what democracy meant to him: it meant carrying out the law. (He was still too green to realize that law was not all that democracy required.) Aside from his insistence on the law, however, he was "regular"—a staunch Republican, upholding the faith against those who had been corrupting it. In 1884, having made his mark —with the people, not the machine—he ventured to run for Congress and, in a whirlwind campaign, won again, and carried his gospel of freedom to Washington.

During his three terms in the House of Representatives La Follette crossed many bridges. He learned slowly because he was learning from experience; but about the question of the railroads he did not have much to learn. He saw that they were strictly incapable of obeying the law, and he did not hesitate to attack their representatives whenever they crossed his path. La Follette's severity made many enemies in politics; he was able to keep in

---

[2a] The La Follette saga is treated skeptically in D. Thelen, *The Early Life of . . . La Follette . . .* , Loyola University Press, Chicago, 1966. It misses the point in imagining that idealism connotes weakness.

politics only because at that time his moral eye saw no deeper than obvious sin. He admired McKinley, for example, being much taken with his charm and dignity; he approved the Interstate Act of 1887—with reservations, of course—and helped to frame the protective tariff of 1890. He was, in fine, a party man set on purifying his party. Even so, it was only his personality and inexhaustible energy that kept the Republican leaders from ridding themselves of him.

It was during his career as a Congressman that he cultivated an individual approach to the people which served him to the end. At a personal expense which in the early years kept him poor, he made certain that his constituents were constantly aware of his efforts in their behalf. He sent them copies of his speeches and bills, advised them on local matters, and warned them of issues immediately important to them. Democracy was, for him, an ever-widening process of enlightenment, and he practiced what he thought. He was therefore bitterly disappointed as well as stunned when, in 1890, Wisconsin went overwhelmingly Democratic and buried even him, its champion, in defeat. Discouraged, convinced that he was done with politics, he returned home to a private law practice.

It was at this time that he had an experience which he later described in his autobiography as the turning point of his life. He was approached by a millionaire railroad Senator with an offer of a bribe.

One might reasonably wonder how anyone who had so much as seen La Follette, let alone had previous dealings with him, could think of such a thing. Bribery, however, was common; the situation happened to be embarrassing, and the Senator evidently saw no harm in his offer. But to La Follette that offer was a revelation. He suddenly understood the railroads' method of controlling the government. Full of indignation, and no doubt seizing opportunity, he broadcast the insult to the state and stirred up angry retaliation by railroad partisans.

The winter of 1891 was the sorest ordeal of La Follette's life. A movement was set afoot to destroy him. Friends deserted him; clients left him. La Follette had never realized that outraged honesty could bring such consequences. But now, attacked by an implacable enemy himself, he saw how the whole country was being victimized. He realized that democracy could not co-exist with the politico-economic interests that were hounding him.

Having made up his mind, La Follette now began single-handed a crusade which represented for him a struggle between the people and autocracy. He fought in Wisconsin with something of the desperation, the bottomless sincerity, of the Socialists, inspired by similarly ideal visions. He harangued and recruited volunteers and developed party workers, not for Socialism but for democracy. It was hard, uphill work, but he thought it could be done. And while he labored he decided not to break with the Republican Party, but to capture it—and to capture it without sacrificing principle.

His battle was soon taken up in other states, and while the Interstate Commerce Commission was rapidly stripped of such power as it had been given, a separate movement for railroad control mounted in strength. In Wisconsin party lines broke down before La Follette as reactionary Republicans banded with reactionary Democrats to defeat his slates. La Follette lost the state elections in 1892, but his machine was strengthened in the struggle. He ran for Governor three times, losing in 1894 and again in 1896, and still again in 1898. There were gains in each election, however—gains which were not fully registered by the election returns.

In 1899 the railroad interests in Wisconsin were driven, in self-defense, to adopt pledges from the La Follette platform—pledges which they of course betrayed. Their stratagem, however, was in vain. When La Follette ran again in 1900, with a plank demanding direct primaries (which would give the nomination of candidates back to the people) and a plank calling for railroad taxation, he won.

The five momentous years of La Follette's governorship fulfilled his hopes. He came to direct grips with the railroads and resisted them as no other American had done before. Incessant propaganda from railroad sources in particular was poured out to discredit him in the state and beyond—propaganda which was so successful that when Steffens came to see La Follette he was convinced that he was dealing with an unprincipled demagogue. All the while La Follette ruled his machine with an iron hand, but it was a hand directed by principle. Having won the Governorship, he rallied the state solidly behind him and changed the statute books one by one.

After a three-year fight with the opposition in the state legislature, he won the direct primary. The railroads were now made subject to equitable taxation. Knowing that this was not enough—

LA FOLLETTE

Drawn by Art Young

the railroads could make up their losses through exorbitant rates— La Follette won a state railroad commission which in actual strength shamed the Interstate Commerce Commission, and which proceeded to make public the affairs the railroads had hitherto kept secret.

During those five years La Follette achieved other revolutionary and advanced legislation—legislation that placed Wisconsin second only to Oregon in laws and ahead of Oregon in practice, and caused Frederic C. Howe to call Wisconsin an experiment in democracy. (During his service under Tom Johnson in Cleveland,

Howe had become America's foremost authority on municipal affairs, and his opinion was very much worth attention.) La Follette's reforms extended far, including not only railroads but education and forestry, taxation, civil service, and insurance. He organized a state industrial commission, passed workmen's compensation laws, and otherwise forced the labor issues to their democratic conclusions. But his greatest triumphs were, of necessity, his railroad and public-utility laws—models of legislation which roused strong envy in other states and troubled the meditations of Congress. When he was elected to the United States Senate early in 1905, it was as though La Follette was going to Washington in person to see what changes he had wrought there since the beginning of his fifteen-year war with the railroads.

The issue now before the country was not railroad regulation but government ownership of the railroads. The demand for government ownership, sharply posed by the Socialists, was no less vigorously urged by other groups and the longer the railroad issue was allowed to fester, the more bold became the government-ownership advocates. In 1901 the Hill-Harriman duel for control of the Chicago, Burlington & Quincy Railroad Company—a duel that all but precipitated an economic crisis—doubled the clamor. The Elkins Act, passed by Congress in 1903 as a reform measure, impressed no one who knew the facts involved. It was aimed specifically against discrimination and rebates; but it was framed by Senator Elkins, who was far from being a reformer: he was a railroad man, and the purpose of his bill was no more than to protect the railroads from being forced to grant exorbitant rebates to their shippers. The ordinary passenger and shipper received no relief by it.

Theodore Roosevelt was well aware of the national sentiment with which he had to deal. He knew very well the anti-railroad work La Follette had been doing, and he knew that the people were learning about it. Roosevelt's own friend Steffens was helping spread the facts, and Bryan in his *Commoner* was holding forth radically to appreciative audiences on the railroad question.

From half a dozen approaches the muckrakers were making startling and understandable the complex questions of railroad management and manipulation.

There was, for example, the irritating question of passes. For over twenty-five years the gift of free rides had been a ready means of corrupting legislators, purchasing lawyers, and otherwise degrading representatives of the public. Mark Sullivan, looking backward from today, finds much to tolerate in such practices. In *Our Times* he tells how being the possessor of a pass was a privilege, an honor bestowed by a time-worn custom, and in his personal memoirs he admits jocosely that he himself received and used a railroad pass when he was the twenty-year-old editor of a local newspaper in Pennsylvania. Of course one accepted such privileges! But when one learned what was behind them, one registered such a protest as Sullivan's own earnest *Collier's* article, which listed the crimes of the Boston and Maine Railroad in its control over New Hampshire and singled out the business of "courtesy passes" for special condemnation.[3] Actually, the free-pass practice became, in the hands of the muckrakers, a symbol of railroad misrule, and it strengthened the nation's determination that the railroads must be regulated.

Among the muckrakers who had seized upon the railroad issue and made the most of it, before La Follette arrived in Washington, B. O. Flower with his *Arena* was one of the most effective. Railroad regulation had been a major issue for Flower since his start; no magazine had more consistently opposed the unhampered expansion of railroads than *The Arena*. Although ordinarily this magazine failed to combine fresh, significant fact with moral purpose in the manner of the best muckraking article, it had succeeded in doing so with the railroad question, which was its inheritance from the Populist revolt and with which Flower was thoroughly familiar. In July 1904 *The Arena* had brightened up with more pictures, more life, a new format, and Flower himself had led off with a powerful article, "Twenty-Five Years of Bribery and Corrupt Practices," which detailed unforgotten sins and caused deserved comment. Then *The Arena* had settled down to a long campaign of education and agitation ably sustained by Professor Frank Parsons, seconded by Carl S. Vrooman. Parsons had written on railroads as far back as 1895, and his work had become more and more extensive. Under his direction, articles on passes,

---

[3] "The Way of a Railroad," August 11, 1906.

rebates, the private-car evil, the accident and death rates of the railroads, and proposals for railroad legislation had made the pages of *The Arena* fascinating.

The railroads' accident rates were particularly disturbing to the public. The increase in railroad mileage and transportation facilities had not been accompanied by a corresponding increase in safety devices. Semaphore and danger-light systems, to say nothing of grade-crossing elimination, involved more money than the railroads cared to spend. The result was that shocking accidents were a commonplace in the news of the day; the death toll mounted steadily, and no relief for either employees or passengers seemed near. Nor were the muckrakers alone in pointing to the frightful facts. *The Review of Reviews, The Science Monthly*, and even *The Nation* published grave accounts of accidents which played no favorites but took the president of the Southern Pacific Railroad as promptly as it did the humblest unfortunate passenger. The death rate could have no direct defenders—only apologists who argued about the meaning of the fateful statistics or blamed them on "negligent" railroad employees. Even Frederick Upham Adams, brilliant writer and inventor, who had deserted the radical movement, was moved to write so critical an article as "The Dollar and the Death Rate," [4] in which he deplored the greed in high circles which deprived the public of necessary protection in travel.

It remained for Ellery Sedgwick, of *Leslie's*, to give the accident issue enough momentum and drama to make it national. Sedgwick did not account himself a muckraker, but he had in *Leslie's* a magazine which always courted popularity, and just now he was seeking a theme that would be not "sensational" but constructive and, incidentally, popular. He found it in the accident problem. And so, to the future editor of the *Atlantic Monthly*, and to his magazine *Leslie's*, must go credit for a campaign which did much to bring government regulation of the railroads. At first glance accidents had nothing to do with government regulation—or the lack of it; at least Sedgwick so thought. He ran appreciative articles about railroad magnates at the same time that he deplored the death rate among their clientele. But

[4] In *Success*, January 1905.

the 300,000 readers of *Leslie's*, seeking what they wished to find, separated the relevant from the irrelevant and placed the onus where it belonged.

The *Leslie's* campaign was carefully planned. It protested at the inexcusable statistics and it made the most of the human factors. Sedgwick called America "The Land of Disasters"—and that became one of the slogans of muckraking agitation. Month after month, with fact and comment, the national disgrace was brought home to readers. The readers were urged to write their Congressmen, and were kept informed of efforts in Washington to pass laws ordering the installation of safety devices. Congressmen were interviewed by the magazine's representatives, copies of bills prescribing safety were sent free of charge to readers. Thus Sedgwick took advantage of his opportunities; and although the campaign for safety in travel was foremost in his mind, it lent added vigor to the general campaign for more inclusive railroad legislation.

"We are both practical men," Roosevelt wrote Harriman in friendly confidence, in a letter which preceded his unprincipled break with the railroad leader. But in politics Roosevelt was vastly more practical than the financiers whom he served. Time and again, in private letters and conversation, he told the magnates impatiently that their stubborn inability to adjust themselves to new conditions was making it difficult for him to save capitalism. But they did not read the popular magazines; Roosevelt did, carefully. He knew the temper of the country. He knew what power to convince lay in Charles Edward Russell's extended attack on the "private cars" of the beef barons. He noted how a crowd of imitators arose to follow after Russell, and he understood why: there was a demand for their work. Although Roosevelt managed to sidetrack the Russell exposé, he did not delude himself into thinking that he had scored a victory; he had merely earned a breathing spell. There had to be railroad legislation; there should be such legislation. He therefore set about getting it.

In December 1905 Roosevelt delivered a message to Congress in which he urged "government supervision and regulation of rates charges by the railroads," softening his demand with a warning against "radical" legislation. Soon after, Representative Hepburn of Idaho introduced in the House a Roosevelt-sponsored and

Roosevelt-endorsed bill. The shrewdness of Roosevelt's strategy is evident when one realizes that the Senate was determined to prevent the passage of *any* regulation in the interests of the people. Roosevelt, by setting up the Hepburn Bill, diverted attention from the entire issue of government ownership; he made the fate of *any* regulation precious; and he made himself the leader of the fight for such regulation.

He was aided by the muckrakers, who for the most part followed his lead. After the Hepburn Bill passed the House almost unanimously, the February 24 issue of *Collier's* announced that the siege of the Senate had begun, and cheered it on. Other liberal organs followed suit. Such journalistic support—balanced, of course, by angry admonishments from the conservative press—gave proper atmosphere to the fight.

Best tuned to the battle Roosevelt had mapped and was prosecuting was the series of articles with which Ray Stannard Baker now attracted national attention. No issue better suited his talents than the railroad issue. In the work that had made his reputation,[5] he had already stretched to weariness his fear of capitalist autocracy on the one hand and labor autocracy on the other. But the railroads were different; they had no ground for defense. They were in the same class as his colleague Tarbell's Standard Oil Company: the more one labored to understand their point of view —and Baker had studied them at first hand for months and even years—the worse their case appeared.

Baker's series, beginning in *McClure's* in November 1905 under the title "The Railroads on Trial," led off with a robust exposition of railroad rates. Baker next discussed the rebates question— that long and tiring subject—and gave it freshness and urgency. In January 1906 he added to Russell's interpretation his own interpretation of the private-car and beef-trust situation. Whereas Russell had undoubtedly stirred the deeper currents of popular resentment, being "radical" he did not receive the approval of educators and politicians. Baker closed earnest descriptions of the railroad situation with definite but by no means burning remarks about the need for reform. By March, when he told how the railroads created public opinion—when he told of the bribery and

[5] See Chapter VII.

corruption involved in railroad propaganda, he had touched a new high in public esteem and was having a direct influence on the furious debates which were then echoing in the Senate.

The Senate, elected as it was by the state legislatures rather than by the public, was then reactionary almost to the last man. It was composed of "railroad men" and "steel men" and "oil men," and others who were known agents of special interests. Among the exceptions, Beveridge, of Indiana, a self-made young man who belonged to no corporation, functioned on progressive issues only fitfully because of his unfortunate idealization of material success. Ben R. Tillman, of North Carolina, created politically and formed mentally by the Populist rebellion, was bound by the states'-rights doctrine of the solid South. Such principles as La Follette had brought with him from Wisconsin had no echo in the Senatorial chamber.[6] The Republicans, who made up the overwhelming majority, were absolutely led by the party boss Aldrich and could be moved, as in the case of the pure-food crusade, only by a demand backed by public threats.

The complicated arguments and intrigues which marked the Senate's struggle during April and May of 1906—after the publication of Baker's article on railroad propaganda—were reducible to one question: How much power to regulate would the Interstate Commerce Commission be given? La Follette, listening to the debates, was amazed at the shallowness of the arguments. Twenty-five years of discussion and experience had apparently predetermined that the eloquence of the "distinguished" Senators would be nothing but defiance of popular will. Needless to say, the man who had led the Western revolt against the railroads, and had broken their grip on Wisconsin, had not been given a place on the Senate Committee on Interstate Commerce. Instead, "Senate tradition" was invoked to prevent him from entering into the fight for regulation.

Nevertheless, on April 19, having spent several weeks in careful preparation, La Follette began a speech which extended over three sessions of debate. His fellow-Republicans expressed their resentment by deserting the Senate chamber, whereupon he inter-

---

[6] See *Current Literature*, March 1907, which discusses La Follette's isolation.

rupted himself to make a quiet, prophetic statement:

Mr. President, I pause in my remarks to say this. I cannot be wholly indifferent to the fact that Senators by their absence at this time indicate their want of interest in what I may have to say upon this subject. The public is interested. Unless this important subject is rightly settled, seats now temporarily vacant may be permanently vacated by those who have the right to occupy them at this time.

The Hepburn Bill, however, took the appointed Rooseveltian course. It was uphill work getting even this half-measure passed. "Railroad Senators Unmask!" [7] cried Henry Beach Needham—a favorite journalist and magazine writer—as though the railroad Senators had ever claimed to be anything but what they were! As he worked to get the Hepburn Bill passed, Roosevelt was opposed by his own entire Republican majority. He was forced to make a temporary alliance with the Democrat Tillman, who was his personal enemy, and other concessions. The Bill became law.

Roosevelt emerged as the hero of the battle, the man who had revitalized the Interstate Commerce Commission. Actually he had applied brakes to public sentiment which had been moving rapidly toward drastic action; he had successfully curbed and directed the muckraking propaganda for essential reform. Ever a master politician, Roosevelt never revealed his ingenuity more clearly than in this fight. His policy, siphoning off indignation as rapidly as it mounted, enabled the railroads to weather the most flagrant scandals and exposures. No one could deny, on the other hand, the truth of what Samuel Untermyer, one of the most intelligent and farsighted of the conservatives, observed: [8]

The accomplishments of the Inter-State Commerce Commission are the greatest triumph of modern times in scientific Government. No one who has watched at close range our progress in securing control over the Railroads will doubt our capacity for progressive Government in that direction. It saved us from Government ownership of the Railroads, as the like Regulation of Industrial Corporations will save us from Socialism.

[7] *Collier's*, March 24, 1906.
[8] Address to the Economic Club, New York, November 22, 1911. For further Progressive developments in railroads, see Donald R. Richberg, *Tents of the Mighty*, Willett, Clark & Colby, Chicago, 1930, 121 ff.

XVII. DYNAMITE

PUBLIC concern for the central middle-class problems of the day did not obscure the fact that there was a "submerged third" of the people who had little to anticipate from railroad reform, insurance exposures, and the like. This was the muckraking era, and no challenge to democracy was ignored by the reform writers. Before the era was over the working-class was given a thorough, democratic investigation by men and women who had, for the most part, nothing directly to gain from that class. These investigators were not union people, and they were not employed by labor papers. They wrote because there was a demand for their work, and because they wanted more reform and more democracy.

Millions of workers were drudging for wages that hardly warranted their efforts. Strikes regularly punctuated their struggles to secure higher pay and better hours as well as more tolerable living and working conditions. Their appeals and demands were carried to legislatures and the courts. But it was remarkable how low a standing labor had in the courts. The courts seemed to register seismographically the triumphs and defeats of the classes —no more. One heard of honest politicians, liberal district attorneys, radical lawyers. But who heard of a radical judge? Yet wait —there were a number of them, and we shall hear of one—the greatest of them, and a muckraker—in a later chapter.

Labor struggles in the East were comparatively civilized. That is to say, law—some kind of law restraining the belligerents—was never seriously transgressed after 1877, except during such catastrophes as the Homestead affair of 1892. But beyond the Middle West—that middle-class fortress—conditions changed completely. From Montana down to New Mexico, and all the way over to the Pacific Coast, violence was prevalent: the class struggle existed in its most overt form. *The reason was that in the*

*Far West no influential middle-class was established capable of
acting as a buffer between those who monopolized the natural
resources and the men whom they employed.* These were the
states where vigilante committees were still often the only instruments of law. See that fact in relation to the character of the work
the laborers had to do, and the reason for capital-labor violence is
clear.

Take, for example, the seasonal workers who followed the harvest. Their essentially homeless and disorganized manner of living made them easy prey for their masters, who kept them at
minimum wages. The lumberjacks worked hard, lived hard, and
paid a like penalty for extreme individualism. Thousands of Western workers were, in fact, utterly abject.

The lot of the copper, gold, and silver workers was the worst
of all. The fluctuating fortunes of the smelters, mills, and mines
affected them constantly. Cave-ins, poisonous fumes, long hours
took rapid toll of them. But since they worked under a closer
approximation to Eastern conditions—worked side by side and in
great numbers—the impulse to organization came more naturally
to them. These were the men who later formed the membership
and following of the Industrial Workers of the World, and who
evolved a philosophy and a method. Later still, when they had
reached the zenith of their power under the I.W.W., John Spargo
with his fine logic and learning destroyed their philosophy,[1] but
he did not alter them as men and did not change the conditions
which had made them what they were. The labor unions and the
I.W.W. needed no theoretical justification. For if, as the muckrakers proved, the courts and the politicians were uniformly
against them, and if they were opposed by the highly organized
Mine Owners Association, which never hesitated to use agent-
provocateurs and strikebreakers, what else were they to do in order
to live?

That question was to be fully posed and answered in a number
of ways before the period ended.

The miners made many attempts to organize, but it was not
until 1892 that the lowest-paid enjoyed any tangible gains. In

---

[1] In his *Syndicalism, Industrial Unionism and Socialism,* B. W. Huebsch, New
York, 1913.

that year the miners of the Coeur d'Alene region in Idaho struck and in the ensuing broil the Helena-Frisco mine was wrecked by dynamite, whereupon martial law was declared, the strike was broken, and "order" was restored under conditions of the operators' choosing. Out of this struggle sprang the Western Federation of Miners, which spread rapidly through Idaho into Montana, Colorado, and beyond, and led battles (there is no other word) in which guns and dynamite were freely used. Obviously such desperate warfare was no accidental development. As the most reactionary journals admitted, the rank and file of the union was composed of "decent" people. In the crudest form the warfare represented conflict between labor and capital, and the labor, it should be observed, was purely American in biological and cultural inheritance.

The first great test of the Federation took place in 1894 at Cripple Creek, Colorado—a region which was to write itself into the history of the next quarter-century—when Governor Waite, a fervid and aggressive Populist, stirred the country by acting openly in the interests of the miners. Accused of setting class against class, he retorted that labor had been so consistently mistreated that it was only justice for prejudice, for once, to run the other way! But Governor Waite was only one blessing for labor in a long series of misfortunes. The miners had, for the most part, no other recourse against scabs and company police but terror.

From the beginning the Federation was directed by bold and resourceful leaders—leaders who, it is well to emphasize now, were undoubtedly the choice of the membership, which followed and defended them in their decisions. One notable leader was Ed Boyce, who before Charles Moyer was president of the Federation, and who during trouble in the Coeur d'Alene mines in 1897 urged the locals to distribute guns to the strikers. Another leader was Vincent St. John, who during a strike in the gold and silver mines of Telluride, Colorado, ordered (and undoubtedly received) from a Denver firm two hundred and fifty rifles and fifty thousand rounds of ammunition. But the greatest of all the miners' representatives was "Big Bill" Haywood, the first of the modern working-class leaders of the West.

Haywood's life—he had been a cowboy and a prospector before he had become a miner and a Socialist—read like a résumé of all the hopes and defeats of the miners who finally turned to the Federation for relief,[2] except that in his past there had been no social defeat, and he was not a man whose power and prestige depended merely upon union leadership. Like Debs, Haywood was a union man by choice, in thought as well as action. He joined other miners in the Federation and became a Socialist because he had no stomach for success or petty personal satisfaction. Having come of old American stock, he steered on an even keel into more and more radical waters, becoming famous as the fighting leader of strikes that shook the West and were echoed in labor struggles everywhere else in the nation. It was a long way from Plymouth Rock to a tomb outside the Kremlin walls. He covered the distance in fifty-nine years, by a longer and more complex route than did John Reed, near whom he was buried.

A climax in the mine warfare was reached in the Idaho sector when, in 1899, the $250,000 Bunker Hill mine was totally destroyed by dynamite. Governor Frank Steunenberg, a former trade-union printer who had been elected on the Populist ticket, broke his party pledges and called upon President McKinley for federal troops. Hundreds of strikers were arrested without warrant and herded into bull pens, and the entire region was put under martial law.

Montana meanwhile was being shaken by a unique set of forces. Here the class struggle was complicated by gigantic conflicts between the monopolists. Lawson's—that is, Standard Oil's—Amalgamated Copper Company was fiercely battling interests led by F. Augustus Heinze, a young mining engineer who had risen spectacularly to become one of the outstanding mine-owning millionaires of the state. Heinze fought as the workers' champion against the Standard Oil Trust—no less—and on both sides many miners were recruited in the interests of their employers. The conflict offered a full opportunity for Federation activity, and the Federation took advantage of it.

As serious as was the situation in Montana, it was Colorado that held the center of the stage from 1901 until the magnitude of the Western struggle was fully impressed on the American pub-

---

[2] *Bill Haywood's Book,* International Publishers, New York, 1929.

lic. In 1901 the Telluride miners, having tried often and without success to win the eight-hour day, went on strike. Scabs were imported, and the armed miners prepared to fight. The scabs were ambushed, and a bitter battle followed. Finally the scabs raised a white flag and evacuated the mines, which were taken over and held by the miners.

During the next several years, dynamite, murder from ambush, and open war made the situation in Colorado more and more intolerable. In 1903 the miners of Cripple Creek—Colorado's Coeur d'Alene—threw down their tools because of discrimination against union men. Mines were dynamited; non-union men were killed; Governor Peabody declared martial law. Adjutant-General Sherman Bell, a swaggering, brutal type of soldier, occupied the camp with federal forces and began the now familiar arrests, bull-pen imprisonments, wholesale deportations from the state, and military terrorism.

As disturbances continued in the West, the magazines began to publish articles on the crisis. From the start the muckraking organs struck the keynote of impartiality which they sustained until the San Francisco bombing by the McNamaras, in 1911, drew a line of demarcation between the old and the new reform attitudes. They did not try to minimize the despotism practiced by the operators. They were equally horrified by the tactics of the miners.

Ray Stannard Baker, for instance, taking the Colorado situation in the stride of his work, wrote a vivid account of its history and its personalities.[3] William MacLeod Raine was sent by *Leslie's* to Montana as an impartial investigator to review the Heinze-Amalgamated fight for copper, and in July 1904 he wrote on the policies of Adjutant-General Bell in Colorado. Though he arraigned the Western Federation bitterly, giving it an "appalling record," he could not and did not attempt to deny the harshness of the military dictatorship in the mining regions.

While the muckrakers thus labored to understand a situation which, under the circumstances, seemed to have no solution, the workers themselves were taking decisive and important steps. In June 1905 representatives of unions and labor organizations met

---

[3] "The Reign of Lawlessness," *McClure's*, May 1904.

in Chicago, paid a respectful and symbolic visit to the graves of the victims of the Haymarket riot of 1886, and set themselves to the business of creating a new working-class organization. Present were such militants as Daniel De Leon, Debs, Lucy Parsons—widow of the Chicago anarchist—and others representing unions and labor groups. The aim of the convention was not to form an organization supplementing the American Federation of Labor. Haywood, who was the reigning spirit of the convention, voiced the thoughts of the delegates when he declared that the American Federation was incapable of leading the organized workers, not to mention organizing the unorganized. He himself, because of his duties to the Western Federation, whose secretary-treasurer he was, declined the offer of the presidency of the new alliance, but the temper of the convention indicated that he would inevitably find himself drawn into its major activities.

The new organization was to be not a political party but a working-class *union* which would oppose the craft system of organization as reactionary and class-splitting. It was to be *revolutionary* in practice; one delegate, in fact, warned against taking the proceedings lightly, and prophesied that the tragedy of the ages was about to be played on the American scene.[4] The historic preamble which was adopted stated defiantly that

between the two classes [capital and labor] a struggle must go on until all the toilers come together . . . and take hold of that which they produce by their labor through an economic organization of the working-class, without affiliation with any political party.

Yet it was a foregone conclusion that the I.W.W. would become a banner—a party. No sooner was the organization launched than a fight began for control of it. Straddlers and moderates were driven out by the bloody struggles in which I.W.W. units became embroiled. De Leon dropped the organization in disgust. Debs, although he gave it his loyalty to the end, found himself inadequate for the type of fighting it involved.

Never did the I.W.W. have more than perhaps 5000 members. It tolerated only the most fearless militants. But the great strikes

---

[4] See *Proceedings of the First Annual Convention of the Industrial Workers of the World* (New York Labor News Co., 1905) for a full account of this momentous gathering.

it carried on among the unorganized in the East, and the miners, harvesters, and lumberjacks in the West, gave the lie to those who complained that it consisted merely of outlaws, despised and hated by all "right-thinking" workingmen. It was for the workingman's enemies to prove that the I.W.W. was unwanted.

Frank Steunenberg, the Governor of Idaho who had broken his campaign pledge by calling federal troops to the Bunker Hill mine in 1899, was ruined politically by his turnabout and, at the end of his term, retired to private life and wealth, taking the curses of the betrayed miners with him. On December 30, 1905, Steunenberg was fatally wounded by a bomb explosion at the gate to his home in Caldwell, Idaho. A cordon was thrown about the town, and a search for the murderer began. Public attention now focused on Caldwell, as though in anticipation of what was to be the decade's most important showdown on the labor question.

Three weeks before the assassination, a man had registered in a Caldwell hotel as T. S. Hogan and had let it be known that he was there to buy land for some friends. After the murder he remained in Caldwell, apparently to transact his business. His extreme calm in the face of the prevailing excitement, however, aroused suspicion. His room was searched, and some small amounts of plaster of Paris and bits of explosive were discovered. Under questioning he maintained his innocence, and gave such valid explanations of his activities that he was released.

It happened, however, that among those who witnessed the cross-examination was an Oregon sheriff—later to die in the same manner as Steunenberg—who identified the suspect as Harry Orchard, whom he had seen in Oregon and known as an officer of the Bourne Miners' Union. "Hogan" was held for further questioning and finally charged with Steunenberg's murder. He was transferred to Boise, where he continued to assert his innocence.

To Boise came many detectives, anxious to collect the large rewards that had been offered by the state and by the Steunenberg family. Among the detectives was James McParland, the man who thirty years before had broken up the Molly Maguires and sent their leaders to the scaffold. He was now an old man and general manager of the Pinkerton Agency. He visited "Hogan" in prison and held long conversations with him.

Several days after, he came from the prison with a startling announcement: the prisoner had confessed! "Hogan" was really Harry Orchard, and he had killed not only Steunenberg but eighteen other people during the past eight years! Furthermore, he had acted under the direct instructions of Bill Haywood, Charles Moyer, and George A. Pettibone, a former official of the Western Federation, who had been blacklisted for militancy!

Immediately a cry of protest arose from labor-unionists and Socialists all over the land. Orchard was denounced as a Pinkerton agent and the confession as a studied plot against the Western Federation. Even Gompers hurried to deny that the miners could have committed the crimes with which Orchard charged them. For the Western Federation was an affiliate of the American Federation, and the confession, if true, threatened to compromise labor —conservative as well as radical—seriously.

Meanwhile the prosecution struck quickly. Sheriffs were sent from Boise to Governor Peabody of Colorado demanding extradition of Haywood, Moyer, and Pettibone, who were all in Denver. Since these accused men had not been present at the scene of the murder, nor in the state for that matter, and since they were not therefore fugitives from Idaho, it was a question whether they could be placed in custody. On a Saturday, however—when the courts were closed and they were unable to get out a writ of habeas corpus—Haywood, Moyer and Pettibone were arrested by the Boise sheriffs and kept in jail during the night. The next day they were taken to Idaho under guard.

Debs sounded the alarm to the country. He called for the creation of an army to march on Idaho and forcibly free the prisoners. *The Appeal to Reason* seethed with indignation. The subsequent Supreme Court decision that the "extradition" had been legal increased the fury of the radical and Hearst press, which held that there was a conspiracy to murder the labor leaders and smash the Western Federation. A 4,000,000-copy "Rescue Edition" of *The Appeal* was issued—a feat never to be equaled—and was poured into the forty-eight states and territories. The labor movement was mobilized for the creation of a Moyer-Haywood-Pettibone Defense Committee. In short order $250,000 was raised for

the defendants, and Clarence Darrow, who at fifty years of age
was the country's outstanding labor lawyer, was commissioned
with E. F. Richardson, the great Denver criminal attorney, to
conduct the defense.

Boise had by now become the center of international attention.
Correspondents from all over the country and England were present to report the coming trial, and all agreed that matters looked
dark for the labor leaders.

As the day of the trial—May 9, 1907—approached, national
excitement mounted to fever-pitch. In all parts of the country
citizens bandied frank questions in the street: What would the
mysterious Orchard say? Would the trial be fair? *If Haywood
was guilty, how under the circumstances should he be judged?*

The extraordinary efforts of labor, and particularly of the Socialists and their sympathizers, had changed the whole aspect of
the situation. Had national interest and understanding regarding
the capital-labor situation in the West been no keener than it was
on December 30, 1905, when Steunenberg was assassinated, there
could have been no doubt about the fate of the defendants: they
would have been summarily condemned and executed. But a colossal feat of propaganda had been accomplished. Monster demonstrations had taken place in all the large cities. On May 4, Fifth
Avenue and Lexington Avenue in New York City had been
choked with marchers denouncing the approaching trial as a
frame-up and threatening violence if it were carried through. Such
demonstrations, making a profound impression on the public, had
focused the anxious attention of all classes on Boise.

William E. Borah, prosecutor of the State of Idaho, and newly
elected to the United States Senate, vigorously declared that nothing was involved in the case but Haywood's innocence or guilt.
Among labor sympathizers his plea fell on deaf ears. The circumstances of the case, which involved the very existence of unions,
had dragged labor to its feet to face problems it had hitherto
evaded. The middle-class itself was faced with the necessity for
taking a stand on labor. Labor, in a word, was on trial, not Haywood.

On May 9, before Judge Woods and a jury of poor farmers,
Haywood went on trial for his life.

As Harry Orchard sat stolidly in the witness chair and told his story—a story that chilled the nation with its matter-of-fact de-

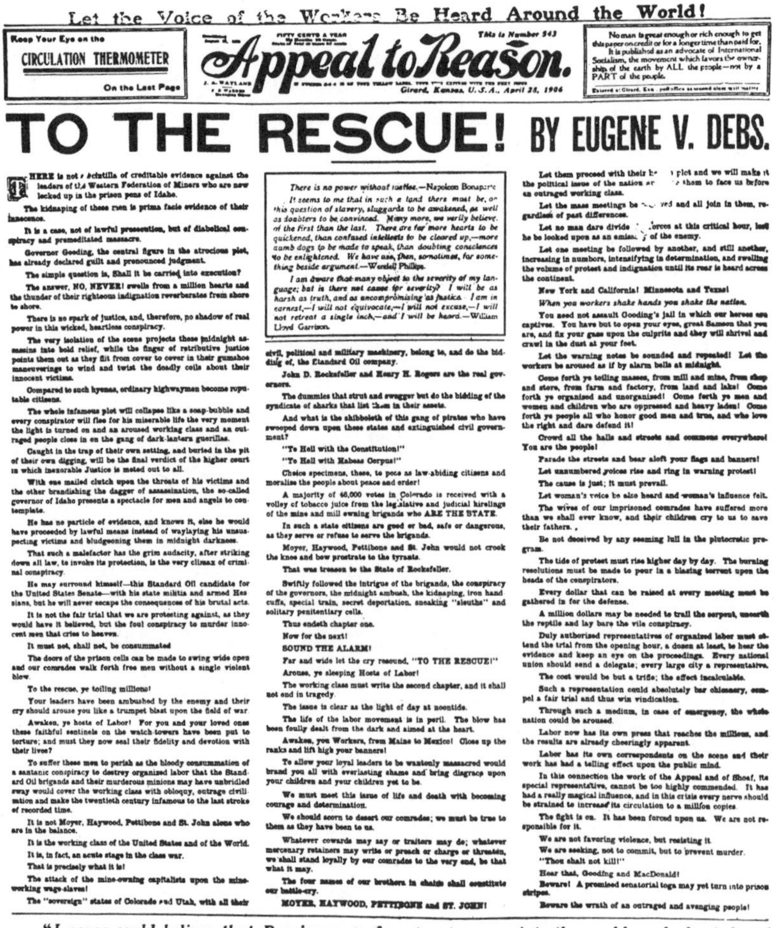

Let the Voice of the Workers Be Heard Around the World!

Appeal to Reason.

Girard, Kansas, U.S.A., April 28, 1906

TO THE RESCUE! BY EUGENE V. DEBS.

(three-column reproduction of newspaper text, largely illegible)

MOYER, HAYWOOD, PETTIBONE and ST. JOHN!

"*I never could believe that Providence had sent a few men into the world ready booted and spurred to ride, and millions ready saddled and bridled to be ridden.*"
—Richard Rumbold, on the scaffold, 1685.

"AROUSE, YE SLEEPING HOSTS OF LABOR!"

tails of fearful crime—it was apparent that he had changed considerably during the months of his imprisonment. Photographs taken at the time of his arrest had represented a weak-smiling, vacant proletarian type. He had paced his cell like a caged beast, snarled at his keepers, hurled back a Bible he had been offered by a visiting priest. He had since that time become religious; he was stouter, had grown a dignified mustache, and altogether presented a grave if negative appearance. His eyes and speech, however, were as cold and characterless as before.

His real name, he said, was Albert E. Horsley. He told of his eminently respectable childhood in Canada; how he had worked in the lumber woods of Saginaw, Michigan, and returned home to marry, and how he and his wife had manufactured cheese and lived quiet, provincial lives. Just why he should have "fallen," as he put it, was not so clear; evidently his feelings at the time were too far in the past to recapture. It was plain that he had no imagination, for his recital was couched in the baldest possible terms, with a simplicity that was more impressive than any drama could have been.

Orchard told of prosperous years and a happy home life which he had varied with apparently unsatisfactory dissipation. It was clear that his moral purposes were weak, not to say rootless; prosperity had only further weakened his hold on reality. His "fall" had culminated in a feeble infatuation with a woman in whose home he was living while he built a factory in another town. He had burned the factory for the insurance and run off with her to Detroit. The affair had been brief; she had returned to Canada, and he had begun to drift . . . to British Columbia . . . to Spokane, Washington . . . to the Coeur d'Alene mines.

It was significant that this part of his story, which he told in narrative form during several days of testimony, was not questioned seriously by the defense. Contemporary photographs showed the little courtroom: Darrow, sensitive and alert; Haywood, his good eye fixed sternly on the witness; the expressionless Orchard, carefully avoiding "Mr." Haywood's gaze. Whatever McParland's share was in the confession Orchard was making—and the unsavory connection of the Pinkertons with the prosecution was being screamed daily to the public by the radical press—there was little doubt that the confession thus far rang true.

In 1897 Orchard, driving a milk wagon in the mining region, saved enough money to buy a sixteenth interest in the Hercules mine near Burke. A wood and coal business increased his savings.

Bad habits, however, prevented him from becoming settled. As drink and gambling ate into his resources, he was finally forced to sell his mining interest—an interest which in several years was to be worth many times what he had put into it. By 1899 he had become a shoveler in the Tiger-Poorman mine at Burke. It was then that his relations with the Western Federation began.

It was at this point, also, that Orchard's story became curiously illogical. The union, he asserted, was run by an "inner circle" of conspirators. This was a typical Pinkerton charge, as the radical press hastened to inform its readers. Yet Orchard, as a union man, must have known that the sentiment of the average unionist was for his leaders. At any rate, he acted as a union man in those earlier days.

Continuing his story, Orchard claimed credit for blowing up the Bunker Hill mine and for an explosion in another mine. He told of his first visit to the Federation headquarters, of his meeting with Moyer, Haywood, and Pettibone, of the regular union business which he indubitably carried out for them, and of numerous and horrifying attempts to murder Governor Peabody, and the murder of several incidental mine detectives and operators.

What he did not tell was that while he was carrying on mysterious and debatable dealings with the Federation, he had also done work in the employ of various detectives and employer associations.

The defense flung the evidence of his double-dealing into his face, waved it in the faces of the jurors, brought witnesses to the stand to testify against Orchard.

Like Orchard, the other witnesses which Borah was able to bring to the stand fared worse than the witnesses for the defense. They were disreputable, shifty men who did more to hurt the prosecution than to help it. If McParland was being honest, bringing strikebreakers and others to corroborate Orchard's despicable if breath-taking tale, then he had never chosen a poorer time for honesty! It became clear that the defense grew stronger every day.

Orchard was undoubtedly a murderer—days of questioning failed to shake his story—but it was impossible to prove Haywood's complicity in his crimes. Haywood himself faced Borah firmly and gave a detailed account of his activities up to and including his arrest and imprisonment. If there was little question that he believed in class war and the use of terrorism, and if there was more than a suspicion that he had been involved in at least several of the bombing incidents, it was also plain that he was no boon companion of Orchard, and that if he had "used" Orchard, it was certainly not on Orchard's dissolute terms.

But *had* he used him? Borah insisted that he had. He hurled at Darrow the accusation that if Orchard had *not* confessed, Darrow would now be passionately defending Orchard instead of impugning him. The labor and Socialist press ignored the argument and its implications; the conservative press repeated it with Borah's heat and indignation; the muckrakers covering the trial, and they alone, treated it with fitting sobriety and honesty.

Why hadn't Orchard told of his relations with strikebreakers and provocateurs? Did he imagine, in his new devoutness, that the Federation was better off purged of its leadership, that his case was better not compromised with unfortunate facts? While Borah reaffirmed his belief in Orchard's story, Richardson, for the defense, enumerated the pros and cons of the evidence, tore into the prosecution, and execrated Orchard as a vile criminal and a monumental liar.

But it was Darrow's eleven-hour speech that was the high point of the trial. In moving and dramatic phrases he painted the history of the Federation and spoke of it as a haven of the miners, their militant champion against the operators. He blasted the testimony of Orchard and compared the man with Haywood, whose life was dedicated to the welfare and defense of the workers. He declared that the sole purpose of the trial was, not justice, but the murder of Haywood, and added that whether or not Haywood died the class struggle would go on.

When the prosecution and defense had completed their summings up, the case went to the jury. Judge Woods gave a clear charge to the jurors, warning them explicitly that Haywood could not be condemned unless evidence of his direct relationship to the crimes committed by Orchard had been shown.

No such evidence of his complicity had been presented, and Haywood was freed. A wave of relief swept the country, which had been tortured by the problems the trial contained. Haywood's acquittal provided a breathing spell, at least.

Haywood became labor's reigning hero, even being proposed as the next Socialist candidate for President. He declined the honor, preferring to return to policies and associates that later led to his expulsion from the Socialist Party.

As for Orchard, he was sentenced to die—Borah had pledged that he would be prosecuted to the limit of the law. His sentence was then commuted to life imprisonment. He became more and more religious, voluntarily undertook the support through handicraft of the wife and child whom he had deserted years before in Canada, and presented his life as a moral lesson to would-be sinners.

Labor, and particularly the Socialist Party, took the ground that they had smashed a conspiracy of the capitalists and emerged triumphant over them. And yet the trial had been fair—notably fair. And by consent other than that of the Socialists its fairness was due to the muckrakers, who had insisted upon trying to find the facts. *This stand was held against them by those who feared that the facts might establish a basis for convicting Haywood.* Those who preached the necessity for class war exclusively were unable to realize that the great body of citizens who made up public opinion were not to be won to Haywood's cause merely by passionate references to labor's wrongs. Only the muckrakers had been able to draw a picture of the trial and its principals that convinced because it was evident that they had made every effort to arrive at the truth.

There was, for example, Orchard's charge that the Western Federation was run by an "inner circle." The violent denials of the radicals had won over only those who were already heart and soul for the defendants. It was the muckrakers who brought the deeper meanings of the charge close to the great body of neutrals who held the balance. For the accusation that an "inner circle" existed *was* superficially true. The countless dynamitings certainly had not happened accidentally. Just whom they involved, however, was a more difficult question to answer. One thing was sure: dynamitings in the mines were not planned by callous individuals, and they were not necessarily planned by any of the leadership. (There had been violence in the Pullman strike, for instance, even though Debs had been an outspoken opponent of violence and had pleaded against it.) Above all, the dynamitings were never planned except by desperate men (or provocateurs). The miners' union was not a building-trades union overrun, as some were, by racketeers; it was thoroughly proletarian.

It was such careful explanations on the part of the muckrakers —as contrasted with the Socialists' flat assertions of innocence— that sowed doubt in the minds of many skeptics who had been originally inclined to accept Haywood as a terrorist and to think him guilty as charged. And first among the muckrakers who contributed to public understanding in this crisis was Christopher Powell Connolly, whom *Collier's* sent to report the trial. Connolly had long been the upright district attorney of politically corrupted Silverbow County, Montana, before he returned East to take high place among the other journalist-reformers with a series of dramatic exposures that amounted in essence to the history of the state from which he had come.[5] When Haywood came to trial, *Collier's* had seized upon the earnest and brilliant Connolly as its correspondent. With the Socialist and labor-union press shouting that the capitalists were in conspiracy to prejudice the nation against the defendant, *Collier's* had drily remarked that it could not speak for the other capitalists, but that it was determined to try to arrive at the truth—and that this was more than the Socialists were trying to do.

Connolly, combining the lawyer's acumen with the literary man's imagination and courage, wrote in great detail about the long and controversial history of the labor struggle. For his pains, he was called, by an Idaho miner, a "seller-out" to the capitalists. Connolly stood for hours trying to convince the miner that there was need for the truth. The miner cared nothing at all for the truth: this was class war, he repeated; Haywood must go free, and he and his fellow-unionists were determined that he should.

But if the truth seemed less important to the miner than acquittal, it had not seemed so to the public at large—that public which ultimately determined the verdict. It approved, for example, the

[5] See particularly the following series written for *McClure's: The Story of Montana*, August-December, 1906; *The Fight of the Copper Kings*, May-June, 1907; *The Fight for the Minnie Healy*, July, 1907. Shortly before his death, Connolly was to recapitulate his story for a new and unbelieving generation in *The Devil Learns to Vote*, Covici-Friede, New York, 1938.

enterprise of McClure, who during the trial ran some of the most important and sensational articles of the entire era. To interview Orchard he sent George Kibbe Turner, who had become the top-ranking McClure writer under circumstances which will be presently mentioned.[6] Turner had obtained Orchard's confessions for his magazine. These were run immediately, being supplemented by an introduction and notes to which even those who resented the wide publication of the confession gave reluctant approval. In *McClure's* the Orchard memoirs were hardly less impressive than the newspaper accounts. They were written with a blood-chilling simplicity which seemed to fit the personality Orchard had exhibited on the witness stand. Samuel Hopkins Adams, reviewing the published volume [7] for *Bookman*, expressed very well the conviction it inspired, despite all the damaging evidence the defense had marshaled. McClure, true to the tradition of muckraking—which never operated at a consistently higher level than in this emergency—did not fail to offer Haywood, through Darrow, a huge sum for an article giving his side of the case. The offer was refused.

Paradoxically enough, it was this very willingness to give Orchard an opportunity to tell his story which helped turn the tide in Haywood's favor. As the magazines insistently pointed out, acquittal of Haywood had *not* meant conviction of his innocence. So one of the jurors had explained in telling how the jury had arrived at its verdict. Connolly, in *Collier's*, shrewdly added that probably the jury had, "with a healthy repugnance for so inhuman a murderer as Orchard, made a distinction between believing the facts he presented and hanging a man on his testimony." *Collier's* later engaged in a debate with Darrow, whose high indignation failed to establish that *Collier's* had been unfair to him.

The muckrakers, in brief, had educated the public to the complex problems involved in the case, and it was because they had done this successfully that the public, respectful of questions which were not to be summed up in a simple indictment, had given the benefit of the doubt to Haywood. That was clearly to be read in the animated discussions that were carried on, once tension was

[6] See Chapter XVIII.

[7] *The Confessions and Autobiography of Harry Orchard,* McClure, Phillips Co., New York, 1907.

relaxed and reasonable argument was once more possible. The nation as a whole, the middle-class in particular, by giving ear to the muckrakers, showed itself dissatisfied with unctuous warnings concerned with the imminence of class war. Labor had been on trial, not Haywood; and labor had been vindicated—but only because it had been proved that its case was just, not because the nation had bowed to threats of force and violence.

XVIII. THE SEARCH FOR DEMOCRACY

GEORGE W. ALGER, the lawyer who was to draft important labor and child-labor laws for New York and who, like many other primarily non-literary men, sought and found support for his ideas through the magazines, wrote for the *Atlantic Monthly* an article on "The Literature of Exposure" which had a wide circulation.[1] Commenting on the muckraking magazines, he asserted that they did not go to the roots of trouble; that they merely "disheartened" the reader with arraignments of people who had succumbed to temptation; that, in a word, they were doing nothing constructive. Alger represented a school of thought which was, to speak simply, wrong. Even *The Bookman*, which rarely held a brief for the muckrakers, took issue with him. The critic cited Tarbell's work as a model of constructive criticism, and went so far as to give Charles Edward Russell credit for using a scientific method in his beef trust exposé. Furthermore, *The Bookman* critic concluded, muckraking did show results: the insurance men who had laughed at Lawson were not laughing any more; Standard Oil, the railroad barons, and grafters of every kind were on the defensive.

Neither Alger nor *The Bookman* writer, however, saw very far into muckraking. The aim to find constructive remedies for corruption was inherent in the muckraking articles, particularly in those which most bravely and conscientiously sought to analyze entire situations as a prelude to prescribing for them. The muckrakers, to repeat what has been said before, had to learn like the people: through inquiry, study, and experiment. Steffens, for example, wrote *The Shame of the Cities* before he wrote *The Struggle for Self-Government* (a book which compared the relative state of democracy in various sections of the country) for the sim-

---

[1] Reprinted in *Moral Overstrain*, Houghton Mifflin & Co., Boston, 1906.

ple reason that he did not know enough to write the second book first. Like George W. Alger he was a professional man who had been born and bred among certain outmoded ideas; unlike Alger he was determined to dig down until he understood conditions thoroughly and only then to name the correctives. On the other hand, he was not a political theoretician. His contribution to muckraking consisted of feeling and imagination. *The Struggle for Self-Government*, for instance, was dedicated to the Czar of Russia (just then reorganizing his empire, after the 1905 revolution), whom he advised to grant his people everything they wanted: then, Steffens promised, like the American people they would give their privileges away to individuals.

Alger might have found nothing suggestive in Steffens's irony; other readers of his book did. But Alger might have found something in Steffens's definition of political corruption; namely, that it was the process by which a representative democracy was transformed, through party evolution, into an oligarchy representative of special interests. An elementary definition? It focused attention on parties, at least, and it gave a first principle for evaluating La Follette and Folk, "Boss" Cox's Cincinnati, Tom Johnson's Cleveland (in the chapter "Ohio: A Tale of Two Cities"), and Jersey City, of the "traitor state" of New Jersey, the maternity ward of trusts, where Mayor Mark Fagan, a religious man and an undertaker, was in sharp conflict with the utilities.

Labor laws were certainly worth getting passed. They were the tangible memorials to popular victories. But propaganda against intolerable conditions, "disheartening" though it might have been, was a necessary groundwork for Alger's "constructive" legal work in labor legislation. Alger, like many another, ignored his debt to the muckrakers.

Every muckraker restlessly considered alternatives to the conditions he was describing. The entire purpose of *Frenzied Finance*, as Lawson time and again repeated, was education for change. Again, Upton Sinclair constantly professed to have the solution for the country's ills: Socialism—modern democracy. In the absence of a Socialist victory at the polls, he undertook to give a practical demonstration of his beliefs. He invested the money he had made from *The Jungle* in Helicon Hall, a colony, run on a co-operative basis, which incidentally became the target for countless malicious and libelous attacks. The colony was a valuable project from any, including the public, point of view. To it were attracted many of the outstanding intellectuals and radicals, as well as others who were to become outstanding—Harry Sinclair Lewis, for example, who left Yale to become Helicon Hall's furnace man. When Helicon Hall burned down, to the concerted jeers of the press, which took special delight in baiting the sensitive and argumentative Sinclair, the loss was real, for Helicon Hall had pioneered the way for other and more ambitious projects.

Everybody's made a more extended and deliberate search for democracy. It sent Charles Edward Russell about the world to write a series called "Soldiers of the Common Good,"[2] which would acquaint Americans with the efforts other nations were making to achieve democracy. Russell reported on the famous Rochdale Co-operative in England, told how Germany, Italy, and France were handling their government-ownership problems, elaborated on Switzerland, the classic land of successful democracy, and was properly impressed by New Zealand's triumphant paternalism. In his autobiography he was to admit that New Zealand's arbitration boards had fooled him (he was actually convinced that the problem of strikes had been settled) but, again, experiment had to come before knowledge, and Russell, who was one of the most sincere of the muckrakers—a martyr type, as Steffens called him—had fewer errors to confess than others who chanced less and accomplished less.

Muckraking was, first of all, constructive and democratic. Sensationalism as an end in itself was to become the property of writers who had nothing else to contribute. After the muckrakers, in incredibly few years, had educated the country to new conditions and solutions, they advanced—or rather began to advance—to more sophisticated planes of discussion. They discarded outmoded methods of debate, which straightway became the property of less sincere and less talented writers.

The city, wrote Frederic C. Howe, is the hope of democracy. And yet it might have seemed to those who read *McClure's, Suc-*

[2] Published in book form as *The Uprising of the Many*, Doubleday, Page & Co., New York, 1907.

cess, *Arena,* and like magazines in 1906 that America had never been so flagrantly corrupt as now. Trials of eminent and pre-

"CURRENT LITERATURE"

Drawn by E. W. Kemble for *Collier's,* March 25, 1905

eminent men were taking place in scores of cities. The Oregon land frauds several years after having been disclosed, continued to be aired in the press. Francis J. Heney, who had become a national figure through his handling of the case, was now in San Francisco acting as special prosecutor against Mayor Schmitz and investigating, among others, Patrick Calhoun, the famous traction magnate. The prosecution, only temporarily halted by the great earthquake, continued down to 1909 in an atmosphere of terror and stench.

Similar situations existed in Philadelphia, Chicago, and other major cities. It was almost as though, perversely, the old-time political bosses were offering the muckrakers opportunities for exposure. Actually, of course, they were only continuing disreputable practices because they knew no other ways of carrying on business and politics. Those practices were the ones by which they had grown and flourished. They fought reform stubbornly, blindly, because reform rendered them useless.

In practice, it was the reformers who had to learn resistance, for the odds were heavily against them. The muckraking organs were more than encouraging to the reformers in their work; they were essential to prevent the isolation of reform campaigns—as was true when Folk reached an impasse in St. Louis and Steffens came to his aid. The magazines, in brief, gave the reformers a chance to voice their aims and difficulties, taught them what other reformers were doing, and otherwise sustained them in their individual crusades.

Among the muckrakers themselves, Brand Whitlock was an illustration of the political reformer (he detested the term) who, being fundamentally literary, was acutely conscious of what his work involved. He was no lawmaker, like W. S. U'Ren, of Oregon; no robust, practical Single-Taxer, like his friend Tom Johnson, who had made Cleveland the best-governed city in the country. Whitlock had the temperament of the artist, and he had been inspired by "Golden Rule" Jones to believe that the fight for democracy must go on. After Jones's death in 1904, Whitlock took up the work of "practical Christianity" where Jones had left it, and served four times as Mayor of Toledo.

Why did not Whitlock devote himself freely to literature, as he longed to do, rather than to his "duty" as a politician? Whitlock wanted more than other muckrakers to step out of his times and produce "pure" art. There being little of that in America, he read eagerly the work which the last line of English masters— Hardy, Conrad, and the others—was creating, and struggled for leisure to do his own writing. He believed that literature as he conceived it, cool and finished and classical, could be developed out of the broken soil of the era. It seemed to him that muck- raking was only a half-step to frankly political work: one might just as well go the whole way. At any rate, it was with no feeling of triumph that he became a municipal statesman (he later recog- nized those years of his service as the best years of his life [3]) and he was many times to wish that "Golden Rule" Jones, with his calm, indomitable faith in his fellow-men, were beside to advise and direct him.

Whitlock inherited the hatred which all the organized groups of the community had accorded Jones. Sensitive and imaginative, Whitlock was never able to read indifferently the malice and mis- representation which capitalists, churchmen, and Socialists alike directed at him. Yet it was, curiously enough, the Socialists to whom he most quickly turned cold. They too were idealists; and because he was an idealist, it seemed to them that he deserved less consideration than others who were frankly corrupt or igno- rant. When, in 1907, Whitlock published *The Turn of the Bal- ance,* in which he summed up all his intense feeling about the injustices of which life was capable, Socialist fury against him only increased. A man capable of such social understanding had no right to be less than a Socialist; it was his duty to join the only party of truth and righteousness! Whitlock, who read seriously and thought seriously, was revolted by their indifference to his point of view, their assumption that only a desire to be comfortable— actually, there were millionaire Socialists who received whole- hearted party approval—prevented him from taking the one course which honesty and courage would have dictated. They closed their doors to him, and Whitlock henceforth ignored them.

Whitlock saw that common people, uninspired and unprophetic, had at least the virtue of human nature, if not always of human kindness. He found himself at war with every organized element

[3] See *The Letters and Journal of Brand Whitlock,* D. Appleton-Century Co., New York, 1936.

of Toledo, but he himself shrank from hurting anyone. Like Jones, he saw no gain to society in the harassment of criminals and prostitutes. They had to live; the duty of society was to purify itself. And it was to the task of purification that he addressed himself as best he could.

For eight years he immersed himself in work which was as exhausting as it was disheartening. Very often he felt like Tom Johnson, "even such a strong man as Tom Johnson," whom he reported to have said: "I wish I could take a train to the end of the longest railway in the world, then go as far as wagons could draw me and then walk and crawl as far as I could and then in the midst of the farthest forest lie down and rest." [4]

Still, he had chosen his work, and it was good work. He and those others who had dedicated themselves to it were able to look upon charters and laws which established landmarks of municipal order, and to call them their own.

In 1912 Whitlock declined the nomination for a fifth term as Toledo's Mayor. If he was ever to write his novels, he would have to leave politics now. Instead, he wrote *Forty Years of It,* a sensitive and true account of his long struggle for achievement. It was meant to be merely a summary of the long years before a new, and literary, career began. The career to which he actually turned was a diplomatic career, upon which Upton Sinclair in *Money Writes!* so unfairly and inadequately commented.

Whitlock wrote novels, but they were not the novels about which he had dreamed. (*Uprooted*—a title of significance—as published in 1926 was representative of his several later efforts in novel-writing.) He was unable to transmute his profound experience, at least fictionally, for use in the late Tens and the Twenties. *Forty Years of It,* however, even more than the stirring *Turn of the Balance,* contained all the art of which Whitlock had dreamed. It was not fiction, but, had he known it, had criticism been able to tell him so, it had enduring qualities such as major works by his literary heroes possessed—granting that democracy, and the struggle for democracy, were as important as he and others of his generation believed.

[4] Quoted in Whitlock, *Forty Years of It,* introduction by Filler, Press of Case Western Reserve University, Cleveland, 1970 ed.

Such were some of the human factors in the struggle for representative government. The development of a *mechanism* for good government proceeded along parallel lines. From the theoretical point of view, if one had honest men in power, any framework of politics was as good as another. It did not much matter whether a city was ruled from the state capitol or from the city hall; whether the voter had a long, complicated ballot on which to register his vote or a short, simple one; whether there were bosses, city councils, or city boards of directors. Hard experience had nevertheless shown that the casual, brutal, dictatorial rule which obtained in the cities was, to say the least, unscientific. Under such rule it was physically impossible for the citizen to cast a meaningful vote.

Well aware of such truths was *The Arena*, which throughout the era had been a sort of theoretical organ of reform. B. O. Flower placed a great deal of emphasis upon methods of conducting a real democracy. He ran articles on the Australian ballot and experiments in city rule. He conducted pages for public-ownership news, printed notes about co-operatives, and otherwise encouraged all plans to simplify government and give it improved form and character.

McClure's also consciously sought the way to better democratic city government. When, back in 1901, Galveston, Texas, had been destroyed by a tidal wave, the office of the mayor and the council had been summarily abolished, and entire responsibility for the restoration of the city had been placed in the hands of five commissioners, one of whom had been called the "mayor president." The Galveston Plan, as commission government came to be known, had since shown such powers of efficiency that news of it had spread over the country. McClure had pricked up his ears: this was just the kind of scheme he had been seeking. His dream of government had been government as it was found in England and on the Continent: efficient, simple, and, incidentally, class-biased. McClure had been willing that it need not be class government in America; in any event, it could be efficient.

A revolution had taken place in his offices. His associate John S. Phillips had resigned, and with Tarbell, Baker, and Steffens, as well as Finley Dunne, and William Allen White, had taken over *The American Magazine* (as *Leslie's* had recently become) which they quickly pushed to the front rank of muckraking organs.[5] Despite this, McClure had dauntlessly reorganized his staff and set out to publicize municipal experiments. He himself had already outlined the negative phase of city rule in his December 1904 article "The Increase of Lawlessness in the United States." Now he sent George Kibbe Turner to the new Galveston to report developments, and Turner came back with an article that immediately placed him high among the magazine writers.

"Galveston: A Business Corporation," published in October 1906, was the first of Turner's articles on municipal government to make a deep impression on the country. (As late as December 1909 McClure was to notice, with pardonable pride, that the article was being frequently published and republished in pamphlet form and in the newspapers.) By April 1907 Turner had ready for *McClure's* another article, "The City of Chicago," an unforgettable picture of the reigning immoralities of drink, gambling, and prostitution which McClure had himself earlier drawn from the editorial standpoint. An editorial on "Chicago and Galveston," pointing out the wide interest the articles by Turner had caused, now mentioned efforts that were being made to push commission government in various states of the Union. Thus McClure once more struck a major note that arrested thoughtful readers—a note he was to strike with continued success until, finally, his magazine was taken away from him.

The Galveston Plan caught on. But continued experiment with it revealed defects. Practice showed that, too often, the commissioners were mere politicians who did not know how to direct public health, works, and utilities, and the fire and police departments. The proposal was then made, in connection with the city-manager plan which Des Moines created, that a city should be run not by commissioners but rather by directors with power to select and appoint competent managers. This plan succeeded the Galveston Plan in popular interest and spread rapidly. It was supplemented by amendments providing for the recall of unsatisfactory city officials and for other democratic needs, and was otherwise modeled into a standard form for city government. By 1915

[5] Tarbell's *All in the Day's Work* (Macmillan Co., New York, 1939) narrates in detail the reasons and results of this revolution.

it was recognized as an American method of municipal control that had already developed a history.

It was not wholly premature in 1910 to issue a book [6] which declaimed the end of the old methods of city rule. The book was written in a key that was much too triumphant for any realist, and yet it was startlingly true. The old bosses were gone. Municipal affairs were being conducted with an efficiency that "Boss" Croker, Ames, Cox, and the others of Steffens's immortal gallery would not have recognized, and—this was significant—in 1910 the muckrakers themselves were no longer busy exposing arch political criminals. This sort of agitation had become the concern of local newspapers dealing with local affairs. There were bosses, of course, but the bosses were, by and large, no longer the picturesque and bold characters whom the muckrakers had challenged. The new bosses were merely integral units in a larger system.

The cities had become regulated. And, it is true, not always by impeccable men. New Jersey, for instance, was among the first of the Eastern states to give state-wide sanction to the commission form of government. Under the Walsh Act, Jersey City came under that variety of rule, and in 1916 it elected Frank Hague to the proud office of mayor. Reformers like Frederic Howe, watching officials like Hague, cried despairingly that regulation was not enough, that monopolists and politicians had adjusted themselves to it and preferred it for their business and careers.[7] But that despair simply drove Howe and others to the logical next step of demanding socialization and economic equality. This was what Howe and other mature muckrakers and reformers, flanked by a healthy, trained, radical youth, were turning over in their minds when war broke their moorings and scattered them into helpless isolation.

Meanwhile one could understand Brand Whitlock's strange mixture of despair for American democracy as he viewed it in the Twenties, and pride in his old achievements. The younger men did not realize how much trouble it had been to achieve reform. They accepted and held lightly forms and modes of government

[6] *The Dethronement of the City Boss*, by John J. Hamilton, Funk & Wagnalls Co., New York, 1910.

[7] *The High Cost of Living*, Charles Scribner's Sons, New York, 1917.

that had only been won through sacrifice and persistence.

They were unimpressed by such a career as E. A. Filene's of Boston. Filene was a businessman—a leading department store owner—but his concerns were both local and national. His interest in customer service was reminiscent of Edward Bellamy's ideas. Filene's "automatic bargain basement" was intended to bring the best buys to the most people. The chamber of commerce concept which he initiated in Boston was pushed by him as a national and even an international design, intended to involve businessmen in social service.

Brandeis believed Filene was always creating instruments for the use of the "enemy," but the concept of the businessman as a foe set dark perspectives for an American future. Filene was wiser to help create the credit union in the United States, and the Co-operative League, and, finally, to endow the Twentieth Century Fund as a constant factor in American social and economic planning. If his hopes that his employees would take his store away from him did not materialize, and if his expectation that the American economy would turn from a competitive arena to a cooperative one moved instead in an orbit of prosperity and depression, nonetheless his theory and example provided experience for any would-be innovators.[8] Filene was a reformer. And it was for younger people to prove, if they could, and discern some benefit in doing so, that his reforms had not been worth the winning.

---

[8] Filene merits extended investigation such as he has not yet received. See Gerald W. Johnson, *Liberal's Progress*, Coward-McCann, New York, 1948, and Mary La Dame, *The Filene Store*, Russell Sage Foundation, New York, 1930. See also Steffens's *Autobiography*, 598 ff.

XIX. "THE TREASON OF THE SENATE"

ALL signs now pointed to a muckraking blast against the Senate as the enemy or, at best, the bad servant of the people. The House, too, was fettered by reactionary forces. In 1901 Representative Joseph Cannon, "Uncle Joe" Cannon—or, as he had been dubbed because of a particularly coarse speech in the Nineties, "foul-mouthed Joe"—had saddled himself upon his colleagues and proceeded, by control of special powers, to dictate conservative policy. He was a separate problem. But the Senate was openly, flagrantly, admittedly, the most reactionary body in the government. Elected as the Senators were by the state legislatures rather than by popular vote, they were direct represenatives of special interests. They composed an "upper House," as Alexander Hamilton had said, whose purpose was to represent the wealth and vested interests of the country.

La Follette, a free man and a progressive, was in the Senate, but there was only one La Follette. Even Beveridge and Tillman, erratically liberal, were exceptions. For the most part the Senate was made up of men like Tom Platt, the boss of New York; Boies Penrose, the boss of Pennsylvania; Clark of Montana, whose noisome services to his state had been revealed in detail by C. P. Connolly; Chauncey Depew, the "railroad Senator"; and Bailey, stipendiary of Standard Oil. There was barely a handful of Senators who did not represent one corporation or another. Aldrich of Rhode Island, the boss of the Republican Party as well as of the Senate, virtuously represented them all.

As the muckraking era reached its brilliant zenith in 1906, the reactionary character of the Senate stood out in bright relief. The Senate came out frankly and aggressively against reform laws. On the pure-food question, the railroad question, the tariff question, the Senate was always to be found brazenly adamant. Federal reform laws were achieved, so to say, only by breaking through stone walls of the "upper House." The walls were sturdy, and the leading Senators had every intention of maintaining them as a permanent defense against progress.

For years the existence of a "millionaires' club," as the Senate was called, was a theme for bitter but futile denunciation in the radical press. It was the old story: "What are you going to do about it?" What, indeed, was to be done? The Socialists demanded the abolition of the Senate as an anachronism, an unendurable affront to democracy; those who clung to the states'-rights theory —and that meant the majority of the population—conceded the usefulness of such a body but urged the democratic antidote: direct election of Senators.

Cynics like Ambrose Bierce scoffed at the alternative. If the people were incapable of electing state representatives who would represent their will in the election of Senators, how were they capable of electing representative Senators themselves? Bierce was ignoring the significance of tradition: tradition had *dictated* that state-elected Senators might, and even should be, reactionary; giving the power of election to the people meant a break with one of the oldest traditions in American history. Far from being an impotent panacea, direct election would be essentially revolutionary. It was one of the prime objectives that democracy had to achieve if it was to chart a successful course.

In any event, there seemed little possibility of any such reform. The Senate carried on proudly. Being the organ of plutocracy (which was a scientific if belabored definition of trust and boss rule), it identified itself with plutocracy's fortunes. It presented a challenge which only the outright revolutionary—that is, the Socialist—dared to meet.

Menacing signs of protest against the Senate appeared, however, early. *The Arena*, for instance, stood squarely against the Senate and its works. Being concerned primarily with protests against the passage of reactionary legislation and the approval of progressive legislation, *The Arena* made only a slight impression on its readers, and the Senate itself stood intact and unmolested, a titled and powerful arm of the government. But the guerrilla attacks increased. Writers circled moodily about the Congress, berating individual Senators for one or another misdeed, and denouncing the Senatorial body as a whole for its obdurate unconcern for popular needs. Steffens, in his stories for *McClure's*, had more than one occasion to report sordid acts of Senators, and most of the exposés of reactionaries involved them. But no one dared to dream of a muckraking exposé that would be as thorough as were other of the carefully documented investigations. The Senate was composed of individuals; the individuals were among the richest and most influential men in the country. Attacking them was more dangerous than attacking corporations—soulless legal creations whose revealed sins their rulers could easily impute to understrappers overenthusiastically looking out for their company's welfare. Each Senator represented a possible libel suit, and all of them together meant some unimaginably frightful retaliation.

It was Charles Edward Russell who first conceived the notion of coming to grips with that garrison of reaction. Sitting in the gallery of the Senate one day in 1905, he was suddenly struck with the thought that hardly a man had any reason for being in the chamber except to serve a trust in its battle with the people. He took the idea to Cosgrave and Ridgway of *Everybody's*, who put their lawyers to work upon it. The lawyers shook their heads: it was too much of a risk. (Yet at this time Lawson was running his Amalgamated and insurance exposures in that very magazine!)

Meanwhile portentous changes had taken place on *Cosmopolitan*. It had fallen on hungry if not evil days, for John Brisben Walker had become so absorbed in the manufacture of automobiles that he had quite neglected his magazine—had, in fact, stripped its treasury to bare essentials and reduced it as a whole to secondary significance. However, *Cosmopolitan* was in sound condition, and he was anxious to sell it so that he could devote himself to his new interest. Hearst, who had been anxious to enter the magazine field, now stepped in to take *Cosmopolitan* off Walker's hands. He brought East his old editor of the San Francisco *Examiner*, Bailey Millard, who had discovered "The Man with the Hoe," and making him editor of *Cosmopolitan*, gave him a full purse and instructed him to turn the magazine into a success once more. Millard plunged into his work. Money was spent, new writers and finer articles were found, Socialists and other radicals of every description were furnished a new avenue for expression. A great breath of air was let into the magazine, which immediately began to revive and capture attention.

Bailey Millard now snatched, out of the currents of popular unrest, the idea of indicting the Senate, and he set out to make it a reality. Who could write the series? What writer had the power, as well as the courage, to limn the Senators and recount the outrages they had perpetrated, in such form as to win that writer the support of the public? Charles Edward Russell had gone off on his quest for democracy. Alfred Henry Lewis was not quite the man for the work: the ex-cowboy's hatred of cowardice and injustice was not properly focused; he saw too much in individual terms, and he was apt to miss the point while making otherwise valid indictments. Millard finally hit upon David Graham Phillips as his man.

Millard did not then know Phillips personally, but he knew all he needed to know. For one thing, Phillips had already contributed a number of strong articles to *Cosmopolitan* under Walker. Moreover, Phillips had made a reputation since 1901, when he had first broken with newspaper work. After fifteen years of journalism in Cincinnati, and in New York under Dana and Pulitzer, he had ventured to become a free-lance writer and novelist. But always he had charted a deliberate course. He had from the beginning determined to be a novelist, and he had worked on the newspapers to learn the facts of American life as an apprentice. His apprenticeship served, he began a new career cautiously, experimentally, with miscellaneous articles and with novels.

In 1906, at thirty-nine years of age, Phillips was tall, arrestingly handsome, and well-dressed. He worked incessantly, and with a seriousness that exasperated and annoyed many people. Opinion was that only great novelists should take their work so seriously, and that Phillips should work more slowly, with less concern for immediate issues, if he hoped to be a great novelist, as he apparently did. Great novelists did not write every day, whether they were in the mood or not; they did not produce two novels a year, as well as a host of lesser fiction and magazine articles.

Phillips, who was well acquainted with the methods of great novelists, knew better. But, that aside, he had made up his mind as to what method suited him best, and he went his own way, issuing books which became progressively larger, more closely knit, and better expressive of his intentions. He had built for himself the famous drafting table at which he stood every night— even during vacations, when he traveled—and smoked innumerable cigarettes while he produced enormous quantities of manuscript for typing and revision. Friends, passing through Gramercy Park in the small hours, would see his quiet light high up in the modern apartment house and observe: "There's Phillips, pounding away at his old black pulpit."

For Phillips, despite his insistence upon his work as just a "job," despite his hatred of the cant and sentimentality which made up current literary conceptions, had a mission that was second only to his passion for producing the very best fiction of which he was capable. Like all the muckrakers, he had seen in his lifetime the breakdown of the old moralities, the old modes of life, that had constituted the bases of a past democracy. If democracy were to be recaptured, new moralities and modes would have to be developed. And not only that: the older ones would have to be broken down completely, discredited and annihilated; they could not be revived, for they were a dead hand on the present, the means by which the trusts and their allies continued to grow toward that logical end of individualism: oligarchy.

In *The Master-Rogue*, a rude and vital novel issued in 1903, Phillips had sketched the portrait of the modern millionaire; other novels, too, had identified Phillips as a searching analyst of modern life and character. In 1905 he had scored his first major success with *The Plum Tree*, which recounted the evolution and rise of a president-maker. By 1905, moreover, Phillips had so organized his life that he felt free to give himself to novel writing entirely, to attempt the large-scale plans upon which he had mused for years, and to give them his wholehearted care.

It was therefore with mixed feelings that Phillips received Bailey Millard's offer to undertake the research and writing for a series on the Senate. It should be done, Phillips admitted, but he did not want to break into his other writing; he wanted to get away from magazine assignments, to be known as a novelist altogether. He urged Millard to approach William Allen White and others who were familiar with politics and political figures. But when White was approached, he refused the task; anyway, his articles on leading lights in Washington and elsewhere had never quite approximated the detail and point of view Millard required. Since other possibilities for the job seemed simply inadequate, Phillips loomed ever larger as the logical and necessary man.

Millard, who had become a friend of Phillips's since their first discussion, urged him again and again to reconsider the proposition. He appealed where he knew he could score: to Phillips's social conscience; and at last the novelist consented. Gustavus Myers and Phillips's brother Harrison, a Denver newspaperman, were commissioned to help him gather the material for his work. Phillips himself prepared to give it attention in the only way he knew how—completely. Putting aside his other work, he went to Washington to consult friends and acquaintances. His wisdom in going to Washington was later proved by Millard, who revealed that some of the most telling points in Phillips's articles were provided in secret by some Senators who were anxious to cast off the yoke of the system to which they were bound.

The reception for Phillips's exposé was carefully prepared by *Cosmopolitan*. Hearst himself in an introductory article promised that no one was to be spared. Requests came in from rural newspapers in the West for permission to reprint the articles as they appeared. Tension increased among all observers who knew what was in the wind.

In March 1906, *Cosmopolitan* appeared on the stands with the first article of "The Treason of the Senate," bannered with the solemn quotation from the Constitution (Article III, Section 3):

Treason against the United States shall consist only in levying war against them, *or in adhering to their enemies, giving them aid and comfort.*

What happened to copies of *Cosmopolitan* went beyond the wildest of Millard's expectations. The clamor for the magazine was a clamor such as only *Everybody's* had experienced, when *Frenzied Finance* had begun. The newsstands were swept clean of the first issues and requests for issues and subscriptions flooded the magazine's offices.

The first article, an acid introduction concerned chiefly with

Chauncey Depew as an example of the kind of men who were sent to the Senate, reverberated throughout the country. It was immediately apparent that there was an extraordinary reason for the article's success. Phillips had previously written mordant articles about official crime and criminals, but never before had he attempted such a large-scale indictment, challenged so large a body of distinguished men, with such revelations of planned corruption as to pose publicly the question of their role in government. He was doing in the field of politics what Lawson had just finished doing in the field of finance. But Lawson was a financier himself: it was only this fact that had given *Everybody's* the courage to print *Frenzied Finance*. Phillips was a writer, not a politician. No wonder Phillips's manuscripts were examined word for word by Hearst's lawyers before they were allowed to go to press!

"Glory Hallelujah!" ejaculated one of the countless readers who wrote in to assure *Cosmopolitan* of his approval and support. "You have found a David who is able and willing to attack this Goliath of a Senate."

Phillips was jubilant, too. He had known that the people would back him in his fight, he told Millard, and he was glad he had gone into it; something would come of it.

In his second article, he began to grapple with the fundamental issues that concerned the Senate. He described that body's "central mechanism" composed of Aldrich and the committees through which Aldrich exercised his control. Then he drew a vivid picture of Gorman, "the left arm" of the Senate leadership and the leader of the Democratic minority. The differences between Aldrich and Gorman, Phillips showed, were only fractional. Phillips also invented the term "the Interests"—a term that impressed itself on American speech—to describe the constituency for which Aldrich and Gorman worked hand in hand. As he developed his thesis with facts and documentary proof, he drew Senator after Senator into an enormous picture as pieces in an organized and deliberate conspiracy for circumventing the needs of the masses.

With the appearance of Phillips's first article, a cry of protest and denunciation arose from the conservative press and magazines. Phillips received threatening letters. His name was brought up for castigation in the Senate. Writers were hastily commissioned to write in the Senate's defense.

Theodore Roosevelt, who had been tolerating the less "impartial" exposés with diminishing patience, now lost all restraint. He was particularly stirred by the attack on "poor old Chauncey," as he told Steffens later when that realist called him up to warn him that the muckrakers were his best support. On March 17, at a dinner given by Speaker Cannon to the Gridiron Club, in Washington, Roosevelt spoke informally of "the man with the muckrake" who "in newspapers and magazines makes slanderous and mendacious attacks upon men in public life and upon men engaged in public work and at the same time defends labor leaders who were guilty directly or indirectly of murderous assaults upon officials who opposed their schemes." [1]

Speeches given at the Gridiron—a newspapermen's club—were always supposed to be kept strictly secret, but rumor of Roosevelt's assault spread widely. Roosevelt, having determined to elaborate on his opinion, decided to make it part of an address on the laying of a cornerstone of a new office building for the House of Representatives. He explained his intention to Ray Stannard Baker in a letter on April 9: [2]

> One reason I want to make that address is because people so persistently misunderstand what I said that I want to have it reported in full. For instance, you understand it. I want to let in light and air, but I do not want to let in sewer gas. If a room is fetid and the windows are bolted I am perfectly contented to knock out the windows, but I would not want to knock a hole into the drain pipe. . . . I disapprove of the whitewash brush quite as much as of mud-slinging, and it seems to me that the disapproval of the one in no shape or way implies approval of the other. This I shall try to make clear.

Roosevelt's practice of balancing attacks on the right with attacks on the left usually reduced his statements to platitudes and

---

[1] Quoted in Joseph Bucklin Bishop's *Theodore Roosevelt and His Times. Shown in His Own Letters* (Charles Scribner's Sons, New York, 1920). The labor leaders referred to were, of course, Haywood, Moyer, and Pettibone, as Roosevelt explained in a separate letter in which he condemned defenders of men "whose organization certainly, if not they themselves personally [*sic*] were accessories to murder before the fact. . . ."

[2] *Ibid.*

allowed him to use reasonable arguments for partial purposes. He was here merely repeating more vigorously the false argument which George W. Alger had detailed in his *Atlantic Monthly* article.

On April 14, however, Roosevelt laid his cornerstone and delivered his speech, taking as text a passage from Bunyan's *Pilgrim's Progress* regarding "the Man with the Muckrake, the man who could look no way but downward with the muckrake in his hand, who was offered a celestial crown for his muckrake, but would neither look up nor regard the crown he was offered, but continued to rake to himself the filth of the floor."

In time men were to point out that Roosevelt had torn the Bunyan quotation out of its context, and to ask who had prepared the muck. But not on that day. The President's speech was what the reactionary journals had been looking for since exposure had first begun. The speech won headlines from coast to coast, and was followed by countless articles and editorials expressing fervent approval. The epithet of "muckraker"—for epithet it was supposed to be—was fastened with delight on all the reformers, and with most delight on Phillips. Some judicial heads attempted to draw a distinction between "good" muckrakers like Steffens and "bad" ones like Phillips, but such reasoned classification took no public effect. Exposure was muckraking: it could be an accolade or an insult. Men like Lawson, Russell, and Sinclair, taking up the challenge proudly, called themselves muckrakers. Spargo insisted on the distinction between muckraker and Socialist educator. Ida Tarbell herself was to wonder whether she had been a muckraker or an historian. But for better or for worse, the term "muckraker" had come to stay.

Roosevelt's speech did not stop "The Treason of the Senate." Phillips was hurt but not deterred. And when Roosevelt, who tried to conciliate everybody (who was *anybody*), attempted to arrange a meeting with him, he angrily refused to consider it. Three times emissaries were sent to him before he decided to meet the President. Phillips, who was fascinated by character and personality, no doubt found Roosevelt worth meeting, but politically he never held him to be more than an opportunist.

So "The Treason of the Senate" continued. Even in Washington billboards were placarded with announcements in large type of forthcoming issues. Public interest in *Cosmopolitan* soared. The President had delivered his historical speech on April 14, and that

HEARST DISSENTS

month *Cosmopolitan* had sold 450,000 copies. That was the popular answer to Roosevelt's denunciation. Muckrakers were good; the President was as powerless to prevent misapplication of his muckraking parable as Bunyan had been before him. Nor was Phillips simply responsible for a temporary sensation. There were some observers capable of realizing that he had prepared a veritable storehouse of facts, as well as living descriptions of Senators and their careers, which was long to serve as an arsenal for reformers throughout the West.

"These men want Socialism!" cried Ellery Sedgwick in exasperated disapproval of Phillips. He was mistaken: what Phillips was after was the truth. In a Pollyanna age (as one observer was to call it) truth was a mania to Phillips.

> I used to try to point out to him [his friend Russell writes [3]] that occasions arise in which it is needful for even the best of men to compromise with the bald truth, but he would never admit this. . . . He and I were at Carlsbad one season and walked about the streets and hillpaths discussing this with one invariable result. "Well, I don't see how you can say so," says Graham.

That was the distinction of "The Treason of the Senate." Most muckraking articles were necessarily limited to specific indictments, to specific individuals. Muckrakers usually made anxious efforts to show that their indictment went so far and no further. Phillips, in taking up the opportunity Bailey Millard presented to him, went the entire way. He made clear from the outset that he was against corruption, in every shape or form, as it sprang from a system. When he traced tariff frauds, deliberate and prepared jockeying in the interest of one or another of the trusts, and the systematic execution of necessary legislation, it was bad enough for the reactionaries. But when he applied his creative talents to the Senators themselves, when he painted them as personalities and then showed them as the inevitable resultants of a *process* of governmental decay, when he forced upon the reader the realization that the mere removal of present Senators would not in itself accomplish permanent reform—why, then he was an anarchist, a revolutionist, or, as Sedgwick called him, a Socialist.

What is certain is that Phillips was for change—thorough, unequivocal change. For sixteen years, ever since the beginning of the Populist uprising, the middle-class had been struggling to give expression to its hatred of the moral, mental, and physical degen-

---

[3] In a letter to the author.

eration which had overcome the country. "Austere" documentation could not alone express that feeling; eloquence and human description were demanded. These were the elements that went into "The Treason of the Senate." The time had come for change, and the age had found its voice.

The popularity of the series, therefore, increased rather than diminished. Each issue aroused further storms of discussion. Phillips called for the direct election of Senators, but he also continued to propound all the questions which the bewildering varieties of treason called forth. *Cosmopolitan* continued to grow, but only through the support of its readers and despite ever more bitter attacks by its critics.

Suddenly, in November 1906, the series ended. It did not receive a reprint in book form like many lesser muckraking exposés. It was too desperate a work, and too dangerous. The gallery of Senators which Phillips had created was never, therefore, to be available to history, was to be buried in the original issues of *Cosmopolitan*, and in another generation conventional Senatorial memoirs and biographies were issued which were not subjected to critical analysis.

Phillips by his work had set himself apart. He was now known to be incorrigible and uncompromising. His early experimental writing had been noncommittally received, for the most part; after "The Treason of the Senate" literary criticism revenged itself upon him by means of a studied and deliberate contempt for his novels. Although Phillips's later books sold in the hundreds of thousands and excited controversy on many scores, barely a trace of their existence—or of Phillips's—is found in the books and magazines which serve as a guide to the literary history of the time.

"The Treason of the Senate" had at least broken down those adamant walls of the Senate. Freer discussion of Senatorial personages and powers followed. A number of Senators were unseated in the next elections, and others were dropped from the rolls in succeeding years until, by 1912, the composition of the chamber had changed completely. Public discussion of the House, too, was now freer and enlightened. For Phillips had drawn a sharp line between the useful and useless members of the Congress as a whole. He thus strengthened and accelerated the development of a progressive bloc which was to have so marked an influence on the national life.

In 1911 Senator William E. Lorimer, the boss of Cook County, Illinois, was expelled from the Senate for vote buying. The situation had changed since 1900, when Clark of Montana successfully bought his way into the Senate by means of unparalleled corruption. Lorimer's sins were minor in comparison, but they were the last straw to an indignant public. An amendment to the Constitution was drafted and triumphantly adopted, and the power of direct election of Senators was at last given to the people.

This was the political consequence of "The Treason of the Senate." Another fact, obscured by the bitter controversies that raged over the series, was that "The Treason of the Senate" represented the high point of muckraking in its exposure phase. Phillips voiced all that indignation felt by citizens who had been confronted by revelations of corruption in every avenue of public and private life. After this series indignation would never be enough. There had been reforms in the hectic elections and legislative sessions of 1904 to 1906, but minor reform had only emphasized the need for more sweeping, *national* reform. With the conclusion of Phillips's series *the citizens had been made acquainted with their country.* They knew now that events a thousand miles away affected them directly, and they reacted to news with a maturity that had been wholly lacking a few short years before.

"The Treason of the Senate," then, marked an epoch. But it suggested still another thought. This was expressed in an extraordinary article in Hamilton Holt's *The Independent,* which was no muckraking organ but was the most open-minded of the weeklies. On March 22, 1906, the brilliant and versatile Edwin E. Slosson, literary editor of the magazine, in an unsigned article entitled "The Literature of Exposure," took cognizance of a phase of muckraking which had, in the excitement, altogether escaped any but malicious attention. His words are memorable:

Fifty years from now, when the historian of American literature writes of the opening of this century, he will give one of his most interesting chapters to the literature of exposure, and he will pronounce it a true intellectual force, a vital element in the creative activities of later years.

Like all realities of the mental life of a people, it came unheralded and swiftly. In 1900 it did not exist. Two of three years later, a magazine article here and there betrayed a slight vermilion tint, like maple tree buds in early spring. Then, all at once, the news stands, from Seattle to St. Augustine, blossomed forth in every hue of rhetorical red, from the aniline cerise of Miss Tarbell's tale of Standard Oil to the Tyrian crimson of Mr. Lawson's story of Amalgamated Copper. It will disappear as quickly as it came. . . .

It will disappear, we mean, as a reigning passion in journalistic literature. Journalistic exposure itself, of public and private wrong-doing, is not in the least novel, and it will go out of style. But between the matter of fact output of steady-going journalism and this sociological *Erscheinung* there is a difference.

Literature is more than a tale of facts, as architecture is more than a tale of bricks. Literature and architecture are products of the creative imagination. Yet they are more also than the poet's vision and the builder's drawing. They are substantial things, constructed of facts or of bricks. They are art, because they fashion and combine their materials to the magic esthetic form, because they reveal the creative personality of him who fashions them, and because they have power to move him who reads or beholds them.

Judged by these tests, the recent work of Lincoln Steffens, of Miss Tarbell, of Mr. Lawson, of Sinclair and Phillips, is literature, beyond a peradventure. It has taken the tale of facts from the year books and the official reports, from the statutes and the decisions, and from unwilling witnesses before investigating committees, and has wrought them into narratives that stir the blood. Its writers have seen in the dead materials that which only the imaginative insight ever sees—their significance, their relation to life, their potential striking force.

We cannot expect, however, that the literature of exposure, more than other developments of literature in the past, will give to the world an indefinite number of writers of true creative power. Already the masters have imitators, and the quality of the output must inevitably deteriorate. . . .

And even if these inherent tendencies of all true literary evolution had not to be reckoned with, there are laws of human nature that must bring the literature of exposure speedily to a period. The public cannot stand at attention with its eyes fixed on one spot indefinitely. It is bound to get restive, and seek diversion in other interests. When that happens the literature of exposure has done its work, at least for a time. To keep on creating it, even though its creators waved the wand of the wizard, would be to waste enchantment. Nay, it would be to weary and to irritate, and to make the public out of sheer annoyance lose some of its present fervor of indignation against unrighteousness.

All right-thinking men must rejoice that the literature of exposure came into existence when it did, and all sane men will be glad if it gives place to something less fervid, in due time. It has accomplished a great purpose, and the American people will be sounder, more sincere, more fearless in right doing, henceforth, because of it. The public conscience has been awakened and wrong-doers have been stricken with wholesome fear. But henceforth the work of exposing evil must be transformed into a steady-going constructive effort to prevent it. . . .[4]

[4] Phillips continues to reside in a gray world of "history," which treats him as author of "muckraking" novels and of *The Treason of the Senate*, and as a pre-World War I writer who compares badly with Theodore Dreiser. See my "The Reputation of David Graham Phillips," *Antioch Review*, Winter 1952, and "A Tale of Two Authors: Theodore Dreiser and David Graham Phillips," in *New Voices in American Studies*, Ray B. Browne *et al.*, eds., Purdue University Studies, W. Lafayette, Indiana, 1966, 35 ff.

XX. THE CRY FOR JUSTICE

THE legend was now developed that muckraking was dead, that "The Treason of the Senate" had completely discredited an already disreputable movement, and that the President's speech had given it the final thrust. It was agreed that the public was thoroughly "tired" of muckraking, and that the few remaining muckrakers were mere outlaws with no following. This legend was stubbornly sustained until muckraking actually did come to an end.

The truth of the legend can be judged by the fact that *McClure's, Success, The American Magazine, Everybody's, Collier's, The Arena, Cosmopolitan,* and a dozen other magazines which gave space to the muckrakers were at full growth and selling to ever-widening circles of readers. The real truth was that "The Treason of the Senate" had marked a turning point in muckraking. The focus now shifted from exposure to reform—although exposure, of course, remained the essence of muckraking—and the reforms aimed at were so broad, so interrelated, that they predicted a full change in American life and thought.

Earlier muckraking had occupied itself chiefly with the antisocial nature of the old way of life, the dominant trusts and the economic and political malpractices which conservatives held to be reasonable and democratic. The public now began to hear of new organizations and new ideas which had sprung up in the last few years and demanded attention. The muckrakers, having exposed American institutions to popular expression and discussion, brought home to their readers the urgency of issues which could only be called constructive, and gave a forum, ready-made, to men and women who were professionals in the fields in which those issues lay.

If women's suffrage could hardly be called a new issue, the problem of women in industry and of child labor was new. The prohibition of liquor presented as old a question as the labor-union movement, but the relation of the saloon to prostitution, the workingman's budget, the boy who worked in the streets, was a fact as new as it was socially vital. The Negro question in its modern phase dated from the Civil War, but it was entangled with all the problems not only of the South but of the North, to which hundreds of thousands of freedmen had migrated.

Economic thought had caught up with these facts and made them arresting and important, despite the fact that there was available hardly any organized knowledge concerning them. It became the task of pioneer sociologists and social workers, as well as muckrakers, to gather information basically necessary to a government operating for the people. The Labor Bureau (there was no Department of Labor) had not at that time accomplished much.

In 1904 Sarah Platt Decker, of Colorado, a militant suffragist, was elected president of the General Federation of Women's Clubs. She took the platform with words that were as rousing as they were unprecedented:

Ladies, [she said] you have chosen me your leader. Well, I have an important piece of news to give you. Dante is dead. He has been dead for several centuries, and I think it is time that we dropped the study of his Inferno and turned our attention to our own.

That was the spirit of the new time. The year 1904 saw the formation of the National Child Labor Committee, under such tried investigators as Owen R. Lovejoy and Homer Folks. The National Consumer's League was already in the field, led by the experienced Florence Kelley. Two years later, the American Association for Labor Legislation was to be launched. The Women's Trade Union League grew through the tireless work of William English Walling, a millionaire Socialist and writer, who in the liberal (not muckraking) organs explained aspects of the labor, child-worker, and Negro questions and who, in 1908, issued *Russia's Message*, a large, powerful study of the country and the revolutionary movement under the Czar, which included in its sympathetic scope the exiled Lenin as well as dissident liberals.

Magazines that expressed the aims of such organizations were vitalized by purposeful editors and contributors. The pages of *Charities*, Jane Addams's *Survey*, *The Annals of the American*

Academy, and *Education* contained robust reports on social conditions in the nation. *The Woman's Home Companion* sponsored the Anti-Child Slavery League. *The Ladies' Home Journal* carried on a sober controversy about women's suffrage—Bok soberly concluding that women did not want it. Many articles on such topics appeared also in the liberal *Outlook*, *The Review of Reviews*, *The Living Age*, and other journals.

Just what the status of such questions was can be gathered by comparing Colorado with Kentucky in regard to the women's-suffrage question. In 1897 the women of Colorado were granted the political franchise. As late as 1898, however, the women of Kentucky were barred by law from making wills. This backward situation was the occasion for *Sally Ann's Experience*, Eliza Calvert Hall's classic story which Walker accepted for *Cosmopolitan* and which was printed and reprinted in magazines and newspapers. Its purpose was, briefly, to show the inequality of the old common law of England in regard to property rights of married women.[1] Aunt Jane of Kentucky was persuaded to tell the homely story of a prayer meeting in which the men of Goshen were dragged over hot coals by the spirited Sally Ann for mean and parsimonious treatment of their wives.

Such a story was radical, however, because it expressed heart truths, not because it faced the modern scene. It remained for the muckrakers—free-lance writers and investigators—to capture the imagination of the country with stirring accounts of social injustice, and in that way to act as the connecting link between those who legislated and those who fought for legislation.

Judge Ben Lindsey, of Denver, Colorado, was one of those who approved Ellery Sedgwick's denunciation of "destructive" muckraking, and wrote in to commend him warmly on his editorial article. Lindsey, like others, was against "sensationalism" and for honest social reform. Like others, too, he was to find that he had misunderstood the muckrakers. To his own bewilderment he found himself at odds with the society which had condemned the muckrakers, saw himself classed with the muckrakers by that same society, and discovered himself in a long war with forces he had not properly evaluated.

[1] "Why I Wrote *Sally Ann's Experience*," by Eliza Calvert Hall, *Cosmopolitan*, July 1908.

Lindsey was a Southerner of good and not undistinguished American stock. He came poor with his family to Denver in 1880, at the age of eleven. In the next twenty years he was permitted to view the growth of a city from outpost to capital of a thriving state, and to be impressed with the Populist administration of Governor Waite, who was so forcefully determined to have a government that represented the people.

Later, when he wrote his fighting autobiography,[2] Lindsey recognized that he had been part of a general movement of revolt. In the eventful days in which he made his reputation, however, he had to learn as all reformers learned—by trial and error. Beginning as a Democrat, he dreamed of returning the party to the principles of Jefferson—as Charles Edward Russell had once hoped, and as Robert La Follette still hoped, to return the Republican Party to the practices of Lincoln. Lindsey's original naïveté enabled him to make a start in life; or perhaps it is more correct to say that his ideas and background placed him on the road he finally took. In 1894, after doing common work and fulfilling a legal apprenticeship, he was, by reason of the liberal statutes then in force, admitted to the bar.

He early learned that he was a better defender than prosecutor. On one occasion his passionate appeal in behalf of a man he had just convicted caused the amazed judge to advise him to avoid prosecution work. His very first case involved "burglars" who turned out to be mere children, and in their defense Lindsey prepared a brief that was less an appeal than it was an indictment of the laws of Colorado.

By 1897 Lindsey had an active law practice and was taking cases which set him against smelting, street-railway, and other corporation interests. He entered politics to push necessary bills through the state legislature, and soon found himself fighting the bosses and special agents who dominated the state.

In politics for the first time Lindsey saw the clear tracks of the corporations who opposed his reforms. He learned slowly; as late as 1904 he was still trusting enough to appeal to an official of the

[2] *The Dangerous Life*, edited by Rube Borough, Liveright Co., New York, 1931. See also Charles Larsen, *The Good Fight: the Life and Times of Ben B. Lindsey*, Quadrangle Books, Chicago, 1972.

Denver Union Water Company for aid against the politicians who were making one of their repeated attempts to crush him. But he pushed his dramatic fights for what became known as "Lindsey bills," and year after year he added basic statutes to Colorado law.

In 1899 the Democrats won a state-wide victory, and Lindsey, having been an ardent party worker, was rewarded with an appointment as public administrator. The reason for the appointment was clear: to keep him from interfering with the Democratic machine. As public guardian of orphan children and other dependents, he could not do much harm, and the position did not pay well. Political Denver had as much contempt for this idealist as it had wholesome fear of his energy. To Lindsey, however, the work was congenial and profitable and, as he recognized—but only in after years—it provided him with the background he needed for the work he was to do.

His honesty and strenuous efforts made him more and more popular, and in 1901 he was elected county judge. While he was judge, one morning occurred the famous incident that marked the turning point in his life. A boy had been arrested for petty theft. As Judge Lindsey prepared to dispose of the case, he was taken aback by wild shrieks from the rear of the courtroom. They came from the child's mother: she was beating her head against the wall, as though against injustice. Lindsey looked at the case again. What was it about? What had the child done? Why had the case been brought into a criminal court at all?

The case had been brought before him so that the court officials could collect fees!

Lindsey now visited the prison in which the juvenile delinquents were housed, and he was shocked to see that they were placed in the same cells with hardened criminals, who taught them the practices and ideals of gangland. He visited the home of the delinquent who had been brought before him, and found it to be a poverty-plagued ménage where the father was ill from lead poisoning and twelve hours a day in a smelter. Lindsey next visited dives which were schools of ruin for boys and girls and which were openly and legally institutions of the community.

What could be done—especially for the children? Lindsey believed that there are no innately good children and no innately bad children, but merely children who are molded by their environment. Many of the most "incorrigible" offenders, he found, were brighter and more courageous than others who had simply not been exposed to temptation. Lindsey looked for a means of saving them for society. He found his answer in the Colorado school law which ruled that school children who had committed offenses were not criminals but wards of the state. Most of Lindsey's "kids" were not school children, but they might well have been, and in any event, Lindsey had made up his mind that they must be saved, legally or illegally.

He now had all cases of juvenile delinquency transferred to his court, and his colleagues were glad to pass them on to him. He made friends with the children and convinced them that he wanted nothing but to help them. He drafted laws in their behalf. He conducted studies that showed three-fourths of all crimes being committed by children under twenty-three. He organized the Kids Citizen's League, and every other Saturday held a Court of Probation.

The years 1902 to 1904 were the heydays of the Juvenile Court. Judge Lindsey troubled public functionaries and private firms with his complaints and requisitions; but after all he was "the kids' judge," and who would not do anything to help the kids? Lindsey also entered into a campaign against criminal-creating jails and brothels. For his reward he was called "crazy" by the police commissioner and was himself "investigated." His career might have ended there and then had he not rallied his "kids" to give testimony about Denver social conditions that shocked and outraged even Governor Peabody, who was a machine politician.

In 1902 Lindsey's fight against official graft resulted in serious attempts to unseat him, involve him in scandal, and actually assassinate him. Yet for the most part he had the forces of law and order with him at that time. The Chamber of Commerce applauded his work, the Fresh Air Fund was glad to co-operate with him. In 1904 he was given an honorary degree by Denver University.

Lindsey's troubles began when he broadened his activities. He subscribed to women's suffrage; that was radical, but not criminal —Colorado had already granted the franchise. But then a cotton mill opened in Denver, and Lindsey was frowned upon in certain quarters for opposing child labor. In 1902 he and his friends formulated the first bill for a Children's Bureau to be submitted to Congress, and he straightway became an "enemy of prosperity." When he campaigned against ballot stuffing, he was disowned by both parties. This event placed his Juvenile Court in jeopardy, because each two years he had to defend it in public election. In 1904 only the support of the Woman's Club of Denver, and the fine propaganda of the army of children he had befriended, enabled him to continue his work.

When Lindsey learned that Governor Peabody had made a deal with the Colorado railroads and the Denver public-service corporations to allow them to select justices for the state supreme court, he saw plainly who the real enemies of society were: not the petty thieves and hooligans, but those who acquired special privileges, who subverted justice at its source. Was it any wonder that such a murderer as Harry Orchard was brought into being? With such thoughts in his head, Lindsey became a fighter of privilege, which meant of capitalism. He now fought for sound election laws and denounced franchise steals. And as he struggled he saw the churches and colleges band together with the politicians to destroy him. By 1906 there were for him no more honorary degrees and no more official praise. Only in the East, among the muckrakers and social workers, was the truth about Lindsey's work told. Most famous and influential of the articles that were printed about him were the two by Lincoln Steffens which McClure published.[3] The "Just Judge," Steffens called Lindsey, and despite calumny that indicated the reputation he made among men of good will.

Other juvenile courts were modeled after Lindsey's. Most famous, perhaps, was Judge Mack's Juvenile Court in Chicago. In various sectors of the country the principles of child welfare were extended and modified by experience, and a host of career officials for child welfare were created. What was immediately apparent was that Lindsey's humane procedures *saved money for the states;* they were economical.

Lindsey might have remained behind, consolidated his victories, and become important and imposing. He carried on, instead, and paid a measurable price for his determination.

[3] Later reprinted in *Upbuilders* (Doubleday, Page & Co., New York, 1909), a book of portraits and stories of reform.

In 1906 he was practically cheated out of the Governorship. At the same time he was subjected to such a barrage of defamation, he was accused so violently of being a hypocrite, a sex pervert, a "hypnotist" (because in defiance of public opinion he had developed the probation system successfully with toughs and criminals), that even among his own followers he was often held in suspicion. In 1908, again, he was able to save his now legally established Juvenile Court only by the most desperate efforts of his friends and co-workers.

Also in 1908 Lindsey prepared a story of his long fight for justice and submitted it to *Everybody's*. For all his creative imagination, he was not a writer (his three most important books, including *The Companionate Marriage*, were to be written in collaboration), and this story particularly, he had written hastily and under strain. The manuscript was all but rejected when John O'Hara Cosgrave gave it a serious reading and decided that it had possibilities. He sent Harvey O'Higgins, a highly trained and intelligent though pedestrian writer, to Denver, to live there eight months and to work with Lindsey over a fresh draft of the story of Lindsey's war for reform.

The result of their joint efforts was "The Beast and the Jungle," which *Everybody's* ran sensationally during the latter part of 1909. The beast was privilege. In the course of the narrative, Lindsey explained his political evolution, his slow recognition of brutal, triumphant capitalism. In 1908 Lindsey had published also a pamphlet called *The Rule of the Plutocracy*, to make clear to voters that he stood against plutocracy in its anti-democratic features. Were features of it democratic? Now, at the crest of the reform movement, Lindsey—despite himself, despite the original ideas that had motivated him—stood with the muckrakers. It remained to be seen what fate was in store for the causes he championed.

Lindsey's evolution was typical of that of all the reformers, who began with charity and relief organizations and became sponsors and agitators for laws which, at bottom, represented a fundamental break with tradition. Yet even in Lindsey's case muckraking, far from being merely an overflow of his own concrete work, or merely explanatory of it, had been decisive. The many articles by and about Lindsey had given him the strength to persist. He himself attributed the success of his 1906 election to the Steffens articles, which had introduced him to a woman who came to Denver to help him conquer.

The issues of working women, child labor, care of criminals, prison reform, and prostitution—this last deserves a separate treatment—were so massive and complex that they could not have been successfully undertaken by Lindsey, or any other reformer, without supporting propaganda from the muckrakers.

In the matter of prison reform, for example, Brand Whitlock's *The Turn of the Balance* excited as much protest and, ultimately, produced as much amelioration as did the famous Dr. G. W. Galvin's revelations in *The Arena* of injustice in the Massachusetts penitentiaries. Nor should one fail to mention the moving and sensitive novel by James Hopper, one of the fine writers of the period, who in 1909 wrote "*9009*," in collaboration with Fred R. Bechdolt. In its brief pages this book condensed a passionate hatred of the barbarism the muckrakers were finding behind the prison walls. Prison reform, however, was a special field, and was likely to attract specialists rather than professional muckrakers. An exception was Charles Edward Russell, who was in many ways the leader of the muckrakers and contributed important studies in almost every field in which they ventured.[4]

The woman- and child-labor issues were wider, more immediately interesting and all-embracing. To them all the muckrakers contributed personal experiences—Upton Sinclair, for example, who printed "The Children of Packingtown" in *Success*, on the heels of *The Jungle* sensation; and Ernest Poole, who made firsthand studies for the National Child Labor Committee.

From the direct literary point of view, David Graham Phillips undoubtedly represented best the popular feeling about the question of the status of women, to which the child-welfare problem was so profoundly related. He had many years before made up his mind that no main social difficulties would be settled until the status of women was settled. After doing "The Treason of the Senate" he set himself to recording his perceptions in the way he

---

[4] See the influential "Beating Men to Make Them Good," printed in the September and November 1909 issues of *Hampton's*.

knew best—that is, in fiction. His *Old Wives for New*, a cold, uncompromising story of divorce, was a literary feature and topic of argument in 1908. *The Hungry Heart* was the passionate but restrained tale of a woman caught securely on the horns of old moral traditions. While he wrote other novels involving the same theme, Phillips worked year after year upon his masterpiece, *Susan Lenox*, trying to give it everything he had dreamed an American saga should have.

Modern social investigation was set on its feet in 1905 with *Poverty*, written by Robert Hunter, another of the millionaire Socialists and brother-in-law to Graham Phelps Stokes. This book was not based on statistics and public records: they did not then exist. Hunter had to depend almost entirely on his own observations and those of his associates, and to collate what substance he could get out of the books of Jacob Riis, Josiah Flynt, Florence Kelley, and others. He had to bring a trained mind to this pioneer work; he had to explain his book's aims and limitations, and to write for the ambitious social worker as well as the lay reader. But the reception he received was the now familiar story. The book was highly commended in every quarter except among social workers who denounced it as biased and overdrawn. However, it inspired his friend and party comrade John Spargo to write *The Bitter Cry of the Children* and *The Common Sense of the Milk Question*. Valuable also was the work of Lewis W. Hine, a photographer of genius, whose portraits of exploited children stirred many an American conscience and encouraged the creation of settlements and commissions to study the problem.

The exploitation of children in industry was less a "social work" question than an economic and political problem. It remained for Edwin Markham to strike off the great child-labor sensation of the time in "The Hoe-Man in the Making," which *Cosmopolitan* ran during 1906 and 1907. Markham applied an irony and erudition that were Biblical in their strength to the subject that stirred his readers to fury. He told of the yearly sacrifice of "golden boys and girls" in the canneries, in the cotton fields, in the factories. The National Child Labor Committee was given a tremendous push ahead by this great series, and *Cosmopolitan* itself sponsored the Child Labor Federation, with Gustavus Myers as secretary, which carried on its own fight against child exploitation.[5] *Cosmopolitan* and Markham only led the fight of the muckrakers: in many of the other magazines, strong and effective articles reported and encouraged the battle for law in the states.

As late as 1914, Markham's series had not spent its force. It was reprinted in the famous *Children in Bondage,* along with

WOODCUT FOR "THE HOE-MAN IN THE MAKING"

Drawn by Warren Rockwell for *Cosmopolitan*, September 1906

supplementary essays by Lindsey and the meteoric young George Creel, who had come to Denver in 1909 and within a few months set his indelible mark upon it. As reform journalist and as police commissioner Creel gave the city its greatest impulse forward since Judge Lindsey had begun his work.[6] Meanwhile he poured out articles for the muckraking magazines on woman suffrage, child labor, and Denver generally. Within a few years this flaming radical was to receive one of the highest—and most ambiguous—honors in the land.

[5] "*Cosmopolitan* Readers Agree That This Disgrace Must Go," *Cosmopolitan*, November 1906.

[6] "The Fortunes of Citizen Creel," *Collier's*, July 19, 1913.

In 1907 Mrs. John Van Vorst printed in *The Saturday Evening Post* widely publicized articles on child labor as she had found it in Alabama, Georgia, and in the North.[7] Senator Beveridge, who respected Lorimer's magazine highly—and for good reason, since he had made his own reputation through its pages—was sufficiently stirred by the articles to look further into child labor. The result was that he drafted and pushed the first of the child-labor laws that were to become national issues, and in doing so took a long step beyond the conservatives in the Senate with whom he had previously worked in relative harmony.

In succeeding years agitation for laws to protect children from exploitation was to result in new reforms, and to make the hope tangible that a national child-labor policy would come into being. "Conserve the child" was a leading slogan of the time. All the major issues were ultimately questions of conservation—"constructive" criticism could mean only that. America had been granted the best resources in the world and the aristocracy of the sturdy poorer classes of Europe. Just as the forests had been devastated, so the younger generations were being broken in the sweatshops and tenements. No wonder the Socialist Party and the Progressive bloc in Congress grew apace.

Ida Tarbell failed to see this point in her *American Magazine* articles on the status of women.[8] In her opinion women should think less about the suffrage and more about making their homes more livable and their children more upright. She forgot that some homes were too poor to have a "tender touch"; she ignored the mother and child in the sweatshop, and woman's inferior position before custom as well as before the law. There was no question as to her honesty; she simply had not given the subject the same attention she had once given Standard Oil.

The child-labor issue was, then, intimately connected with the issue of woman's rights and her situation in society. Among those who gave the point adequate attention was Benjamin Hampton, especially through his writer Rheta Childe Dorr. In 1907 Hamp-

[7] Reprinted in *The Cry of the Children*, Moffat, Yard & Co., New York, 1908. (Not to be confused with John Spargo's *The Bitter Cry of the Children*.)
[8] Reprinted in *The Business of Being a Woman*, Macmillan Co., New York, 1912.

ton, who had been with the American Tobacco Company for years, and was a brilliant advertiser and executive, took up the old *Broadway Magazine*, a nondescript organ with a circulation of 12,000, and within three years ran it up to 480,000. He did this not on the muckraking platform Hearst had consciously demanded for *Cosmopolitan* but by the "constructive" policy the best of the muckrakers earnestly sought. Ben Hampton repeatedly promised that his magazine would print only the "facts," but he soon had to acknowledge that if facts constituted muckraking, then *Hampton's* was a muckraking magazine. Hampton was a genius of an editor—at least two writers, Frederic Howe and Rheta Childe Dorr, credited him with teaching them how to write—and his superb sense of news aroused the admiration of many of the literary fraternity. *Hampton's* "firsts" were numerous, and it was for one of these firsts, as we shall see, that this most phenomenal of all the magazines was destroyed overnight—because it dared to carry exposure to its logical conclusion.

Rheta Childe Dorr was Ben Hampton's creation. Her lifelong determination to make a place for herself as a free woman and the equal of any man had broken up her otherwise secure marriage, and had sent her off to New York to become one of the new-style women journalists and feminists.[9] Like the Van Vorsts before her, she worked in factories and sweatshops in order to acquaint herself with actual conditions, and she criticized her predecessors justly:

> The Van Vorsts understood nothing of the significance of the woman's exodus from home to factory work. What passed before their eyes was a series of rather repellent pictures. The girls beside whom they worked remained utter strangers to them. The tasks accomplished [by the Van Vorsts] bore no relation to the life of society or to their own sheltered lives. . . .

Dorr set out to avoid such deficiencies in her investigations. She worked as a laundress, seamstress, and factory-hand, and sent in her reports to William Hard, of *Everybody's*, with whom she had arranged to collaborate on a series. After months of such work, she was outraged to receive a brief note from the young editor informing her that her services were no longer required,

---

[9] See *A Woman of Fifty*, Funk & Wagnalls Co., New York, 1924.

and that, in a word, the series was to be his own. The implication was that she had been nothing but a secretary or research worker.[10] Court action forced the editors to add her name as co-author of the series, but Rheta Dorr lost interest in it. She had wanted to show the bondage of women in industry; "The Woman's Invasion," as Hard presented it, was a triumphal march of women into industry. Although the series aroused interest, Rheta Dorr saw to it that its utterly different representations did not become available in book form.[11]

Hampton now took Rheta Dorr in hand and, with caustic criticism and abuse, taught her how to write. He brought her to a level of craftsmanship that he had established. She became, in no small sense, the woman's muckraker. *What Eight Million Women Want*, a book made chiefly out of articles that had appeared in *Hampton's*, gave the concise, complete story of women's clubs, women's work, and the fight for suffrage and against the double standard. It carried its message to half a million readers and placed Dorr in the forefront of the crusaders for reform.

In 1912 the Federal Children's Bureau was created. Victory for the woman-suffrage advocates was only a few years away. In 1916, and again in 1919, child-labor laws were passed in Congress but declared unconstitutional.

Such victories and defeats were only high points of reform campaigns and education that covered the whole country. The muckrakers, and the organizations which were rapidly absorbing the work they had begun, continued to work toward their goals ardently and hopefully. They felt that the victories they gained were permanent, whereas the defeats were events that further education would make impossible in the future. During the earlier years of the second decade, at least, this optimism seemed not merely reasonable but inevitable.

[10] *Everybody's* position was, according to Mr. John O'Hara Cosgrave, that she was just that.

[11] It should be added, however, that William Hard was a brilliant and talented writer, and in such articles as "De Kid Wot Works at Night," and in his important articles on workmen's compensation (reprinted in *Injured in the Course of Duty*, Ridgway-Thayer Co., New York, 1910), he made a not inconsiderable contribution to the literature of exposure.

XXI. UP FROM SLAVERY

THE South, too, was a part of the Union. This was a fact the average Northerner—more than the Westerner—was likely to forget. The Civil War had accomplished its main objective: it had opened the West to Northern enterprise; and the South, and particularly its Negro population, had been straightway forgotten. The former slaves had become the worries of philanthropic societies and volunteer educators whose achievements, commendable though they were, had had no ultimate effect on the postwar generation.

The two decades following 1865 saw a struggle for power between the old feudal aristocracy and the poor whites who inherited a ruined domain. The landowners and their offspring were preoccupied with nostalgic memories of a good time when they and their slaves had lived, so they said, in happy harmony. The poor whites had no time for such tinted pictures. They were fighting for bread and opportunity, and they were producing leaders who mixed Populist radicalism with ignorance and a malevolent hatred of the colored freedman, whom they recognized as their economic rivals in the new age the war had borne. Through those years the Negro was less a problem than an issue. He was the pawn of the carpetbaggers, who used him to crush the revolt that brewed in the Southern states, and after they left he was beaten down by terror and disenfranchisement, and rendered politically helpless.[1]

But oppressors even more redoubtable than the carpetbaggers came down from the North: industry and competition. The Negro, tilling his farm, threatened to become a power in agriculture, and, however humbly, he elbowed the white man from his place in the new factories. Not only this but miscegenation, previously practiced under white domination, loomed as a menace

---

[1] See *A Fool's Errand*, by A. W. Tourgee (Fords, Howard, & Hulbert, New York, 1879), which fictionalized carpetbagger experiences.

to "white supremacy." The Ku Klux Klan came and was succeeded by mob lynchings. Laws were passed segregating the Negroes and humane efforts to develop peace between the races were denounced. The kindly novelist, George Washington Cable, was practically driven from his native South because he urged fair treatment of the colored people.[2]

By 1900 the situation had been "stabilized"; that is, the Negro had been reduced to the ignominious status of sharecropper on the land and had been everywhere suppressed. The poor whites, who were themselves living close to abasement, were now led successfully by such politicians as J. K. Vardaman in Mississippi, Jeff Davis in Arkansas, and the famous Ben Tillman. The Negro was recognizably a problem; four million had become eight million, and they were to be found not only in the South but in the large cities of the North, to which they had fled in appreciable numbers. Lynching and race riots had become substantial features of Southern life; they occurred above the old Mason-Dixon Line as well, the North not always being ready to accept the presence of colored people or to grant them equal rights.

Meanwhile, quietly, the Negro had been prescribing on his own account. Once it was clear that the generous slogans of the Abolitionists were not to be fulfilled, he bestirred himself. Howard University was created as far back as 1867, and the next year Hampton Normal and Agricultural Institute had opened its doors. From such colleges and training schools had come young men and women to cope with the new freedom with which their race had been endowed.

Frederick Douglass typified Negro aspirations before emancipation; his appeal for equal rights had no meaning to a generation faced with specific economic and social dilemmas. Now came Booker T. Washington, also out of slavery, and a graduate of Hampton, to preach the gospel of work as the only solution to Negro problems. In 1895 in his famous "Atlanta Compromise" speech, he declared his willingness to submit to inequality so long as his people could advance themselves in the crafts and so prove their right to existence. Tuskegee Institute, a normal and indus-

[2] See Cable's *The Negro Question,* Charles Scribner's Sons, New York, 1890.

trial school he had established, set a practical example of his teachings.

Washington was branded an "Uncle Tom" by more militant Negroes, but he made steady progress in his work, and he emerged in the 1900's as the most influential figure of his race. Washington, born a slave, sponsored a conservative platform. W. E. B. Du Bois came from New England, a free man from birth and a graduate of Harvard and Heidelberg. He began as a brilliant social investigator and co-worker with Booker T. Washington, and in time he made historical and sociological studies of the Negro which quickly placed him in the front rank of the socially-minded intellectuals. A striking and superior man, he might have been regarded no more as a Negro than Dumas *fils*, as William Archer later observed. This was America, however, and his scholarship and intelligence won him no general esteem. He accordingly waxed more radical, rather than less. In 1905, when the famous Niagara Falls Conference of Negroes, in opposition to the movement led by Washington, pledged an uncompromising fight for complete liberation, Du Bois—who had been won over to the militants of the gathering—came out as the leader of the Negro radical forces in the country.

Kropotkin, who was already world-famous for his philosophic and radical studies, laughed loud and long when he heard that there were conservatives among the Negroes in America. "What on earth do they have to conserve?" he asked. He might also have asked, How radical are the radicals? It was in the nature of the problem that its solution could not be accomplished by the Negro race alone, that any solution would require the wholehearted co-operation of the whites. It remained to be seen how much co-operation would be forthcoming, and whence it would come.

During the Negro struggle for liberation, numerous crude attempts were made to set up an impasse against progress in race relations. The attitude of representative Southerners—they alone "understood the Negro"—their unprincipled adherence to states' rights, their sullen fear of being browbeaten by an antagonistic "Yankee" government, meant, in theory as well as practice, nothing less than a determination to hold the Negro down and, if possible, rid the country of him. Liberalism—the barest lip-service to liberalism—was anathema to such men of the South. Their thinking was well reproduced in that infamous work *The Negro a Beast*, by Professor Charles Carroll, who spent, so he wrote, twenty years and many thousands of dollars in order to prepare his "scientific" justification for the repression of the Negro race. Nor was Carroll a lone crusader. Typical of many books was the one by a Tulane University instructor [3] who appealed more logically to reason but no less certainly, beneath the surface, to the basest brutality of conservatism. Dr. Franz Boas, of Columbia University, was denounced as though he had been a criminal because he dared to question whether the Negro was biologically inferior to the white man.

Taken in its modern setting, the South was as predisposed to democracy, was as willing to co-operate with strains of progressivism in other sections of the country, as it had in pre-Civil War times.[4] This was disheartening, and to whom in the South could one, looking to the uplift of the Negro race, turn for aid? Northern philanthropy and Negro sacrifice built the Southern schools which were the great hope of the colored people. Oswald Garrison Villard, in his vivid autobiography,[5] told of an extraordinary trip into the deep South taken by a group interested in Negro education: the details of the trip read like those of an armed truce. Of vigorous thought in the South, even radical thought, *Tom Watson's Magazine* could be taken as representative. Watson was an outstanding Georgia politician, a product of the New South, a Populist and an historian. His magazine contained anti-trust articles which sounded much like those of the most militant of the muckrakers. Yet the magazine was, as a whole, marked by a distressing lack of perspective and, on the Negro question, Watson differed not a hairbreadth from the most virulent Negro haters at home.

Who, then, could help the Negro, faced with such forbidding barriers? It was the Northern reformers who carried the brunt of

---

[3] *The Color Line, a Brief in Behalf of the Unborn*, by William Smith, McClure, Phillips & Co., New York, 1905.

[4] See the significant *Sectionalism Unmasked*, edited by H. E. Tremain (Bonnell, Silver & Co., New York, 1907), a valuable compendium of social and political opinion in North and South.

[5] *Fighting Years*, Harcourt, Brace & Co., New York, 1939.

constructive work after the turn of the century, and the muckraking organs gave them their vehicle of expression.

Race riots and disenfranchisement of the Negro were occasions

"IN GEORGIA: THE SOUTHERN GENTLEMAN DEMON-
STRATES HIS SUPERIORITY"

Drawn by Robert Minor for *The Masses*

for important articles, particularly in *The Independent*, which was
clear-eyed and dispassionate on such questions. The articles were
important but not sufficient. What was needed was a systematic
analysis of the situation, and it was McClure, to whom such projects came as second nature, who set writers to furnishing that
analysis.

Such an article as Carl Schurz's "Can the South Solve Its Negro Problem?", published in *McClure's* for January 1904, might seem at first reading to have been mild. The venerable statesman, having reported on conditions in the South at the close of the Civil War, he was hardly the man to say the final word on the problem as of more recent date. Yet his article was news, and it remained an important reference for many years. It was answered by the novelist Thomas Nelson Page, also in *McClure's*. Page, a Southerner, gave "the other side," since Schurz supposedly represented Northern opinion.

In 1904 Page also issued his book *The Negro, the Southerner's Problem*, which exhausted impartiality in order to prove, as Page itemized, that (1) the Negro, lovable as he had been in old plantation days, was the white's inferior; (2) the North should attend to its own affairs and leave the Southerner to his; and (3) the Southerner, at whatever cost (that is, to the Negro), must be "satisfied."

The value of the *McClure's* articles lay in the fact that they opened the topic to inquiry and discredited the moralistic, eloquent, and otherwise futile studies that had formerly passed for serious opinion. The Schurz and Page articles contained facts and figures which could be, and were, made the basis for discussion. Negro writers like the brilliant educator Kelly Miller picked up the argument and carried it further. The demand for information was, in fact, so stimulated that almost every periodical was constrained to admit to its pages articles on the Negro. Such a periodical as *The Arena*, of course, needed no special stimulation; B. O. Flower was bold in his denunciations of lynchings, sharecropping slavery, and racial segregation.

Booker T. Washington, Du Bois, and others had reason to appreciate the spadework done by the muckraking editors generally, and in the first place McClure, who opened the liberal and even the conservative organs to them.

After 1904 appeared a number of articles on aspects of the race question, and, gratuitously, on the problem of the South as a whole, which aroused public interest. Notable was one by the journalist Richard Barry, who in the March 1907 issue of *Cos-*

mopolitan printed an article on peonage, which was attacked in Congress by Southern representatives. But no other muckraker achieved such eminence in this work as Ray Stannard Baker, who was taken into it by McClure and given the opportunity to write what was, by and large, his most distinguished book. McClure was well aware that Schurz and Page had not covered the question and that they lacked the modern approach it required. He therefore sent Baker to report on lynching, and early in 1905 he published Baker's two articles, which were written with a care that approached the scientific and were made vivid by photographs of actual lynchings.

These articles attracted immediate attention. They justified Baker's contentions that he was engaged in educational labors of the highest importance. The Socialists might protest that Baker had not sufficiently emphasized the economic reasons behind the lynchings; but as a study Baker's articles would have been hard to match. The picture he presented was complete to its last detail: it explained the motives—or rationalizations—of the lynchers, the types of humanity involved, the pretexts furnished by the unfortunate victims. Baker compared lynching in the South with lynching in the North and pointed out similarities and differences. His conclusions were, of course, Rooseveltian: there was right and wrong on both sides; there was sore need for education; there would be no lynchings if all the laws in the statute books were enforced. Baker walked a tightrope in summing up; but it was not for his conclusions that his articles were read.

In 1907, when Baker was already with *The American Magazine*, he attacked the race problem with an energy that made him an authority on the subject. "Following the Color Line" he called the great series which extended into 1908 and which he supplemented with further investigations after his book had come from the press. Using the Atlanta riot of 1906 as a take-off, he plunged into the ghastly record of rumors, murders, and panics that accompanied race riots, and from there he ventured into social investigations that took in Negroes, whites, and their communities throughout the South and North. But now, significantly, he was no longer the impartial observer he had tried so hard to be. *Outlook*, reviewing his book, called it "essentially journalism"—

the usual tribute paid to the real and first-hand investigations of the muckrakers—and noted that he had not "succeeded in understanding the feeling of those Southerners who . . . are inexorable in their determination that the white race shall remain distinct." Baker was biased! Despite himself he recognized that the Negro was struggling against the greatest possible odds, and that those who held the reins deserved less "understanding" than opposition. This was not to be read in his "conclusions," but it was woven into the texture of his story, and it could be no more easily overlooked than his tragic tales of Negro enslavement could be forgotten.

Education, time, and patience—Baker's panaceas—might solve the Negro question. But meanwhile, human feelings could be harrowed by immediate instances of suffering and humiliation which tempted one to take a stand against those who—inadvertently or deliberately—caused suffering. It was a relief for Baker to come down from Olympus and engage in common earthly struggle. Baker was not ready to take a stand, and he clung to the role of educator, but so long as he continued to give his luminous pictures of things American he continued to belong to the radicals and to be a force for a better national life.

While Baker wrote on, it remained for others to follow the logic of his book and create the necessary machinery for action. Among them was William English Walling, a Southerner as well as a Socialist—there was no better combination for an understanding of the Negro problem—and Walling soon found his chance.

In 1908 the country was shocked by the outbreak of a race riot in Springfield, Illinois—Lincoln's home town. For two days the riot raged; Negroes were killed and maimed, and thousands of them were driven from the city.

In the September 3 issue of *The Independent*, Walling wrote his indignant story of "Race War in the North," in which he declared that

Either the spirit of the Abolitionists, of Lincoln and of Lovejoy must be revived and we must come to treat the Negro on a plane of absolute political and social equality, or Vardaman and Tillman will soon have transferred the race-war to the North.

Mary White Ovington, who had studied the question for four years, responded to his appeal. At that very moment she was living in a Negro tenement in New York City, investigating the foul conditions under which the colored people lived. Early in January of 1909 she held a preliminary meeting with Walling and Henry Moskowitz.[6] Their decision as to the next step was that Oswald Garrison Villard's aid must be enlisted—a decision which was to Villard the greatest compliment he had ever received.

Villard, as editor of the New York *Evening Post,* had been no startling figure during the muckraking period. He inherited the Godkin brand of journalism, and we have seen what that was. Villard was a liberal in the old tradition. Yet it was surprising how often he turned right side up, at crucial moments, when other more militant figures had fallen by the wayside. He was critical of Roosevelt, he saw the value of Tom Lawson's exposés, he broke the famous Allds scandal in 1910, he stood out against America's entrance into the World War, and he crowned a distinguished newspaper career with the publication of the secret treaties which the Bolsheviks had released from the Czar's archives.[7]

Now he received Walling and Ovington with enthusiasm, and he drafted for them the famous Call for the Lincoln's Birthday conference and helped give it the widest publicity. It was interesting to note the names subscribed to that Call—Jane Addams, of course; John Dewey, William Lloyd Garrison, Jr., Charles Edward Russell, Hamilton Holt of *The Independent,* Lincoln Steffens, Du Bois, and various distinguished social workers and Negroes. Socialists, muckrakers, and liberals—a cross section of the best Northern opinion. (Ray Stannard Baker did not sign the Call.) Shortly after, the National Association for the Advancement of the Colored People was formally launched and began its career of struggle against lynch law, ignorance, and economic inequality.

The years 1905—when Baker began his work—to 1915 were only a decade. Yet in that time the Negro problem was taken out

---

[6] See Ovington's pamphlet *How the National Association for the Advancement of Colored People Was Founded,* New York, 1914.

[7] His record is told in *Fighting Years, op. cit.*

of the hands of reactionaries and scattered forces of well-wishing individuals and societies, and it was raised to its rightful place among the most important social issues. *The Crisis,* edited by Du Bois, took over the work of the magazine scribes and provided a constant organ of comment and opinion regarding the race question.

A landmark in educational propaganda and in the work of pro-Negro reform groups was the strong and directed wave of protest that followed the release of *The Birth of a Nation* in 1915. This motion picture, crammed with anti-Negro prejudice and misrepresentation, was based directly on the book *The Clansman,* written by the viciously reactionary Thomas Dixon. Wrote Dixon in response to popular condemnation: "The silly legal opposition [of the N.A.A.C.P.] . . . will make me a millionaire if they keep it up." The box-office value of the film, however, was but one phase of the matter. Much more important was the proved power of the new organization to hound such a prejudiced if brilliant production from city to city, and to demonstrate by its success that a strong feeling against slander of the Negro had been developed. It was perhaps a testimonial to the work of the Association that D. W. Griffith, director of *The Birth of a Nation* and a native Southerner himself, later made remorseful gestures toward the Negro in his famous *Intolerance.*

If, then, the problems of the Negro had been multiplied, his power to meet them had been extended. Business associations, urban leagues, and other centers of power had been created by talented and capable members of the colored race. Sentiment for Negro emancipation existed everywhere, even in the South among poor whites who were beginning to feel dissatisfied with the results of a "white supremacy" that, in the end, brought them nothing.

James Weldon Johnson, one of the new-generation Negroes, who had already made a name for himself as a songwriter and diplomat, expressed well the possibilities that lay ahead of his race at the end of the muckraking period: [8]

[8] In *The Autobiography of an Ex-Colored Man* (Sherman, French & Co., Boston, 1912; reprinted with an introduction by Carl Van Vechten, Knopf, New York, 1927). Contrary to general impression, this is not a book of memoirs but a novel concerned with a Negro who has "passed"—that is, been accepted as a white.

Several years ago I attended a great meeting in the interest of Hampton Institute at Carnegie Hall. . . . Among the speakers were R. C. Ogden, ex-Ambassador Choate, and Mark Twain; but the greatest interest of the audience was centered in Booker T. Washington, and not because he so much surpassed the others in eloquence, but because of what he represented with so much earnestness and faith. And it is this that all of that small but gallant band of colored men who are publicly fighting the cause of their race have behind them. Even those who oppose them know that these men have the eternal principles of right on their side, and that they will be victors even though they should go down in defeat.

Men who had learned to take their country seriously, however, had learned a second thing—namely, that there could be no victory if the Negro were defeated.

XXII. THE HOUSE OF BONDAGE

PROSTITUTION naturally became the most sensational of all the social evils that were opened wide to the public eye. The facts about it had long remained ungathered. Josiah Flynt had not treated it in his studies of the underworld, the anti-corruptionists had avoided its implications for the most part, and the women's-rights partisans had not been educated to see it frankly. Recognition of the problem offended not only conservative economics but the national tradition of prudery. Intelligent treatment of such a social evil needed, therefore, a background of exposure to inform the nation.

"Golden Rule" Jones, of Toledo, who understood the significance of the prostitute better than many of his fellow-citizens, was one day waited upon by a committee of ladies and gentlemen who ordered him summarily to enforce the laws of chastity and drive "the girls" from the city. Jones asked where he might drive them—it had not occurred to the committee that the women would have to go somewhere—and presently, with great sincerity and patience, said:

"I'll make you a proposition. You go and select two of the worst of these women you can find, and I'll agree to take them into my house and provide for them until they can find some other home and some other way of making a living. And then, you each of you, take one girl into your home, under the same conditions, and together, we'll try to find homes for the rest." [1]

His proposal was not accepted, but it emphasized the lack of realism, or of sophistication, that characterized moral indignation about "fallen" women.

Prostitution was more than a sin; it was a product of civiliza-

[1] Told in Brand Whitlock's *Forty Years of It*, D. Appleton & Co., New York, 1914.

tion. Europe had recognized that fact centuries before, and its systems of regulation, ultimately inadequate though they were, showed maturity of attitude and, perhaps, in certain countries progress. Prostitution was, too, a symptom: it came of leaving immigrants to shift for themselves, of allowing low wage standards for men as well as women, of tolerating the liquor and opium traffic. It resulted from the housing situation, which crowded the poor into run-down apartments, and above all it derived from municipal politics, which drew revenue from the evil and permitted it to flourish. It derived, in fine, from everything that made up society, and it existed in its most anarchistic form in America. But old though it was, it had not yet been "discovered" here.

The one attempt to deal with prostitution seriously was made in St. Louis from 1870 to 1874, when segregation and medical inspection were unsuccessfully tried. In the Nineties, too, the Reverend Charles Pankhurst led crusades against brothels in New York City. He did not end or even curb prostitution, but he did show that the police were implicated in the business and, in that way, he contributed to the education of the muckrakers. So far as wider understanding went—Anthony Comstock remained a power in the land, and public enlightenment remained on his intellectual and moral level.

But speakers at medical congresses pleaded for statistics concerning the prevalence of social disease, and there was a wide and oppressive consciousness that prostitutes were daily recruited from society in general rather than from any special class. Startling stories concerning the disappearance of girls appeared sporadically in the press. "Red-light" districts continued to exist flagrantly without investigation or explanation. The convention was sustained that prostitutes were inherently vicious, that they attracted only degenerates, and that, as a problem, they did not concern normal people at all.

In 1900, however, there were startling disclosures in the newspapers concerning the amount of prostitution in New York City. The direct reason was the spread of the so-called Raines Law hotels, which provided the best facilities yet known for prostitution. The Raines Law had given a favored status to hotels in regard to the sale of liquor on Sundays, and saloons had therefore provided themselves with enough rooms to pass under the definition of hotels. The rooms became centers of prostitution, and were especially useful to "cadets," as pimps were known, who needed facilities for their work.

A Committee of Fifteen, including such notables as George Foster Peabody, Jacob H. Schiff, and Charles Sprague Smith, the founder of the People's Institute in New York City, began an investigation. Their work coincided with that of a campaign against tenements that had been built without regard for sanitary conditions in order to profit from the waves of immigration into the city. The Committee co-operated for the enactment of a Tenement House Bill—the first since 1867—with specifications for new buildings. It also gave out to the newspapers its findings on prostitution, showing how Tammany protected panders and their brothels. The consequence was that 1901 became a reform year, and a new city administration made gestures toward "cleaning up vice" to reassure the more easily placated citizens.

More important than the help the Committee gave in "overthrowing Tammany" was its publication, in 1902, of *The Social Evil*—the first substantial attempt to lay facts about prostitution before the public. This contained an historical review of the subject (Alvin S. Johnson, who prepared this, had to use foreign authorities exclusively, there being no reliable American sources) and a special section devoted to conditions in New York.

In 1905 the Committee of Fifteen was succeeded by a permanent Committee of Fourteen, whose task it was to make investigations of prostitution and keep itself abreast of developments. Information about those developments continued to be almost inaccessible to the public, for only *Charities* and like social-work magazines provided any discussion regarding the evil. As late as that year O. Henry's masterpiece, *The Unfinished Story*, was rejected by several newspapers and magazines before it was taken finally by McClure. The reason was that it told of a girl who, working for six dollars a week in a department store, sometimes felt herself tempted to venture beyond her monotonous routine. Even O. Henry, who rarely brought "social implications" into his stories, could not expand his human sympathies without drawing down disapproval on his head.

The need for enlightenment, then, persisted, and a few encouraging signs of it appeared. Theodore Schroeder, a New York lawyer who had dedicated himself to the furtherance of civil liberties, organized the Free Speech League and propagandized against "purity" legislation and censorship of literary and other productions dealing with sex. Help came even from less radical sources, since the effects of prostitution were to be felt beyond the tenements. Edward Bok himself was shocked to learn of the high proportion of babies born blind to innocent mothers whose husbands had neglected to tell them of premarital experiences. *The Ladies' Home Journal* thereupon conducted a campaign for education on the subject of syphilis, despite outraged protest by those whom it exposed or who felt it to be indecent. Other liberal voices were raised in defense of the education of the public regarding sexual problems.

As early as 1902 Reginald Wright Kauffman, a magazine editor and novelist and a student of the "social evil," wrote *The Things That Are Caesar's*, the first of his stories about prostitutes. But it was not until 1907, when George Kibbe Turner published his article on Chicago (previously referred to [2]), that muckraking went into its stride on the prostitution issue. Describing the "great business of dissipation," Turner told of the fantastic sums the people of Chicago paid annually for liquor, cocaine, gambling, and prostitutes. He told of the gang wars which made the streets unsafe for passers-by, and of the police protection that set official approval on as lawless a state of affairs as could be found in the civilized world.

The effect of this single article was indescribable. Coming as it did four years after Steffens began his investigations into municipal crime, it found a national audience ready and able to appreciate it and apply its lessons at home. Prostitution had hitherto been mentioned in generalities; it was significant that the public now seized upon it rather than upon municipal corruption as a whole. Prostitution was the subject the people wanted elaborated.

As the phrase "white slavery"—a sadly racist concept—inflamed the reading public, articles appeared which followed tentatively after Turner. George Kennan, in his study of San Francisco for *McClure's*, entitled "Criminal Government and the Pri-

[2] See Chapter XVIII.

vate Citizen," showed—what Fremont Older had already shown to a local audience—that vice had been made a regular industry. McClure himself, in one of his influential editorials, told of the increasing insecurity of women on the streets—a startling fact about life in the great cities.

Meanwhile the ground for more vivid and more personalized exposés was being laid. Turner's article brought together a group of Chicago reformers to crusade against vice. Legal trials of professional seducers were given larger proportions of space in the newspapers. The juvenile courts carried on work in behalf of wayward girls, and the new American Society of Sanitary and Moral Prophylaxis released information which gave the medical aspect of prostitution. In 1908 President Roosevelt proclaimed America's adherence to the international white-slave treaty, and the immigration law was strengthened to make the importation of women for prostitution more perilous for the importers.

By the beginning of 1909 the outline of prostitution as a factor in society had been drawn for the public, although the realities behind it were still only dimly understood. In the following months a veritable barrage of magazine articles on the subject was laid on American readers. Theodore Schroeder wrote for *The Arena* a sharp discussion of prostitution as a social problem; *Harper's Weekly* printed a story of the making of a prostitute; Arthur Gleason in *Collier's* described the Raines Law hotels. Like articles attacked the evil confidently and more realistically than ever before.

Again it was George Kibbe Turner who made the deepest impression with his series of articles and stories. One of these was an account of Tammany rule in which Turner showed that prostitution had been practically licensed in New York.[3] Another, and even more stirring, was his "Daughters of the Poor," in which he recounted the melancholy tale of the immigrant girl in New York, caught in what had become one of the world's greatest centers of white-slave trade.

That same important November issue of *McClure's* contained an article by New York's ex-Commissioner of Police, General

[3] "Tammany's Control of New York by Professional Criminals," *McClure's*, June 1909.

Theodore A. Bingham, who had already captured national attention with an article, several months before, in *Hampton's*, on the corrupt police situation in the cities. McClure himself contributed "The Tammanyization of Civilization," in which he outlined Gustavus Myers's history of Tammany and reviewed efforts that were being made in Chicago, Pittsburgh, and elsewhere to control vice.

In succeeding issues McClure had reason to note that these revelations were producing results. Such people as Maude E. Miner began to work—she to organize Waverley House, where prostitutes were cared for—and to lobby for humane methods of procedure in the lower courts. Tammany was defeated in the fall of 1909 because of its known relations with gang chieftains. Rheta Childe Dorr, in *Hampton's*, varied her stories of women's fight for justice with the theme of the "prodigal daughter," and told of the pitfalls in the way of the working woman, as well as of the efforts that were being made by religious and non-sectarian committees to sustain her in her struggle.

White-slave investigations moved forward. John D. Rockefeller, Jr., heading a grand jury in New York, reported findings that focused national attention on the trade in women and, particularly, on the New York Independent Benevolent Association, through which much of the traffic passed. (This investigation was precipitated by Turner's articles, as was another and even more important inquiry in Chicago.) Vice commissions were organized in city after city until they included all the outstanding centers of population; and meanwhile the state legislatures were urged to pass laws defining crime in prostitution. Finally, on June 25, 1910, the Mann Act was passed by Congress, and so for the first time a national policy on the issue was established.

From the literary point of view, and for Americans, the novel which became the *Uncle Tom's Cabin* of white slavery was not Elizabeth Robins's *My Little Sister*, as Mark Sullivan asserts in *Our Times*, but rather *The House of Bondage*, by Reginald Wright Kauffman, issued in 1910. *My Little Sister* dealt with England and English girls, and was a horror story rather than a novel about prostitution. Kauffman's novel, written with superb technique and understanding, was thoroughly native and mature. In a sense, it supplemented or exemplified another book he published that year, *What Is Socialism?*, which made clear for uninformed readers the principles and history of the movement. *The House of Bondage* demonstrated the effect of economic forces upon women, and did so with details gathered from long observation. It ran from edition into edition, and was translated into the major foreign languages. It was not a great book as *The Jungle* or *Frenzied Finance* or Jack London's *Martin Eden* was great; full though it was of realistic knowledge about brothels and their inmates, it was nevertheless more sociological than it was creative. It was, at any event, an impressive and satisfying work, and it served well those who were agitating for a better understanding of this social problem.

Other books on prostitution followed. Kauffman issued *The Girl That Goes Wrong*, a book of sketches which had been printed in *Leslie's Weekly*. General Bingham wrote, out of his police experience, *The Girl That Disappears*. Upton Sinclair issued *Sylvia* and *Sylvia's Marriage*, novels emphasizing the danger of disease through prostitution, and novelized Brieux's *Damaged Goods*, a play on the same theme which started controversy and drew good audiences in 1913. The best of all the books involving these themes could not, strictly speaking, be classed with the others. Rumor and calumny did that for it. It is true that David Graham Phillips thought of calling this book—which was issued years after he died—*A Girl of the Streets*. But *Susan Lenox* was the story of women's problems as a whole; prostitution was for Susan a means of livelihood at crucial periods of her life, not an all-pervading fate. The books by Sinclair, Kauffman, and Bingham, on the other hand, were produced to meet a definite demand along narrow lines. That demand in the early 1910's reached a point that shocked and frightened easily frightened members of the church and press.

Such were the social and literary aspects of what quickly became a full-bodied campaign for reform. Prostitution, however, was more than a record of statistics and economic necessity. It involved sex in its most brutal expressions, and thus involved the passions and repressions of every person. Few were able to view the "kept" woman to say nothing of the harlot, rationally. Once the great taboo on the subject had been broken, therefore, scribes and careerists appeared who appealed to the ignorance, morbidity and vices of the reading public itself.

White slavery was real enough, veiled though it was by corrupt police and the double standard that condemned a woman as "lost" once she had been seduced, by whatever means. In the hands of sensationalists prostitution became no more real, no more truthful, than the old dime novel. The earnest fact-finding of the muckrakers was beyond the ability of such exploiters of the morbid. They developed fantasies of the underworld that thrilled and scared those who followed with difficulty the content of more serious investigations.

Brand Whitlock, in Toledo, was forced to deal constantly with the wild rumor and hysteria that grew out of agitation for saner laws and attitudes. Like "Golden Rule" Jones he took the human approach, recognizing that prostitution was not to be ended by decree. He closed criminal hangouts. With his director of public safety he tolerated and experimented with modified regulation of prostitution. Nevertheless he could not ignore a story which went the rounds of two continents and was firmly believed by nine-tenths of those who had heard it. Briefly, it involved the kidnapping of a prominent citizen's daughter, who was rescued from "a fate worse than death" by an heroic social worker—or was it a policeman or a minister? Disappearances did occur, but never to the extent that rumor had them, and hardly ever accompanied by the lurid adventures with which they were embellished. The one case Whitlock thoroughly investigated turned out to be a lie from start to finish:

> It is a subject which only the student of morbid psychology, I suppose, can illuminate properly, [he wrote [4]] . . . and out of all this arose a new conception of the prostitute quite as grotesque as that which it replaced. She was no longer the ruined and abandoned thing she once was, too vile for any contact with the virtuous and respectable . . . ; she was not even that daughter of joy whose dalliance is the secret despair of moralists too prudent to imitate her abandon; she became the white-slave, a shanghaied innocent kept under lock and key.

Elsewhere in the nation raids and revival meetings outside "hells of iniquity" increased. It became a fixed popular conviction

[4] In *Forty Years of It, op. cit.*

that women were covertly given injections of cocaine in crowded
streetcars or theatres, and then dragged off in cabs to houses of
prostitution. In such accounts of sex in the underworld the only
approach to the truth revealed by muckrakers was vague references to "economic conditions" which sometimes helped pave
woman's way downward.

The new moving pictures, just coming into vogue, took up the
theme and, laughable as they may seem in review, they seriously
disturbed the thousands who saw them. *Outlook,* summarizing
this trend, noted that sex had been "discovered," and quoted influential readers who felt that such films as *The Traffic in Souls*
and *The Inside of the White-Slave Traffic* were bound to encourage youth to enter into vice. *Current Opinion* went further,
commenting upon the nation's fear of "slavery" and quoting in
particular the New York *World,* which asked how far the delusion of public danger was to go:

> If the popular imagination is to become heated to the point where it
> discerns an attempt at abduction in every dizzy feeling of momentary
> illness suffered by a young woman in a public place, [wrote the *World*]
> it will be unsafe for a man to offer the slightest civility to a person of
> the opposite sex whom he does not happen to know.

These sins of sensationalism were charged to the muckrakers—
who were held responsible for all the "excesses" of the time.
There was not, of course, the barest reason behind such charges.
Muckraking was factual; it tried to define the phenomenon of
prostitution and trace it to its sources. Lesser writings were invariably moralistic and uninformed; they were a sign of public
and personal disturbance, an overflow of the need for reform.
Whitlock recognized that they helped, if nothing else, to give a
trace of humanity to the public conception of the prostitute, even
though they fixed upon the pander as the chief and only villain
of the piece. The pander was also a product of society; he had his
function, and the sentimentalized accounts of reformed pimps, so
valuable to the evangelist, had no important bearing upon reform.

The wave of misinformation about prostitution constituted only
the froth of the reform movement. But it coincided with the decline of muckraking, foretelling an era when "popular" literature

"FOR GOD'S SAKE, COME AND GET ME."

Mildred Clark's frenzied cry that rang out in the night as the Gypsy Smith great parade was passing through the vice district. Chapter I

AN ILLUSTRATION FOR CLIFFORD G. ROE'S "THE PRODIGAL DAUGHTER" (such as the gangster story), far from being in the van of social progress, would be no better than the dregs it described. The reforms that accompanied the muckraking agitation, on the other hand, were tangible and permanent. Ten years of national concern with prostitution resulted in a marked improvement in the situation. The Raines Law hotels were wiped out. Public educa-. tion regarding venereal disease and its prevention was begun. In New York the Bureau of Social Hygiene was created to fill needs pointed out in the investigation by the New York Grand Jury, and the Bureau prepared publications which treated social hygiene scientifically for the first time. *Commercialized Prostitution in New York City,* the first of the studies issued under the Bureau's auspices, was a record vastly superior to that which the Committee of Fifteen had brought forth eleven years before. The federal government, too, began to take official notice of the prostitution evil and to prepare information for the use of professional social workers and educators.

Once the hysteria had passed, prostitution took a somewhat more normal place among the social problems. It was recognized as an effect, not a cause, and as such ceased to concern the radicals who succeeded the muckrakers. Prostitution itself did not noticeably increase nor decrease; like the death rate it was observed to fluctuate with social conditions.

Such facts tended to discourage some of the less soundly informed of the crusaders who had seriously expected to eradicate the evil entirely and for all time. Such crusaders were well dispensed with. The few who remained sane in the fevered years that followed the reform agitation recognized that it had more than justified itself. Agitation had, as George Kibbe Turner believed, been overworked. The worst that came of this was that it confused the efforts of the reformers and gave opportunities for slander to those who were interested in discrediting reform. But this, too, was unavoidable.

XXIII. THE SPIRITUAL UNREST

TO those who saw beyond immediate issues it was clear that more was implied by those issues than specific reforms. The age was one of crisis; it was bound to come to a climax. Whether that climax was to be Socialism or anarchism, or whatever else was predicted by the reigning prophets, remained to be seen. But the fact of its imminence placed upon each person the weighty responsibility of clarifying for himself the convictions by which he would stand or fall.

Charles Edward Russell, for one, believed wholeheartedly in the historic necessity for muckraking. He saw it, amplified by Socialism, as the final answer to the enigma of democracy—the one perfect weapon for correcting its abuses on an imperfect but undoubtedly progressive course. To others the future was more uncertain, and the conflict of allegiances more troublesome. The muckraker was vexed with doubts as to whether he was truly strengthening the middle-class in its war with the trusts or simply making inevitable a conflict between the laboring-class and capitalism. Men could be certain only that the old social frameworks had been shattered, and that social adaptation to new conditions of life was lagging badly.

As for the public, the position of the church and its leadership could readily be taken as an index of popular response to the crisis. That position was not secure. Although Professor Faulkner has shown that church membership increased by sixteen millions between 1900 and 1914,[1] this figure was not a tribute to new-found faith in the established churches. It indicated rather the influx of immigrants from Europe, social organization among the Negroes, and the general increase in population; moreover, it did not take into account the breakdown of dogma and tradition. Disbelief was

[1] *The Quest for Social Justice*, by H. U. Faulkner, Macmillan Co., New York, 1931. See "Religion and Reform."

already undermining the churches so perilously that they were compelled to modernize themselves in both teaching and practice. Science did "continue to give opportunity for theological exegesis and doctrinal controversy," [2] but in this age of reality it would have been indiscreet for clergymen to take full advantage of it. The secure strength which in the nineteenth century had allowed the churches the luxury of schisms and debates had been shaken. The masses were now in no mood for cabalistic discussion: they demanded sermons and practical help that bore a relation to every-day life.

The churches were openly suspected by many citizens of having been consistently aligned with reaction—with that reaction which had been mercilessly unmasked in the past years. Churchmen who earnestly felt that religion could play a progressive role in the new time, therefore, formulated liberal policies and took their place beside those who were working for reform. Dr. Washington Gladden, who had been a pioneer in propagandizing from the pulpit in behalf of the workingman, was still active and militant. Many younger and more radical men among the clergy, speaking out against class-biased injustice and oppression, were tolerated by conservative church leaders who, in another time, could have disposed of them with little trouble. Other radical church workers were not so fortunate. George D. Herron, for instance, was removed from his church for espousing Socialism, and was subjected to one of the most bitter campaigns for character assassination that ever disgraced the press. Despite such sacrifices, however, reaction in the church was visibly being forced to retreat. The revival meetings of such curiosities as "Billy" Sunday and "Gipsy" Smith, Barnumesque though they were, indicated that the masses were to be attracted only by appeals to their personal lives.

Significant was the attitude of thinkers like Shailer Mathews, Dean of the Divinity School of the University of Chicago, and editor of the liberal *The World Today*. In a series of articles entitled "The Awakened Church" he pointed out the church's advance in social service and educational techniques. Such promotion was badly needed. If past generations had fought great

[2] *Ibid.*

battles in behalf of a separation of church and state, the church now was constrained to show what useful connection, if any, it had with society. Like other social institutions the church was on the scales, and it could not afford to take the test lightly.

The attitude of the muckrakers regarding religion was catholic. Most of them had come from homes in which the church, or religion, had been a recognized and valued part of family life. They were not inclined to take the violently anti-ecclesiastical stand which the more uncompromising of the Socialists and the frankly revolutionary I.W.W. had adopted. The churches and their adherents were real, and were not to be waved aside with any such slogan as "Religion is the opium of the people." The cosmos was likewise real, and the nature and history of humanity had questions for those who asked whither the fight for bread tended.

It was just this question that John Spargo considered in his lecture, before the People's Institute in Cooper Union, entitled *The Spiritual Significance of Socialism*.[3] Socialism, he said (dissenting comrades to the contrary), did not ignore the basic dilemmas of life. It looked toward a social order which would allow for more honest and intelligent contemplation of those dilemmas; it would free the masses from unscrupulous leaders who appealed to fear and superstition. Socialism constituted a release from dogma, not enslavement to new dogmas.

Such was the spiritual perspective. In practice the muckrakers busied themselves less with religious speculation than with direct consideration of the churches in their day-to-day activity. This was less violent than wholesale negation; actually, the investigations of the muckrakers, although constituting the source material for denunciation of the churches, was far more influential than those denunciations. The muckrakers were plainly reformistic. They did not attempt or intend to "destroy" the religious motive among their readers. They attempted, and were competent, to clarify the difference between the progressive and the unprogressive elements in the churches. And this, it should be added, was more than Socialism, with all its broad ambitions, could begin to do.

[3] Published by B. W. Huebsch, New York, in 1908, and dedicated to Rufus W. Weeks, vice-president of the New York Life Assurance Company and a Socialist Party comrade in good standing.

Muckraking in the spiritual sphere began with fundamentals. We have seen what happened when "Golden Rule" Jones took literally the teachings of Christ regarding prostitutes. He was branded a Socialist for his unorthodox behavior, and was condemned as sacrilegious by those who were outraged by his familiar interpretation of Christ's sayings. There were others who found the Nazarene more helpful as a man than as a god, and who were castigated in the lay as well as the religious press, for reasons which began with theology but wandered far afield. To sum up, the muckrakers were—and it will bear repeating—more for practical Christianity than against it.

Meanwhile the social unrest had produced new fashions in religious thought, and sects multiplied. John Alexander Dowie, the "second Elijah" and founder of Zion City, Illinois, reached the height of his success when, in 1903, he invaded New York City with his cohorts. (The invasion was the beginning of the end for Dowie personally, but it did not end the many stammerings of spiritual dissatisfaction.) Christian Science and New Thought, the latter an offshoot of the old New England Transcendentalism with features of Eastern philosophy, made a more national impression. Although they did not properly touch the masses at all, they were nonetheless symptomatic of public uneasiness. Christian Science in particular grew astonishingly, and in a decade was to become established in wealthier and middle-class circles.

Among the muckrakers Christian Science captured only one adherent, B. O. Flower, who was never a harsh realist and who in the Nineties had been so taken up with theories about the "psyche." If his long and eloquent defenses of Mrs. Mary Baker Eddy's tenets represented a retreat from reality, that retreat was harmless, for *The Arena* continued to carry on with a social platform which went so far as to approve and respect Debs and his work. Less sympathetic toward Christian Science was David Graham Phillips in his earnest and truth-seeking novel, *The Mother-Light*, which appeared anonymously in 1905. Although the book sold well, it was coldly received where it was not boycotted, and its authorship was never publicly acknowledged. Mark Twain could afford to be more bellicose, and he showed less restraint in his attack on the new religion and a lesser sense of proportion in warning of its spread. Mark Twain notwithstanding, Christian Science neither seized the government nor corrupted the schools; it did, however, establish itself beyond the control of any power but dictatorship—happily nonexistent.

The muckrakers were on safer and surer ground when they pointed not to philosophic defects in the religions but to malpractices by those who ruled churches and theological centers. In January 1905 Samuel Hopkins Adams, for instance, had an article in *McClure's* on tuberculosis as constituting the real "race suicide" in the country.[4] In this article he found reason to attack the Trinity Church Corporation (as distinguished, obscurely, from Trinity Church) for its conduct, as landlord, of some of the worst tenements—containing the worst brothels and saloons—in New York. The Tenement Commission, Adams noted, had had many occasions to run afoul of the Church and had found it a hard fighter; the Church had, however, a salutory respect for the Board of Health.

Trinity now undertook a brief and dignified correspondence with McClure, finally concluding the issue to its own satisfaction.[5] It did not reform its policy, and in 1908 Charles Edward Russell took up the question at length in an article for *Everybody's* and in an even more powerful one for *Hampton's*, in which he evaluated Trinity according to its history. For his article "Trinity: Church of Mystery," he was widely denounced, even being accused of having brought on the death of Morgan Dix. But the article inspired a contemporary drama, *The Writing on the Wall*, which had a successful run, and in April 1910 Hampton was able to announce editorially that Trinity had torn down four blocks of the worst tenements and had partly cleaned up others.

Muckraking articles on the churches continued to appear in the magazines. Among the notable ones was the long and exhaustive exposé of Mary Baker Eddy and Christian Science, by Georgine Milmine, which McClure ran in 1907. Another was the survey of Mormonism published by Ruth and Reginald Wright Kauffman

[4] President Roosevelt had noted with horror the decreased birth rate among native Americans, as contrasted with that of the immigrants. His picturesque phrase, "race suicide," took the popular fancy and was widely used.

[5] *Correspondence Between the Corporation of Trinity Church and McClure's Magazine*, printed by order of the vestry, 1905.

in 1912—a survey which culminated many bitter attacks by such writers as Burton J. Hendrick and A. H. Lewis.

None of these articles, however, attracted the attention which was given to a series by Harold Bolce, that ran in *Cosmopolitan* during 1909. Bailey Millard was no longer editor of the magazine; he had been succeeded by a lesser man, and *Cosmopolitan*, Hearst-wise, had begun to lose the balance which had originally set it so high among the periodicals. This explains why Harold Bolce, a journalist of long experience but no distinction, and more reactionary than progressive, was commissioned to undertake a study of current religious thought in the colleges and universities for *Cosmopolitan*. He had no principle but sensationalism to guide him. The series, in fact, was originally considered as not of the first importance, and only three articles were planned.

The first article, printed in May 1909 and called "Blasting at the Rock of Ages," caused an astounding degree of comment. It consisted of quotations from the lectures and books of prominent college professors, and was supposed to indicate revolutionary teachings that were undermining the church in the minds of youth. The inference, if any inference was to be grasped, was that Bolce disapproved of these teachings. Bolce, however, preserved a reportorial air, and took pains to show that it was not he, but the scholars, who made the assertions. The "teachings" themselves varied from the frankly cynical and aristocratic variety to the innocent principles of science. It was clear that—to quote the title of Bolce's second article—there were "Polyglots in Temples of Babel."

Here was, perhaps, a revelation that lively if not always lucid voices were sounding in the colleges. President Woodrow Wilson, of Princeton, believed that there was a need for a "new civilization." Professor Barrett Wendell felt that the American Revolution had been fought to maintain a delusion; namely, that all men are created equal. Professor William Z. Ripley spoke for the trusts, and Dr. John Bates Clark for the survival of the fittest. Like opinions, formal, scholastic, and platitudinous, were served up by Bolce with scare headlines and comment, to indicate that the ground was weak under tradition.

Perhaps this aspect of Bolce's work explains the excitement that the series created: facts about the colleges had not before been accessible to the common man, and a certain awe of learning still prevailed. The series had, at any rate, no other distinguishing feature. Bolce committed himself to nothing, and he followed up the series with a second one, "The Crusade Invisible," which purported to do for the women's colleges what had been done for the others, and which balanced quotations defending traditional Christianity against others which presumably threatened it. The second series, like the first, was dishonest in principle and vacuous in content. If they were, as Professor Faulkner says, "interesting" and "helped to awaken the church to a realization that a new day had come," it was certainly not because of any intrinsic merit they possessed in themselves. They were products of, or a sop to, unrest rather than an instrument of education. They likewise showed into what confusion the reader was carried when he tried to distinguish the worth-while from the futile in an age that was not self-critical but creative.

The muckrakers were, of course, touched personally, though not so naïvely, by the same unease that affected the common man. They were haunted by the need for certainty. If David Graham Phillips was content to work at picturing his time in novels, and if Upton Sinclair was vocalizing loud and clear for Socialism, others who were less sure of themselves found the future difficult.

"Charles Edward Russell has gone over to the Socialist Party," Steffens told Ida Tarbell. "Is not that what we should all be doing? Should we not make *The American Magazine* a Socialist organ?" [6]

There was no danger that Ida Tarbell would catch fire. Steffens soon after left the magazine to work with *Everybody's* and satisfy his feeling for social experience with free-lance writing.

Now Steffens had become much impressed by the example of practical Christianity set by "Golden Rule" Jones, and he read the New Testament, "without reverence, with feet up on a desk and a pipe in the mouth, as news." He was struck by its content of truths as modern as his own latest revelations. Christianity, he reflected, could be made to work.[7] He thereupon began to develop his thoughts into the point of view which he consummated in the unsuccessful book *Moses in Red*, published in 1926. Badly as the theory came out in literary form, it came out even worse in practice, as we shall see.

Steffens did not, after all, join the Socialist Party, but he did free himself from the McClure brand of impartiality as practiced by his associates. This had outlived its usefulness quickly. There had been some reason for it, in the earlier days: at that time muckraking had been new, causes and effects unclear. In the light of the insurance investigations, the Haywood trial, the pure-food fight, impartiality could not but begin to seem inadequate. Muckraking had made it fully clear that individuals were not to blame for crime; the great exposés had revealed opposing systems of life which could be defended or attacked. It was, in a word, becoming increasingly difficult to stand above the battle, and Steffens, for one, had no desire to avoid entering it.

Ray Stannard Baker, too, was bothered by the dilemma. His theme—education—still carried power, was still radical and compelling. Nevertheless, Baker himself felt the need for intellectual peace. Upton Sinclair, later accusing him of having become a "back-to-the-land sentimentalist," was hasty and mechanical in his analysis. What happened to Baker was more complex and was in response to contemporary trends. Through 1907, 1908, and beyond, Baker continued his muckraking investigations, facing the scene as boldly as he could. But in 1906 he was already narrating his adventures in contentment under the pseudonym of "David Grayson." He created this second personality, as George Gissing in England had earlier created Henry Ryecroft, as a personal reaction against the stirring injustice and social disorder he had been forced to witness. It is remarkable that his similarity to Gissing was never pointed out, for the psychological elements in both cases were strikingly alike. Baker was unable to adjust his vision dishonestly, as Frederick Upham Adams had done; yet he had to escape, and by way of David Grayson he did.

It's real creative art, Baker [wrote Steffens of Baker's articles, with all his capacity for appreciating human permutation], far above and beyond reporting. I respect reporting. I have great ideas of what can be done by telling the facts and telling the stories of life about us. I would have the *American* report and report and report, till men had to see in what a state of serviture they are in [sic], and fight for very shame. But what I'd have men stirred up for would be only to raise them to a state of mind into which you put them without effort in these articles.[8]

But "Grayson's" effortlessness was only a token of Baker's great need for serenity. It was not triumph, but escape. The "serviture" continued to exist and, being life, would have to furnish and did furnish the basis for such "real, creative art" as Steffens conceived. David Grayson did not solve or dissolve the battle for existence; he failed as Ryecroft failed; he was only calculated to arouse impatience in the mature reader. Baker's "understanding" —perfect and Olympian at last!—as represented in the mind of David Grayson was a maze of rustic sophistry and half-truths which could not withstand sharp scrutiny.

Baker increased and variegated his *alter ego* in the books of his later career, but never to the extent of influencing significantly American life or thought with them. The question during the muckraking era was, What effect will David Grayson have on Ray Stannard Baker? The effect was not immediately apparent. Baker kept his eyes on current strife while Grayson, on the farm and unruffled by Negro, labor, or political questions, enjoying nature, work, and the social amenities, invited his soul in peace.

In time Grayson became more troubled and alert. He evinced concern for his country's problems—not to the extent of investigating them at first hand, of course, and certainly not with Baker's descriptive powers. As Grayson waxed, Baker waned, until at last there was nothing but Grayson, a writer, journalist, and historian who had, presumably, written Baker's works in a more troubled, more perspicacious past.

All this, however, was clearer in another era, which had no deep concern for either Baker or Grayson.

Meanwhile Baker issued in 1910 the most cogent of all accounts of that spiritual dissatisfaction that touched all but the extreme reactionaries and the extreme radicals of the time: *The Spiritual Unrest*. This consisted of a series of articles that had been printed in *The American*, and told with supreme clarity of the predica-

[8] *The Letters of Lincoln Steffens*, Harcourt, Brace & Co., New York, 1938.

ment of the church and the efforts that were being made to give it new vitality and meaning. The story of Trinity—the richest church in the country—was related, if not so mordantly as Russell's story, still with great effect. Baker then appraised the condition of the Protestant sects generally and, after this, told of the disintegration of the Old World Jewish communities in New York, now broken into economic groups, their synagogues (so much admired by the muckrakers) deserted by the younger generation, which sought to fit itself into a totally different environment. In contrast, Baker described the new institutional churches, showing how they were attempting to make religion acceptable to those who needed practical comradeship. He told of the Emmanuel movement, an outgrowth of the tendency toward "faith healing"—a subject on which he had elsewhere written at length. He concluded with an account of the "New Christianity" as it was being practiced by the very modern and progressive Professor Walter Rauschenbusch, of Rochester Theological Seminary.

This was a strong and ambitious picture, and he painted it with forthrightness and sincerity. One might wonder why it should have been criticized as it was by reactionaries. Baker's intentions were generous.

Baker was not alone in his concern for religion. Even the Socialists were wont to refer to Christ as "Comrade Jesus"—to the great indignation of their enemies—and to assert that Christ, were he to appear today, would have no home in any church. That was the theme of Upton Sinclair's novel, written in the Twenties, entitled *They Call Me Carpenter*. (Sinclair reserved a less flippant reverence for the Thirties.) Other works of less importance and merit, dealing with the same theme, appeared from time to time.

It was a serious question for the muckrakers whether Christianity was practical or not. If it was not, what principle was? There was, of course, Socialism. Russell, Spargo, and Ghent were satisfied with its practice, and there were others—"step-comrades," as Ghent recalls Hillquit naming them—who played fellow-traveler roles. But their friends and colleagues resisted Socialism's call. Many of them reproduced the attitude of David Graham Phillips, of whom John Spargo writes: "Sometimes he proclaimed that he was a Socialist, and at other times with equal vehemence and intensity proclaimed that he was not a Socialist. This did not mean that he was vacillating or uncertain, or that he was superficial." What it did mean was that Phillips, and men like Phillips, wished to be free and unhampered; they wanted to do their work, and the work of muckrakers could not be done while they were

PREACHER: "YOU MUST BE BORN AGAIN!"
MIKE (TIRED OF THE STRUGGLE): "ONCE IS ENOUGH, DOC!"

Drawn by Art Young for *The Masses*

harnessed to party politics. Steffens alone, in that section [9] of his memoirs in which he analyzed the intellectuals in their relation to action, saw this fact clearly. The intellectual was not made of the same stuff as the politician: his training, abilities, and point of view were different. His achievement was, ultimately, the capture of experience, not action as such, whatever practical work he happened to accomplish.

Experience, on the other hand, had to be pertinent to the reader. The experiences of the muckrakers were first of all that. It remained to be seen how long they would continue to be so.

[9] See page 633 of his *Autobiography*.

XXIV. THE PANIC OF 1907

A DEPRESSION was long overdue, for the development of trusts, now in its final stage and not to be halted by muckrakers or reformers, could not be accomplished without human sacrifice. The schemes of the Morgans and the Rockefellers led directly to an economic breakdown, not for them, certainly, but for those who were touched by their activities. Panic had all but broken loose during the Hill-Harriman fight for ownership of the Western railroads; it had threatened again in 1903, and many times during the following years when the muckraking attacks shook public confidence in the insurance companies and other business corporations in which it had invested. If exposure focused attention on palpably dishonest manipulations, like the shipbuilders' trust, it did not arrest or even deter the concentration of business. Free competition could not be enforced by either public demand or law. The banks dealt as they pleased with their reserves, and they dealt, as was to be expected, in the interests of those who controlled them. The irony and indignation of the muckrakers only emphasized that finance had been centralized and that the middle-class had been deprived of any ultimate control of it.

In January 1906 Jacob H. Schiff predicted that there would be a panic unless the currency system were reformed.[1] Schiff was primarily worried for the banks rather than the country at large; yet his warning was a reminder that no governmental effort had ever been made to lighten the effects of economic crisis, that no concern had ever been manifested by the government for the economic welfare of the nation except when wholesale bankruptcy and the stoppage of business had made action imperative. In those days each bank stood alone and a run on any one bank meant ruin to it. This had been relatively "fair" in the earlier time when banks were independent entities and reflected the policies of indi-

[1] See *Current Literature*, February 1906.

viduals. Now a bank was part of a system, unacknowledged but no less real; its directors were also directors of numerous other banks and companies. The ruin of any bank reacted upon other institutions, and the fall of an important bank was bound to have national repercussions.

To Socialists financial tragedy seemed the normal and inevitable concomitant of capitalism. For the depositor the issue of safety was more immediate, vital. Changes in the social system concerned him only when they touched him directly; and capitalism was acceptable so long as it did not destroy him. Whenever it threatened his peace or existence, and only then, his thoughts turned to government ownership and like radical solutions. His knowledge sometimes went beyond his practice, but never to the extent of influencing it.

When it came, the panic of 1907 formally introduced the new capitalism to Americans, and the sharp criticism that followed only served to stabilize and secure the new capitalism. This effect of criticism accounted for the bitterness of those radicals of later years who accused the muckrakers of having "saved" capitalism instead of allowing it to disintegrate through inefficiency and corruption. Most men during the crisis, however, and they included the broad masses of the population, were thankful to the muckrakers for their work, feeling that they not only had prevented chaos but also had laid the ground for further reforms. It is to be remembered that the movement of middle-class revolt was ascendant and was not intended to stop at any given point.

The spokesmen for capitalism blamed the muckrakers, and even Roosevelt, for capitalism's troubles. They contended that there would be no panics or depressions if they were let alone and allowed to conduct their businesses as they chose. Their point was undoubtedly true. But the terms upon which the financiers and capitalists could have stabilized their control would have meant an end of trade unionism, the public vote, in a word, democracy. It would have meant dictatorship with everything which that implies.

The idea of dictatorship was not distasteful to many business men and their intellectuals. Examples were culled from ancient history to prove that rule from above had resulted in "golden ages" of art and commerce. "Democracy" was not, at this time, a catchword for conservative demagogues; use of the word brought heaps of abuse on President Roosevelt among others. A fine contempt for the masses was frankly and even indignantly voiced in the more aristocratic of the magazines.

To the possibilities of financial dictatorship the muckrakers stood resolutely opposed. Their attacks upon the trusts and their concern for the small tradesmen bore witness to their determination that business as well as politics should be subject to popular will. It was, therefore, no accident that they should have followed the course of the Standard Oil Company of New Jersey and its subsidiaries so relentlessly. They struck often at the other trusts, but it was understood that the future of Standard would in all respects be the future of its brother corporations. From the publication of Tarbell's history until 1911 a full stream of criticism was directed at the ethics, history, and practices of the trust.

The hatred voiced by the muckrakers for large-scale business was shared by most citizens and the feelings of some citizens occasionally got out of hand. In 1905, for example, when Rockefeller contributed $100,000 to the American Board of Foreign Missions, Dr. Washington Gladden publicly denounced the acceptance of "tainted money" by his church. The matter became a subject for national controversy, heated arguments being conducted as to whether ill-gotten money—Standard Oil money— could conscientiously be used for worthy causes. Even John L. Sullivan, lecturing in behalf of temperance, gave his opinion. In the confusion it was entirely forgotten that Rockefeller had not been offering "conscience money." On the contrary, he had been importuned for a year by the American Board before he had consented to give them the money. Despite Dr. Gladden's protest, the money was spent, and was not returned. The willingness with which the public accepted the legend that the gift had been "refused," its satisfaction with the "rebuff" given the magnate, indicated a vengeful public mood which could not be placated by all the defenses and explanations of Rockefeller's agents.

Such public excitements were insignificant when compared with the prosecutions of Standard which the states undertook. In Kansas determined steps were taken to curb Standard's monopolistic and rebate activities; in Texas the famous Waters-Pierce Oil

Company, a subsidiary, was indicted for carrying on business in restraint of trade; and similar action of a kind not seen in twenty years was begun in other states. These suits were palpably of the highest importance. If future events were to prove that competition could not be revived in its older form, it was nonetheless felt that the suits were crucial tests of the power of government. No wonder the muckrakers kept an anxious eye upon them. Ida Tarbell, wielding the most influence, explained the Kansas situation for *McClure's* readers, and then, taken out of her role of historian, drew a portrait of Rockefeller as a man and as a type which proved that there were limits to her impartiality. As for Rockefeller himself—"Not a word. Not a word about that misguided woman," he said. He had been deeply hurt by the public's cynicism and its refusal to credit his religious and charitable convictions.

By 1907 the struggles between the government and Standard had come to a head. Early in January of that year the trust was indicted in the Ohio courts on five hundred and thirty-nine counts involving rebate practices. Two weeks later the Interstate Commerce Commission published what was recognized as a scathing indictment of Standard Oil and its leaders. On May 19 the Commissioner of Corporations issued a report charging that the oil trust had, by reason of its control of transportation, a practical monopoly over the petroleum industry.

Such was the tide of public antagonism against Standard that all the trust's news and publicity agencies could not check it. Nor was it by any means certain that the people's feelings could be controlled at the point of action. Rockefeller was sufficiently disturbed to issue an autobiography (published in *World's Work*) to offset biographies of him that had already been written. Frederick Upham Adams was commissioned to write in eloquent defense of the Waters-Pierce Company. Standard Oil was moved to the extent of purchasing space in such organs as *Collier's*, in which it appealed to American decency and impartiality.

Standard Oil, commented *Collier's*, was fighting for its life. This seemed hardly true, but it was not easy to foretell what the future would bring—particularly after the thunderbolts of the next several months had fallen. In June an Austin, Texas, jury rendered a decision for the state of over a million and a half dollars against Waters-Pierce, and recommended that the company be banished from the state because of its criminal activities. This action was sensational enough. But, in August, Judge Kenesaw Mountain Landis, sitting in judgment of the Indiana branch of Standard, electrified the country by imposing a $29,240,000 fine, following an earlier indictment of the corporation on 1,462 counts for the acceptance of rebates. Since the Indiana branch did not possess sufficient assets to pay the fine, Landis ruled that the holding company—that is, Standard Oil of New Jersey—must pay it. Landis's decision sounded, to the public, like the millennium. Rockefeller, however, vowed malevolently that Landis would be dead a long time before the fine was paid. The fine was not paid, and a "higher court" ordered the government to pay the costs of the prosecution.

At the time when news of the ruling was written large in headlines, a current of hope vibrated throughout the country. When, in September, Government Prosecutor Frank B. Kellogg brought suit for the dissolution of the trust under the Sherman Act, savage controversies began which seemed to point to the most violent showdown on the issue of big business in the history of the country. Standard Oil was not alone in the docket. The Harriman railroad lines were being investigated, and the American Tobacco Company was undergoing examination. In 1908 the Harvester trust was dissolved.

It should be remembered, however, that this pressure on the trusts was being exerted by men who would hardly have seemed fit instruments for revolution. Kellogg and Landis were not radicals; they were not even apostles of Populism. And the rulers of the Harvester trust were not made paupers through the dissolution; their profits, in fact, increased. Those who were profoundly excited by the antitrust proceedings failed to see that antitrust measures alone could not break up the financial system.

But meanwhile the panic and accompanying events helped to clear up certain confusions in men's minds and to explain—by bitter experience—what was happening to the country.

The depression was first indicated—but not frankly acknowledged—on March 14 when panic carried twenty standard railroad stocks to their lowest point in three years. The stock market continued to stagger and, later in the month, fell still further. All through the spring and summer it remained at ebb, and by October 24 it was many points lower than it had been at any time during the year.

This was the story of depression according to the ticker tape; and more was to come. In October, F. Augustus Heinze, the Montana copper king, attempted to corner United Copper. It shot up in value from 37¼ to 63, but dropped quickly to 36 and then, catastrophically, to 10. Heinze had bungled his corner. The stock-brokerage firm belonging to his brother was forced to close, as was another Stock Exchange firm through which Heinze had operated. The Mercantile National Bank, of which he was president and whose funds he had used, had to ask the Clearing House to meet its debit balance. The House did so, but not until Heinze and his directors had been compelled to turn in their resignations from the bank.

It would be proper to say that Heinze was sacrificed to his rivals in Wall Street, for his baronial methods of manipulating stock were not unique. Honesty did not triumph when the Mercantile was rid of his presence. Heinze had simply made the mistake of leaving an opening for opponents who did not approve of his power. This aspect of affairs was not publicized to any degree, for Wall Street was not in the habit of discussing its private business with the public.

The quick action of the Clearing House apparently saved the situation, closing up the ranks in business with no damage except to those who had investments in copper. Nevertheless, rumors concerning an unsteady condition of the banks circulated and fear became widespread. When the National Bank of Commerce sent out notice that it would not clear for the Knickerbocker Trust, one of the largest banks in America, which had been involved in Heinze's speculations, a frantic crowd collected at its doors, demanding money. Its president, Charles T. Barney, immediately resigned, but the damage was already done: $8,000,000 were paid out during a sensational run, and then the Knickerbocker closed its doors.

Panic was now in full swing. The stock market crashed completely, and banks all over the country found themselves unable to meet their obligations.

After the Knickerbocker Trust failed, the Trust Company of America became the second point of attack for depositors; it was all but closed on its first day, when it paid out $12,000,000 from its vaults. By that time it was certain that every other bank would be similarly besieged unless immediate action were taken to sustain all of them. J. P. Morgan, taking control of the situation, called upon all the financial leaders to help him break the panic. Rockefeller responded with a pledge to back him as far as necessary, and co-operation was offered by others of influence. Secretary of the Treasury Cortelyou put $25,000,000 of government money at the disposal of the banks, and announced his readiness to deposit with the national banks of the country $150,000,000 and more up to the limit of the law.

The Trust Company of America was saved. Public assurances that a united front among the financiers existed, and would continue to exist so long as it was needed, soon ended the runs which had threatened to destroy the banking system of the country.

So the panic ended. But the effects of the panic lingered as a depression. As Mark Sullivan has it, the country had to find its own "slow way to normal recovery." As for Morgan—he was hailed as a savior who had, almost single-handed, stopped the panic at its worst. It was true that he had emerged, mysteriously, with greater power than ever; it was likewise clear that Wall Street had been tolerating a system of banking which made banks vulnerable whenever co-operation among bankers was not forthcoming. But these considerations were not allowed to detract from Morgan's glory: he had saved the country. To quote Sullivan again, the financiers had come to him for guidance, some out of "voluntary deference," many "drawn irresistibly by that subtler and more powerful force" which individualized him. The public accepted this tale, if one can judge by the unreserved encomium which was accorded him. In any case, the panic was over, and there was no one else to praise for its termination.

The panic had been worse than the panic of 1893 and yet, significantly, it had done less damage. The reason, believes Professor Faulkner, was the "fundamental prosperity" of the country. It is also likely that the stakes of reform that had been driven into law saved the working-classes from being compelled to carry the full burden of the crisis. However the panic was analyzed, it was certain that common men would not again, in that generation, consent to suffer alone for such adventures in speculation as were launched in 1907.

There was another version of the panic. Upton Sinclair, visiting Edmond Kelly one day before the panic began, found him in great distress. Kelly, an internationally famous lawyer, a wealthy man, and a Socialist who had written important books on radical theory, told Sinclair his fears.

He—Kelly—had just left his friend, Charles T. Barney, the president of the Knickerbocker Trust, who had opened his heart to him. Barney had been in dire straits. Morgan had determined to ruin him, he said, and had therefore deliberately led him into entanglements and given him promises of support. Morgan had repudiated his pledges that very night. The Knickerbocker was doomed, and several other institutions were also marked for slaughter.

This was the gist of Kelly's revelations to Sinclair. That same night the press carried the story that Barney had committed suicide, and the next day his bank failed. The panic now reached its alarming proportions, threatened to get entirely out of hand, and was finally stopped.

So, while Morgan received plaudits for his statesmanship, Sinclair harbored what was not precisely a secret but was very close to one; namely, that Morgan was no deliverer but a man who had acted in the same way and with the same motives as Heinze, who, having failed, was being condemned as an irresponsible adventurer.

Sinclair now visited *The American Magazine* and offered to write a story on the theme. His subject was approved, a contract was signed, and Sinclair began to prepare his manuscript. Shortly after, however, according to *The Brass Check*, John S. Phillips came to him and begged to be released from the contract. Certain interests were displeased, it seemed, and might revenge themselves upon the magazine if the manuscript were published. Sinclair, therefore, freed Phillips from his obligation and set himself to finding another publisher.

Ida Tarbell denies the story: there was no "pressure" involved, she says, in *The American Magazine's* refusal to print Sinclair's

The Money-Changers. The manuscript was, she insists, rejected for no other reason except that it was second-rate. This remark can be compared with Sinclair's other reminiscence concerning the book. It was rejected also by Walter Page, of Doubleday, Page, on the grounds that it was inartistic work. When Sinclair heard this from Page's lips, he looked the editor in the eye and reminded him that a new novel by Thomas Dixon was being issued by his firm. He asked Page to tell him whether *that* was art.

Undoubtedly the subject matter of Sinclair's book had much to do with the fact that it was finally issued by a small and unimportant firm. It was noteworthy that no question about art had come up when *The Jungle* was finally accepted: that book was recognizably art. The truth is that Sinclair did not follow up *The Jungle* with anything of like power. *The Overman* was quite valueless; so was *The Metropolis*, for all its arresting gossip about the mad manners of smart New York. *The Money-Changers* had an important story to tell, but its characters were puppets, and the book hardly rose to dignity on any page. Not until 1909, when he published the novelette *Samuel the Seeker*, did Sinclair raise his style of fiction above mediocrity; then he achieved a certain Voltairesque brightness which compensated somewhat for the shallow story and trite characterizations.

And so the editors of *The American* were justified in their attitude at least to the extent of having been unwilling to wage a battle to defend, against inevitable criticism, such a slight work as Sinclair had to offer. The panic had greater significance than anyone realized who was merely concerned for his personal savings or investments, and it is by weighing such a book as *The Money-Changers* that we can fully grasp the power and importance of more substantial muckraking works that drew from that crisis in capitalism.

Although finance could not be taken out of the hands of the Morgan and Rockefeller circles, the muckraker could publicize facts which would end the cruder forms of speculation and protect the masses against men like Heinze. The middle-class was, unconsciously, digging in to preserve its outposts against destruction. Many writers now made contributions to exposure literature which helped to round out Lawson's dramatic story of gross fraud in high places.

Edwin LeFèvre's novels and stories of high finance only capitalized, perhaps, upon the desire of the magazine and book reader to know more about the processes of business. They did, however, help him to such understanding and entertained him while doing so. Will Payne, also, drew from his experiences as a financial reporter and editor to write such fine stories as *The Automatic Capitalist*, which explained how finance was conducted and explained in the human terms the reader best understood.

Everybody's prided itself on its financial features. In June 1906, John O'Hara Cosgrave began Merrill A. Teague's series on "Bucket-Shop Sharks," which helped to reduce the number of such frauds. After the panic had passed Cosgrave printed a symposium on its causes, giving the opinions of men like James J. Hill, William Graham Sumner, and Lawson. Lawson's comment, written in his most vigorous style shortly before he repudiated muckraking, blamed "fictitious wealth." *Everybody's* also printed Charles Edward Russell's series "Where Did You Get It, Gentlemen?", in the course of which Russell raked over the careers of Thomas Fortune Ryan, William C. Whitney, Yerkes, and others, asking sardonically why anyone need be poor when such easy roads to wealth as these men had found were still open.

Other magazines were hardly less alert to the importance of the financial subject, particularly about the time of the crisis. It was *Success* and *Collier's*, however, which best told the truth about the stock market from the point of view of the small investor. Frank Fayant, who wrote the critical biography of Lawson, ran a series for *Success* entitled "Fools and Their Money" in which he treated financial firms and syndicates with startling familiarity. He also solicited correspondence from his readers and advised them regarding the solvency of specific firms. Elliott Flower, for his part, wrote for *Collier's* "The Diary of a Small Investor," and in it followed the actual path of the common man to the extent of recording real transactions, describing the "sucker's" market and elaborating on the question of promoters and their "references." Burton J. Hendrick and, later, John Moody and George Kibbe Turner also added chapters to that history of the financiers which was being written from so many approaches.

Such writings pioneered in the financial world, reduced considerably the effectiveness of brazen schemes for mulcting the public. By 1910 financial features were appearing regularly in the magazines. *Collier's* was even conducting a financial department for the benefit of its readers.

The centerpiece of all such writing, however, received no public honor. Gustavus Myers, completing his monumental *History of the Great American Fortunes,* could find no publisher for it. No

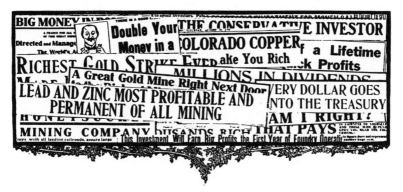

AN ILLUSTRATION FOR FAYANT'S "FOOLS AND
THEIR MONEY"

wonder he resented a "latter class of writers, intent upon pandering to a supposedly popular appetite for sensation," and denied the value of muckraking save as a reflection of disordered times. Myers, now a Socialist, felt that the work of such men as Teague and Fayant and Elliott Flower was worthless when compared to the results of his own long investigation. Their work was not, of course, worthless; it was only less persistent and unrelenting in its probings; but it left its mark on the times. Myers' book was finally issued by the Socialist Kerr Company of Chicago.

The striking fact about all these books is that they were, first, bent on winnowing out fraud, and second, providing checks and balances upon finance. It seemed evident that centralization of financial power could not be indefinitely continued without pushing democracy into the discard. That danger accounted for the government's feverish efforts to purify finance and dissolve the trusts, and likewise for the earnest work of the muckrakers.

The difficulty was to determine how much purification and dissolution could be accomplished short of state Socialism. In 1909, for example, when the Hughes Commission on Speculation in Securities and Commodities conducted a timid survey and accomplished little, few commentators besides Lawson were able to say clearly just why the survey had failed. Wall Street had its place in the life of the country; honestly run it could benefit the nation. But it functioned entirely by individual enterprise, which was not easily controlled, and surely individualism in the form of the Rockefeller trust or the Morgan firm was dangerous. Agitation for a Federal Reserve Act, which would prevent such currency panics as had been witnessed in 1907, was finally begun among conservatives. Conservatives were also among those who approved the breaking up of the Standard Oil oligarchy, as well as among those who saw with alarm Morgan's domination of finance. Even millionaires were no longer safe, according to the rules of free competition, as Arthur Edward Stilwell could testify.[2]

The situation was further complicated by the fact that American finance had been drawn into international competition. Standard Oil, for example, no longer took its products about the world freely, for in 1903 the Royal Dutch Company and British Shell amalgamation had given Rockefeller a more formidable competitor than he had ever expected. Like mergers made it necessary for American finance to present a common front against foreign rivals. Tariff protection no longer sufficed to preserve old-style capitalism.

From 1909 to the time when President Wilson took the matter completely in hand, it was this need for adjustment which strengthened the campaign for curbing and defining capitalism. In 1911 the Standard Oil trust was dissolved. Shortly after, the American Tobacco Company was likewise ordered to dissolve by the decision of the Supreme Court. On another front, the Federal Reserve Bank was created to insure finance against such experiences as that of 1907. Louis D. Brandeis was to be found in the thick of such reforms; and when the Pujo Committee of 1912

[2] *Cannibals of Finance.* "Fifteen Years' Contest with the Money Trust," Chicago, 1912.

met to discuss whether or not a money trust existed in the country, it was Brandeis and men like him who were requisitioned to determine the facts. Brandeis later wrote the best account of these investigations for his friend and admirer Norman Hapgood, who had become editor of *Harper's Weekly*,[3] and in his account expressed the feelings and ideals which had motivated the antitrust campaigners.

Centralization of business had been completed, but that did not mean that capital was free to act as it chose. More than ever did capital have to consider the aims and demands of organized labor. Industrial anarchy was definitely past; no one individual or group of individuals could any longer disorganize national affairs. What remained to be done, from the standpoint of those who had no place in the "higher brackets," was to continue such fights as political insurgents and magazine investigators could best carry on.

Government ownership as the next step in reform was the theme of Charles Edward Russell's book *Business: The Heart of the Nation*. A "moral awakening" no longer sufficed for him, as it had in 1905 when he investigated the beef trust. He amplified his more mature conclusions in the frankly Socialistic book in which he derided "government bunk" on the subject of the tariff and pointed out that the "dissolved" trusts had reorganized and were carrying on business as usual.[4]

That is to say, in the end the muckrakers were at the beginning: competition was not to be enforced, and the country was constrained to arrive at some utterly new understanding about a capitalism which was changing unpredictably—and beyond all question in ways that would affect the great reform movement to its foundations. Government ownership of essential industries was one solution that seemed to have possibilities, and Socialists talked often and at length of the advantages that would accrue to the public if capitalists were "bought out." The capitalists themselves had no enthusiasm for the proposal, and proletarian leaders scorned the idea that they would voluntarily surrender any of their power. If government ownership were the solution, it would have to be passed upon by those who stood between the political extremes.

[3] Published in Brandeis's *Other People's Money*, Stokes Co., New York, 1914.
[4] *Doing Us Good and Plenty*, Kerr Co., Chicago, 1914.

XXV. TAFT

TAFT represented a victory for everything that was least progressive in Roosevelt. The great love which bound the two men, as it has been described touchingly and at length by dozens of their friends and aides, contained scarcely a glimmer of common interest relating to reform. It had to do with social standing, political advancement, favors asked and favors given. When Steffens visited Roosevelt, it was to discuss the unrest seething outside of the White House. Mark Sullivan also brought news of the world as it was to be seen from the windows of *Collier's*. Taft came only to sun himself in the President's energy, and to deliver reports that were commendable for clear wording and little else.

The essence of Roosevelt's conservatism was his dependence on party politics; of Taft's, his adherence to the law. Roosevelt, that is to say, was a politician; his friend was a lawyer. As a jurist Taft gained for himself a well-deserved name for his ability to interpret in the interests of the *status quo*, and so he ensured his rapid advance in public life. The high light of his earlier career was his unequivocal sponsorship of the use of injunctions in labor disputes. This practice endeared him to McKinley but not to trade-unionists. As Governor-General of the Philippines, he followed a course of conservatism which other ambitious men, for fear of destroying their future, hesitated to take.[1] For his principles Taft received the gratitude of the administration, and was even approved by the popular magazines, which were less principled in their attitude toward foreign and colonial policy than they were in strictly domestic affairs.

Taft was selected by Roosevelt to be Secretary of War, and in that post he distinguished himself only by his ardent appreciation of Roosevelt's work. This made him, nominally, a progressive, if

[1] See Moorfield Storey's analysis of *The Philippine Policy of Secretary Taft*, issued by the New England Anti-Imperialist League, Boston, 1902.

Roosevelt was a progressive; actually he was recognized to be a stand-pat party man, a thread in the hands of Roosevelt, who had mastered the art of weaving policies that escaped the displeasure of Morgan and the muckrakers at one and the same time.

Why, then, did Roosevelt choose Taft as his successor in the White House, rather than Governor Hughes of New York, who had by this time made it clear that the insurance investigations were not to be followed by any action similarly drastic? It was, perhaps, Taft's plasticity which determined Roosevelt's choice; that plasticity reassured Roosevelt that his political leadership need not end with his second term. Hughes, solidly constructed, was likely to initiate a Hughes policy rather than a Roosevelt policy. Taft frankly admired and earnestly applauded his chief's handling of affairs. Taft disliked the progressives, ranging from La Follette to Beveridge, who were slowly formulating a new approach to public problems that was based on the momentous experiences of the recent past. Taft knew, however, that though Roosevelt used the progressives when necessary, he had no stomach for insurgency and no desire to have it operating from the inner recesses of the Capitol. Roosevelt felt, in fact, that the worst of reform was over; that the hectic sessions of Congress had taken sufficient care of the public demands that had been inspired by scandal and expressed in propaganda for social change. He conceived himself as having done a great work, helped and hindered by various impetuous radicals and reformers. The present task in his view was that of organizing the results of his labors, and he believed that Taft's legal experience would be of good service—particularly if it followed the lines of reform Roosevelt himself had laid down.

In so reasoning Roosevelt misread the signs of the times. The need for reform had not abated; the insurgents did not represent a "lunatic fringe," but a type of politician which was, in reality, to inherit the political field. It is true that "The Treason of the Senate" was followed by no comparable series of exposure, but one reason for this was that exposure, ceasing to be novel, had taken its place as a normal part of the news. These quieter years were for the reformers years of organization and construction. The magazines, recording the trend, concerned themselves largely with personalities who were putting reform into practice; only in gross cases of fraud were the corruptionists given headlines.

Yet even if Roosevelt had correctly read the times it is doubtful whether he would have taken any other course than he chose. If the insurgents were to inherit of the new time, Roosevelt was certain to align himself with them—but not to the extent of placing one of them in the White House, and taking for himself a subordinate place. Better Taft than La Follette! When his administration ended on March 4, 1909, Roosevelt reviewed the man whom he had lobbied, coached, and carried into the Presidency, and who was to take up the work he had left—and reviewed him with some qualms, but not to the length of thinking wishfully of other men who had supported his administration. Instead Roosevelt went on his trip around the world, to receive such homage as he could hardly have expected had he remained at home to match talents with men whom he now joined in the second rank.

The Taft administration has not come down to us as a memorable one, and there are few people who would make claims for it as having been better than Roosevelt's. Yet, soberly considered, why was it not better? During his very first Congress, the Sixty-First, Taft recommended and had enacted into law many bills of the first importance—bills for railroad control, the publication of political campaign expenditures, the limitation of the use of injunctions, the creation of a postal-savings system. Under Taft the trusts were subjected to such government criticism and restraint as they had not previously known; and before Taft's term was over many more landmarks of legislation were passed than Roosevelt could point to as having originated with him.

It is true that revival of the Sherman Anti-Trust law stabilized the trusts rather than destroyed them. It is also true that many of the best laws passed during Taft's term of office were to be credited to the efforts of insurgent Senators and Representatives, as well as to numberless nonpolitical figures, rather than to Taft himself. But this had also been true of Roosevelt in his time— witness, for example, the pure-food and the railroad struggles. An important difference between the two administrations is that Roosevelt had the gift of keeping fire and meaning in his compromises, while Taft developed a humorless pomposity that quickly alienated the reformers and created a chasm between him and them. Taft also left his real relations with the reactionaries open to public view—a mistake Roosevelt had not made.

The fact that more actually progressive law was enacted under Taft than under Roosevelt cannot, then, be explained by their different personalities. The explanation is that the reform movement was beyond Taft's control, being the end product of demands and exposures begun under the previous administration. Taft was as powerless to prevent reform as he was to prevent his own undoing. He made, in fact, every effort to halt reform, but he did it ineptly. He appealed to principle when demagogy would have been more effective; he broke promises which he should not have made or, having made, should have broken more adroitly.

Roosevelt, too, had promised an income tax; he, too, had promised a downward revision of the tariff. But he kept so many political irons heated that his failure to fulfill either promise was never listed to his discredit by the reformers. Taft, on the other hand, burdened with the weight of the Presidency, failed to preserve a fitting human demeanor; he made the old error of identifying criticism of him with criticism of his high office. His well-publicized heartiness and joviality left him entirely. Taft, as Upton Sinclair observed, was good-humored so long as he was not crossed; when he was crossed, he became malevolent and vindictive. With the muckraking movement at its crest, he was fated for opposition. The muckrakers, in fact, mistrusted him from the first, and his subsequent conduct put them at swords' points with him.

Taft was a bulwark against reform; he had been so appraised by the financiers, who did not concern themselves with Roosevelt's logic or ideas and who knew what they wanted. That Taft failed to prevent reform was not their fault but the fault of Roosevelt, who selected him and saw him into the Presidency. Roosevelt, who so often protested against the shortsightedness of his capitalist allies, here made a fearful and, as it turned out, a gigantic blunder. It would hardly have been so bad had his estimation of the forces of reform been correct. Since muckraking was presumably dead, according to Roosevelt, little sensational stimulation for reform was to be expected of the magazines. The nonjournalistic reformers were carrying on work for separate and fragmentary ideals which, good in themselves, nevertheless did not constitute a platform. If muckraking was dead, thought Roosevelt, the major parties could fight over their differences with no danger to themselves, and Taft could look forward to four years of honor and good weather.

Muckraking, however, was not dead, and the muckrakers were no less bent upon establishing democracy upon firm and unshakable foundations. They were somewhat depleted in numbers; those who had casually fallen in with them, with the intention of reaping some of the attention they had arrested, were now beginning to follow other leads having nothing to do with exposure. But those to whom muckraking was more than a passing fashion were rooted in their work and determined to see it through to the end. They encouraged the progressives in Congress, helped to deepen the differences in the Republican Party. They seized wisely upon conservation of natural resources as the most significant issue in national affairs and, with this issue chosen, set up a standard by which progressivism could be judged.

Taft was hardly a few months in office before the muckrakers intervened in his administration with such effect that it became invalid. In doing so they revealed how strong they had become, how much a part of the substructure of national affairs they were. Following the Ballinger affair, Taft's prestige was gone, and so was his strength to influence national affairs.

It is hardly likely that Roosevelt, had he gained a third term, would have been similarly hamstrung. Yet he could not have checked insurgency any more than Taft. Reviewing the Ballinger case, Roosevelt remarked that he was not yet persuaded that Taft could have acted otherwise in the affair. Roosevelt was at that time excusing his friend, explaining his position in a matter involving law and justice. His remark, however, was truer in another sense; namely, that Taft could not have escaped that position in which he found himself. Roosevelt might have handled the situation differently; before his term expired, he was planning to do so. But would he have been more effectual in halting the tide?

XXVI. THE BALLINGER CASE

CONSERVATION, now becoming a national issue, was well symbolized by the aims and ideals which motivated Gifford Pinchot. This tall, lean, ascetic man was a reformer, whose political acuteness might be measured by his adoration of Roosevelt. He had graduated from Yale in 1889, spent three years studying forestry in Germany and Switzerland, and then returned to America to begin, in the private Vanderbilt mountain lands at Biltmore, North Carolina, the first systematic forestry work in the United States.

Pinchot was not the first to know America's need for forest conservation. John Muir had advocated forest reserves as far back as the Eighties, and in 1891 the Boone and Crockett Club and members of the American Forestry Association had agitated successfully for a Forestry Reserve Act. Pinchot, however, was the first to attack the problem of conservation from a modern viewpoint. Under Hoke Smith, Cleveland's Secretary of the Interior, he was chosen to report plans for a rational forest policy, and in 1898 he became forester and chief of division in that unit of the Department of Agriculture which afterward became the Bureau of Forestry. The Bureau was a small department with an annual appropriation of only $40,000, but Pinchot and the earnest young men he gathered about him accomplished great volumes of work, and Pinchot himself achieved a fame which rarely came to subordinates. His main interest was in trees, but he developed a concern for other natural resources—ore, coal, water power—and therefore followed closely the activities of the General Land Office of the Department of the Interior, which ruled over those resources.

Pinchot's enthusiasm touched the most sincere of Roosevelt's political feelings. Although Pinchot looked up to his friend, it is likely that in conservation matters he exercised more influence upon Roosevelt than Roosevelt exercised upon him. Roosevelt withdrew millions of acres from public entry—that is, from private hands—and sponsored the National Conservation Commission, with Pinchot at its head. The Commission did educational and propaganda work of vast importance.

Roosevelt did this for conservation, but many who later felt that they were fighting for a "continuation of the Roosevelt policies" forgot that he had also other deeds to his credit. He encouraged various financiers to look into Alaska's possibilities, for instance, and so interested George Perkins—a Morgan man—as to cause him to create the Alaska Syndicate, which acquired copper mines and sought to buy the Cunningham claims, with which the public was soon to become familiar.

Furthermore, it should be observed, Richard Achilles Ballinger was not created by Taft or by Taft's co-workers: Ballinger was appointed Commissioner of the General Land Office in March 1907 by recommendation of his old Williams College schoolmate Secretary of the Interior Garfield—Roosevelt's favorite, who had earlier interfered in Charles Edward Russell's beef-trust fight. Ballinger was a Seattle lawyer and jurist, who had been elected "reform mayor" in 1904. He was an expert in mining and land law, and a successful corporation lawyer who had no standing—none whatever—with reformers of a muckraking persuasion. Those who so thoughtlessly approved Roosevelt's policies and Pinchot's energy would have done better to have kept their eyes on Ballinger. The innocent, unquestioning acceptance of this unknown man as head of the Land Office showed that the public had much to learn about conservation in theory and practice.

On November 12, 1906, Roosevelt withdrew from public entry 100,000 acres of Alaska coal lands. Before this was done, however, some nine hundred claims to the land had been filed by companies and individuals who were by no means willing to pull up their stakes. The aims of the conservationists—and of Roosevelt, in this case—were clear: to preserve government ownership of the rich territories which had not yet been taken over by exploiters, and to establish regulation of what might become private property. The law relating to claims such as those that had been made in Alaska was also clear. The land which the government decided to release was to be turned over to small owners, pioneers and explorers, rather than to the type of combine Wall Street trust-makers might wish to form. Alaska, in other words, was to be spared control by monopolists. That was what the conservationists understood, and that was the law. The law's interpretation was likely to be a more complex task, of course, particularly as one's sympathies drifted away from the common people, as the sympathies of government officials were liable to do.

Of all the claims which had been pending in the Territory before entry was refused, the most important were the Cunningham claims, named after Clarence Cunningham, a Westerner who had gone to Alaska in 1903 and located thirty-three claims in the rich coal regions for interests which included Morgan and the Guggenheims. On its face, each of these claims was separate and distinct; collectively they were not to be consolidated, once they were approved. Yet what was to prevent individual claim holders from deciding to merge their interests, later on, if they should so choose? As conservative journals never tired of repeating, trusts made for efficiency and economy and were therefore good as well as inevitable.

In 1905 a special agent for the General Land Office, H. K. Love, began to suspect that some of the coal claims were fraudulent, deliberately arranged by monopolists, and he reported his suspicions to the Department of the Interior. Further research increased his doubts. In the fall of 1907 Louis R. Glavis, a young Land Office investigator who had become chief of the Field Division of the Territory and who was of a singularly loyal and conscientious makeup, made discoveries in Seattle which showed that at least some of the claims were not bona fide. Meanwhile Ballinger, newly appointed to the Land Office, ignored the Love report and ordered Glavis to grant the Cunningham claims entry. Glavis submitted his discoveries, and Ballinger revoked the order.

Glavis, unsupported by his superiors, persisted with his original investigations. Ballinger, having tried in vain to persuade Congress to validate the Cunningham claims, resigned his post in March 1908 and returned to private law practice, taking with him the praise of Roosevelt and Secretary of the Interior Garfield for his work in reorganizing the Land Office and putting it on an efficient basis.

When Taft assumed office the following March, one of his first acts was to dismiss Garfield, whom Roosevelt had expressly asked to be kept in the Cabinet. Garfield was humiliated, and it was for this reason, perhaps, rather than for ideals, that before leaving office he withdrew from entry hundreds of thousands of acres as water-power sites, and left the work of dealing with the situation so created to Taft's new Secretary of the Interior, who turned out to be none other than Richard Ballinger, Garfield's erstwhile subordinate.[1]

Ballinger set out to reorganize the Department as he had already reorganized the Land Office. With the approval of the new President, he canceled the Garfield withdrawals. He then sent a peremptory request to Louis Glavis for a report on the Cunningham claims showing why they should not be granted entry. This request was followed up by a telegram stating that the report must be submitted within sixty days. Glavis, bewildered, explained that it was impossible for him to report in that time. His investigations had brought new evidence of fraud to the surface, and this evidence required further research and study. The best he could do was promise to expedite his work as much as possible.

The very next month Ballinger and his associates attempted to pass the mysteriously persistent Cunningham claims, but were overruled by Attorney-General George W. Wickersham, to whom Glavis appealed for support.

When the sixty days were up, Glavis was forced to ask for more time to make his report. He was now aware that Ballinger, for reasons of his own, was personally determined to give away to monopolists what Glavis thought to be some of the most valuable lands in Alaska. Glavis was also aware of other facts relating to Ballinger's interest in the matter, but feeling the need for abiding by discipline, he respectfully explained his position. Now he received instructions which became more and more imperative, and he was finally informed that the claims were to be passed upon in July, and that another official in the Land Office was coming to Seattle to take over his duties at that time.

Glavis, in desperation, turned to Gifford Pinchot and asked him to intervene. Glavis was, of course, breaking discipline in appeal-

[1] The Taft viewpoint is best expressed in Henry S. Pringle, *William Howard Taft*, Farrar, New York, 1939.

ing over the head of his superior to a man in another department;
he was also openly impugning Ballinger's motives. But Glavis
could see no other course to take. Pinchot, thoroughly stirred by
his tale, did intervene and forced a postponement of the land-
grant trials until October. The young Land Office chief, however,
understood that entry had only been forestalled, not stopped:
Secretary Ballinger was not likely to wait idly for him to submit
his report. Glavis then asked Pinchot for a letter of introduction to
the President, and with that letter he obtained an interview with
Taft, to whom he related the entire story of his work and the
treatment he had received for it.

On September 13, 1909, Taft wrote a long letter—or sent a
letter signed with his name—to Ballinger, stating that he had
reviewed the matter completely and studied the evidence submitted by Glavis, Ballinger, and others. He had reached a decision: Ballinger had been fully justified in his actions, and Glavis,
on nothing but "shreds of suspicion," had taken it upon himself
to defy his chief and step outside his rights and duties. Taft approved Ballinger's procedure and recommended Glavis's dismissal.

Glavis was accordingly dismissed. A young man in an insignificant government post, he had dared to reach independent conclusions and run afoul of his superiors.

Glavis's downfall might have ended the incident, but Pinchot
was not satisfied to have it so. Not only had a grave wrong been
done to Glavis, but what was more important, valuable lands were
marked for delivery to monopolists. Pinchot was likewise concerned for the public water-power sites, which Ballinger was dispensing freely.

Rumors of differences between the Chief Forester and the Secretary of the Interior now began to be heard. Charges and counter-
charges began to leak out. The public, on the other hand, though
still unaware of the facts relating to the claims situation, was becoming more interested in Alaska. The opening of the Alaska-
Yukon-Pacific Exposition at Seattle was drawing attention to issues
involving territory far beyond the usual orbit of popular consciousness and understanding.

It was *Collier's* that first gave the Ballinger-Pinchot rumors an
examination in print. As early as June 22 *Collier's* had com-

mented on the fact that Taft was not keeping his tariff promises. Norman Hapgood did not accuse him outright of having broken his word; he simply mentioned that Taft had not kept it to date. One month later Hapgood was ready to declare that "Ballinger Should Go." The Pinchot-Glavis charges were catching interest, and it was evident that Hapgood and his fellow-editors had been keeping their eyes upon the new Secretary of the Interior. Details about Ballinger, Glavis, and the Cunningham claims were not yet public, and Hapgood and Collier were forced to rely upon independent analyses of Ballinger's work for proof of maladministration. They emphasized his dealings with Senator Heyburn, of Idaho, an anti-conservationist (for all the interest he had shown in the pure-food fight [2]) who had persuaded Ballinger to eliminate certain state forests from the national reserves. The Secretary had also been "reorganizing" again—sending experienced men away from posts at which they were eminently useful.

Less than a month later, Collier's repeated its sober demand for Ballinger's dismissal, and this time it pointed out that his differences with Pinchot were by no means personal. Policy was involved. The Department of the Interior had been throwing government land open to entry and had not been giving settlers preference. It was giving water-power sites away without notice to the Forest Service. Simple departmental courtesy, to say nothing of regulations, would have called for such notification.

More arresting, though at that time not sensational, was the revelation that Ballinger, after leaving the Land Office and before taking up his duties as Secretary, had acted as attorney for the Cunningham interests. This action had been plainly illegal. Government workers were cautioned against accepting positions with private companies whose affairs they had been considering from the government's standpoint. Collier's, though it lacked complete information on the Glavis case, was still able to point out that many lawyers had been disbarred for doing what Ballinger had done—and certainly had not been allowed to return to government work, to a Cabinet office, afterwards.

It was lack of information that kept the Collier's editors from coming to grips with Ballinger. Their instincts were, however,

[2] See Chapter XII.

right. In October they began a series of articles by the historian Agnes C. Laut on the fight for water in the West, and they tied up this subject with the battle being waged by Pinchot and the other conservationists. As for Ballinger himself, they went so far as to ask editorially whether the letter signed by Taft eulogizing the Secretary and calling for Glavis's dismissal had really been written by the President. The letter did not ring true. Taft, *Collier's* believed, was good-natured, an "easy mark," and misled.

On November 6, *Collier's* announced that the most important material yet available on Ballinger would be presented in the following issue. With that announcement the controversy ceased to be factional and became a public issue.

Glavis had been impressed by the gratuitous support from *Collier's*. When he was offered $3,000 for his story by another magazine, he refused it and, instead, arranged a meeting with Norman Hapgood, for whom he offered to write the story. Glavis stipulated that he was to receive no money for this work.[3]

On November 13, *Collier's* appeared with a cover bearing the question: "Are the Guggenheims in Charge of the Department of the Interior?" Glavis's article, entitled "The White-Washing of Ballinger," was a factual, unvarnished account of the mishaps to which he, Glavis, had been subjected. For attempting to prevent the loss of some of the most valuable lands in the Territory, he stated, he had been removed from his work. For attempting to call the attention of the President to injustice, he had been treated like a criminal. Glavis asked the public to judge whether or not his actions had justified this treatment.

The article stirred the country and called forth demands for a Congressional investigation of Glavis's charges. The conservative press declared sensationally that there was a conspiracy afoot to discredit the President and force upon the public the issue of a third term for Roosevelt. *Collier's*, in reply, printed a chronological list of its many commendatory and well-wishing statements regarding Taft, and repeated that it was interested only in getting to the bottom of the Pinchot-Ballinger feud.

[3] See Norman Hapgood's *The Changing Years*, Farrar & Rinehart, New York, 1930. The best account is Alpheus Thomas Mason, *Bureaucracy Convicts Itself*, Viking Press, New York, 1941.

In the meantime *Collier's* had been joined in its campaign by another magazine whose policy had been leading it directly to the present controversy. That *Hampton's* was almost as influential as *Collier's* in causing the ruin of Taft and his Secretary of the Interior has been entirely forgotten. *McClure's* and other magazines joined in the general protest against misconduct in high office, but none of these exerted *Hampton's* influence. *Hampton's*, in fact, took about the same position among the muckraking magazines that *McClure's* had taken earlier. It printed amazing quantities of articles that were original, precise, and popular. *Hampton's*, in 1909, was much more nearly indispensable than *McClure's*.

In October 1908, for example, Eugene P. Lyle, Jr., published his article "The Supreme Court," which showed the importance of the judiciary in the coming elections. The following April, Charles Edward Russell began the series "The Heart of the Railroad Problem," which was to be so fateful for *Hampton's*, and, therefore, for the entire muckraking movement. In June of that year John L. Mathews began, with "White Coal Mines and Water Farms," his truly great series on the importance of water power in the life of the country.

Mathews was no casual journalist but an expert in his field and a persuasive and compelling propagandist for conservation. In the course of his series he explained how water power was destined to succeed coal and wood in importance, and how, unless water-power sites were preserved for the public, those who controlled them were bound ultimately to control the nation. Coming down to present cases, Mathews described so tellingly the activities of General Electric and other concerns that he impeded and prevented several land and water-power grabs, including that of Muscle Shoals, which would have had far-reaching effects upon the standard of living in many parts of the country.

By the time Judson C. Welliver (later to become a corporation executive) began telling the story of the sugar trust in Congress and Cuba—this was Ben Hampton's next contribution to the larger story of trusts and natural resources—the Ballinger affair was being forced into the news by *Collier's*. John L. Mathews was sent off to report the matter for *Hampton's*. In November 1909 he reviewed the water-power aspects of Ballinger's policy and gave them a significance *Collier's* had failed to achieve. He devoted his next article to the Alaskan claims, which were of greater public interest if only because they more clearly involved the cross-purposes of individuals, Glavis and the Secretary of the Interior in particular. In considering the claims Mathews disentangled their complexities and brought to the surface obscure and apparently innocent questions of property rights and government procedure. He showed the importance of the few railroads that extended into the Territory, proved how necessary it was for monopolists to control them, and, fixing on the Cunningham claims, demonstrated how those who owned the coal resources of Alaska would finally gain control of the copper mines in the vicinity.

Eugene Lyle had been running important articles on the history of mining in America, which articles included in detail the story of the rise of the Guggenheims. Now Mathews stated boldly (as *Collier's* had not yet cared to do) that the Department of the Interior was in collusion with the Guggenheim and Morgan interests to facilitate the passage of Alaskan coal and water-power resources into private hands. Mathews did not hesitate to name Taft himself as a party to the conspiracy. Taft, of course, did not consider it a conspiracy, but the muckraker's interpretation was not one Taft or his friends could argue in the open. Mathews, for example, reported an interview with Ballinger in which the Secretary delivered himself of coarse and careless expressions full of anti-conservationist feeling—expressions which he was forced to deny publicly. Mathews repeated the conversation, and in the January issue of *Hampton's* printed a detailed and notarized statement of the interview. The statement was not answered.

Collier's, continuing its own campaign, printed the opinions of readers and sympathetic newspapers. It satirized Taft for having termed Glavis's charges "shreds of suspicion," and brought up new evidence of Ballinger's relations to the "Morganheims." C. P. Connolly, who had written many telling articles for *Collier's* since his series on the Haywood trial, was now brought into the case. On December 18 he published his famous article "Can This Be White-Washed Also?", which contained legal analyses and revelations that carried public interest in Ballinger to the highest point yet.

It was this article which finally forced a Congressional investigation of the accusations leveled at Ballinger by Glavis and Pinchot. Pinchot was now in Glavis's position, and like Glavis he had gone out of bounds: he had released government information to the newspapers and had been immediately dismissed by Taft for insubordination. Just as Glavis had had no honorable alternative, so there was nothing else Pinchot could have done; but whether or not he would be vindicated rested entirely with the public and, presumably, with the investigating committee.

In the House and in the Senate committees were now chosen. Speaker Cannon, the "Czar" of the House, now busily fighting the insurgents who were attempting to break his absolute power over them, tried to name the representatives who would participate in the investigation. In the ensuing debates he was defeated—this being the first of his major defeats. As Norman Hapgood later decided when reviewing the case, Cannon's failure to control the House at this juncture saved the day for the conservationists. It made possible the appointment of Democrats to the committee and heartened those who hoped that the trial would be honestly conducted.

Payne Whitney, the son of the traction magnate, was an "insider" in politics, having been an important subscriber to campaign treasuries. He was also a liberal and a friend of Robert J. Collier's, and he was sympathetic toward Collier's editorial purposes. Now he came from Washington to inform his friend of serious developments: he had secret information to the effect that high Republican leaders were determined to teach *Collier's* a lesson. The committee that was to judge the charges of Glavis and Pinchot—the majority of the Committee were Republicans—had instructions to whitewash Ballinger completely. *Collier's* was then to be sued for a million dollars on the ground of slander.[4]

Under the circumstances it was practically impossible for this plan, which had been prepared in the offices of the Department of the Interior—or in the White House—to fail. The charges of the defendants, Glavis and Pinchot, were vulnerable in that there was no final, positive proof that Ballinger and the President had

[4] See Hapgood's *The Changing Years, op. cit.*

acted improperly. If the Committee chose to be unconvinced that they had so acted, no circumstantial evidence, though a thousand times multiplied, would break that attitude. And the Committee's conclusions would have a damning effect on *Collier's* in the courts.

An emergency council of war was held by the conservationists. At the New York office of Henry L. Stimson, then acting as ex-Secretary Garfield's adviser, were convened a number of interested persons. Pinchot and his brother Amos, as well as Pinchot's attorney, George Wharton Pepper, and Garfield, Hapgood, and Collier were present. They discussed the choice of a suitable attorney for Glavis and approved Hapgood's suggestion of Louis D. Brandeis. The Boston lawyer was offered $25,000 by Collier to conduct the defense, and having accepted the commission, he secluded himself for a week in order to study the evidence, seeing no one in that time but Norman Hapgood. He pored over the complex and voluminous records of the Land Office, broke them down and mastered them; and when he finally appeared before the investigating committee he was practically as familiar with the material involved as were those who had prepared it and manipulated it for their own ends.

As the investigation began, *Collier's* and *Hampton's* continued to drag into the open information which showed that the Glavis incident was no matter involving trifling justice or injustice. Ballinger had been made Secretary of the Interior to carry out specific public purposes. In his letter exonerating the Secretary, Taft had asserted that the Secretary committed no offense in having acted as attorney for the Cunningham interests. Ballinger's acquaintance with the details of their claims, said Taft, had been merely "formal," and he had taken on work for them in good faith, ethically, as any other lawyer might have done. But *Collier's* and *Hampton's* both showed that Ballinger's acquaintance with the claims had been anything but formal. The "Morganheims" were deeply interested in the functions of the Department of the Interior, and Taft's choice of Ballinger, clouded though it was by rationalizations, had been deliberate—the consequence of earnest planning by interested individuals. Exculpation of Ballinger would therefore mean more than a victory for him; it would mean vindication of an official attitude toward the public domain, and, concretely, of a determination to deal with the public domain in a way which rightly or wrongly was calculated to outrage the muck-rakers and, to judge from popular response to their articles, the general public.

Connolly, speaking for his magazine, described Ballinger's policy as constituting a raid on the public lands. Hampton himself summed up the material which had been appearing in his magazine, doing so in an article he prepared himself and published under his own name, in order to demonstrate his responsibility for the accusations that had been made editorially in *Hampton's* and in the Mathews articles. Hampton advocated a clear program for Alaska and for government reserves in general, and his program premised public ownership of resources and railroads. It is worth underscoring that Hampton thus showed he was ready for state Socialism and was more consistently, more responsibly, so than Hearst had been. His program represented the clearest and most courageous conclusions of muckraking thought; and certainly the Ballinger campaign showed the power of these convictions in action.

On March 26, *Collier's* devoted the major part of its issue to the case that was being tried in Washington. Its cover was illustrated with a bill of indictment against Ballinger. C. P. Connolly contributed the article "Ballinger—Shyster," which so aggravated the Secretary that one of his aides, during a session of the hearings, made an unrestrained attack upon Connolly, calling him a yellow journalist and a coward who had deserted a ship in distress. This curious libel was due to his having confused C. P. Connolly with the sea-story writer, James Brendan Connolly, also a contributor to *Collier's*, who had described a personal experience aboard ship in which, as a matter of fact, he had been anything but a coward!

The magazine campaign continued to keep Ballinger and his Department in the news, but matters remained uncertain in the committee hearings. These were being conducted under the chairmanship of Senator Knute Nelson of Minnesota, a reactionary who spared no efforts to confuse and hinder the defense. If the public accepted Ballinger as a tool of monopolists, it seemed probable that the investigation would end without having drawn a convincing picture of corruption. The public could not digest the countless details involving Alaska, governmental powers and obliga-

Collier's
THE NATIONAL WEEKLY

COURT OF PUBLIC MORALS

THE AMERICAN PEOPLE
against
RICHARD A. BALLINGER

INDICTMENT

A TRUE BILL.

UNCLE SAM
Foreman.

A "COLLIER'S" BROADSIDE

tions, and personal intentions. Glavis's narrative, honest and organized though it was, was not easy to grasp, and it mentioned no single instance of flagrant crime which could be laid to the Secretary. The exoneration of Ballinger having been prepared, therefore, the American Dreyfus Case (as *Collier's* called it) seemed fated to take the same course the French trials had originally followed—with like results, and for the same reasons.

One night Brandeis, in a mood of great excitement, asked Hapgood to take a walk with him. As they walked he asked the editor whether he had noticed anything "queer" about a report on the Glavis case by Attorney-General Wickersham, which Taft had submitted as part of the evidence upon which he had based his conclusions. (Although Wickersham had at first intervened to prevent entry of the Cunningham claims, further investigation and study of Ballinger's own report had apparently convinced him that Ballinger had acted and was acting in good faith.) Hapgood answered that he had noticed nothing strange in the Wickersham report, and Brandeis now explained.

Taft's letter to Ballinger was dated September 13, 1909. Wickersham's report to Taft was dated September 11. The Ballinger report of half a million words had been given to Wickersham to study *just one week before he sent his own report to the President*. The Ballinger report was not all the Attorney-General had required for his study: he had had to consult Glavis's version of the facts, the Land Office regulations, and other supplementary material—for his report was thorough in its references to many intricate documents.

How, demanded Brandeis, could Wickersham have mastered all that material *within a week*, even if he had done nothing else and had not needed time to prepare his own report?

Hapgood, stunned, was asked to consider the possibility that the President, when he made his decision, had not had the Wickersham report on hand; that this report had been written *afterward* to give authority to Taft's opinion, and then had been predated.

This frightening theory marked a turning point in the hearings. Brandeis, following up the clue, found his proof in a casual passage in the Wickersham report which mentioned an event that had not occurred until *after* the date on the document. He bided his time. And now, miraculously, a secretary was enlisted to support the accusation of fraud. Ballinger and Taft were then drawn into falsehood before they were finally forced to confess that the Wickersham report had not been prepared until after Glavis's discharge. Taft's last defense—namely, that the false date had been appended "merely to stress" the time when the Attorney-General rendered an oral report—made no impression on the listeners. Taft and his Secretary of the Interior now stood exposed as having deliberately sacrificed Glavis in order to be free of a persistent obstacle to the illegal allocation of public property.

It was the lying, Brandeis later observed, that undermined the President and Ballinger. Had they brazened it out, stood by their policy, and merely asserted that they had done what seemed to them just, Glavis and Pinchot would have been defeated at the hearings, the public would have forgotten, and *Collier's* would subsequently have been destroyed. But the fact that Taft and Ballinger had concocted evidence against their subordinates told the public more than anything *Collier's* or *Hampton's* had been able to tell: it suggested collusion of the most secret and vicious kind.

The investigating committee, with its Republican majority, reported that Ballinger was competent and honorable. The minority report gave a different story, and this was the one which the public accepted. *Collier's* was not sued for slander, and in the fall elections of 1910 popular revulsion against Taft lost for the Republican Party its majority in the Lower House.

Collier's and *Hampton's*, however, redoubled their demand for Ballinger's dismissal, and now that his "usefulness was impaired," Taft asked for his resignation. Amazingly, Ballinger refused to resign. Why? asked Hampton sardonically. Why didn't the President dismiss him anyhow? Was Taft afraid of him? Did Ballinger know something Taft would not want publicized? Such distressing comment continued to be heard until Ballinger did finally resign and relieve the administration of his embarrassing presence.

Conservation, with all it implied, was triumphant in that year. The Cunningham claims were not granted. The magazines continued to familiarize the public with details of Alaska which Jack London had not described, and warned of the need for keeping alert to developments there. Pinchot published *The Fight for Conservation,* in it expressing his generous conservationist convictions. Such novels and studies about conservation as Stewart Edward White's *The Rules of the Game* were read attentively. In September 1910 the conservationists met at St. Paul and held the most vigorous sessions in their history.

Meanwhile *Hampton's* cracked down on the sugar trust. Judson C. Welliver showed its relationship to the Mormon Church and showed also how the beet sugar industry, fostered by the government, had been absorbed by the trust in order to protect its tariff. As a direct result of this article, the monopoly was placed under investigation by the Federal Department of Justice and was subsequently forced to reorganize.

"Never before in the history of journalistic enterprise," Hampton announced proudly, "have such big and prompt results been secured from an exposure of this kind."

Hampton went on to say that his magazine was being sneered at as the last of the muckraking organs. He warned against that misapprehension. It was true that there had been an apparent lag in muckraking during the last year of Roosevelt's administration—a lag that had made *Hampton's* outstanding for its principles and clear-sighted understanding of trends. But the Ballinger exposé, the excitement it had stirred up, the approval it had received, should show, Hampton insisted, that muckraking had by no means gone out of style. It was just becoming efficient. So long as there was muck, there had to be muckraking: it was a necessary agency in American life. So long as its spirit endured, Hampton declared, democracy as it was understood by Americans would prevail.[5]

[5] The contrast of events and principals with the later Watergate affair of the 1970's is striking. For a retrospective view, see pp. 412-413, and Filler, *Appointment at Armageddon.*

XXVII. CROSSROADS

MUCKRAKING in 1910 was free, virile, and aggressive. It was based confidently on the wide reading public which turned to it for guidance as well as entertainment. The magazines that had no other goal but to "entertain"—such magazines as *Book News* and *Putnam's,* as well as the standard and respectable periodicals— were vastly weaker than the muckraking organs in content and influence. The success of muckraking, which was a cultural as well as an educational force, showed that the masses were socially conscious to an unprecedented degree.

It is significant that the readers supported their magazines with money as well as with approval. *Success, Hampton's,* and others, despite the contempt of more aristocratic publishers, did not hesitate to ask for such support on the basis of their public-service campaigns, and they received it. They sold large blocks of stock to readers who felt that financial aid to such benefactors constituted not merely a mode of investment but also a personal and patriotic duty.

The big circulations of the muckraking magazines attracted the financially necessary advertisers who, although they suffered from the exposures, nevertheless wanted to use such popular organs. The crusading magazines were, after all, primarily businesses rather than philanthropic institutions—even though Ben Hampton, to take a notable example, was now living no better than he had before he pushed his magazine to the front and tied up all his money in the venture. Being businesses, the magazines depended on advertising support.

Dependence upon advertisers showed itself in many turns of policy. This does not mean that the muckraking editors, or even the publishers, were necessarily insincere or opportunistic, even when they happened to lack the full crusading spirit of a B. O. Flower. The magazines selected by the corporations for advertis-

341

ing purposes were often chosen by what Upton Sinclair was to call "artificial selection"; that is, since all the magazines were not equally set against all the corporations, each magazine could come to terms with some corporations.

B. O. Flower himself, to illustrate, was not prevented by his muckraking convictions from becoming the dupe of R. C. Flower, whom *Collier's* exposed as a notorious quack.[1] B. O. Flower was president of the "R. C. Flower Medicine Company" (although it should be added in extenuation that he served in that capacity before the great exposés in the field of patent medicines). He was also president of the League for Medical Freedom, which consistently propagandized against government supervision of medicine. As chief pamphleteer, Flower denounced compulsory medical inspection and official warnings against the possibility of the spread of the bubonic plague, terming these part of a plot by the American Medical Association to "monopolize" the field of medicine. Flower felt that proprietary medicines were less harmful than doctors!

These were extraordinary convictions for a man who otherwise held to an unchanging level of radical thought and sympathy, but they could be traced to his interest in "spiritual" things and, specifically, to his interest in faith healing and Christian Science. These convictions made him no more pleasing to those who were antagonized by his muckraking crusades than to the muckrakers themselves. But they were of great service to advertisers—in this case, to patent-medicine advertisers.

The strength of the muckraking magazines, however, lay ultimately in the public demand for exposure. The magazines were as strong as their strongest articles rather than their weakest; and it was the muckrakers proper, rather than their editors, who continued to satisfy the public demand.

Politically the muckrakers found their best support in the Republican Progressives, led by La Follette, who began to multiply about 1909 and, by the following year, had important victories to their credit and were recognizably a movement. Heretofore

---

[1] See *Collier's*, June 3, 1911; also George Seldes, *The Freedom of the Press*, Bobbs-Merrill Co., Indianapolis, 1935.

reform had been achieved despite, or regardless of, party platforms. The increase of the Progressives made it plain that the base of reform had been widened, and that a thoroughly roused public was intent on seeing through a work which had been started, approximately, with the beginning of the *McClure's* campaigns. How far that work was to go, no one knew—it had long since slipped from the hands of its original managers—but the Progressives had already adopted major planks from the Socialist platform and were no longer frightened by its daring. They took pains, it is true, to draw sharp lines of distinction between their proposals and those of the Socialists, dilating on the "essential" differences between Socialism and democracy, but even this practice showed, although negatively, that the impulse toward government regulation had gone farther than ever before in the nation's history. If Progressivism had the air of having come from nowhere, actually it was an end-product of all the movements that had challenged social conditions and institutions.

One of the most influential progressive groups was The People's Lobby, which owed its existence to *Success*. As early as September 1906 *Success* announced that it had received a remarkable suggestion from its contributor, Henry Beach Needham. Washington, said Needham, was overrun with lobbies: there was a railroad lobby, a lumber lobby, a beef lobby. Why should there not also be a People's Lobby? It was certain to work, he declared; it was a vital, democratic necessity. It could be made unreservedly nonpartisan, the mouthpiece of the great, truth-seeking public, a positive and decisive influence upon Congress.

Success spoke to a ready audience, for its crusades had been many and successful. Paul Latske had exposed the telegraph trust; Frank Fayant was exposing the wireless telegraph bubble; Gilson Gardner, Washington correspondent, was telling about the "Third House" of the lobbyists; and Samuel Merwin was about to print his famous series, "Drugging a Race," the material for which he had gathered during a long journey through China. The proposal for a People's Lobby was, then, received with enthusiasm.

Success now set out to make the idea a reality. The next month it was able to print a list of outstanding reformers who had accepted places on the governing board of the Lobby. These included Francis J. Heney; John Mitchell, President of the United Mine Workers; William Allen White; Benjamin Ide Wheeler, President of the University of California; Mark Twain; and Lincoln Steffens—journalists, labor-unionists, politicians, educators. Other important names were quickly added. Readers were urged to support a permanent bureau in Washington, and Needham himself, pointing to the various "press muzzles" that were to be found in the Capital, explained how the bureau would function.

Data collected by experts would give the facts about the various issues confronting Congress. Truthful letters—factual, explanatory, impartial—were to be sent to subscribers and to the newspapers. The hope was expressed that

when the newspapers, which are almost wholly honest [sic] can get this accurate and truthful letter, they will cease to accept the tainted letters of the corporations, and we shall have honest public opinion throughout the United States.

Such expectations are likely to seem farfetched to modern readers, but it is important to remember that they were not merely voiced; they existed at a time when heavy social pressure was being applied to achieve reforms. If the expectations did not materialize, they were at least tested. Before The People's Lobby had outplayed its role, in fact, real results were obtained by those who directed it.

On November 21, 1906, officers of the Lobby were elected, and the organization was formally launched.[2] Mark Sullivan was its president and Henry Beach Needham its secretary. The workers of the Lobby, becoming part of the entire muckraking movement, rapidly found their stride. *Success* reported the Lobby's activities and supplemented them with a department, "The Inside of Washington," which was conducted anonymously and released news of important intrigues inside Congressional circles. The development of this organized muckraking lobby coincided with and assisted organized opposition to the autocracy existing in the House and Senate.

Joseph Cannon, Speaker of the House, was the direct target of this opposition. David Graham Phillips had already expressed

---

[2] For a later People's Lobby of distinction, Benjamin C. Marsh, *Lobbyist for the People*, Public Affairs Press, Washington, D.C., 1953.

popular opinion of Senator Aldrich, and a progressive bloc, small but determined, was tirelessly preparing his downfall. Cannon had as yet been accorded no similar consideration. On May 23, 1908, and again on May 30, William Hard attacked the "Czar" in the pages of *Collier's*. Sporadic criticism of the Illinois Representative continued to appear in that magazine until, on March 6 of the following year, Mark Sullivan took over the work and put it upon a firm basis.

The few articles Sullivan had published under his own name since joining *Collier's* had been strong but fugitive. He now emerged as the magazine's expert on Congressional affairs, and from the first struck powerful blows which quickly gave him high rank among the muckrakers. Congress to him meant Cannon in the House and Aldrich in the Senate, and he made it clear that he had no interest in writing petty, equivocal Washington gossip in the manner of the ordinary correspondent. He meant to deal only with principals. Cannon and Aldrich had to go, and whoever defended them had to go likewise. Whoever opposed them—"insurgents," Sullivan named these fighters—Western Representatives like Charles Lindbergh and Victor Murdock, Western Senators like La Follette and Beveridge—deserved support and encouragement.

While Sullivan pounded away at Cannonism so persistently that he came to be known as the "official journalist of the Progressive movement," *Success* carried on its own fight against the "Czar" and his works. It excoriated him in an article about "The Barnacles on the Ship of State." In April 1909 it congratulated its readers on the influence they were exerting in Washington through the People's Lobby, and explained the need for taking from Cannon his arbitrary control of the House committees.

Readers were now pouring letters into the offices of the Bureau in protest against this dictatorial power. Judge Lindsey, more than ever alert to such official crime as he had uncovered, wrote in to offer his approval and encouragement in the fight. So much excitement did *Collier's* and *Success* stir up that Cannon was driven to answer their attacks in an article, prepared for *Century*, in which he explained that there was no lack of democracy in the House—the contrary was true—and that he was being baited by the magazines for sordid and mercenary reasons.

Success, with Samuel Merwin now at the editorial helm, printed its reply to this article. It was true, said *Success,* that Cannon's powers were few; he had only the power to appoint the working committees—that was all! It happened, however, that he appointed a conservative Republican majority to the Committee of Rules, which interpreted and administered the eight volumes of rules. He appointed all the Republican members of all the committees, and saw to it that opponents were kept securely in their places and punished when they became intractable. He simply ignored anyone who ventured to suggest amendments to the rules.

That was Cannonism, and that was the method of House procedure which *Success* and *Collier's* resolved to end. Their campaign continued; it was parallel to that which involved Ballinger and the Department of the Interior, and it gained influence through it. While what Sullivan was later—much later—to call a "spirit of rebellion for rebellion's sake" won adherents in Congress, the strength of the Progressives mounted. By January 1910, *Success* was warranted in printing an exultant article, "The End of Cannonism," by Judson C. Welliver, which prophesied the Speaker's early defeat. It was this issue of the magazine, with its realistic and therefore unflattering picture of the "Czar," used as a frontispiece, which caused Cannon to exclaim: "Damn *Success!* Who in hell is Edward E. Higgins?" [3]

Edward E. Higgins was the publisher of the magazine and had been its directing hand ever since Orison Swett Marden had lost the right to print anything but his personal expressions of uplift and optimism. Cannon was not asking an irrelevant question, and Higgins, as well as Samuel Merwin, who besides editing the periodical had also invested in it, were to hear an answer to that question.

Meanwhile George W. Norris of Nebraska, a leader of the insurgents in the House, studied the rules and precedents governing it and tried to discover a means by which Cannon's power could be challenged. He failed to find a legal weapon, but fortunately the time had passed when procedure could by itself determine power. A rising tide was making progressivism invincible.

[3] See George French's "The Damnation of the Magazine," *Twentieth Century Magazine,* May 1912.

On March 17, 1910, after a wild session during which Cannon tried vainly to control his forces, Norris moved that the Committee on Rules be hereafter elected by the House as a body instead of being appointed by the Speaker. The ensuing furious debate lasted twenty-nine hours, and the Republican insurgents, uniting with the Democrats, finally carried the day, winning by thirty-five votes.

The muckraking magazines were triumphant. "What Is 'Joe' Cannon?" asked A. H. Lewis bluntly in *Cosmopolitan*, and he answered in terms the speaker could understand. *Success* took due credit for its part in the victory, and as for Mark Sullivan, "Next, Aldrich!" he cried. The movement for freedom from committee rule was irresistible, and within three months the master of the Senate was compelled to join Cannon in the rout.

The overthrow of the Republican machine was complete. *Collier's* printed a "History of a Political Revolution," which consisted of a series of facsimiles of Sullivan's pages on Congress. Naturally *Collier's* did not recognize the work of *Success*, which work was of a type likely to seem "sensational" to Hapgood and his colleagues, but it hardly gave itself undue honor for the triumph. Cannon might well have damned Sullivan as well as *Success*, although Sullivan, as he was to explain, had fought him impersonally and was, long after, in *Our Times* and in his autobiography, to pay eloquent tribute to the Speaker's "bigness" and "realism." In any case, Cannon was dethroned and so was Aldrich. *Collier's* printed one of its inimitable pictures showing Cannon standing in the shadows observing the sunset, and being told by the Rhode Island Senator that it was time for them to go home.

The fall elections completed the Republican debacle. Taft lost the House to the Democrats, and his majority in the Senate was narrowed to ten. It was only a year and a half since he had assumed office, and already he had yielded new life, such life as they had not had since 1896, to the Democrats. It was not even certain that in 1912 Taft could control his own insurgents—those who had contributed so much to his defeats.

The Progressive movement offered the straightest road to genuine democracy. The Progressives, and in the first place their leader La Follette, could be expected to assume responsibility for measures to carry the revolution against monopoly to its permanent conclusions. That, broadly put, was the point of view of such muckrakers as Mark Sullivan and of reformers who found their way into movements such as that for woman suffrage.

It was the current unrest and the difficulties of battle that led some men and women to more radical expression and even carried a number of them into the Socialist Party. It was the times that made fervid revolutionists of men like Arthur Bullard and the heir to Chicago newspaper millions, Joseph Medill Patterson, later editor and proprietor of the New York *Daily News*. Not only Charles Edward Russell, but such writers as Ray Stannard Baker, surveyed the political scene and saw signs that the old parties were on the way out.

Many muckrakers, like Rheta Childe Dorr, became "highbrow Socialists" and "explored," as she says, the variegated radical movement of the new intellectuals which was beginning to shape itself in centers such as Greenwich Village. *The Masses* was created in 1911. One year later *Poetry: A Magazine of Verse* was founded in Chicago by Harriet Monroe. Now the "little magazine" movement was in full swing. The younger writers evidently did not find muckraking sufficient for their needs. They had no will to carry on the work the muckrakers had so painfully established; they found no joy in the solid family virtues, the middle-class virtues, which served the muckrakers as foundation stones. The middle of the road suited them not at all. They came to New York like John Reed to be poets, and like Reed to identify themselves with the cause of labor. Or, like Floyd Dell, they followed the arts.

Randolph Bourne was almost alone among the younger intellectuals in that he was not impatient to tear himself loose from the middle-class tradition. Like his fellows he was more concerned with literature than with life as a whole. Unlike them, he recognized that in occupying himself with literature he was merely working a field that was being separated from the larger field the muckrakers had been forced to till. The contempt for "journalism" which so many of the new intellectuals professed was clearly a contempt of the middle-class from which they had come and from which they were determined to escape.

"What Are You Going to Do About It?" Charles Edward Russell asked in a series for *Cosmopolitan* in 1910. In this last of the important series on graft which the muckrakers produced, Russell detailed corruption as it was to be found in many states. His articles found their audience, but not among the younger readers. These read muckraking literature only in order to determine what they were to do with their own lives; they were not concerned with graft. Graft, carried on crudely or with modern flourishes, was for them a logical product of capitalism, and part of it. Socialism alone could end it, and Socialism was to be achieved only through the liberation of the working-class. Already the younger men were repeating the revolutionary slogans which had previously belonged to Continental movements.

The elders whom the young radical intellectuals admired and sought out, and to some degree imitated, were people like Emma Goldman, Clarence Darrow, Bill Haywood, and—among the muckrakers—Upton Sinclair. Even Hutchins Hapgood, who with his pleasure in art and freedom found himself at home among the younger experimentalists, had no common status with them, because of his individual, rather than Socialistic, approach to their problems and ideas. The new radical generation made a fetish of labor—working-class labor—although, in practice, they busied themselves with preparing careers that were to become balanced and substantial, among the best talents, in the postwar years. The possibility of war itself had as little place in their consciousness as in that of the muckrakers.

Labor, to be sure, had come a long way since the Haywood trial had shown its dimensions to the nation at large. Momentous strikes had knit the unions together and provided news to supplement the muckrakers' accounts of business unification. If business had been centralized, so had labor. It would seem that the muckrakers, with their informed, factual understanding of social issues, had never been more necessary than now. But labor, in its I.W.W. phases, had no desire for muckraking interpreters. It preferred the passion and partisanship of the younger radicals to such appreciation as the muckrakers had to offer.

The Socialist Party thrived on such tendencies, but the I.W.W., if it won the full admiration of the radical intellectuals and furnished a graph of class war in America, did not grow in numbers.

It was not the I.W.W. but, as in the case of the Haywood trial, an A. F. of L. unit, the Structural Iron Workers' Union, which in 1911 provided the formula for the new age that was being superimposed on the muckraking era. Although reform mounted step by step until the World War engulfed all the reformers, muckraking ceased being a major influence before that time. The McNamara case, which involved muckrakers, Socialists, and labor officials—and of course their opponents—created at least one dividing line between the old and the new.

Lincoln Steffens now thought he was finding his way "out of the muck." He was tired of exposure, for although a good thing in itself—good at any time—it still did not probe to the bottom. Muckraking had to be supplemented by something else: Socialism, perhaps. Many of Steffens's younger friends confidently expected him to join them in the Socialist Party.

Steffens was not likely to give his energies to a party. He had too much interest in individuals; he had too much appreciation of the human virtues as well as failings that were to be found in any man, capitalist or proletarian. Yet he knew that there must be some principle, some motive, that would induce men in the mass to work for common and progressive goals. Had Steffens been a European, his cynicism and clear view of reality might have made him a revolutionist; it all but did so years later, when he was old. But as an American he valued democracy and knew that, to have a future, democracy must be able to provide a solution for class troubles.

That he should have hit upon the Golden Rule as a working principle may seem incredible, but it should be remembered that he had seen it work for "Golden Rule" Jones. Steffens himself had often made Wall Street consciously pay the expenses of radical campaigns and projects. The entire muckraking movement, with its quest for justice, involved an appeal to the Golden Rule. The Golden Rule could be made to work, despite the fact that labor, in its most desperate forays, in its most direct clashes with capital, did not ask for justice, but simply fought for life.

"When justice is on trial, there is no justice," said Bill Haywood. There must be, Steffens decided—justice and mercy both; and when on October 1, 1910, the Los Angeles *Times* building was destroyed by a dynamite blast, and fifteen men were killed and half a million dollars' worth of property was demolished, Steffens felt the urge to interest himself in the case.

While Steffens busied himself with plans for sending reports to various newspapers, the case assumed national proportions. Why the *Times* building should have been singled out for wrecking was no secret. San Francisco possessed a strong labor movement, but Los Angeles was open-shop; and one of the prime reasons for the situation was General Otis, the owner of the *Times*, a fierce old man who was labor's most determined foe. The Structural Iron Workers' Union had fought him on many occasions, and a fight against the open shop was now in progress. Feeling was so high that it had divided the city and made the radical and labor forces powerful enough to threaten politically those who controlled municipal affairs.

Dynamite had been a weapon in building-trades disputes before, but never had it taken such a toll. When the McNamara brothers, officers in the Structural Iron Workers' Union, were arrested and charged with the crime, Steffens assumed that they were implicated, and he was amazed at the attitude of the radicals with whom he discussed the matter in New York. They, who had so often advocated "direct action," now vehemently insisted that the McNamaras were innocent and that the case against them was nothing but a frame-up. It was the Haywood case all over again, but with this difference: the new generation of labor defenders was less honest than the country at large had been in 1906. They were admittedly advocates of class war; yet it was still impossible to preach I.W.W. gospel in the courts and at the same time hope for acquittal. Then—"Let capital prove its case," the radicals said. To Steffens it seemed that in standing behind a fiction of innocence, in demanding acquittal instead of telling the country why dynamitings occurred, the labor defenders lost something true and significant from their purposes and opened the way for lies that might finally enmesh them completely.

Steffens, for one, wanted the truth. Perhaps it was the Haywood case all over again, and he might just as well have been George Kibbe Turner interviewing Harry Orchard, or C. P. Connolly studying the evidence with earnestness and precision. Steffens differed from them in one respect at least: he was a friend of the defendants, who felt that they, too, had a case; and he was not so much concerned with the evidence as with devising some means whereby he could make their case clear to the world.

This was beyond all question a forward step in muckraking thought. If exposure was not enough, then evidence was not enough. If the muckrakers had saved Haywood by simply giving the facts, they would have to do more to save the McNamara brothers, who as certainly deserved saving as Haywood, if they were to continue to be decisive factors in labor disputes. So, while C. P. Connolly was sent by *Collier's* to Los Angeles to do what he had done in the earlier case—to report the facts—Steffens, keeping in mind that justice was on trial, went in a more positive frame of mind.

Steffens could hardly have found less encouraging circumstances for his kind of justice than he found in Los Angeles. That city was in ferment. Sympathy for the defendants had so multiplied Socialist support that it seemed probable that Job Harriman, Socialist candidate for mayor, would be elected. The conservative forces were frantically determined to see the McNamaras to their death. The prosecution, and the defense headed by Clarence Darrow, were fighting with every means to insure verdicts in their favor. Large sums of money to carry on the fight had been raised on both sides, and the money was being spent with no regard for legal restrictions. This was, indeed, class war.

Steffens soon convinced himself that the labor leaders were guilty as charged. Since he had come West not to judge them but to help them, he was neither surprised nor daunted. If they were guilty, so were those who had driven them to seek redress with dynamite. That had to be made clear. Above all, justice had to be achieved in their trial, and this meant that those who were planning the condemnation of the McNamaras, who were set upon having their lives in atonement, would have to be persuaded that they would lose by revenge. The class struggle was not to be stopped by terror; the death of the McNamaras was certain to intensify it. Confident in the power of the Golden Rule, Steffens was determined to convince the prosecution of the value and justice of a compromise.

The temperamental Darrow, now in despair, now certain of victory, listened to him reluctantly. Since Darrow, a veteran of labor disputes, had known venom and fraud at close range, it was hardly to be expected that he would hear Steffens's proposal with patience. But Darrow was desperate; he knew what evidence the prosecution had, and he was more than afraid the McNamaras would be convicted. He reflected (says Steffens), considered, but then threw up his hands. Would the local employers let the prisoners go? And if, by some fantastic chance, they could be persuaded to do so, would the Eastern employers who had suffered from dynamite acquiesce? It was impossible.

Nevertheless Darrow gave a free hand to Steffens, on condition that the journalist would in no way implicate the defense or suggest that it was anxious to effect a compromise. Steffens went ahead to beard the "big, bad men," the "few men who actually govern this town . . . the kind of men who act off their own bats, don't have to consult others, and who, when they set out to do something, good or bad, put it over." The entire story is told in his *Autobiography:* how he won over the politicians, the businessmen, and finally General Otis himself, the arch-enemy of labor, to the idea of a compromise based on mercy as well as justice and practical sense.

Upton Sinclair was to complain that his younger friends of the postwar period refused to believe his stories of the muckraking era and declared that such events could not have really happened. Perhaps that explains why Steffens's account of his dealings with the Los Angeles capitalists made no impression when it was told to a new generation of readers, and why it brought about no new review of the McNamara case. It was evidently read as a good story rather than as a serious version of past and important events.

Extraordinary Steffens's story was. *But what significant relation did Steffens's dealings have to what finally occurred in the case?* On November 28, Darrow was accused of having been caught red-handed in an attempt to bribe a juror! Steffens never believed that he had made such a move; Darrow was apparently aware that Steffens's negotiations with the prosecution's backers were going satisfactorily. Yet did Darrow really have faith that those negotiations would come to anything? Did he ever actually prove that he had not participated in an attempt to bribe?

At any rate, the McNamaras confessed to the dynamiting, and

confessed *before* election day, to the ruin of Socialist Party hopes. This development led objective reporters to conclude that the McNamaras had been *forced* to confess, that they had accepted a compromise based on Darrow's personal negotiations, rather than that they had consented, in the interests of justice and enlightenment, to a compromise arrived at by Steffens—and then had been betrayed. Was the defeat of the Socialists, in other words, part of the agreement which Darrow ultimately arrived at with the prosecution? So C. P. Connolly suggested in the important story he wrote for *Collier's* entitled "The Saving of Clarence Darrow." Connolly did not doubt the altruistic motives of Lincoln Steffens; he felt that Darrow had used the muckraker as a screen in order to prevent a total collapse of the defense.

In any event, labor now stood disgraced. Los Angeles was strewn with the Socialist campaign buttons which disillusioned voters had thrown away. Darrow faced prison for criminal complicity in bribery, and as for Steffens—"I am going to kill that Golden Rule fellow," a labor leader vowed to a group of New York radicals who were stupefied by the dramatic close of the case. There can be no doubt that the labor leader's feeling against the man who was being called a Red by everyone except the Reds was shared by comrades who believed that Steffens's interference had somehow helped to bring on a miscarriage of "working-class justice."

C. P. Connolly was satisfied with the close of the case. It had, he insisted, cleared the atmosphere. Bribery must be condemned no matter who perpetrated it; muckrakers like himself could excuse no one. But if Steffens was damned on all sides, Connolly was doomed. This is easier to say today than it was in 1912. For Connolly continued to receive respectful hearings in the magazines. His series "Big Business and the Bench," printed in *Everybody's* in 1913, was as strong as his earlier articles. For it he was slandered by a Memphis lawyer, whom he afterward sued successfully in the courts. But Connolly's work no longer touched central issues, and Connolly ceased to be a dominant muckraking figure.

Steffens, on the other hand, had at least attempted to intervene in the McNamara case, and in the interests of labor. "I have always assumed," writes one muckraker, "that Steffens [in his accounts of the Los Angeles affair] wished to protect Darrow."

This was a widely held suspicion. But even if correct, it still showed Steffens's pro-labor bias. Times were changing, and, for better or for worse, such a positive bias became necessary to the writer who wished to exert radical influence.

Steffens was forgiven by the radicals, but he returned to New York marked by his exploits and unable to sell his manuscripts to the popular magazines. He was no longer able to write for that audience which he had first won with his "Shame of the Cities" articles. By that time, in fact, that audience had all but disappeared.

Apparently of deeper significance than the McNamara case—of overwhelmingly greater importance to the nation in its immediate worries—was the fight for political control of the country which culminated in the Presidential elections of 1912.

During the holiday recess, in the last days of 1910, outstanding progressives met at La Follette's home in Washington and there drafted a Declaration of Principles and a Constitution. The National Progressive League was formed, with Jonathan Bourne as president, Frederic C. Howe as secretary, and Charles R. Crane as treasurer. Taft was bitterly assailed as a reactionary, and it became certain that a new party, with La Follette as its logical candidate, was to compete in the election.

With the Progressives setting the pace and receiving wide support, the Republican and Democratic Parties were driven to advocate policies that would have been unmentionable a few years before. Since Bryan could no longer speak in terms the country was willing to hear, the Democrats looked elsewhere for their candidate. Taft, unpopular and under suspicion, began the desperate antitrust drive and sponsorship of advanced legislation which characterized his final span in office.

Roosevelt now proved himself to be a master of political strategy. He kept his opinions in rein and, in the meantime, sounded out public feeling about his own availability for the Presidency. Roosevelt was as popular as ever—more so, in fact, since Taft's failure had given his own record added luster. He held himself in check, letting La Follette fashion the insurgent machine which was stirring up so much enthusiasm. It was understood that La

Follette would lead his group at the decisive time, for who else could speak for Progressivism?

Roosevelt now seized principled pretexts to break with Taft, and then, after a personal campaign of speeches, presented himself at the Republican National Convention as a candidate. The expected happened: the Progressives found themselves marked for discrimination. Fully a fourth of the convention seats were disputed by two sets of claimants, and the National Committee settled the contests in such a fashion as to give Taft his majority. The Progressives bolted the convention. Meanwhile, however, an opportunity had been taken to slander and destroy La Follette as a leader of his caucus; he was stripped of his power and prestige. Then, after Senator Beveridge, as temporary chairman of the Progressive National Convention, gave the keynote slogan of "Pass Prosperity Around," Roosevelt, his cards having been played to perfection, emerged as the Progressive candidate.

La Follette would have been a better expression of insurgency, but Roosevelt was—Roosevelt. As a candidate he would prepare such an election campaign as had not been seen for years. If he should be elected, the two-party system would be at an end. And whom did he face? There was Governor Woodrow Wilson, of New Jersey, the Democratic choice. Here was his erstwhile friend Taft, standing on his achievements. And the Socialists, who had so often cried, "Socialism by 1912!" were thrusting Debs forward with unparalleled fanfare and optimism.

One must turn to the Hearst election campaigns of 1905 and 1906 to find analogies for the frenzied election campaign that followed. Roosevelt and Taft buried each other in recriminations. Wilson, standing on his "New Freedom" platform, uttered ringing slogans that thrilled even supporters of insurgency. William English Walling, then a left-wing Socialist, and a man of more integrity than many of his party, later evaluated the Presidential promises made by the Democrats and insurgents, and tendered them a respect never before given by radicals to nonradicals.[4]

Wilson won, but it was the Socialists who furnished the major sensation. Far from having been buried by Roosevelt and the ren-

[4] *Progressivism and After*, Macmillan Co., New York, 1914.

ovated old parties, they seemed to take their place beside them as representative of a substantial sector of national opinion.

The importance of the Debs vote in that year [wrote W. J. Ghent [5]] has never been, so far as I know, sufficiently dwelt upon. Against a liberal candidate [Wilson] and a radical liberal [as Roosevelt was for that year at least] Debs polled within a fraction of 6 per cent of the total vote. To have polled even half of that vote would have been a marvel. The Rooseveltians in that year wearied themselves in efforts to capture the Socialist vote, and their platform contained 19 planks lifted bodily from the Socialist platform.

If insurgency did not triumph, at least Wilson entered the White House flanked by Progressives and supplemented by a Socialist Party which, to all intents, had established itself firmly, despite the McNamaras and the class-war-minded radicals and artists. Democracy had gained ground. And where had the muckrakers been in the campaign? Some had supported Debs; many more had aligned themselves with Roosevelt.

Norman Hapgood concluded that more was to be expected from Wilson than from the ex-President, but Robert Collier and Mark Sullivan were ardently pro-Roosevelt. This difference of opinion climaxed a change of relationships in *Collier's* offices which had begun with the death of old P. F. Collier in 1909. A quarrel followed, and Hapgood left the magazine.

Similar differences among liberals and radicals were precipitated by the issues and personalities of 1912. Progressivism was no longer easily distinguished in the confusion, and men who had worked in harmony for years found it difficult to tell friends from foes. But progressivism as such was apparently to be found everywhere, and it was possible to view its variations optimistically, as representing democracy on a higher, more complex plane.

The spirit of the time was illustrated by a story which the muckrakers liked to repeat, and which could be heard in many versions.

A wealthy Alaskan miner called upon a newspaper editor to urge a political crusade upon him. He explained what he had in mind with such evidence of having given it deep thought and

[5] In a letter to the author.

consideration, that the editor, much impressed, remarked: "Well! You certainly are a progressive, aren't you?"

"Progressive!" the miner exclaimed. "Progressive! I tell you I'm a full-fledged insurgent. Why, man, I subscribe to thirteen magazines!"

Thirteen *muckraking* magazines—no one had to explain that. But the story belonged, properly, to a period that ended a year or more before the 1912 elections. In 1912 George French, a magazine writer, looked about him in amazement and asked, "Where are the popular magazines?" He, too, was referring to those practicing exposure, but change had come so quickly that it was not easy to fix the meaning of "popular." For by that time the muckraking magazines either had dropped catastrophically out of existence or had lost their muckraking hue, and of the influence they had been wielding only fragments remained.

CARTOON IN THE LOS ANGELES TIMES, BEFORE THE DYNAMITING

XXVIII. ARMAGEDDON

THE movement to put a stop to exposure was systematically begun by those who felt that they could no longer tolerate interference in their affairs. If no executive council met solemnly to discuss ways and means to corrupt or liquidate the muckraking magazines, it was only because enough minor disagreements existed among the interested parties to make such co-operation impossible. It is no less true that the destruction of the magazines was deliberately planned and accomplished in short order—in the case of individual organs, within a few months.

It was not enough for the trusts to develop private publicity bureaus, nor even to influence the independent press. So long as the muckrakers were at large and had a forum, they were dangerous—more dangerous than the Socialists, who scorned reform and were therefore less able to cope with tendencies of big business to the extent of forcing them to follow popular will. The corporation leaders were content to take their chances with class war so long as they could rid themselves of the obstinate journalists. Since reform showed no signs of abating, of becoming respectable, the reactionaries had to deal with its advance guard severely and summarily.

This move was no sudden inspiration among those who hated and feared the muckrakers. Ambitious attempts had already been made to meet the muckrakers on their own ground. Standard Oil, for example, in an effort to build up an organ sympathetic to its principles, had subsidized *Gunton's Magazine. Gunton's*, however, lacking the stamina to compete with the national magazines, had been discontinued in 1904. *Leslie's Weekly* [1] had later been given like support, but though it struck a more popular—and shallow— note, it had failed to make the kind of impression its sponsors

---

[1] Not to be confused with the monthly Ellery Sedgwick had edited which became *The American Magazine*.

required. Now there was nothing to do but recognize that the muckraking magazines had the best and most influential writers, and to make attempts to corrupt or cripple those magazines by way of the advertising bribe or boycott.

Until 1910 the strength of popular demand, as well as the disunity between advertisers, more than counterbalanced the efforts of reaction to check the muckrakers. But the urge to combat exposure could hardly be expected to wane, despite the optimistic predictions of some muckrakers that a good time was coming when business would be perfectly free, competitive, and honest. The cheerful avowals of the less realistic muckrakers simply proved that they did not understand their own success. Men who believed that "honesty is catching" were not likely to survive the shock of disillusion. For reform could not proceed on its own momentum. Big business was not to be argued into social consciousness; it had its own convictions. The farther reform progressed, moreover, the more basic became the issues involved in it.

Collier's, when it began in 1907 its long campaign against "tainted news," showed its awareness of the fact that honest journalism was not to be expected of the trusts. Mark Sullivan and Samuel Hopkins Adams, out of their extensive newspaper experiences and investigations, gave searching descriptions of trust methods. With the definitive series on the subject which he wrote for *Collier's*, and which extended through 1911 and beyond, Will Irwin crowned the protest against those methods as they were revealed by scores of investigators in a dozen periodicals. But what Irwin and Sullivan and Adams failed to understand and record was that the trusts were not to be reformed by exposure. Their bureaus were intended for permanence, which meant that either they or muckraking would have to go. Both could not exist side by side, and the reform magazines, if they were to continue, would have to be as highly organized as the trust agencies.

Collier's might therefore have been concerned for the fate of its fellow-publications instead of holding itself aloof from them. Editorial differences did not make any muckraking organ more palatable to those whom it exposed; and *Collier's*, for all its half-million circulation, had a stake in the future of even such a periodical as *The Arena*. But *Collier's* did not acknowledge that stake.

The American News Company, handling magazine distribution, singled out B. O. Flower's magazine for anti-reform discrimination and ruled that copies of it which had not been sold by the newsdealers could not be returned. The aim of this action was to make dealers reluctant to handle a magazine which they might not happen to sell and which they would have to keep at a loss. Similar forces were brought to bear on *The Arena*. Flower was unable to stimulate enough support to preserve control of it, and in 1909 it was taken away from him and merged with *Christian Work*. Thus *The Arena* was the first of the muckraking organs to succumb to the advertising boycott.

Flower then took over the insignificant *Twentieth Century* and, almost immediately, brought it to the level of his old magazine. Newton D. Baker, Rose Pastor Stokes, the Socialist William Mailly, and such tried contributors as Hamlin Garland, Charles Zueblin, Debs, and Charles Edward Russell, responding to Flower's call, tempered his doubtful essays on Christian Science with articles affirming the need for progressivism and freedom of speech.

Free speech had once meant the right of minority groups to express opinions in a hostile atmosphere, and had usually been cited with reference to radicals and labor agitators. The muckrakers, secure with their public, had been more than generous in advocating free speech for everybody. Now the right to free speech took on more subtle implications for muckrakers as well as radicals. One of these implications was that advertisers had no right to discriminate against periodicals that practiced exposure; another was that banks were duty-bound to deal with their clients impartially.

The muckraking magazines were, as we have seen, businesses for the most part, and several of them were to be corrupted not by outside influences directly but with their own money. Still, before the end, all of them appealed to moral principles against the forces that were depriving them of their proper place in society. However, they had not come into being through moral appeals but in response to public demand. This latter point only made it patent that the ground had slipped from under them, and that moral suasion could help them no more than it had helped the Populists years before.

When late in 1909, President Taft and Postmaster-General Hitchcock made a sudden attempt to pass legislation aimed at the magazines, all of them arose fighting. Magazines had for decades been given special postal rates by the government. Hitchcock now pointed to the Post Office deficit and urged the passage of a law raising the postage on magazines from one cent to four or five cents.

In *Collier's* Robert J. Collier printed an open letter in which he asserted that he wanted no favors from the government. If it could be proved, he said, that such a rate on periodicals was necessary, he would be glad to test the interest of *Collier's* readers by continuing on what must be inevitably a ruinous postal rate for magazines selling at ten cents. He asked only for the facts on the situation—Hitchcock had not given them.

Success, less defiant, more fearful, analyzed the proposed Taft-Hitchcock recommendation at length. Samuel Merwin noted that it particularly discriminated against periodicals having voluminous advertising and a heavy percentage of Western readers. No magazine could meet the new rate unless it had a huge fortune and a conservative policy behind it. *Ship* subsidies, he observed, had Taft's approval, but subsidies—if they really were that—for purposes of popular education, did not. Canada's rate on periodicals was one-fourth of a cent!

Ben Hampton asked sardonically why Taft and his Postmaster-General did not simply list the muckraking organs slated for destruction and have done with it, instead of preparing elaborate postal schedules which in reality meant nothing.

Although this particular attempt to strike at the magazines failed, it showed which way the wind blew. The magazines could expect no consideration from Washington should they happen to find themselves in difficulties.

Early in 1910, E. J. Ridgway sold *Everybody's* to the Butterick Company for $3,000,000. No change in policy was immediately noticeable, but the next year, John O'Hara Cosgrave, beginning to feel a pressure to which he was totally unaccustomed, resigned as editor of the magazine, and after negotiating with Robert J. Collier and Norman Hapgood, who promised him a free hand, he began anew with *Collier's*. Cosgrave entered upon his duties with enthusiasm, having formulated a campaign against Stock Exchange practices which Lawson would have endorsed.

But in the meantime the magazine had begun to experience rough sailing. The younger Collier, unlike his father, was a reckless businessman, and he had saddled his property with so much debt that he was forced to borrow heavily from his friend Harry Payne Whitney. No doubt Whitney would have been willing to extend credit and support, but his bankers intervened and ordered *Collier's* to curb its muckraking campaigns. A business manager was put over Mark Sullivan and Hapgood. Cosgrave himself lasted just eleven weeks with the magazine. Observing that a number of articles he had passed for publication had been omitted, he resigned and quit the magazine field entirely.

In time it became clear that *Collier's* was defeated. As clear an indication as any other was its prosperity, which allowed the editors to cut its price from ten to five cents. Hapgood followed Cosgrave out soon after. With Charles R. Crane as "angel," Hapgood kept *Harper's Weekly* in the field until the advertising boycott became too powerful.

In the interim, *Success* came more dramatically to grief. Having completed its most useful year with the overthrow of Cannon, it was ready to follow *Hampton's* into the bolder ways of exposure. Surveying the magazine field, it asked whether it was true that the muckrakers were being stalked by enemies. Publisher Higgins and Samuel Merwin wrote confidently, but they were plainly troubled; and it was noteworthy that they should have emphasized that they did not consider the other organs of exposure "competitors" but colleagues who were doing similar work. In those uncertain days it was heartening to feel that there were friends.

What of *The American Magazine?* Merwin asked anxiously. For it had become allied with the Crowell Publishing Company, which was controlled by Thomas W. Lamont and J. P. Morgan. Newspaper stories appeared stating that the *American* was to do no more muckraking. Was the lariat to go over Tarbell, Baker, John S. Phillips, and Finley Dunne? Although these editors announced that they contemplated no changes whatsoever in policy, there was reasonable doubt that they would be allowed to print whatever they chose.

The doubt was sound. Tarbell, Baker, and the others stopped a campaign against the reactionary Diaz regime in Mexico at the demand of Americans having interests there, and even published articles in defense of it.[2] They made further concessions. By the time they had lost the magazine entirely it was hardly recognizable as the organ they had launched so bravely in 1906.

Success, confident that Morgan himself could not stop its own rise or influence, floated a second periodical, *The National Post*, a fortnightly which was to interpret current affairs. Within three months it was forced to combine the two properties. . . .

The rest of the story was told in fitting fashion by Margaret Connolly, in her *Life Story of Orison Swett Marden*, which summed up that optimist's achievements in just such terms and from just such a standpoint as he would have appreciated. *Success*, she wrote bitterly, had been under Marden the greatest of all the popular magazines. It had been esteemed for its uplift motives, patriotism, and fine ideals. But then—

Rival magazines [sought] some weapon with which to challenge his [Marden's] position. Many ingenious plans were evolved without avail, until "muck-raking" attacks upon big businessmen and politicians were launched. These magazines, in attempts to command public attention, directed assaults upon American politics and civic life; upon the personalities and methods of our great industrial leaders, and upon some of our institutions. And for a time they succeeded. "Muck-raking" swept the country like a pestilent wave. To speak well of a man or an institution became a "lost art." A period of destruction and confiscation of character and property set in. . . .

So great became this wave that it forced its insidious way even into the magazine founded on faith in God and man. Inside groups in Doctor Marden's own *Success* "household," through ingenious methods, playing on his faith in man and his associates, maneuvered until they secured control of the magazine. They vetoed his principles, reversed his policies, joined the "muck-raking" writers; and entered upon a regime of exploitation and what they believed to be "expansion"—until one day the climax came.

[2] See John Kenneth Turner's *Barbarous Mexico*, Kerr Co., Chicago, 1910. Later editions contain further information on the methods employed by pro-Diaz journalists and industrialists.

The splendid structure, the institution that Editor Marden and his ideals had built, collapsed. Like modern Samsons, the "muck-rakers" had pulled down the temple on their own shoulders.

Like all large publishing plants, *Success* had monthly bills running into the thousands of dollars with printers, paper makers, and others. The expense of getting out a single issue of such a periodical is enormous, and its income from subscribers and advertisers is spread over a period of months. Consequently, the life blood of a great magazine is credit.

In swerving from Doctor Marden's fixed standards, and attacking "big business," *Success* laid itself open to counter-attack below the water-line, in its most vulnerable spot—its financial credit—and this is just what occurred.

It was dealt a staggering blow when a great banker—evidently offended by these articles on big business—stated politely, but firmly, that its loans must be curtailed. Demand notes were called in. Printers and paper men grew insistent, and *Success* suddenly found itself upon the financial rocks. It was forced into the hands of a receiver—and this despite its hundreds of thousands of reader friends.

Success failed after a large Christmas number which promised many literary and educational treats ahead. What remained of it was absorbed into *The Circle*, an innocuous family magazine of the time. Samuel Merwin, cast adrift by this disaster, abandoned reform and began a new career as a writer of light fiction.

It was almost at the same moment that B. O. Flower lost the editorship of *Twentieth Century* because, although he had built it into a paying venture, he was unable to find the credit necessary to continue it. Urging his readers to support the new sponsors, he began his last important series of articles for the magazine: his memoirs. Flower evidently felt—and felt rightly, as it turned out—that the time had come to sum up. *Twentieth Century* itself was little helped by the change in editorial personnel, and after struggling for a little more than a year it was forced to close up.

Human Life, a Boston periodical which A. H. Lewis edited, had shorter shrift.

Inside of five years Lewis had built it into a substantial organ that seemed as unlikely as *Success* to go to the wall. He had just signed a contract with the University Press at Cambridge, which was henceforth to print the entire magazine. *Human Life* was unique among the muckraking organs because of the amount of personalia it printed. It was the magazine "about people"; it published material on muckrakers and reformers which could not be found in any other journal. Lewis himself contributed many autobiographical chapters to its pages.

As a muckraker Lewis was uncertain, but for that very reason worrisome. He actually defended Ballinger, simply because he knew the Secretary personally and liked him. He became a "convert" to insurance at a time when evidence of criminal manipulations were still being unearthed. But at the same time he joined the fight against Cannon, whom he did *not* like, and printed articles by Bailey Millard, Upton Sinclair, and his friend Charles Edward Russell. Above all he kept the muckraking "tone" which was so hateful to special interests—a tone which gave notice that he intended to print whatever he chose, and whatever he deemed interesting to his readers.

Just how *Human Life* was dispatched, and by whom, was never told. Apparently trouble was precipitated by a novel of Lewis's entitled "The Chief," which he was running in serial form and which dealt intimately with the New York police. The magazine suddenly changed ownership, and publication of "The Chief" was halted in mid-course with the new owners' comment that they did not care to "wash their linen in public" regarding it. As usual, there were no warnings that catastrophe was imminent. With the July issue of 1911 control of *Human Life* slipped from Lewis's hands, and within two months, despite the bright promises of the new publishers and their editor, Francis Hackett, the magazine was deserted by its subscribers and ceased to exist.

Other periodicals were killed in the same fashion, but it was *Hampton's* that best showed how determined financial interests were to rid themselves of the incubus of exposure and to what measures they were prepared to resort. Since *Hampton's* was the greatest of the muckraking organs, its shocking end had an indubitable effect on the morale of other organs with like inclinations.

In 1910, Charles Edward Russell was running his definitive series on the rise and practices of the great railroads. In the course of his work he took up the story of the New York, New Haven & Hartford and showed how it had secretly gained a monopoly over all New England traffic, including that of steamship lines and street-railways. (This was several years before a Congressional investigation brought out that the conduct of the company had made one of the worst records in railroad history.) While the article was still in proof, and apparently was known only to its author and publisher, Ben Hampton received a visit from a man who introduced himself as representing Charles S. Mellon himself, president of the New England railroad. Mellon, he said, understood that an article "full of lies," as he described it, was to appear in *Hampton's* attacking him.

In discussing the article Hampton's visitor showed such a remarkable familiarity with its contents, that Hampton was taken aback. He brought out the article and reviewed it line for line with his visitor, and in the end he satisfied himself that the man had no information disproving Russell's statements. Nevertheless Hampton was threatened with ruin if he dared to print the article. Convinced, however, that he had no reason to discuss the matter further with the railroad agent, Hampton closed the interview and in his December 1910 issue printed "The Surrender of New England."

From that time on Hampton was marked.[3] Spies ferreted their way into his offices, and one in the accounting department found the opportunity to copy out the entire list of Hampton's stockholders. Each stockholder was separately visited and regaled with stories of how Hampton was misusing company funds. Wall Street agents of the railroad made extraordinary bids for the stock in order to indicate that it was losing value. Hampton, who had a credit of three hundred thousand dollars with the paper makers, was unable to raise thirty thousand dollars to pay his current bill, and was arbitrarily ordered to pay the money in advance.

Seeing trouble ahead, he convened a committee of stockholders in New York City, and a group of a dozen men, whose combined

[3] Hampton's own account of these proceedings was given in Upton Sinclair's *The Brass Check;* see also Charles Edward Russell's *Stories of the Great Railroads* (Kerr Co., Chicago, 1912), "Prefatory Anecdote." Hampton abandoned reform in disgust and began a new career in the motion picture field; see his *A History of the Movies,* Covici-Friede, New York, 1931.

fortune exceeded $2,000,000, endorsed for him three notes of ten thousand dollars each. The paper was taken to the bank and accepted. Hampton checked against them, drew money on them—and on the following day was ordered to return the money and take his notes from the bank. Such banking practice was illegal, but the manager of the bank told Hampton that he was powerless to do anything else; "downtown" people were giving the orders, and he had to take them.

Hampton now tried and failed to float a loan. One banker who declared that he would stand by Hampton in his crisis, whether the "Morgan crowd" willed it or not, was forced to stop his transactions and was himself put out of business within several months.

Within ten days Hampton had to turn his affairs over to his lawyers. Facing receivership, he chose what seemed the lesser of two evils: he relinquished his magazine to a group of promoters who offered impressive introductions and gave promises that the magazine would be fully supported. In a few months Hampton became convinced that the new owners had no intention but to loot the magazine. He was later told by the bookkeeper that they abstracted $175,000 from the property, and then took the books down to the East River and threw them from a bridge.

Hampton tried to indict the new owners for criminal practices, but when the trial came he was unable to prove anything. He could prove that *Hampton's* had been extremely valuable, but he could show no evidence that its affairs had been criminally mishandled. The records were gone. And, in the meantime, the magazine had been destroyed.

This caused little concern among Wilsonian Progressives or the new young radicals. Herbert Croly, founding the *New Republic*, scorned muckrakers as sentimentalists of democracy. He, young Walter Lippmann, and others intended to create a new elite to run the country. They turned from the broad middle classes of town and farm, and defined their middle class center as located in Sinclair Lewis's admirable satires. This defined a point of view which affected Progressive hopes for decades.

S. S. McClure vigorously denies (what Upton Sinclair claimed) that his magazine was taken away from him by special interests. It was "bad business methods," he feels, that gave the West Vir-

HAMPTON'S
MAGAZINE

?

Will the Magazines Remain Free?

Will They Withstand the Attacks of Wall Street and Big Politics?

PRESS CENSOR

HAMPTON SAW TROUBLE BEFORE IT CAME

ginia Pulp and Paper Company ownership of *McClure's*. Perhaps. But "bad business methods" do not explain why McClure immediately lost public influence upon the change of ownership. He was at that time only fifty-five years old, and the most distinguished editor in the country. He had built his syndicate and magazine out of nothing, not through good business methods primarily, but by popular demand. When McClure lost his magazine, it was because muckraking was "on the spot."

Yet the last of the muckraking organs had the fire and courage, if not the editorial genius, of *Hampton's*. It was, surprisingly, *Pearson's* which took the wandering muckrakers out of the cold, as Russell has it, and gave them a final haven—*Pearson's*, which had been the "Easy-to-Read" magazine, and had played almost no part at all in exposure.

Arthur West Little, its publisher, head of the J. J. Little & Ives Company, was not a muckraker, but he was a firm friend and admirer of the muckrakers and was more than willing to give them a forum. He took over the subscribers' list of the defunct *Hampton's* and, in his April 1912 issue, announced that *Pearson's*, seeing how reaction had taken the offensive in journalism, was determined to oppose it. *Pearson's* was to be a free organ of opinion, and Little knew that meant he must be independent of advertisers; for this reason, he announced, *Pearson's* was dispensing with pictures and would be printed on pulp paper. Its one attraction would be its subject matter, and Little was confident that an audience existed for that.

During the next four years, until Frank Harris took over the magazine and turned it into an organ expressive solely of his personality and interests, *Pearson's* held its post as the last of the muckraking magazines. It was "The Magazine Which Prints the Facts That Others Dare Not Print." This claim was, perhaps, unfair to *The Metropolitan* which, under Carl Hovey and supported by Payne Whitney, opened a new career at the same time, but as a quasi-Socialist periodical. Yet the claim was true in the sense that *The Metropolitan*, being "radical," disdained muckraking subject matter and gave space to more "advanced" material, of which Morris Hillquit's series on the theory and practice of Socialism was representative. Special interests were not sorely disturbed by it—less disturbed, at any rate, than by articles which exposed their immediate plans and activities.

The Metropolitan accumulated subscribers and prestige . . . and its Socialist features were finally dispensed with. *Pearson's*, on the other hand, from the time it threw down the gauntlet to "the interests," never lost a certain desperate and harassed demeanor.

Arthur Little's friend, David Graham Phillips, was already dead when Little embarked on his venture in reform. (Phillips had been shot down by a manic-depressive who fancied that one of Phillips's novels, *The Fashionable Adventures of Joshua Craig*, was directed at him and his family.) Little's friend Charles Edward Russell, glad to find a new avenue for his work, became *Pearson's* leading writer. Alfred Henry Lewis also contributed to *Pearson's* until his death in 1914, although his writings hardly constituted muckraking. Bolton Hall carried on the campaign for the Single Tax; and Gifford Pinchot, C. P. Connolly, Judson C. Welliver, and others of the original reformers, as well as such Socialists as Allen L. Benson, Robert Hunter, and Harry W. Laidler, also helped to make *Pearson's* required reading for earnest Americans.

It was of more than casual significance that *Pearson's*, without pictures, without the diverting features which had tempted readers of *McClure's* and other periodicals of late influence, should have received considerable support. Those who said, and have said, that muckraking "died" because there was no further demand for it, might have asked themselves what class of readers followed Russell's documented exposures and the political analyses that *Pearson's* presented unadorned.

Those who insisted that muckraking just died never accounted for *Pearson's* health and substance. Unerringly the magazine seized upon the Nonpartisan League, just then gathering strength, as the most likely center about which a new democratic movement could be built. The Progressive movement had quickly disintegrated under the leadership of opportunists. The new Nonpartisan League, beginning from scratch, concerned itself, as was proper, with the basic grievances of the farmers. When *Pearson's* became its official organ, Charles Edward Russell wrote articles about the

League which he later collected to form his last ambitious muck-raking book.[4]

The League, led by Governor Frazier of North Dakota, fought important battles in the Northwest, and if it did not capture national attention as Progressivism had done, the reason was that greater issues had arisen which it was unable to understand, let alone master. But it functioned commendably, and so foretold the coming of days when the political pendulum would swing again toward the aims and program for which it stood.

It was the World War that completed the work of reaction, that took the scattered and demoralized reformers and herded them into strange alliances with men and movements they had previously opposed. The professional trust-defenders by themselves could never have carried on effective propaganda for war. They lacked the intellectual equipment, the direct contact with the masses. An issue involving so somber a question of life and death required men and women who could convince because they were convincing—and only those who had been muckrakers were able to do that.

The years from 1914, when war ceased to mean the differences between several small European countries, to 1917, were the time during which America was prepared for participation. While George Sylvester Viereck edited his pro-German magazine, pro-Ally propaganda was released through a thousand channels. The reformers were aroused sufficiently to clamor for swifter and more comprehensive reforms that would make the country independent of foreign catastrophes and insure democracy. Charles Edward Russell wrote that it was Kaiserism which had plunged Germany into her great adventure, and insisted that such "Kaiserism" as had started the latest class war in Colorado would have to be ended if Americans were to resist embroilment in Europe's affairs. Allen L. Benson (one of the Socialists who approved the sensational Ford plan for distributing profits) urged a referendum on war.

While peace parades vied with "preparedness" campaigns, the issue was at last resolved by the final declaration of war. Many

---

[4] *The Story of the Nonpartisan League*, Harper & Bros., New York, 1920.

joined the patriotic front out of sheer relief that a decision had been made for them, and assured themselves that they could support their country as any citizen should. Others, throwing overboard the ideas and companions they had cherished until now, went to war with passion and determination. Rheta Dorr sent her son into the service, and she herself became a fiery propagandist for war.

Down in the streets, in Union and Madison Squares [she wrote [5]] and all over the East Side, scores and hundreds of loud-mouthed alien Socialists were pouring out in execrable English, denunciation of the President, of our flag, of the army and navy, and of the "capitalists" who were forcing the country into war. What did they know about America, except that we had been so senseless as to let their slaveminded lot in? . . . It was time they were beginning to let Americans fight.

Dorr was speaking in terms different from those she had used in the battles for factory regulation and women's rights—those battles by which she had made her reputation. (Woman suffrage came, but under banners less bright than those that had heralded it.) Upton Sinclair also joined in the great crusade, but without such venom for those who broke with him on the issue.

It was my task, self-assumed [he wrote [6]] to hold the radical movement in line for Woodrow Wilson's policies. Needless to say, I never asked or received a cent from anyone, and the little magazine [7] which I edited and published cost me a deficit of six or eight thousand dollars for the ten months of its history. . . .

How could I have been trapped into supporting the war? I thought that Woodrow Wilson really meant his golden, glowing words; I thought he was in position to know what I couldn't know, and would take the obvious steps to protect us against diplomatic perfidy. I knew nothing of the pre-war intrigues of the French and Russian statesmen against Germany, which had made the war inevitable, and had been planned for that purpose; I knew nothing of the secret treaties which bound the allies for the war. . . .

Others did not have so much of a past so that they would have to explain why they submitted; the cause needed no explanation.

[5] *A Woman of Fifty*, Funk & Wagnalls Co., New York, 1924.
[6] In *Money Writes!*, A. & C. Boni, New York, 1927.
[7] *Upton Sinclair's*.

As Hermann Hagedorn, who was made president of the Vigi-
lantes in the American League of Artists and Authors for Patriotic Services, put it:

> There are strange, unexpected ways
> Of going soldiering these days.
> It may be only census-blanks
>   You're asked to conquer, with a pen,
> And suddenly you're in the ranks
>   And fighting for the rights of men! [8]

The choice was as easy as that. One was, perhaps, only a writer
or educator, faced with the choice of standing for or against war.
One found one's services in demand, and was lifted into high and
influential position. And suddenly one, too, was in the ranks and
fighting for the rights of men.

The Socialist Party was split in two. Jack London was already
dead (the best fate a muckraker could have asked, commented
Sinclair, who lived into the Coolidge prosperity era); worn out
by the personal and social contradictions that hounded him, London had taken his own life. Gustavus Myers, infected, wrote such
an article as "Why Idealists Quit the Socialist Party" and a book,
The German Myth, exploding, or attempting to explode, German claims to culture and enlightenment. And when Charles
Edward Russell's eloquence was finally enlisted for war, it was
clear that no more anti-war support could be expected from any
of the veteran scribes. Russell had been a hero to the younger
generation because of his firm and principled adherence to exposure, and it was because he joined the war agitators with firm-
ness and principle that he was showered with abuse by his former
admirers. But, as he later noted in his autobiography, he did no
worse than Clarence Darrow—or, he might have added, Ben
Lindsey or Frederic Howe, who were less revered for their
powers of leadership and hence were less condemned for their
roles in the war years. Or Herbert Croly.

George Creel was made chairman of the Committee on Public
Information, and with Arthur Bullard he turned it, within six
months, into a machine which dominated every agency of propa-

---

[8] "How Can I Serve?" in *Defenders of Democracy*, John Lane Co., New
York, 1918.

ganda.[9] Seventy-five thousand "Four Minute Men" covered the country in a whirlwind campaign of speeches. On or co-operating with the Committee were such people as Harvey O'Higgins, Will and Wallace Irwin, Ernest Poole, Samuel Hopkins Adams, Louis F. Post, Ray Stannard Baker, Ida Tarbell—indeed, it was a roll call of the muckrakers.

The Bolshevik revolution gave the muckrakers the *coup de grâce*, ending their efforts to deal as independents with their new associates on the political and cultural fronts. The overthrow of the Czar delighted them: this was democracy coming out of war; this justified their patriotic zeal. But the uncompromising determination of the proletarian leaders to continue the battle against the allied governments, and under a working-class dictatorship, pushed the ex-muckrakers to the other extreme. It was, Rheta Dorr saw with horror, the French Revolution all over again. In *Red Friday*, a prophetic novel of a Lenin come to America, George Kibbe Turner abandoned the famed McClure objectivity to portray his fear of class war on the Russian model. Charles Edward Russell and William English Walling gave better documented evaluations of the "democratic centralism" espoused by the Bolsheviks, although in order to do it they were constrained to ignore the point of view, the desperate situation of the Bolsheviks. As for John Spargo, he issued one voluminous study after another to prove that the revolutionists were liars and dictators who were determined to wipe out democracy. He left reform to become, improbably, an expert on American ceramics.

It was this abandonment of objectivity by the ex-muckrakers, this confession that as middle-class writers they could not act as a determining force in the international crisis, which broke off all their relationships with the vital radical movement. For better or for worse, the old reformers were now with those who dominated the democracies and, as it happened, controlled their thoughts. They were no longer able as before to criticize big business; many no longer desired to do so. When the war ended, they quietly retired. But there was evidence in such a book as Frederic C. Howe's autobiography that all were not entirely satisfied with their conduct during the War. They had been party to hysteria,

---

[9] *How We Advertised America*, by George Creel, Harper & Bros., New York, 1920.

hardly the role for educators and reformers; they had tacitly condoned the cruel raids which brought suffering and death to radicals; they had condoned the imprisonment of Eugene Debs. Necessary though war might or might not have been, there had not been such democracy behind the lines in America as the ex-muckrakers had demanded of the Bolsheviks.

For all the old reformers' contempt of "parlor pinks," this minority had asked sane questions—questions not reported correctly in patriotic newspapers or the freshly groomed magazines. Lincoln Steffens, one of the "pinks," had refused to be involved in the massacre of free speech, and had even consented to write an introduction to a volume of essays by Leon Trotsky, crediting the leader of the Red Army with sanity and earnestness.

The War was over, but not its effects. An age set in which held reform lightly. Capitalism had no further fear of reform, but even sponsored it whenever it might smooth the road for organized business. The younger generation was completely uninterested in reform, having learned through hard experience that there were greater issues abroad. Russia and Italy, far away though they were, were organized nations intent upon carrying diverse programs out to the finish; but in America reform had shown itself incapable of resisting class pressure. Although Harding scandals and labor troubles roused Progressive actions, they could not offset the vitiating effects of prosperity.

In 1918 Upton Sinclair began to write what his biographer Floyd Dell has called his "great pamphlet-histories." These furious, detailed summaries of his experiences with American customs and institutions were the last of the muckraking books. It was unfortunate that the younger radicals took them for histories rather than for what they were: polemics. But it is likely that if Sinclair had attempted to give the picture of his times, rather than the Socialist version of affairs, he would not have been believed. Even the memory of muckraking was gone, and those who avidly accepted his conception of the muckraking era were seeking an answer to the late war, and would not have been able to comprehend the psychology of the movement for exposure even if they could have been persuaded to believe it. The young radicals, the "lost generation," had no roots in the past and no faith in the future.

The Profits of Religion, the first of Sinclair's books, was written with the high indignation of muckraking. *The Brass Check,* the most famous, concluded with an appeal for funds to found a newspaper which would be entirely free and impartial in content (Sinclair later withdrew this chapter). *The Goose-Step, The Goslings,* and *Mammonart* continued his story of capitalism as it had influenced the schools, the colleges, and literature. By 1927, when *Money Writes!* was published, Sinclair's tone had changed, if not his manner. There was no audience for exposure; there was much more of an audience for literary gossip. He pleaded for a little patience from the reader while he gave background to his opinions of Sherwood Anderson, Dreiser, Cabell, Mencken, Hergesheimer, and others who were the literary lights of the day. Even this device was vain. Having sold many thousands of copies of *The Brass Check* despite a newspaper boycott, Sinclair now could find no way of catching the interest of the reading public.

It was not to be wondered at, then, that others who had no stake in Socialism lost contact with radical thought. There were jobs in abundance for such trained writers as the ex-muckrakers—paying jobs, influential jobs—but they were rarely accompanied by the dignity that had once distinguished them.

Ray Stannard Baker, coming out of the war, in which his close relationship with Woodrow Wilson had made him eminent, reviewed labor troubles of the early Twenties in *The New Industrial Unrest.* In method this book was as good as his former muckraking work; but it lacked strength and vitality, that quality of movement that he had earlier given his writing, and it caused not a ripple of interest. He retired, subsequently to undertake the definitive and authorized biography of his war-time chief.

Samuel Hopkins Adams wrote *Revelry,* a novel of the Harding administration. This was a muckraking subject and, what was more, had drawn public attention. But Adams's treatment of it was a travesty on muckraking. Embarrassingly, for those who knew his earlier work, he curried his plain style in an attempt to compete with the brilliant new-generation writers on their own flapper-slang-hipflask level. It was a pitiful comedown, and although *Revelry* sold well, it was only for the same reasons which gave Kathleen Norris, Harold Bell Wright, and Edgar Rice Burroughs their vast publics.

Wallace Irwin, forgetting verse and the Japanese schoolboy, joined the movement in second-rate fiction, as did Henry Kitchell Webster, Reginald Wright Kauffman, and others. Will Irwin, who had written the most mordant account of "kept" journalism, was now convinced that it had reformed. Finley Dunne reviewed his memories of President Harding—as though the creator of "Mr. Dooley" needed these for fame!

A barrage of books praising and explaining conservative and hard core personages high-lighted the times. Carl Hovey wrote of J.P. Morgan, George Kennan (who had attacked the Southern Pacific) of E.H. Harriman, William Hard and Will Irwin both of Herbert Hoover, and Tarbell of Judge Gary and Owen D. Young. Charles Edward Russell, however, turned to biography not as a means of explaining new convictions but in order to develop long-cherished interests; and his studies, particularly those of Julia Marlowe and Theodore Thomas, were solid contributions to contemporary writing.

Popular literature, as Norman Hapgood realized, had ended in banality. He himself, perhaps because he had been less violently the muckraker, preserved a cooler head in this post-War age which had no respect for muckrakers. It was a paradox that he, who had been so bitterly opposed to Hearst, should have learned to value that journalist; and Hapgood served him as editor with real satisfaction. But the new magazine work had little to offer a man who had once commanded the earnest attention of the nation. The vast circulations of the "reformed" magazines meant simply that an America that was swifter, more complex, and more highly populated than many had truly believed it could become was better able to satisfy its unthinking desires for romance and escape. The middle-class had lost a certain self-respect in giving way to those desires, and its more lively representatives poured contempt upon it through such organs as *The American Mercury*. But popular education? There was no demand for it; there was apparently no need for it. *Collier's, Cosmopolitan, The American Magazine, Everybody's* (which became *Romance Magazine*)—these magazines, to be found on every newsstand, were now only organs for entertainment.

XXIX. T. R. AND F. D. R.

THE year 1929 put a period to the eclogue of art and radicalism which had been ushered in so excitedly a short decade before. Overnight it became painfully clear that the quest for Cytherea and moon-calf attitudes, to say nothing of simple thoughtlessness on the part of the ordinary citizen, would never suffice for this crisis.

The ex-muckrakers were helpless to explain their point of view, and it is doubtful that they would have been heard if they had tried. Radicals who harbored extreme solutions for industrial ills, who had learned from the Soviets, were alone approved among the desperate. They waxed more confident; they increased their factional battles and redoubled their propaganda. If they spoke in terms drawn chiefly from Europe's experiences, it was because Europe had been unable to blind herself to the realities of class war and now offered the clearest portents of disaster. Again, it was because the gap the World War created between the old America and the new had affected the radical movement as much as every other. Even La Follette's last bid for the Presidency, in 1924, did not stimulate memory; his campaign faded into the limbo of pre-War issues and no one did them honor.

Babbitt lost control of current affairs as surely as the muckrakers had before him. He could not solve the depression; he had scarcely been able to understand prosperity. Obscurely he identified prosperity with the American Way. But the way back—granting that it could be found, or was worth finding—was not to be discovered at a moment's notice; and meanwhile strikes and appeals for relief were distressingly inadequate; worse still, this inadequacy showed that crisis was national, and there was no way of telling how long it would continue to be so.

Public attention was focused upon the laborer: his plight could not be ignored. The middle-class was also in travail, but its sorrows struck no popular chord of sympathy. Holding on to their individualism, the "petty bourgeoisie" responded to the situation in just such a fashion as their radical critics could have asked and predicted: they made frantic efforts to save themselves; they made vain prophecies of an upswing; they grasped at straws of reform.

The radicals, with their grasp of economics, with their firm understanding of the needs of labor, were able to command more attention and as the dark days of 1931 and 1932 came they spoke with increasing emphasis and effect. Since the economic fear towered over every other problem and interest, it was not amazing that a shamed and aimless intelligentsia—that part of it which was not indifferent to the deluge: the unpossessed—should have met the radicals' arguments and accusations half-heartedly, and should have felt, some secretly, some openly, that service to the working-class was the least excuse one could offer for existence. So the working-class was idealized at the expense of the middle-class in much the same way as the "progressive" had been idealized a generation before, but with much less realism. On the one hand, the laborer was a crushed, bewildered slave whose sufferings only a coldhearted reactionary could bear; on the other hand, he was the proud, indomitable bearer of the future—of that future when the middle-class opportunist should beware. "Let the bourgeoisie tremble!" Marx had written.

The trials of labor, the futility of panaceas, the trend toward revolution, were expressed in countless volumes of fiction and polemic. Grace Lumpkin, taking up the tale which Edith Summers Kelly earlier had begun in *Weeds*, a superb story of backwoods enslavement, made in her *To Make My Bread* one of the few notable efforts to link her newfound Communist convictions with matters intrinsically American. But her climax, with its overtones of revolt, was the least vivid section of her book. Other writers, more impatient of the past, more contemptuous of the background of American tradition and ideals, wrote fables of revolution that charmed the very audiences whose life-lines they tried to sever.

Meanwhile a second Roosevelt, speaking with a persuasiveness which not T. R. himself could have equaled, announced his determination to save the country. The "Square Deal" had been pushed through with a waving of fists and with invective; NRA and its "Brain Trusters" now were met with a cry of horror above which one could barely hear the caustic criticisms of the Communists. Still the crisis did not break, and the babel of dissatisfaction mounted. Technocracy had its day. Would-be leaders emerged: Father Coughlin, Huey Long, Townsend, Father Divine, and—wonderful to be told!—Upton Sinclair who, with EPIC, all but carried California against the two party machines. Veblen's "leisure class" was discussed, and also Sumner's "forgotten man," but not so thoroughly as to explain who or what Veblen and Sumner had really been, or socially represented. Hence the leisure class and the forgotten man remained catchwords for debate rather than subjects for consideration. Even Henry George's teachings were not to be heard outside the Henry George School of Social Science. The American Approach, in other words, remained where it had languished before the coming of crisis: in disrepute—considered inadequate for pressing needs.

It would have been false to term the new radicals, or the New Dealers for that matter, muckrakers; and no one thought of doing so. Democracy, with all it connoted, with that realistic concern for American institutions that it presupposed, was not a pivot of thought. There were experts who specialized in middle-class affairs—Schlink and Kallet, J. B. Matthews and Stuart Chase—and it was noticeable that they spoke not for themselves, as the muckrakers had done, but for a constituency, for co-operatives and other consumers' organizations. But there was no phenomenal growth of such organizations, and their spokesmen found themselves driven nearer and nearer extreme radical theory. Such theory held the stage and provided the idiom of controversy.

Streams of books on Russia indicated that the history and possibility of revolution were being considered by thinking groups of Americans. It is not too much to say that the chief characters of the great Communist "experiment" were better personalized, were given more detailed and more careful treatment, by the *littérateurs*—as well as by those many writers who had lost faith in literature—than were many American leaders who were presumably to settle the future of the country. If Judge Gary had been able to say, years before, "We are all Socialists today," it was even truer that Communism, for all that it did not capture a vast following, captured a devout one, and its psychology attracted wide respect, particularly among the brave young people who were most willing to believe that violence was the one way out.

Still, there was relief for the foodless and homeless. Vast agencies attended, although inadequately and without clear purpose, to urgent need. Whereas muckraking had been released in good times and had represented the middle-class on the offensive, it was now the working-class that led the way and won to its cause capable leaders from other social groups. WPA, PWA, ERB were created not for the college hordes and those thrust out of careers in business (these were given the task of administering assistance) but primarily for the unskilled and the semiskilled who would otherwise have starved.

The wheels of industry meanwhile refused to turn, and New Deal critics who appealed to American ideals and upbraided the President as only Theodore Roosevelt had been upbraided, could propose no counter-measures which Hoover had not already tried. The Communists, on the other hand, took the lead in quickening public awareness of mass misery. But if they encouraged discontent, they could not be held responsible for it. The paradox of poverty in the midst of plenty was an objective fact, and if the crisis was not to pass of itself, if reaction was not to be persuaded to make necessary concessions, then certainly there was no way out but revolt.

The fall of the German republic presented a final argument to those who argued the necessity, inevitable or otherwise, of Communism. Hitler was a reality that could be no more ignored than hunger pangs. He derided majority rule even more savagely than did the leaders of the Third International. Since the massed strength of radicals and democrats had been unable to forestall Fascism, Americans asked anxiously, What could? Some blamed the Communists themselves for the German debacle, holding that it was their aggressive determination to have revolution that had precipitated Fascism; but others, particularly among the unemployed and in the unions, could not deny that the Communists had looked first and foremost to the proletariat's needs. Anyway, if no choice but between Fascism and Communism were to present itself, the latter promised more to the dispossessed.

The prospect of revolution, then, was accepted by people who would in other days have been Progressives and Socialists, not merely because of the romantic aura events had given Communism, but because Communism overwhelmed them with its possibilities. The hasty efforts to "Americanize" Marxism were the evidence. Despite the fact that Communism was supposed to be based upon science and history and, of course, upon the working-class, argument on the subject was carried on with feeling and impatience—that is, from compulsion rather than confidence. There was need for convincing, for being convinced, rather than for learning; and, from the point of view of the converts, those who kept themselves free of party entanglements and were reluctant to submit themselves unconditionally to label and discipline merited more contempt than outright foes. It was for the foes that fear was reserved.

It was to be expected that people with Marxist beliefs—or compulsions—should build up influence in the unions, in organizations set up to agitate for relief, and in the relief agencies themselves. Nor did that influence go unrecognized in *status quo* circles. Relief and work projects were wrung out of government only over the opposition of political and industrial leaders who were frightened by the prospect of a standing army of citizens dependent upon the government for sustenance. Worried conservatives pointed out—what required no further emphasis—that there was no guarantee that these dependents would ever be reabsorbed into private industry. They foresaw an end of the American spirit of individualism. The official interference in private enterprise which they visualized made T. R.'s administration days look like a time of untrammeled industrial freedom.

It seemed frightful that the government was giving work to avowed enemies of the capitalist system. Responsible administrators tolerated known Communists; they dealt with groups which made only the slightest secret of advocating or tolerating Communism. Government-sponsored bureaus might well become instruments of insurrection, as the Soviets had. Indeed, it was reported that when the President heard the suggestion that if his plans succeeded he would go down in history as the greatest American executive, he remarked that if he failed he might well be the last one. In any event, there could be no doubt that the agencies he created were hotbeds of unrest.

Relief meanwhile continued to be consistently inadequate, and security for the average citizen seemed as far away as ever. As the Thirties deepened, there was no sign of a turn for the better.

Radical thought, thought roused by repression and despair, surely held its own during those years. For conservatives, radicals were termites undermining the foundations of the state. In their own estimation radicals were formulating the only possible conclusions from the conditions they witnessed. The tenets of "democratic centralism," of absolute adherence to party decisions, which Lenin and his aides hammered out to protect their underground party and to insure united action, dominated the radical circles and made their power felt afar.

Steffens, for one, approved of radical tactics and of the opportunism and double-dealing that marked them in practice. He assimilated just enough Bolshevik theory to round out his life's thought and to make him a critic of those muckraking achievements which he recognized as constituting his claim to remembrance. The end, he believed, justified the means. Unfortunately, and for his Communist friends annoyingly, he also approved of Mussolini's use of this maxim! For Steffens was not to be reduced to the mechanical use of clichés in the manner of unionists and revolutionists who solicited his support. He gave that support, but he preserved a kind of freedom which keeps some men self-contained if not always influential.

To be influential it was necessary to speak in slogans and in conventional modes. One had to lump business and politics into one reactionary mass consisting of "Bourbons" and "counter-revolutionaries." One argued the possibility of a "proletarian" literature, and one "used" reformers and vacillators for "higher goals." Those who criticized as unreal the Communists and neo-Communists portrayed in *The Big Money*, by John Dos Passos, were merely unable to recognize themselves and the psychological pressure to which they had been subjected. For if Dos Passos put robot characteristics in his protagonists, it was not because he had no feeling for character (few other novelists had so much as he) but he saw that his characters had been affected by what could only be called thought alien and unnatural to their personalities. Such an interpretation of this novel would have been construed as red-baiting in those fevered days; but it was true in the sense that the jargon and gestures of those who led the forces of unrest were not drawn from American soil. The Bolsheviks might or might not be the sole heirs of Marx, but they were Russian, and it was a fact that even those who borrowed from them eclectically were unable to develop an approach natural enough to threaten the strength of the New Deal. The New Deal was strong because it responded only to pressure from American sources. To think otherwise was to dream like *Pravda,* which hopefully printed a photograph of barricades purportedly set up during the San Francisco General Strike.

The cry for bread was not a cry for revolution—not yet, at any rate. If revolution was truly on the way, it marched with shorter steps than revolutionists willingly supposed. As for radical intellectuals, the yearning for revolution arose from the need of filling one's inner void, of experimenting in personal life with a philosophy that challenged the void. One could always hope that such a philosophy would somehow force events to a showdown.

Still there was no business revival. Perhaps business was contemptible, the gross body of American capitalism, but it was nevertheless what Charles Edward Russell had called it—the heart of the nation. With the C.I.O. now secure in the field; with relief agencies that were formed for temporary needs now being incorporated in the government structure; with an economy of scarcity being accepted in practice—unrest should have intensified rather than diminished.

Instead there appeared a revival of interest in democracy—sudden, definite, insistent. In the groping for the democratic tradition shades of Jefferson and Lincoln were vaguely but earnestly invoked. It is true that those radical writers who hurried to meet the new demand were unable to meet it consistently or confidently, for they had just been describing democracy as an abstraction, a trick of speech used by demagogues to confuse the public—as it had often been, indeed. Again, these writers had called for a "working-class history" of the United States, evidently to offset such studies as Dr. Charles A. Beard's. No such history had been produced, but neither had any other of a vital, democratic quality.

Yet the precedents for this sensational about-face were to be found in the very radicals who had made sport of democracy. John Chamberlain, for instance, had called the book he issued in 1932 *Farewell to Reform,* but he by no means had bade farewell. Radical trends had influenced him just far enough to cause him to revive the memory of Populist and muckraking achievements in order to demolish them. That done, he could not bring himself to a direct advocacy of revolution, but quibbled with the term until it became a new version of reform.

While talk about democracy increased, there was no security for the radical; but in one form or another, there was work to do—or relief, if no work came to hand. And one could not sustain the high expectations of revolt indefinitely. There was accordingly a general entrenchment in whatever *modus vivendi* offered itself. Relief was not adequate, but it somehow provided for life. The task of the radical became, then, to agitate for further relief, for better and more numerous government projects, for an extension of government participation in industry. And so the agitators who had attached social significance to the personal quest for relief admitted that the quest was, after all, materialistic. As the excitement that raised obscure protestors into well-paying, government-given positions died down, it was plainly to be seen that they had those positions and benefited from them. Since opportunism could not entirely hide itself in such a situation, many others who had cheered and supported messiahs now asked themselves what *they* stood to gain. Revolutionary promises, in short, had materialized no more than those of the blunt and self-seeking conservatives.

Realism came in through other doors, too. War, which in its *What Price Glory?* phase had been a feared generality, now presented itself as real and, according to all signs, inevitable. Hitler was perhaps a madman, but he had armed his nation. Mussolini was not deterred by "moral condemnation" from marching his legions into Ethiopia. The League of Nations mocked Wilson's designs with its very existence. War was close and, as in 1917, cast its shadow into every home.

It was fear, then, that encouraged the trend toward democratic isolation—fear of Fascism as well as Communism. Americans were, of course, no more cowardly than men of other nations, but even those who had learned that there were worse fates than death—hunger and humiliation—still lacked ultimate convictions favoring war. Behind was 1917 to suggest that men could die in vain, and the prospect of Hitler's fall gave no assurance that he would be followed by a better man. If Hitler was "mad," then Germany was mad. But whatever happened abroad, a few realized that there was work to do at home, and, by contrast, it seemed worth doing.

If the collapse of the Madrid government ended hopes for Europe, the Moscow trials had already completed general disillusion with revolution in America. Whether the confessions were true or false, in neither case did they make dictatorship more attractive. In America the fear that one's skepticism about the trials would class one with Red-baiters, with irresponsible individualists, with anti-unionists, produced a stifling atmosphere in the same radical circles that had once thrived on dissension. And gradually that fear was transformed into a renewed interest in free speech. Hence additional interest in democracy—the right to express personal opinions, to evaluate Fascism and Communism without danger of ostracism, to burst through the walls of doctrine that cramped. Even Communist circles, while their propaganda and organization remained regimented and intact, were stirred sufficiently to add their own eager voices to the chorus, and to affirm (perhaps vainly) that Communism was "Twentieth-Century Americanism."

But if democracy was no idle dream, no futile escape from a reality consisting of militant Fascists and Communists, then it must work today as well as yesterday. Jefferson and Lincoln were mere names; they furnished no guide for eliminating unemployment, war fear, class repression, insecurity, and all the other evils the crisis had brought to the surface. If revolution was not the way out, then reform was: not the reform of fanatics and dilettantes, but reform that would meet head on the obdurate defiance of reactionaries.

If anything was Americanism, this was. But it would not develop of itself. It was important to realize that the radical tide had been vainly spent because it had not concerned itself with the concrete institutions of America. The reformer would not repeat that error. He would examine not institutions in the abstract, symbolized by Truth, Equality, and Liberty, but institutions that involved real political, social, and economic practices to which the masses were subject, and that had not yet been proved entirely diseased. Businessmen, he would grant, were better than ogres or idiots, and no manner of insult could prove that they were not. He would see that if Sinclair Lewis's satire had not caused an uprising, the less accurate portraits, the mere invective, of the doctrinaire radicals would be no more successful. He would not venture to condemn the middle-class *en masse*. And as for the proletariat, he would know, as Josephine Herbst had written (and proved beyond her expectations), that pity was not enough, that sacrifice and despair were not enough. Realism that did not stop at epithets, at descriptions of sex experience, at detailing the horrors of poverty, was in order; a realism that respected reality by recognizing facts that did not fit into smug theory, and which affected others beside oneself, needed to be elaborated.

XXX. THE ANGUISH OF CHANGE

"I have read . . . La Follette's *Autobiography* which seemed to me the book of an honest man, fairly shrewd about other men, but very simple about the nature of social phenomena"[1]—this, in 1924, from a brilliant young Britisher, admired by the American elite for socialist concepts which kept him close to the tugging forces of revolution until his death in 1950. Writers and intellectuals like Laski patronized the old muckrakers and Progressives and even used their materials when these fell conveniently into their hands; as Laski also wrote: "I read a book attacking the Churches (*The Profits of Religion*) by Upton Sinclair which, though done in the muck-raking style which I heartily dislike, did, I think, really say and say effectively what was needed about those who preach about the great mission of Christianity and nonsense of that kind."[2]

This patronizing point of view affected many would-be critics of the American condition in the several decades following the decline of the original Progressive movement. Even when such critics sought to reach common readers, as in the radical press, their will toward focusing on the "working class" and its putative international allies gave a cast to their criticism which limited its appeal to doctrinaire minds.

That conditions in the Twenties were unripe for Progressivism and muckraking could be seen in the fact that, while there were vigorous exponents of both traditions, they were able to make only a meagre contribution to the work of their times. Thus the 1920s had such unqualifiedly creative personalities as Senators James Couzens of Michigan and Thomas J. Walsh of Montana, fearless and articulate spokesman for honesty in government, but corrup-

---

[1] Harold J. Laski to Oliver Wendell Holmes, Jr., October 4, 1924, in Mark DeWolfe Howe, ed., *Holmes-Laski Letters*, Harvard University Press, Cambridge, Mass., 1953, I, 665.

[2] *Ibid.*, I, 247.

tion flourished. Donald R. Richberg was a Progressive from the 1910s whose efforts to set the railroads on a responsible course following World War I deserved more success than they achieved.

Such public figures were, in part, held back by the overpowering prosperity of the 1920s. But that this was not the sole cause of the Progressive debacle could be seen in the fact that the economic crisis of the 1930s caused no Progressive revival. And yet there were notable Progressives working in that era too. In Franklin D. Roosevelt's cabinet was Frances Perkins, whose social work services went back to 1913, when she had fought in Albany for laws protecting New York labor on the job. As Secretary of Labor she entered the Promised Land of fulfillment in her projects. Harold L. Ickes, an old Bull Mooser, as Secretary of the Interior, became notorious for his invective, but famous as a defender of the public domain.

Worthy of special note was Rexford G. Tugwell, Under-Secretary of Agriculture, who dreamed a dream of greening America in ways which would pay back coming generations for all the misuse to which it had been exposed. Tugwell's dream was not fulfilled—money was simply not made available—but it was a Progressive dream which could be picked up again, if the nation ever should prove ready for it.

The land attracted such great figures as Arthur E. Morgan, engineer and social engineer, whose Miami (Ohio) Conservancy District became the model from which sprang the Tennessee Valley Authority (TVA), and Hugh Hammond Bennett, "father of soil conservation." Though such personalities were unable to create the land of milk and honey of their visions, no valid social program could build without taking their efforts and philosophies into account.

It was tragic that such a masterpiece of cinematic art as Pare Lorenz's *The River* (1938), produced under the auspices of the Farm Security Administration, should have had no follow-up, either in the areas of social need, or for its director. Also distinguished in the way which muckraking had been at its best was Erskine Caldwell's and Margaret Bourke-White's volume of photographs and text, *You Have Seen Their Faces* (1937), which portrayed a somber side of southern life.

The problem some political Progressives posed for would-be

followers or emulators could be seen in clearest form in such a personality as Senator Burton K. Wheeler of Montana, a man of conspicuous probity and courage, who had fought to expose the ramifications of Teapot Dome and who, in 1935, pushed through Congress the important Public Utilities Holding Company Act. Yet in Wheeler's resentment of the radical pressures of the 1930s, he permitted himself to be exploited by distinctly fascist adventurers who persuaded him that they represented a fighting "Americanism" which warranted his regard. Progressives cherished individualism, and the world of the 1930s did not seem conducive to such luxuries.

A true muckraker of the time was John Roy Carlson (Arthur Derounian) who, by posing as a Fascist or Communist under sometimes dangerous circumstances, revealed the distasteful Wheeler connections and enormous quantities of other plots and ambitions among political desperadoes. Carlson's *Undercover* (1943) and *The Plotters* (1946) were mementoes of investigation which harked back directly to the heroic age of the muckrakers. But, though his books sold well in their time, they did not address a world firmly resistant to collective or authoritarian pressures, and so the exposés did not inspire imitation, nor did they remain memorable.

Somewhat more the muckraker of the new time was George Seldes, whose foe was big business and what he saw as fascist tendencies. His *You Can't Print That* (1929) carried directly on from Upton Sinclair's argument respecting the press. *Iron, Blood and Profits* (1935) treated as revelatory the international traffic in arms. *Freedom of the Press* (1935) discussed, among other subjects, the manner in which manufacturers had managed to eviscerate the Tugwell Bill of 1934, intended to modernize control of the food industries. This deed, however, created much less trauma and excitement than comparable efforts had in 1906. Americans were changing, and the muckraker would have to rediscover the roots of the public's concerns, if he was to minister to its real wants.

Seldes's *Witch Hunt: the Technique and Profits of Redbaiting* (1940) was a piece of muckraking which revealed the passage of years. There had been ardor and defense during the Progressive era for free speech and fair treatment of radicals. Brave voices and energies had created the American Civil Liberties Union during

World War I hysteria. Such challenging events as the Sacco-Vanzetti case had marshalled partisans rather than investigators. Just what responsibility Progressives had to revolutionaries remained an undefined question.

In 1938 was formed the Special House Committee for the Investigation of Un-American Activities. It featured Representative Martin Dies of Texas, who welcomed a long line of informers to his hearings to tell of alleged Communist plans to seize control of government-sponsored unemployment relief projects, to foster protests, to infiltrate unions, and in other ways to affect loosely-federated democratic organizations. Although HUAC was supposed to investigate fascists as well as communists, it concentrated on the latter, to the outrage of both liberals and Communists. "Dies Lies!" was a slogan popularized by constant repetition, but not sufficiently to prevent the Texan from getting his regular congressional appropriations.

Progressives had appealed to the middle class as the mediating body in the nation. But many now perceived it as being, in Karl Marx's classic concept, ground between the hammer and the anvil. Lewis Corey's *The Crisis of the Middle Class* (1935) saw it as having to choose between adherence to capitalist forces or to laboring and radical aggregations. Alfred M. Bingham's magazine *Common Sense* emphasized techniques for rebuilding society, and so was reminiscent of old efficiency enterprises of the Progressive era. But such techniques seemed not to meet the issue of power, and so attracted as much contempt for being impotent or inadequate as they did respect.

All domestic problems were submerged in the advent of World War II, which not only matched the democracies against fascist powers, but created the Grand Alliance of western powers in conjunction with Soviet Russia. This astounding military union effectively ended the career of Congressman Dies, though his Un-American Activities Committee was to revive its energies after the war. Meanwhile, politics were adjourned, as Franklin D. Roosevelt assumed an unprecedented stature in American affairs. A remarkable Progressive development was the relatively brief but brilliant career of Wendell L. Willkie, who rapidly converted from a stipendiary of big business and its Presidential front man in 1940 to an enthusiast for One World who served as Roosevelt's personal emissary to England, Russia, and the Far East. His sudden death in 1944 at the age of fifty-two created a legend of unfulfilled growth.

The hunger for a world at peace made muckraking, certainly on an international scale touchy, and to an extent dangerous. Diplomacy seemed more useful than exposé. Walter Duranty of the *New York Times*, for example, as Moscow correspondent reported a world governed by Joseph Stalin that took no account at all of its nether side of dissent and torment. Stalin's record as scourge and tyrant, as imperialist, as perverter of history and culture, and as mass murderer was widely dampened and hidden by rationalizations which made muckraking of the subject appear abnormal and repulsive. Only following the dictator's death in 1953 were new judgments popularly entertained, many indirect apologies being offered in the form of praise for Aleksandr Solzhenitsyn's *One Day in the Life of Ivan Denisovich* (1963).

The new prosperity in America, actually unleashed during the war itself, requiring no belt-tightening of any kind, drowned all impulses toward muckraking and Progressivism. Harry S. Truman, succeeding Roosevelt to the Presidency, looked like the plain American incarnate—the American of Main Street. But he conducted a Presidential campaign in 1948 in which he pulled all stops in the Presidential prerogative of promise and expenditure built firmly on deficit spending, and on little else.

The year 1948, indeed, saw the display for the last time in the twentieth century, at least until 1975, of a party dubbed Progressive. Its banner-bearer was the wealthy Iowa farmer Henry A. Wallace who, as Roosevelt's Secretary of Agriculture, had introduced farm subsidies, cutbacks in production, and other measures intended to help all classes of farmers and their families. Although Wallace sought to speak for Progressive goals as he recalled them, he had been "captured" by a radical junta unable to rise to the balanced statement of American debits and credits which the times urgently needed. Worthy and even noble individuals enlisted under this "Progressive" program which only dimly recalled either Theodore Roosevelt or Wilson or La Follette. C. D. MacDougall's *Gideon's Army* (1965) was a record of their sad efforts, which resisted courageously the uglier elements of bigotry across the land. They said little to the larger masses of Americans who were neither rightist activists nor leftist crusaders. Progressivism's last hurrah fizzled into sparks and silence.

Still the prosperity continued, nationalizing all promises and programs. The nation enjoyed fast-building suburbs and over-night trees at the expense of its once surging cities watched over by reformers of every type. The nation also intensely investigated the pleasures of cars, boats, bowling alleys, and drive-ins (and -outs). The idea of pleasure as an end in itself was new, and through advertisements and the more indirect means of fads and gossip-mongering made its impress not only on adults but on their smallest children. Wits and frustrated progressives were helpless to show such goals as demeaning to men who had once lived through bombings, enemy charges, and beach landings, but who now sported beer-bellies, golfing shoes, and casual mistresses. The new Romans were chilled by the taking over of mainland China by the Communists, and more than chilled by the revelation that Soviet Russia had attained the atom bomb; but all this no more than prepared them for the anti-Communist drive which had been held back by aspects of the old Grand Alliance.

Meanwhile the prosperous Americans were treated to a war in Korea which put back into headlines American generals of World War II service, and which divided their countrymen into three camps of right, left, and indifferent. The Truman decision to contain the conflict, rather than to carry it on beyond border disputes into the dangerous terrain of possible all-out war, was highlighted by Truman's lifting of General Douglas MacArthur from his Far Eastern commands. But more important was the establishment of a policy of intervention-without-victory which would prove catastrophic in Vietnam more than twenty years later.

By then old Progressive nationalism—the nationalism of Theodore Roosevelt and Senator Albert J. Beveridge, and even Herbert Croly of the *New Republic*—was worse than forgotten. It was despised as proto-fascism. There was no new formulation of a national character, sponsored by either the Democratic or the Republican party, calculated to give new pride and vigor to an American policy in the world.

Meanwhile the anti-Communist drive at home appeared to have more success. It washed away the Democratic Presidential candidacy of Adlai E. Stevenson in 1952, and would repeat its victory over him in 1956. Stevenson was as progressive a politician as the time produced, and in Stevenson's second appeal to the country he carried with him Estes Kefauver of Tennessee as running-mate. The two of them together, Kefauver because of his senatorial investigations into crime and monopoly, came as close to providing a Progressive ticket as had appeared since La Follette's 1924 bid. Their crushing defeat was a comment on how the nation then viewed Progressivism.

The Eisenhower years were the bland years, not unlike the 1920s, but produced their headlines. Hardly rating as muckraking was the journalistic enterprise which drove from Washington Eisenhower's Assistant, Sherman Adams, and which featured a vicuña coat given as a present to Adams's wife by a New England textile manufacturer, presumably for political favors received. Such "muckraking" was too evidently partisan, and the gifts alleged were almost absurd in the light of earlier and later exposés of venal political dealings.

What was interesting was why the attack on Adams succeeded. He himself was aware that he had exposed himself to becoming a target for Democrats—during an election year (1958)—because he had taken the lead in "hard-hitting" campaign oratory. "I had rubbed rather deliberately some old sores, recalling the military catastrophe of Pearl Harbor and the scientific catastrophe of losing our atomic secrets, and the policies that had lost China to the Reds and led to the Communist invasion of Korea and the war which I described as one 'they couldn't end.'"[3] In retrospect, at least, Adams saw it as "obvious" that he would be an "open target" by appearing before a heavily Democratic investigating committee which had a sheaf of hotel bills incurred by the Adamses but paid by the manufacturer.

Adams thought that it was his admission before the committee that he had been "imprudent" in his dealings with the businessman which gave the reporters an opportunity to build sensational stories around what he insisted had been no more than a friendly relationship going back eighteen years. Whatever the reason, the reporters' imputations stuck to Adams and forced him to leave Washington

[3] Sherman Adams, *Firsthand Report*, Harper & Brothers, New York, 1961, 443.

as an embarrassment to the Eisenhower administration.

In general, since the moral indicators had changed significantly in the country since the 1900s, it seems evident that Adams had stepped into a trap which would not have been fatal for everyone. For instance, President Eisenhower himself received personal gifts which none would have dared question. And he and other Presidents removed their papers from the White House and consigned them to libraries—with tax benefits—as they chose, though these documents were technically public property. Muckraking in the 1950s and after was bound to take dips and flurries of public sentiment into account, if it was to be effective or memorable, and in that era it was unable to be either.

The lurid issue of the 1950s was Joseph McCarthy of Wisconsin, who had in 1947 reached the Senate by defeating at the polls none other than Robert M. La Follette, Jr. Standing on his senatorial immunity, McCarthy made wide-ranging charges of Communist conspiracies. They became notorious when directed against figures in government and society who had received high regard, for they thus arraigned the general public on meagre evidence.

And yet there were those who believed that however wild some of McCarthy's charges, there was a solid base for them. Benjamin Gitlow's *I Confess* (1940) had pioneered a species of muckraking literature akin to that of Harry Orchard's, in revealing undercover plottings to give strength to Communists in civil and governmental affairs. There were numerous other such works, including that covering the entire era by a disillusioned liberal journalist who had once picketed for Sacco and Vanzetti and written about them under the impression that they were innocent. Eugene Lyons's *The Red Decade* (1941) spoke to its time with striking ineffectiveness. Those who agreed with Lyons's interpretation of the time either could not join him in his new enthusiasm, expressed in his *Our Unknown Ex-President, a Portrait of Herbert Hoover* (1948), or hoped yet to work with liberals to bring them back to the relative candor and association with the broader electorate which had once characterized the Progressive era.

More shocking, in any event, were the charges of confessed courier for Communists Whittaker Chambers in 1948 that Alger

Hiss, an advisor to the President and himself president of the Carnegie Endowment for International Peace, had carried on subversive work for agents of the Soviet Union. Chambers implemented his claims with evidence honored in the courts. His own *Witness* (1952) was recognized to be one of the extraordinary self-revelations of the time.

Though arguments raged in the press regarding the truth of one or another charge or confession, the question continued to haunt the public as to how far the law, or even public opinion, ought to reach into private lives and opinions in the name of anti-Communism. By and large public opinion found it easier to despise a divisive fascism in a nation which was wholly composed of minorities, and to agree that a type of terror and hysteria had been fathered by McCarthy. Free speech and privacy were still valued, though communism might or might not be.

Nevertheless the postwar years continued to be a poor time for Progressivism, despite the vigor of Adlai Stevenson's defense of himself as a loyal American who, at the same time, despised Loyalty Oaths and other means demanded by assertive patriots for ensuring that individuals did not infect the innocent with their communist views. As Stevenson said, during his first campaign for the Presidency in 1952:

We must, to protect our Government from infiltration, combine vigilance with vigor. This is a long and continuous struggle—no single action can win the campaign.

And the Democratic administration [under Roosevelt and Truman] has been conducting this fight for a long time. . . .

I have often wondered what the Republicans think they would do to improve the situation if they were elected. The General [Eisenhower] has joined loudly in the clamor about the communist menace in Washington. First he said the communists in government were the result of incompetent, loose security policies. More recently, I'm sorry to say, he implies that the Federal Government is deliberately concealing communists. But he has offered only thundering silence about a cure. What would he do? Would he fire J. Edgar Hoover? Would he fire General Bedell Smith, head of the Central Intelligence Agency and his own former Chief of Staff? Would he discharge General Smith's deputy, Allen Dulles, the brother of his own chief advisor on foreign affairs? Would he discharge the experienced men who now protect our nation's security? . . .

Let us never forget that tension breeds fear, fear, repression, and repression, injustice and tyranny. Our police work is aimed at a conspiracy, and not at ideas or opinion. Our country was built on unpopular ideas, on unorthodox opinions. My definition of a free society is a society where it is safe to be unpopular.[4]

Bold and clear were such asseverations of dedication to classic American dreams of freedom. But evidence persisted that Americans were fated to swing in the camps of both conservatism and liberalism between fantasies of One World and vengeful hatred of imagined enemies at home and abroad. All such emotional excesses kept languid and ineffective old ideals of Progressivism and made potential muckrakers the captive scribblers of politicians and their publicity campaigns.

There was simply an insufficient sensitivity to the realities of American experience, which made it a pawn rather than a guide to evidence. Only this could explain the nation-wide success of Arthur Miller's play *The Crucible* (1953), a vulgarization of American Puritan life which played upon the thought that the anti-Communist drive was no more than a witch hunt. The play's triumph, and the responsiveness of audiences to it, suggested that liberal Americans, in their effort to be modern and to resist the rude assaults of bigots, were weakly grounded in tradition, which they could use as a stick but not as a sword. McCarthy, happily, went down, but because he flailed wildly among public people with his accusations, not because it was proved there were no traitors in the land, let alone Communists.

As essentially shoddy as were such antagonists as McCarthy and Miller, the defenders of McCarthy made no better showing than their opposition. Thus William F. Buckley, a conservative of learning and subtlety, and with not a little of the muckraking temper in his criticism of liberal casuistries, could not resist a defense of McCarthy wholly unwarranted by the facts. Once again, the victim of lines of debate thus drawn was social investigation able to inform wide areas of the public, and to bring out issues of free speech and public duty rather than to obscure them.

[4] *Major Campaign Speeches of Adlai E. Stevenson 1952*, Random House, New York, 1953, 216–218.

Of great and related moment to the future of muckraking was the steady deterioration of the reputation of the old literature of "social significance." All over the land were WPA-inspired murals, in post offices, colleges, and federal buildings—all despised by art critics as "mere representational art." Leading critics closed ranks to defend Ezra Pound, arguing that his anti-semitism and defense of Fascism over the Rome Radio during the war ought to be forgiven because of his services to poetry. Inevitably, the Pound defense also demanded a regard for his poetry, and this at the expense of the work of such poets as Vachel Lindsay, Edna St. Vincent Millay, and even Edwin Arlington Robinson—to say nothing of Edwin Markham, who had, the day following his death in 1940, become an uninvestigated cliché.

More impressive in some ways was the apotheosis accorded T. S. Eliot and the all but popularization of his "The Love Song of J. Alfred Prufrock." For along with the adulation Eliot was accorded came the famous "explication," which derogated "emotionalism" in poetry experiences, in favor of a cerebrated digging into meaning. In callow hands this reduced poetry appreciation to a species of detective-story reading. In such an atmosphere of intellectualization there was little place for poets who might have wished to express larger social sympathies.

Poetry in the 1920s had produced distinguished best-sellers, and at least one poet would have been glad to adjust his verse to new human needs. As Archibald MacLeish pointed out, blank verse, for example, was "spacious, slow, noble, and elevated." The rhythms of contemporary American speech were different: "nervous, not muscular; excited, not deliberate; vivid, not proud."[5]

Such outward thinking affected the course of poetry little, as it ceased to have a popular base and became a plaything of professionalism. In many cases poetry lost all humanistic trappings, becoming a weapon in literary power-politics. Strategic mentors were still able to place favored acolytes in relatively good positions on college campuses. Inevitably, they attracted a following of sorts. But more students stolidly chose other fields than poetry in furtherance of a livelihood and career.

[5] Archibald MacLeish, *Panic: a Play in Verse*, Houghton Mifflin Company, Boston, 1935, viii.

Fiction, too, which had produced rich eras of masters who probed human psychology and conditions, began to take on odd combinations of popular and esoteric characteristics. Thus Ernest Hemingway's tale "The Killers" was enjoyed by casual movie-goers and also explicated on college campuses. His title *A Farewell to Arms* inspired a popular song which began, "Farewell to arms which caressed me." Similarly, F. Scott Fitzgerald was revived as the "flapper-philosopher," memories of whom triggered "Twenties parties" among the youth. His *The Great Gatsby* was rediscovered as one of the great American novels meriting the most intense study as representative of basic American life and circumstances. So dominant was this revulsion from the "social significance" writing of the 1930s that when John Steinbeck was awarded the Nobel Prize for Literature in 1962, the event cast a shadow of resentment over the literary departments of the land, and the author of *The Grapes of Wrath* himself, abashed, suggested that he did not deserve the honor.

The tendency toward introverted and "scientific" analysis—so opposed to that of the muckrakers and those who emphasized human nature—attacked other, related fields. Sociology, which had once studied the neighborhood, the ghetto, the gang, labored to construct hypotheses which could be "tested" and so contribute, minutia by minutia, to a mosaic of absolute knowledge. Economics, once during Progressive days involved in the human condition, constructed "models" of production and distribution which, again, would theoretically take care of all problems in the area for all time. In effect, these disciplines became adjuncts of the advertising and business communities which, in no small measure, included the unions.

All such developments created a widening gap between the youth and the "organization men" of the 1950s. Two landmarks of these differences, and the growing social disruption indicated, were J. D. Salinger's *Catcher in the Rye* (1951), a novel of disaffected adolescence, and Jack Kerouac's *On the Road* (1957), which described an almost mystic search during aimless wanderings over the country, sparked only by simple euphorias and guided by no social goals of any sort. That such works, sensitive and well-experienced though they were, should have struck so keen a note of response in their many readers, measured the distance of the new younger generation from youth of earlier decades, who had expected that their elders would be holding the country together while they sought identities. The latest youth, many of them products of the expanded campuses, did not believe the country worth holding together.

The august affluence should have produced an imperial educational establishment. Instead, it produced a brand of "research professors" who expressed frank contempt for students and lesser faculty. It produced an overflowing cornucopia of gifts and benefits, highlighting the languid jest (referring to the widely read advertisement of a favorite whisky): "As long as you're up, get me a grant." Students—some of the sharpest students—reacted by giving as much or more attention to the off-campus events of folksinging and militancy as to their studies.

Yet the campuses were the key—if any there was—to a possible future of muckraking and Progressivism, since they multiplied at an awesome rate, spawning Ph.D.'s, professors, theses, aides, and lower echelons of instructors increasingly embittered by their lack of dignity and likelihood of distinction. Their definition of muckraking was anything which revealed the reactionary nature of America. Progressivism—and they were aided here by the researches of professors in the field—connoted chauvinism, racism, and a view of foreign affairs which they saw as spitting in the face of the "Third World" of underdeveloped nations.

As has been seen, the drive for Negro rights had been part of the original Progressive drive, and had involved the muckraking power of Ray Stannard Baker, and the united efforts of Negroes and whites which had created the NAACP and the Urban League. All this seemed intolerably meagre to a new generation of writers which thought itself better abreast of events by stepping up its demands, and even by demeaning such "Uncle Toms" as Booker T. Washington, and such backward-looking traditions as Negro spirituals.

The revelations produced by the new crusaders, that there was bigotry and inequality in the land, failed to note that the charges worked both ways. Whatever else they were, the revelations failed to constitute muckraking on older models.

Outgoing Democrats and incoming Republicans will live equally to regret that they did not cut McCarthy down to size when they had the chance. With his congenital cheek and the enormous powers conferred upon him by his key Senate chairmanship, McCarthy promises to become Eisenhower's chief headache. McCarthy is in a position to smear any government official who fails to do his bidding. With much daring and few scruples, McCarthy can make himself the most powerful single figure in Congress and terrorize the new Administration. All these mumblings and rumblings about how Communists are "already infiltrating" the Republicans are indicative.[6]

Thus I. F. Stone in January of 1953 in a commentary which on the surface would have seemed all but prophetic. In fact, McCarthy accomplished little so far as the major parties were concerned except to force them to close their ranks a little more tightly as a shield against McCarthy's wilder charges. Stone's role as a critic of American policy, and of the parties proper, was more effective and enabled him, with reservations, to claim title as an authentic heir of the muckrakers. Stone was not distinguished for uncovering new materials for exposé purposes. But, then, neither had most of the original muckrakers done this to any sensational extent. Aside from Lawson, and the Hearst of the Standard Oil exposures, most of them had taken existing facts, known in part to many people, and put them into patterns of import to all of them. Stone's steady view of government policy added up to a criticism which was coherent and informative.

He saw the "fetich of the Fifties" as security. For this, Americans, and especially their legislators would be willing to sacrifice freedom, privacy, civil rights, legality; and in doing so they would achieve not more security, but less. Communism was not a conspiracy, but a contemporary fact in the world. In effect, Stone saw a need for what would later be recognized as "detente"—a living together between differently premised nations all willing to avoid futile and destructive wars.

In addition, we needed to build up our democracy at home, Stone thought, if we were not to face the world as hypocrites and fools. Stone watched closely the rising efforts to extend Negro rights, especially in the South. He deplored the malicious killing in 1955 of young Emmett Till, a Negro, in Mississippi, a crime for which

[6] I. F. Stone, *The Haunted Fifties*, Random House, New York, 1963, 17.

it was not then possible to obtain justice. And he bitterly noted that it was necessary for the bus-desegregation crusader, Reverend Martin Luther King, Jr., to visit Ghana, which was then being visited by Vice President Richard M. Nixon, in order to have his hand shaken by his fellow-American. "The place to win Africa's friendship is still Montgomery, Alabama," Stone concluded.[7]

Stone worked hard to balance his principles. He denounced the Russians for having run with tanks over the Hungarian Republicans in 1956. During a visit to Moscow he probed with Soviet spokesmen and citizens the qualities of freedom, there and at home. He patiently leaned backward in defense not only of the rights of alleged Communists and the more debatable—and more numerous—category of "fellow-traveler," but sought honor for them as balancing wheels of American freedom. Stone criticized the news media as essentially "managed" by government agencies, though conceding that journalists did not fight them too hard. He deplored the then-recent deportation in 1955 of the radical editor Cedric Belfrage, with none to protest.

If there was any limitation on the analysis or emphases of this latter-day muckraker, it lay in his insufficiently acknowledging the viewpoint of the larger American audience, at least to the extent of meeting their counterarguments. Stone treated as heroes all witnesses at HUAC sessions who refused to testify on grounds of the First and Fifth Amendments to the Constitution. A more broadly-based muckraking approach might have wished to apportion some relative status to one or another witness, and to have assessed whether the witness had any concern for the viewpoint and interests of the common citizen. Involved in such questions, also, were certain human and esthetic considerations which had, in older muckraking days, given weight and body to the writer's prose.

Thus, it might have made sense to denounce, as Stone did, the political persecution which caused Charles Chaplin to leave the country and live abroad, and perhaps even to praise Chaplin's art as precious to our cultural heritage. But to reprove *Life* for joining the chorus of praise for Boris Pasternak's *Dr. Zhivago* but not "defending" Howard Fast when he received the Stalin Award for literature raised questions of esthetics as well as international

<hr>

[7] *Ibid.*, 107–109, 205.

propriety. Stone believed as late as 1963 that "an unofficial black-list still bars some of our best artists and actors and directors in Hollywood and from radio-TV work."[8] Stone was anything but a hack, yet his position on some matters came as close to being politically-directed as anything a hack might have contrived.

How to serve the larger American public without knuckling down to its prejudices was a problem which would-be muckrakers did not solve in that generation. It may have been that the over-powering prosperity made any solution untenable. As contemptible as were some of the pro-McCarthy rationalizations for reckless character assassination, the beset opposition did not always act more wisely. Some of the anti-McCarthy denunciations had the quality of the drunk kicking the lamppost for having assaulted him. McCarthy was not so much a principal as a profiteer from what should have been a reasonable fear of being victimized by traitors. But poor time though the 1950s were, they concluded by despising McCarthy, and, despite conservative protests, by giving him to history as the spiritual parent of "the McCarthy Era."

Both Nixon and John F. Kennedy spoke for American pride and American power in 1960, but Kennedy with overtones of "urban liberalism" which rose out of city machines and promised largesse based on Gross National Product. Neither candidate brought with him social workers, labor representatives, investigative reporters, city administrators, innovators in farm policy, social planners—the sinews of a Progressive movement. Their associates were verbalists, memorandum writers, phrase-makers capable of reaching an absent-minded public with appealing albeit often specious phrases.

The Kennedy "Mafia" was not dismayed by a Cuban policy which revealed appalling ineptness on the part of numerous branches—military, intelligence, and organizational—with respect to Cuba. W. W. Rostow, one of the Kennedy intellectuals—and one in the following Johnson administration—noted that "[t]he trouble with our Cuban operation was and remains that it was mounted on simple ideological grounds."[9] Nevertheless he and his associates

---

[8] *Ibid.*, 252.

[9] W. W. Rostow, *The Diffusion of Power: an Essay in Recent History*, The Macmillan Company, New York, 1972, 654.

were not humbled, nor daunted from dealing with numerous problems all around the world in their most acute phases. They learned no means of learning from others. All over the nation there were experts in the politics, traditions, geography, industry, and culture of the nations of the world who knew—not conjecturally, but absolutely—what the circumstances were in their fields of specialty. They had no way of reaching administrators like Rostow in Washington who pushed buttons, gave orders, and announced policies. The experts were not asked, and they could not contribute.

Phrase-makers were not muckrakers. "Military hardware," "salami tactics" (the Soviet program of slicing off strategic pieces of international terrain, as in Berlin and Suez)—such phrases were perhaps evocative for initiating discussions. They were deathly for determining actions and mobilizing sentiment. Rostow's memorandum of March 2, 1961, was typical of much of the "Mafia's" thinking, and calculated to give ordinary citizens pause. In it Rostow informed President Kennedy—and had no diffidence in informing his later readers—that "if we all work hard" (a favorite phrase of Rostow's) it should be possible for Argentina, Brazil, Colombia, Venezuela, India, The Philippines, Taiwan, Turkey, Greece, "and possibly Egypt, Pakistan, Iran and Iraq" to have attained self-sustaining growth by 1970.[10] It is rude to push hindsight too hard at prophecy. But the frame of mind revealed, though it stirred memories of Herbert Croly and of the Woodrow Wilson movers and shakers, became terrifying under 1970s conditions.

The two great waves of social action which finally overcame in popular concern old fears of atomic war, and of Russian and Red Chinese offensives, were the Negro drive for equality, and the youth drive for an emancipated life-style. Both movements totally pushed away from old premises, though bits and pieces of ancient times were evoked to implement new concepts. Thus, the civil rights movement was begun in the South by a combination of white liberals and Negro crusaders who encouraged themselves by recalling slogans of the American Revolution, Negro spirituals, and other symbols of emancipation.

The gathering crisis saw leadership taken away from white organizers of strikes, boycotts, sit-ins, and other front-line opera-

[10] *Ibid.*, 647.

tions, and assumed by a new young core of Negro intransigents. A new rhetoric among them vowed vengeance and death to recalcitrant whites who stood in their path. The term "Blacks" was popularized in spite of a long Negro tradition which identified the word with bigotry and the work of bigots. And a strong, successful campaign made nationally known and identifiable such names as "Brother Huey," "Angela," "Eldridge," "Rap," and "Stokely." James Forman, a Negro militant, wrote an entire book about one young man whom he described as "the first black college student to die in the Black Liberation Movement." *Sammy Younge, Jr.* (1968) described a boy raised in Tuskegee, Alabama, who had served in the United States Navy, entered Tuskegee Institute, engaged in civil rights actions with the Student Nonviolent Coordinating Committee (SNCC), and who had been shot to death during his attempt to desegregate toilets. Although such tragic tales moved readers and gained funds and human support for Negro militants, they were manifestly linked to radical traditions, rather than Progressive. Indeed, a Jack T. Kirby, in his *Darkness at the Dawning* (1972), identified bigotry *with* Progressivism.

But, whereas the dreadful labor battles of the 1930s had advanced unions and social benefits, it became increasingly unclear just what would be gained under such new slogans as "Black Power" and "Freedom Is to Be Found in the Barrel of a Revolver." Negro militant theoreticians argued that whites, frightened, would grant everything the radicals demanded. But though juries proved reluctant to find guilty some Negro defendants who had patently committed murder, the plodding processes of law did eventually reduce the more arrant challengers to small groups of individualistic terrorists. And the ready funds of government, foundations, and "radical chic" sympathizers of wealth dried up.

The youth movement, mainly white, was larger, and, as it gathered force, drew together such disparate types as sheer seekers for sensation, "free speech" advocates whose cause was contained in a few obscene words, and campus malcontents resentful of empty academic routines or what seemed to them inequities perpetrated by administrators. What gave them strength and unity which they could not have otherwise achieved, despite the laxity and loss of direction of their elders, was the intensifying Vietnam war. Once it was established that there would be no governmental drive for victory in the field, no light at the end of the tunnel, forces of ennui and protest could not but gather ever-increasing strength.

The momentous factor about Vietnam was not the expenditure of funds. It was not the blatant corruption, or even the war deaths and woundings. It was the television, employed originally by the Johnson administration to explain and encourage domestic sympathy for the American interventionist mission. Early special television programs showed Americans as adjuncts—"advisors"—to the South Vietnamese military and civilian personnel. The shows revealed the Americans as allegedly making firmly loyal allies in strategic towns and villages, ferreting out underground Viet Cong —often literally, as the Viet Cong employed tunnels in the earth for storage and movement purposes. The specials were complimentary to the Americans, showing, for example, the rebuilding of devastated villages with fresh lumber and supplies brought in by the military.

The cameras also focused on black marketeers, languid South Vietnamese troops, youthful, almost childish-looking, American troops disporting themselves in brothel strips and other uninspiring locations. The correspondents, once they breathed a free air of communication wholly unprecedented in American annals, gave up not one jot of their new-found prerogatives. Formerly, they had looked the other way while shoddy scandals about contrived shows on television, "payola" arrangements involving corrupt music houses and disc jockeys, and other such embarrassments had been aired. Mike Wallace, a brave and resourceful commentator, had made bold efforts at forthright muckraking of street and road contractors and police conspirators, and been quietly put down by his network superiors. Now, foreign correspondents in Vietnam, facing a multi-millioned television audience of "armchair generals," kept up a steady stream of revelations which accumulated to prove that the war could not be won, and that there was a probability of nothing to win.

This was distinctly muckraking which, though it did not create a foreign policy, clearly impugned existing official policy. The momentous fact was that the living room audience clearly hungered for more. Its attention span also took in other phenomena which made "instant heroes" among the marchers for civil rights in Selma, Alabama, among Hippies and political radicals, and, as the social crisis of the era swelled, among participants in mass demonstrations which increasingly put the normal elements of "law and order" in the wrong. How much this was a product of pro-demonstration reportorial sympathy, how much of audience empathy it is difficult to judge. One Abbie Hoffman became a master of orchestrating protest, and appeared not only on the front pages of newspapers, but in the sections devoted to entertainment and advertising news, explaining his methods for obtaining publicity.

At its highest level the era was highlighted by the force of circumstances which caused President Lyndon B. Johnson to announce his decision not to run for his office again in 1968. The instrument of his fall from the dazzling heights of his 1964 victory at the polls was a moderately well-known senator, Eugene McCarthy of Minnesota, a follower of the better-known Vice-President Hubert H. Humphrey of the same state, and like him a patent progressive. Eugene McCarthy's *A Liberal Answer to the Conservative Challenge* (1964) rang the changes on economic justice, the poor and the working people, the farmer, the elderly, the Negroes, and government responsibility through such agencies as Social Security and TVA. His book was distinctly weak on foreign responsibilities, no doubt because he sensed his countrymen's—and his own—confusion on what they should be. By 1967 his *The Limits of Power: America's Role in the World* had learned from the storm of protest, and was somewhat in advance of his colleagues' ideas in announcing that there ought to be a firm decision in concluding the Vietnam commitment. McCarthy had been a professor, but not for twenty years, and he had kept his penchant for wit and poetry under wraps. However, in announcing, in November 1967, that he intended to challenge Johnson for the Democratic nomination, he became the most immediately available bridge to government that the youthful revolters had, and in the momentous New Hampshire primary, the least reckless youth, those most willing to wear neckties and speak courteously to houseowners whose doorbells they rang, turned out in force in McCarthy's behalf.

It was a quasi-Progressive effort, and it brought Johnson down. McCarthy, however, now highlighted in the news, found himself challenged by still another progressive, a scion of the dissolved Kennedy junta who, in effect, offered a similar program intended to bring back the glory of the late President's "thousand days."

Both McCarthy and Robert F. Kennedy claimed to speak in the name of "the people"—McCarthy entitled his account of his campaign *The Year of the People* (1969)—a concept which looked back to Populist and Progressive days, in form if not in fact. It did not, however, feature muckraking or muckrakers, and did not attract a comparable alliance of supporters.

McCarthy himself revealed an almost frivolous personality during a campaign in which he featured the poet Robert Lowell and his own verse: tendencies which helped explain in part his attraction for a youth which was also receptive to the charisma of such a loser as Che Guevara. A thoughtful critic noted that McCarthy was a politician first of all, and wondered how this fact could have been obscured during his charming but ultimately ineffective presidential campaign:

> Was this, in itself, intuitive politics—a sense that after Johnson people [*sic*] wanted an amateur, *à l'anglaise?* Before the primaries, this could almost have been so. There is a connection in American myth between ineffectuality and integrity, but this stops at the clubhouse door. . . . [I]t may all have been a charade anyway, . . . and perhaps McCarthy knew this and concentrated entirely on making a public record.[11]

The war, however, was no charade, and those who made Nixon President in 1968 by somewhat more of a margin than that razor-edged one which had defeated him in 1960 swept past Humphrey, to say nothing of McCarthy, in order to cling to shreds of patriotism and belief in government and to the hope that politicians would contrive a negotiated peace of which the poet was incapable, a peace with face-saving if not honor.

Progressivism, then, had lost almost all status as a movement, despite the presence of such worthies as Thomas K. Finletter, lawyer and statesman, who wisely balanced our international options, and John W. Gardner, secretary under Johnson of the Department of Health, Education, and Welfare, who strove to make that agency an instrument of humanism and enlightenment and afterwards tried to forge a union of citizen-energies under the rubric of Common Cause. Muckraking did better than Progres-

[11] Wilfred Sheed, *The Morning After, Selected Essays and Reviews,* Farrar, Straus & Giroux, New York, 1968, 124–125.

sivism. It stayed abreast of events through the commentary of Drew Pearson and Jack Anderson, among others. It could claim such a crashing sensation as Daniel Ellsberg's revelations of military policy, given permanent place in American annals as "The Pentagon Papers," which he released from under government wraps in 1971. Outstanding also was Seymour M. Hersh's sad exposé of an American massacre in Vietnam, *My Lai 4* (1970).

American policy abroad was so befuddled as to raise questions about just what constituted muckraking in the field. A foreign policy created independently of public opinion needed definitions which would bring muckraking up to date. It was otherwise with domestic affairs, once the base from which foreign policy had been extrapolated. And now a major figure appeared, or was created, to give muckraking such a forward thrust as it had not in years experienced.

Ralph Nader was revealed as having been persecuted by General Motors for exposing the inadequacy of their automotive engineering in his book, *Unsafe at Any Speed: the Designed-in Dangers of the American Automobile* (1965). Nader had studied automobile accidents and their causes and aftermaths in Connecticut, and had worked with government agencies in Washington to draw up public-interest laws controlling corporate indifference to statistics. He had won the sympathy of Senator Abraham A. Ribicoff, whose investigative committee gave Nader the hearing in which he could protest the surveillance he had suffered. In March of 1966 he was given a national audience for airing his complaint.

Once again, it was television which was the hero of the Nader-centered muckraking sensation. TV audiences which viewed the cleancut-looking young man with the good cause could compare him with the automated General Motors executives who evidently had only their private administrative business in mind. And in their backdoor attempts to dig into his privacy, to trip him with the woman game, to use his ethnic origins maliciously against him, they turned on a flood of sympathy for Nader which swept him into prominence.

Unsafe at Any Speed became a best-seller, though how much effect it had on automobile safety remains problematic. After all, manufacturers were not crusaders. They sought anxiously to anticipate the buyers' wants. They remembered the gigantic failure of the "Edsel," which had dragged down with it in research, engineering, advertising, and prestige huge sums of corporate money and good will. Nader went on to appeal to the country and especially to its youth for aid in renovating the laws to compel production calculated to make a better, finer America.

Nader attracted a wave of young lawyers who helped him study the books and legislative hearings for evidence of weakness in manufacturing, public policy—as, for example, in keeping air and water clean—and adequate controls. He himself helped support "Nader's Raiders" with well-paid lectures before college assemblies and clubs. There was scarcely a single field of human need which his teams did not survey, and about which they did not produce carefully written books: a library of them. The children, the elderly, food preparation, equitable taxes, congressional probity—it was a list to warm the hearts of anyone who recalled the heroic age of muckraking.

And yet . . . the vibrant question arose, whether Nader was a person—a most estimable person—or a movement. Evidence accumulated that the first enthusiasm among his followers for serving the nation progressively waned, as young lawyers ceased heading for Washington and took traditional steps to enter law firms strictly concerned for business and profits. One of Nader's acolytes made almost the entire circuit of public interest groups, working with the Federal Communications Commission, with the Commission on the Democratic Selection of Presidential Nominees, and with Bess Myerson's New York City Department of Consumer Affairs. Moreover, Nader could point to numerous changes in law as a result of the work of "Nader's Raiders," such as the Wholesome Meat Act (1967), the Natural Gas Pipeline Safety Act (1968), and the Federal Coal Mine Health and Safety Act (1969).

In the end the young crusader concluded that laws were not self-administering, that they could often be turned against the consumer, and that little had been accomplished. He now put his faith in a "new" Populism which would, however, be administered by an elite of keen legal minds, self-appointed, he confessed, established in government and especially in the federal courts. They would be able to force recalcitrant malefactors not only to right their wrongs in manufacturing and elsewhere, but to pay court costs.[12] Since that had been essentially the program of such still extant government agencies as the Interstate Commerce Commission and the FCC, barring details of penalties, the new program sounded more like the product of desperation than of revelation.

Watergate, in 1975, still hung heavily upon the nation, and appeared likely to continue to do so for a while. And yet the nation needed to know better what it had involved, and even more what it had implied. Certainly it evoked forces of journalistic agitation, reporter enterprise, and persistent digging for more and more information which resulted in denouement after denouement, with criminals and others exposed and brought to trial or disgrace: all the themes identified with classical muckraking.

And yet there were unanswered questions, indefinite conclusions. The key fact about Watergate was the long public apathy which attended it. The break-in affecting National Democratic Party headquarters was discovered in June of 1972. In the succeeding weeks, Democratic spokesmen sought to make it a focal point for dissatisfaction with the Republican administration, but with no success. In November the President was overwhelmingly re-elected. Not until February of 1973 was a Senate committee assembled to investigate the matter, and not until May did the first hearings materialize. Numerous witnesses, with charges and counter-charges, appeared, and the committee's chairman, Sam Ervin, was hailed as a great man, but a coagulate of charges was slow in forming. The public was unclear about what it expected from an administration, whether Republican or Democratic.

Some common corruption was revealed—notably, outside Watergate, in the Vice President's old Maryland connections—but it was generally realized that corruption was not the main issue. What was central was the management of power. The President was not laid low by revelations of his real estate and income tax dealings, or by evidence that he was inculpated in the Watergate "caper." It was proof that he had been implicated in the "cover up" of this adventure that forced his resignation. And not so much the "cover up," as the fact that the support of his party had been withdrawn

[12] Simon Lazarus, *The Genteel Populists*, Holt, Rinehart and Winston, New York, 1974.

from him. As he said, on resigning, he had lost his "power base." It was an ironic last act for one who had been accused of having tried to accrete a personal power threatening to the democratic process.

Financial corruption could not have been the original point of dispute, in a nation which had been slow to flare up in anger at the "$64,000 Question" exposé on television. Indeed, the public had been more puzzled than angry in determining how much "honesty" ought to be expected from an "entertainment" show. Newspaper editors had hastened to point out that wrestling was notoriously in the hands of fixers, but that this fact did not seem to mar the enjoyment of spectators at wrestling matches. Nor had there been any intelligent inquiry into the value of memorizing an endless variety of "facts" respecting literature, or biology, or anything else. Such revelations, like Watergate, were the results of a species of muckraking. But as they faded into forgetfulness they left questions unanswered about what, if anything, had been accomplished.

A diminished Spiro T. Agnew blamed a "post-Watergate morality" for his fall, and it is evident that it was a pre-Watergate set of expectations which persuaded the harassed President fatefully to hold on to tapes which revealed his complicity in the "cover up." Had he destroyed the tapes, all later realized, the campaign against him would ultimately have ended without consummation, whatever the judgment of posterity upon him. It was the President's confidence in the essential sympathy of the majority of Americans with him which betrayed him. Endless conjecture about just how much he had known would have been one thing that he could not have controlled. But he would have been as immune from ultimate overthrow as had been President Ulysses S. Grant before him.

But the public and its congressional spokesmen had experienced a change of heart. Probably that change went no deeper than appearance's sake. But it did go that deep. The public was fed up. It wanted Watergate finished and done with: taken off the boards. And taken off it was. It needs once more to be recalled that what occasioned the President's overthrow was not any decision of a court or prosecutor or superior court, but a decision of Republican party front-liners who were able to determine whether they would or would not vote for the President's conviction, following impeachment. It was their political decision which ended his "reign," that and not a legal decision.

What, then, was the nature of this epic "muckraking" achievement? It was widely recognized that those who had broken open the Watergate case and shown its ramifications into the highest political circles were somehow disappointing in their account of their exploits.[13] Although they had shown courage, persistence, and inventiveness in tracking down connections between unlikely personalities in government, somehow the sagas of Lincoln Steffens and David Graham Phillips did not come to mind.

What was missing was a Progressive movement. Muckraking by itself tended to veer aimlessly between sensationalism and an appeal to a public morality which was not well defined. Only a political movement manned by leaders who did not depend on corrupt machines, who professed loyalty to the interests of the country, and who worked to balance, with more or less equity, the many social interests of the population—only such a movement could hope to initiate a chain of events capable of reversing the disheartening trend of sordid plots and demagoguery: easily "muckraked," but to no important purpose.

Was there a future, then, for muckraking? Only if there was a future for Progressivism. And there could be no such future if a radical change did not bring a Progressive public back to life. A government study which elicited information after promising immunity to a random sample of 1700 citizens more or less established that 91 percent of those interrogated admitted to having committed one or more public offenses for which they could have received prison terms if discovered. Ninety-one percent. Thirteen percent admitted to grand larceny, twenty percent to auto theft—a mind-boggling statistic which raised questions about the entire project—and seventeen percent to some species of burglary.[14]

With such a public, it seemed unlikely that the millennium was around the corner. On the other hand, a type of realism might be: one that recognized the weaknesses in human nature but that took

---

[13] Carl Bernstein and Bob Woodward, *All the President's Men*, Simon and Schuster, New York, 1974.

[14] *Dayton* (Ohio) *Journal Herald*, May 8, 1975, 14.

pride in an American past which had included some of the noblest of spirits and the most ambitious of democratic enterprises. A more humble attitude toward such a past might suggest to readers as well as writers, to voters as well as politicians, that they would be wise to target for a working society. The agencies of social control— once, during New Deal years, intended to settle problems of jobs and insecurity for all time—needed to be reviewed and done over. A new and dynamic criticism of business and government and labor had to be developed.

Easier said than done, the desperate radical could complain. But was this a challenge to be scorned? Were there viable alternatives? Those who had despised reform had not shown their superiority to it. They had not exhibited firsthand familiarity with the factual and cultural details of their country such as the muckrakers had acquired. Having surrendered reform, the bankrupt "radicals" could be charged with having resigned their right to speak for democracy.

Muckraking in its old form was obviously not to be revived. Yet if it was, as Charles Edward Russell had once thought, the only known instrument for correcting democracy's tendency to veer wildly between anarchy and industrial autocracy, then muckraking as an adjunct of progressivism had never been more necessary.

The vital fact that the Seventies needed to know—and Nader, and Ellsberg—was that the reform writers had not really created muckraking. They had merely been its pioneers. Muckraking was at its best as an expression of popular will. The creativity of new muckrakers would be shown by precipitating the finest impulses in the body politic. People were often at their worst because they were discouraged, and had lost faith in others as well as themselves. The competent muckraker would know how to bring his readers back to themselves, help them align themselves with the best in government and society, teach them to despise demagogues and self-pitying rascals. Almost certainly, given a revived public spirit, poets and fictioneers would surface to express sentiments and scenes expressive of a more vital and varied public than the pornographers and "far out" self-indulgent writers had been able to evoke.

When the bounds of muckraking were clearly seen, it was possible to define partially just what it was the muckrakers had accomplished. They had ushered in modern times. To say this is almost to forget the savage unrest which their work involved, the personal tragedy and philosophic confusion that accompanied it. Men and women of the muckraking period yearned as wholeheartedly for the millennium as those who followed them. If they knew less of psychology and economic forces than those others, they had fewer excuses for failure. For all their social consciousness, they placed responsibility upon the individual. Finally, they achieved tangible results.

They fell short of completing their work, but which movement has succeeded in doing that? The original muckrakers had retreated in the face of organized business attacks, and they had broken down completely in their first experience with international affairs. But before that they had succeeded in uniting the country. America in 1900 had not been a union. The cultural spadework of the muckrakers had synthesized it as surely as had the actual spadework of transcontinental highways. As Ida Tarbell later saw:

> I have never had illusions about the value of my individual contribution! I realized early that what a man or a woman does is built on what those who have gone before have done, that its real value depends on making the matter in hand a little clearer, a little sounder for those who come after. Nobody begins or ends anything. Each person is a link, weak or strong, in an endless chain. One of our great mistakes is persuading ourselves that nobody has passed this way before. . . .
>
> We are given to ignoring not only the past of our solutions, their status when we took them over, but the variety of relationships they must meet, satisfy. They must sink or swim in a stream where a multitude of human experiences, prejudices, ambitions, ideals meet and clash, throw one another back, mingle, make that all-powerful current which is public opinion—the trend which swallows, digests, or rejects what we give it. It is our indifference to or ignorance of the multiplicity of human elements in the society we seek to benefit that is responsible for the sinking outright of many of our fine plans.[15]

Maturity—that had, after all, been the foundation of the original muckrakers' achievements. It might well become such a foundation again.

[15] From *All in the Day's Work*, Macmillan Company, New York, 1939. By permission of the publishers.

CHRONOLOGY

1901

February. Josiah Flynt's *The World of Graft*, which anticipated muckraking, began in *McClure's*.

March 3. J. P. Morgan announced the formation of the billion-dollar United States Steel Corporation.

April 2. Tom L. Johnson, advocate of the Single-Tax and formerly a street-railway monopolist, elected Mayor of Cleveland.

May 9. The Hill-Harriman fight for control of the Northern Pacific Railroad brought on a panic, resulting in a truce and the creation of the Northern Securities Company.

September 6. President McKinley shot while attending the Pan-American Exposition in Buffalo, New York.

September 14. McKinley died; Vice-President Theodore Roosevelt took the oath of office.

December 3. Roosevelt's first message to Congress sounded the keynote for his future policies.

1902

February 18. The government instituted proceedings against the Northern Securities Company, serving notice that the Sherman Anti-Trust Act was not defunct.

May 12. Labor exhibited its strength, as the great anthracite coal strike commenced.

June 18. The Federal Reclamation Act, a first step in conservation of natural resources, became law.

October. *McClure's* published Lincoln Steffens's "Tweed Days in St. Louis."

November. The first installment of Ida Tarbell's *The History of the Standard Oil Company* appeared in *McClure's*.

November. Publication of James Howard Bridge's *The Inside History of the Carnegie Steel Company*.

1903

January. *McClure's* discovered muckraking in an editorial concerned with articles by Steffens, Tarbell, and Ray Stannard Baker in the current issue.

March 26. Scandal in the United States Post Office reached the front page of the newspapers, and stayed there.

May. Dr. Harvey W. Wiley, Chief of the United States Bureau of Chemistry, made his "poison squad" experiments news.

October 27. Land frauds, recently discovered in Oregon, grew in magnitude, as United States Senators and others of high office were shown to be involved.

November 10. Joseph G. Cannon, of Illinois, became Speaker of the House of Representatives.

1904

March 14. The Northern Securities Company dissolved by decision of the United States Supreme Court.

April 13. Thomas W. Lawson, of Boston, declared war on Standard Oil.

May. Edward Bok, in *The Ladies' Home Journal*, opened fire on the patent-medicine evil.

July. *The Arena* made a fresh beginning in its battle against the trusts; B. O. Flower, its editor, led off with *Twenty-five Years of Bribery and Corrupt Practices; or, the Railroads, the Lawmakers, the People*.

July. *Everybody's* announced that *The Story of Amalgamated*, by Thomas W. Lawson, would appear in future issues; Lawson himself framed his challenge to organized finance.

July 12. Death of Samuel Milton Jones, the "Golden Rule" Mayor of Toledo. He was succeeded by Brand Whitlock, who carried on his work for eight years.

July 22. Joseph Wingate Folk, newly famous for his prosecutions of "Boodlers" in St. Louis, was nominated, and subsequently elected, Governor of Missouri.

September. *Leslie's* began its fight against railroad accidents; its editor, Ellery Sedgwick, termed America "The Land of Disasters."

September. Lawson, in *Everybody's*, exposed the New York Life Assurance Company as controlled by the System, thus focusing attention on life insurance as requiring investigation.

November. *The Era* began its attack on the management of the great insurance companies with "The Despotism of Combined Millions."

November 10. Roosevelt re-elected on a wholesale reform platform.

1905

February. Serialization of *The Greatest Trust in the World*, Charles Edward Russell's exposé of the Beef Trust, began in *Everybody's*.

February 14. First annual conference of the National Child Labor Committee held in New York City.

March 22. Ministers protested against acceptance of Rockefeller donation for foreign mission work, opening the "tainted money" controversy.

April 22. *Collier's* informally joined the muckraking movement with evaluations of Lawson's work, the Beef Trust question and other issues.

May. Burton J. Hendrick began his *The Story of Insurance* in *McClure's*.

June 27. The first convention of the Industrial Workers of the World opened in Chicago.

July 2. Armour and other Beef Trust leaders indicted in conspiracy to restrain trade; later sentenced, but conviction reversed.

September 6. The Armstrong Insurance Investigating Committee, Charles E. Hughes prosecuting, began hearings in Albany, New York, culminating internecine war between leaders in the insurance field.

October 7. Samuel Hopkins Adams commenced his story of *The Great American Fraud* in *Collier's*.

November. The fight for railroad regulation was strengthened by Ray Stannard Baker's series, "The Railroads on Trial," the first article of which appeared in *McClure's*.

November 8. William Randolph Hearst "defeated" in New York City mayoralty elections.

December 5. Roosevelt, in his annual message to Congress, advocated a law regulating food and drugs. Senator Weldon B. Heyburn of Idaho reintroduced the often-defeated Pure Food bill.

December 30. Ex-Governor Frank Steunenberg assassinated in Caldwell, Idaho.

1906

January 4. Jacob Schiff, of Kuhn, Loeb and Company, predicted a financial panic, unless the national monetary system was reformed.

January 4. Representative Hepburn of Iowa introduced in the House the Roosevelt-sponsored railroad regulation bill.

January 4. Robert Marion La Follette took his seat in the United States Senate in an atmosphere of isolation.

January 16. Libel suit against *Collier's* began in New York City, prompted by *Collier's* denunciation of *Town Topics* as an organ of filth and blackmail.

January 27. Norman Hapgood acquitted of the charge of slandering *Town Topics*.

February 17. Moyer, Haywood, and Pettibone arrested in Denver, Colorado, on charge of complicity in the murder of ex-Governor Steunenberg.

February. Publication of *The Jungle*, by Upton Sinclair.

March. *Cosmopolitan*, under the new editorship of Bailey Millard, began serialization of David Graham Phillips's "The Treason of the Senate."

April 14. Roosevelt delivered his "Man with the Muckrake" speech in Washington.

April 28. The New York State Legislature, acting on the evidence disclosed by the Armstrong Investigating Committee, completed a program of life-insurance reform legislation.

May 18. Passage of the Hepburn Railroad Bill.

May 22. Senator Albert J. Beveridge of Indiana introduced a Roosevelt-endorsed Meat Inspection Bill.

June 4. Lack of co-operation by conservative Senatorial forces impelled Roosevelt to release the first part of the Neill-Reynolds report on conditions of sanitation in the Chicago stockyards.

June 20. Roosevelt signed the Pure Food Bill, which public indignation forced into law.

June 30. Likewise the Meat Inspection Amendment.

August. C. P. Connolly, former District Attorney of corrupt Silverbow County, Montana, opened his career as a muckraker with *The Story of Montana* for *McClure's*.

September. Edwin Markham's first article on child labor appeared in *Cosmopolitan*.

October. *The American Magazine* taken over by John S. Phillips, Steffens, Tarbell, Baker, Peter Finley Dunne, and William Allen White, who seceded from *McClure's*.

October. Publication in *McClure's* of George Kibbe Turner's influential "Galveston: A Business Corporation"—his first article on municipal problems.

November 4. Charles Evans Hughes elected Governor of New York over William Randolph Hearst by 60,000 votes.

November 15. Mayor Eugene Schmitz and "Abe" Ruef, political bosses of San Francisco, indicted on five bills charging extortion. This climaxed agitation for municipal reform.

November 21. The People's Lobby, sponsored by *Success*, formally launched, with Mark Sullivan as president.

1907

January 3. Death of Ernest Crosby.

January 12. Three-cent fare on street-cars went into effect in Cleveland, crowning Mayor Tom Johnson's efforts in that direction. Conservatives instituted a campaign to do away with it, and ultimately succeeded.

January 20. Death of Josiah Flynt.

March 14. Fall on the New York Stock Exchange gave evidence of the coming panic.

April. Ray Stannard Baker's *Following the Color Line* began in *The American Magazine*.

May 9. "Big Bill" Haywood went on trial for his life; Clarence Darrow defending, William Borah prosecuting.

July. Harry Orchard's *Confession and Autobiography* began in *McClure's*.

July 28. Haywood acquitted of having been accessory to the murder of Steunenberg.

August 3. Kenesaw Mountain Landis, United States District Judge, fined the Standard Oil Company of Indiana $29,240,000 for accepting rebates in violation of the Elkins Act of 1903. This company lacking assets to pay the fine, Landis ruled that the holding company (Standard Oil of New Jersey) must pay it. This verdict subsequently reversed.

September 17. Attacks on Standard Oil climaxed with a government suit to dissolve the trust.

October 21. Speculation brought panic and a run on the Knickerbocker Trust Company.

October 23. The Knickerbocker failed. A united front of financial chieftains, headed by Morgan, ended the threatened collapse of the banking system. Agitation for governmental safeguards increased.

November 30. A United States Treasury agent discovered fraudulent weighing machines on the American Sugar Refining Company's Jersey City docks, by which the government was defrauded of duty.

December 7. Lawson officially withdrew from muckraking.

March 18. Harry Orchard sentenced to die for Steunenberg's murder; later given life imprisonment.

1908

May. Charles Edward Russell published in *Hampton's* "Trinity Church: A Riddle of Riches"—typical of many articles critical of religion and the churches.

June 6. Roosevelt appointed a Conservation Commission with Gifford Pinchot, head of the Forestry Bureau, as chairman.

September 3. *The Independent* printed William English Walling's denunciation of lynch law, "Race War in the North," which resulted in the formation of the National Association for the Advancement of Colored People.

September 17. Hearst, at Columbus, Ohio, released the first of the Archbold letters.

November 5. Charles W. Morse convicted of mishandling funds of the National Bank of North America in New York City, and then sentenced to fifteen years' imprisonment.

November 13. Francis J. Heney, prosecuting the San Francisco grafters, critically shot and incapacitated. His place was taken by Hiram Johnson, who carried on to a successful conclusion.

December. Ben Hampton, having set *The Broadway Magazine* on its feet, announced that a period of constructive criticism had come in which his magazine was determined to participate.

1909

March 4. Taft assumed the Presidency.

March 13. *Collier's*, with Mark Sullivan, began its assault on the Congressional bureaucratic machine.

August. *The Arena* taken from B. O. Flower and merged with *Christian Work*.

August 5. Taft signed the Payne-Aldrich Tariff Bill, taking his stand against the progressives in Congress.

September 13. Taft, having interviewed Glavis regarding his difficulties with

Secretary of the Interior Richard A. Ballinger, wrote Ballinger exonerating him and recommending Glavis's dismissal.

October. *Everybody's* began *The Beast and the Jungle*, by Judge Ben Lindsey.

October. B. O. Flower launched *The Twentieth Century Magazine*.

November. *Hampton's* joined in the Ballinger-Pinchot controversy through its conservation expert, John L. Mathews.

November 13. Glavis's "The White-Washing of Ballinger" in *Collier's* opened the subject to the public.

December 18. C. P. Connolly's "Can This Be White-Washed Also?" in *Collier's* finally compelled an investigation into the Pinchot-Glavis charges of maladministration in the Department of the Interior.

1910

January. *Success*, leader in the fight against "Cannonism," prophesied the Speaker's early defeat in terms that roused its enemies.

January. Congressional hearings on the Ballinger case opened.

February. E. J. Ridgway, owner of *Everybody's*, sold it to the Butterick Company for $3,000,000.

May 20. Ballinger hearings closed.

June 16. Roosevelt returned to America after a world tour.

June 25. Passage of the Mann Act established a national policy regarding prostitution.

October 1. The Los Angeles *Times* building destroyed by dynamite.

November 4. Taft lost the House to the Democrats; Aldrich was stripped of his power in the Senate.

December 7. The report on the Ballinger case revealed the Secretary's usefulness as "impaired."

December. Publication of Charles Edward Russell's "The Surrender of New England" put *Hampton's* "on the spot."

1911

January. *The Masses* was born.

January 14. Will Irwin's definitive study of "The American Newspaper" began in *Collier's*.

January 21. The National Progressive Republican League formed at Senator La Follette's home in Washington, D. C.

January 24. David Graham Phillips died of wounds inflicted by an assassin in Bellevue Hospital, New York City.

March 7. Ballinger resigned.

April 10. Death of former Mayor Tom L. Johnson of Cleveland.

April 22. Arrest of the McNamaras for the dynamiting of the Los Angeles *Times* building.

May 15. The Standard Oil Company ordered dissolved, by decision of the United States Supreme Court.

May 28. Likewise the Tobacco Trust.

July. A. H. Lewis, editor of *Human Life*, lost his magazine in a general movement to put a stop to muckraking. (Although *The American*, *McClure's*, and *Collier's* were not taken out of circulation, they were, during this time, gradually transformed into innocuous periodicals.)

August. Ben Hampton announced the transfer of *Hampton's* to new hands. (The magazine quickly changed character, and then failed.)

October 29. Death of Joseph Pulitzer, owner of the New York *World*.

November. B. O. Flower lost the editorship of *Twentieth Century*.

December 1. The McNamaras pleaded guilty to the dynamiting of the Los Angeles *Times*.

December. *Success* failed.

1912

February 24. Roosevelt announced his candidacy as an Insurgent.

March 16. Dr. Harvey W. Wiley, following persecution, left the Bureau of Chemistry.

April. *Pearson's* announced its new policy: determined to carry on as a free organ of opinion in the face of the advertising and banking boycotts.

April 9. Creation of the Children's Bureau in the Department of Commerce and Labor.

June. *The Metropolitan* took on new life, becoming a quasi-Socialist magazine.

June 6. The Pujo ("Money Trust") Inquiry opened in New York City.

July 13. The Senate voted to unseat William Lorimer of Illinois for buying votes.

September 13. The "Cunningham claims" in Alaska canceled by the new Secretary of the Interior.

October 14. Roosevelt shot and wounded at Milwaukee by a maniac.

1913

January 1. Parcel post was instituted.

February 25. The Paterson Strike (the last great effort of the I.W.W.) began.

February 25. A Constitutional Amendment empowering Congress to levy a general income tax became effective.

March 4. Woodrow Wilson inaugurated President of the United States.

March 6. The Department of Labor began independent existence.

April. *Twentieth Century* suspended.

May 31. By Constitutional Amendment, direct election of Senators was given to the people.

December 23. The Federal Reserve Bill became law.

December 24. Death of A. H. Lewis.

1914

October 15. Passage of the Clayton Anti-Trust Act.

1916

September. Frank Harris took over the editorship of *Pearson's*. Later assumed full control.

November 7. President Wilson re-elected.

November 22. Death of Jack London.

1917

April 6. Proclamation of the President declared the United States to be at war with Germany.

1928

Progressives divide their suffrage between Hoover and Smith "the Lincoln of the City Streets."

1933

Franklin D. Roosevelt inaugurates a "New Deal" which offends some older Progressives as constituting a threat to their ideals of a free economy and limited government.

1938

Dies Committee of the House of Representatives to Investigate Un-American Activities begins a national debate on the rights of radicals or accused radicals which takes varied forms in succeeding decades, all diverting attention from Progressive goals.

1939

World War II begins. The "Grand Alliance" of the democracies and Soviet Russia further expands uses of the Keynesian principles of economics, suggesting that Progressivism is securely in history.

1948

Henry A. Wallace's "Progressive Party" unites liberals and radicals. Their crushing defeat seems anti-climactic to the burial of Progressive issues.

1952

Adlai E. Stevenson's Presidential candidacy for the Democratic Party offers a quasi-Progressive program which is turned back by voters.

1961

John F. Kennedy inaugurates a neo-New Deal program which calls for a "grand and global alliance" to fight such social evils as poverty and war. "Let us never negotiate out of fear," Kennedy declared in his Inaugural Address. "But let us never fear to negotiate."

A NOTE ON BIBLIOGRAPHY

HAVING now prepared a book on *Muckraking and Progressivism: an Interpretive Bibliography*, published by R. R. Bowker Company, I have more perspective on the problem of bibliography.

When I first prepared a bibliography for this work, I was aware that all was yet to be done in the field: that not a bibliography, but bibliographies were needed. I had reason to know, however, that the subject was not sufficiently dead to attract the attention of formal bibliographers, or, for that matter, run-of-the-mill Ph.D. practitioners. There was no point in discussing the punctilios of bibliography when the significance of muckraking itself was questioned by then influential writers and the academic profession. Accordingly, I seized on several books which at least recognized the existence of muckraking, and I called them to the special attention of the reader. One of them still merits his consideration: H. U. Faulkner's *The Quest for Social Justice* (1931) does not treat the muckrakers, but does their times. Another, John Chamberlain's *Farewell to Reform* (1932) is now a curio, since its author has long since abandoned his queer though momentarily successful leftwingism; I have examined him as a phenomenon in "John Chamberlain and American Liberalism," *Colorado Quarterly*, Fall 1957. C. C. Regier's *The Era of the Muckrakers* (1932) was a tepid State University of Iowa thesis which could not discriminate materials and may be passed by for most purposes. Frank L. Mott was not better versed in the art of discrimination, but he, possibly with the help of an occasional aide or two, did raise a cloud of library dust while turning the pages of files of magazines and newspapers. The results of his work are useful as chronicle, even when not impressive as history, as in *A History of American Magazines, 1885-1905* (1957). For uninspired magazine history in shorter compass, see Theodore Peterson's *Magazines in the Twentieth Century* (1964 ed.) There is vastly more inspiration in such an account as Mark Sullivan's *Our Times: The United States 1900-1925* (1928-35). It continues to be a fine trap for scholar or general reader. It is a kind of concentrate of the journalism of the time, with all the odd emphases of journalism and life, and with their own peculiar logic. A live historian will strive to understand this logic, rather than fly off to the security of his own. Matthew Josephson's *The President Makers, 1896-1919* (1940) was by a literary expatriate who came late to historical materials; this fact perhaps contributed to his then fresh and critical approach. Finally, any substantial evaluation must take into account the labors of W. D. P. Bliss, whose compendious *Encyclopedia of Social Reform* (1897, 1908, 1909-10 editions) probed the society of his time from a Christian Socialist point of view and activated great numbers of the reformers themselves in the preparation of particular essays. Much of Bliss's *Encyclopedia* is dead, but so is the League of Nations, and the United Nations is not securely alive. We can afford not to be too arbitrary in judging what is and what is not functional for our purposes. My own *Dictionary of American Social Reform* (1970 edition) has varied aims, many of them relevant to the muckrakers.

This matter of liveliness, of vitality merits an additional word or two. Take, for example, the Yale University Press Film Service, Inc., which circulates "authentic historical filmstrip documents showing how the United States grew from a wilderness into a leader in the world of nations." Unit 17, *The Age of Reform*, edited by Ralph H. Gabriel and others offers such tidbits as: "Under Arthur, the Pendleton Act was passed to put civil service on a merit system." (Cleveland is elected. Next slide.) "[He] further improved the quality of the civil service with strict examinations." (Next slide.) "An Interstate Commerce Commission was formed in 1887 to restrain the railroads." A little later, the Sherman Antitrust Act of 1890 "outlawed such monopolies as the oil industry." Outlawed! No more oil monopoly! Fortunately for this strip's sponsors, they run out of slides and do not have to mention the 1911 Supreme Court decision dissolving the Standard Oil Trust; and we all know how free oil has been since. The slides note the stock market crash of 1893 and the Pullman strike in 1894, but in no form calculated to make a picture of events. The nation "was drawn" into a war with Spain, whatever that means. "Teddy" Roosevelt "strongly supported the Monroe Doctrine" while fighting for reform at home. Taft "furthered Roosevelt's reforms." This slide might have offended "Teddy," but the sequence says nothing which could offend a PTA committee anywhere in the land, or stir a student to mental activity.

It would be good to report that the literature of muckraking proper has grown substantially since I first suggested that one was necessary, but it needs again to be said that all is yet to be done. For a respectable body of work is the product of vibrant social awareness of the need for one. The public and its mentors have been content for the most part to hobble along with old cliches covering the field. These have even been formalized in secondhand treatments accorded the muckrakers in such works as Richard Hofstadter's successful *The Age of Reform* (1955), which proves to its own satisfaction that muckraking, its parent Populism, and its associate Progressivism were backward-looking, bleary with utopian dreams, and smirched by prejudice and status-seeking. The Populists have been knowledgeably defended, and the Progressives are being accorded some academic conversation. But the subject is still in the thrust and riposte stage; it is yet to be moved into a more reasonable arena of interested, yet disinterested inquiry.

Robert H. Wiebe, in his *Businessmen and Reform: a Study of the Progressive Movement* (1962) suggests that "[the] way to reopen the question of the progressives is to start with content rather than with people" (p. 211). It seems to me, on the other hand, that the general reader can still do worse than start with such biographies and special items as I offered in earlier printings of *Crusaders*. For those not only put him in touch with *people,* rather than precious hypotheses; they also indicate the effect upon individuals of great social currents and events. Jack London, William Randolph Hearst, Finley Peter Dunne, Edwin Markham, Robert M. La Follette, Upton Sinclair, Lincoln Steffens—where is the generalization which will cover all of these worthies? Some were scarcely muckrakers at all; some have been closely identified with the very idea of muckraking. Some died with the muckraking era; others lived on to become part of entirely different interests and expectations. Upton Sinclair is happily still with us, and just recently the author of a new and helpful autobiography. Yes, I recommend the study of biography. It can help us become aware of the complexity of muckraking, and its modern interrelatedness with movements of which we are ourselves part.

Slowly, the field opens up. Arthur and Lila Weinberg, eds., *The Muckrakers* (1961) is a journalistic compilation which has helped turn some reader's thoughts to the subject. David Mark Chalmers, *The Social and Political Ideas of the Muckrakers* (1964) focusses on a number of partisans and seeks to distinguish their contributions.

Ultimately, one hopes, there will be a shelf of such works to satisfy public wants for information about these often remarkable people.

Meanwhile, one takes pleasure in the success of Peter Lyon's *Success Story: the Life and Times of S. S. McClure* (1963). It is a vivacious account pieced out of McClure's own papers, and not by an academic. Several academics have complained to me that Lyon does not meet their standards for formal exposition. But considering the kind of statements about muckraking they *have* accepted without criticism or complaint in dreary texts and from ill-informed mentors, one can be grateful for Lyon's industry. And also for W. A. Swanberg's best-selling *Citizen Hearst* (1961). Hearst was not a reliable muckraker, but he was a part of the muckraking story, for better or worse. In this same category belongs John W. Tebbel's *George Horace Lorimer and the Saturday Evening Post* (1948)—not great or even good biography, but about a figure relevant to muckraking, for good and ill.

Among more recent writings which either contribute to aspects of muckraking, or bear upon its workings, some typical productions may be noted. First, the precursors. And let me say a word for Lisle A. Rose's pioneer "A Bibliographical Survey of Economic and Political Writings, 1865-1900," *American Literature*, January 1944; he later prepared several supplements for private distribution. Chester A. Destler's *Henry Demarest Lloyd and the Empire of Reform* (1963) is a hard worked and valuable study of the outstanding pre-muckraker. Arthur Mann's *Yankee Reformers* (1954) deals with Boston reformers of the late nineteenth century, including some, like B. O. Flower, who overlap with muckrakers. It may be profitably read in conjunction with Gregory Weinstein's *The Ardent Eighties* (1928), by a participant, rather than an academic, and with strengths of its own. Also relevant to muckrakers are such works as Arthur E. Morgan's *Edward Bellamy* (1944); Aaron I. Abell, *The Urban Impact on American Protestantism, 1865-1900* (1943) and Charles H. Hopkins, *The Rise of the Social Gospel in American Protestantism, 1865-1915* (1940); Russel B. Nye, *Midwestern Progressive Politics* (1951); Harold U. Faulkner, *Politics, Reform and Expansion, 1890-1900* (1959); and Ray Ginger, *The Bending Cross* (1949), a study of Eugene V. Debs which better handles Debs in his pre-muckraking years than in his great days as a socialist symbol. Nor should so popular a statement of pre-muckraking as Dale Kramer's *The Wild Jackasses: The American Farmer in Revolt* (1956) be ignored. It was by a participant in the farmers' agitations of the early 1930's, and sought to bridge the gap between Populism and later discontent. It made much of that evocative figure, Ignatius Donnelly. It contains ideas and details for general reader or student.

Grant C. Knight's *Critical Period in American Literature* (1951) and Howard H. Quint's *The Forging of American Socialism* (1953) are sufficiently different in interest to suggest other bibliographical possibilities in the area. Richard Welling's *As the Twig Is Bent* (1942) is one of a number of autobiographies relevant to the era, this one by a genteel reformer concerned for the civic education of youth: an unpretentious and benign person who gave the lie to the legend that "goo-goo" reformers lacked humor or a zest for life.

Walter Lord's *The Good Years* (1960) is one of several available popular accounts of the pre-World War I era, and prone to easy recapitulations of difficult matters, in *Life* and *American Heritage* style. But it adds its own researches and memories to those of the more pertinacious and challenging investigator, and the broad-based historian will honor both. Yet I confess myself somewhat impatient with the opinions of Van Wyck Brooks, in his *The Confident Years, 1885-1915* (1952), as in the following (p. 387):

> So while none of the books of the muckraking circle,—nor all of them together,—could be weighed with one of Willa Cather's novels, they represented nevertheless a mood that focussed the minds of writers as the cause of abolition had focussed them sixty years before.

One expects more from a person of Brooks's caliber than of Lord's; Brooks had been a force, with possibilities for good, in the World War I and early post-World War I periods. I happen to admire Cather's novels, but his judgment is sweeping, to say the least, and "focussed the mind" means little that I can understand, or that anyone has found it profitable to explicate.

There is little to report on the muckrakers proper. Upton Sinclair has already been mentioned. Ray Stannard Baker's autobiography, *American Chronicle* (1945), added little that was vital in connection with muckraking. George Creel's *Rebel at Large* (1947) threw light on a basic, somber fact about muckraking: the descent of reform into war. Herbert Shapiro, with Ella Winter, Steffens's widow, published *The World of Lincoln Steffens* (1962), a volume of his writings which could have been more judiciously selected. Winter's own autobiography,

And Not to Yield (1963), added information respecting Steffens's old muckraking methods and purposes only by indirection. Walter Johnson's *William Allen White's America* (1947) clarified little more about muckraking than did White's own *Autobiography* (1946). I suppose White can be taken as evidence that muckraking never amounted to much. I prefer to think that there would be instruction in distinguishing a White from a Charles Edward Russell, or a Steffens, or a Sinclair. There are precious few of the latter. David Graham Phillips continues to be the Unknown Writer in the Arlington Cemetery of American Literature, but his *Treason of the Senate*, at least, attracts some attention, for reasons bearing neither upon him nor American culture. Textbook writers find occasion to use abstracts from this work. It was resurrected entirely by editors of the neo-radical *Modern Monthly*, in 1953, solely as a stick with which to beat the late Senator Joe McCarthy. It was still later announced for publication under academic auspices. It may well precede reconsideration of Phillips's fiction. The historians, with all their faults, are miles ahead of the literature practitioners in sheer animation.

None of the muckrakers has done better than Finley Peter Dunne in point of prestige. A small shelf of books is in the making. It includes my own *Mr. Dooley: Now and Forever* (1954) and *The World of Mr. Dooley* (1962), as well as his own autobiographical chapters, hitherto unpublished and filled out with others by his son Philip, *Mr. Dooley Remembers: the Informal Memoirs of Finley Peter Dunne* (1963), and a legal labor of love, Edward J. Bander's compilation, *Mr. Dooley on the Choice of Law* (1963).

Warren F. Kuehl's *Hamilton Holt* (1960) is not about a muckraker, but it does concern a liberal publicist of their time whose work provides a contrast with theirs. His tragic cause was peace. He was editor of the *Independent*, a journal which had been issued significantly since 1848. He became president of Rollins College, which has issued a *Register of Hamilton Holt Papers* (1964). It does not feature muckrakers, but reminds us how their private papers continue to molder in private possession, or to be thrown out to make room for this season's magazines.

A special word on Benjamin C. Marsh's *Lobbyist for the People: A Record of Fifty Years* (1955). Here was an interested citizen who maintained a public service attitude toward his country not merely during election years, but year in year out. He was a true heir of the muckrakers. His autobiography is pleasing and informative, and moves from reform of the reform era into the 1920's, a period too lazily categorized as anti-reform. Marsh's life reminds us that we need not be summer soldiers, whether our absent-minded neighbors honor us or not.

Philip S. Foner's *Jack London* (1947, new ed. 1964) is distinctly tendentious, but at least keeps the flag flying for its remarkable subject in a time when he is better esteemed in the Soviet Union than in his native America. I have issued a biography of Edwin Markham, rarely thought of as a muckraker, published in 1966. The reader might wish to examine my essay, "Edwin Markham, Poetry, and What Have You," *Antioch Review*, Winter '63-'64. Incidentally, Hamlin Garland has done much better among the litterateurs than his contemporary Markham, and his career, like Markham's, helps us grasp that the muckrakers cannot be understood apart from the cultural problems they pose.

As to the larger problem of muckraking and society, I here offer a completely revised *Crusaders* in order to incorporate views and information I have developed over the years, notably about civil rights and the South, about labor, and about American foreign affairs in the reform era. For it was on such shoals as these that muckraking spilled, to mix with blatant sensationalism and grade B motion-pictures about fearless editors and reporters, as well as to make energetic contacts with writings by George Seldes, Theodore Quinn of *Giant Corporations: Challenge to Freedom* (1956), a tale told by an insider, and, most recently, *Fact*.

Muckraking and Progressivism were not the same thing. Moreover, we need to distinguish between mere contemporary adjustments, such as every politician worries about during election year, and the respect for human personality which the memorable reformer will further. Thus, there are many books in the making about such Progressives as La Follette, George W. Norris, William E. Borah, and others. Pages and even chapters of their lives and works will bear on muckraking. But the most enthusiastic of their biographers will have to deal with such a challenge as Gabriel Kolko's *The Triumph of Conservatism: a Reinterpretation of American History 1900-1916* (1963). It sees Theodore Roosevelt as a conservative, Taft as a more "radical" opponent of the trusts, and Progressivism as "not the triumph of small business over the trusts, . . . but the victory of big business in achieving the rationalization of the economy that only the federal government could provide" (p. 284). Such passages will confuse readers who forget that no victories are eternal, but must all be rescued from their exploiters.

Thus, it is false to estimate the work of either Progressives or muckrakers strictly in terms of *results*. To some extent, these are helpful, of course. But social welfare is not the same as philanthropy or charity, and political and economic reforms are not necessarily the same as particular measures which can become old hat and insignificant. Samuel Haber's *Efficiency and Uplift: Scientific Management in the Progressive Era, 1890-1920* (1964) is a case in point. It helps explain that a growing America needed streamlining as a kind of health measure, but it does not tell us much about the patient. Man does not live by efficiency alone. Henry George not only created the Single Tax; he helped create Tom Johnson, and Brand Whitlock, and numerous other dimensional reformers. E. A. Filene created the bargain basement, but he also created the American credit union and other social apparatus, and, more important, an American dream of production for use. His story is told in Gerald W. Johnson's *Liberal's Progress* (1948) and could use further telling. Incidentally, Filene wasted regard on James M. Curley, of Boston, and some academics seem willing to do the same. Anyone who can praise Boss Curley for the "good" he did his Irish constituents, and not note his dissimilarities from an Al Smith, or a La Guardia, or a Robert F. Wagner limits his possibilities for growth. Steffens long ago indicated the difference in his fine chapter of autobiography, "The Dying Boss." Society always needs to renew itself by loping off its dead branches and sustaining its live ones.

We need to ponder past views and present ones: to re-read William H. Tolman's *Municipal Reform Movements in the United States* (1895), while reading Louis G. Geiger's *Joseph W. Folk of Missouri* (1953), Dayton D. McKean's *The Boss: the Hague Machine in Action* (1940), Ransome E. Noble's *New Jersey Progressivism before Wilson* (1946), and Clifford W. Patton's *The Battle for Municipal Reform* (1940). Marvin Wachman's *History of the Social Democratic Party of Milwaukee, 1897-1910* (1945) evokes attitudes and perspectives which influenced the muckrakers; so does so special a work as that by Miriam Allen De Ford—a writer of varied works, among which is the biography of her husband, a Socialist and popular criminologist, *Up-Hill All the Way: the Life of Maynard Shipley* (1956). Moses Rischin, *The Promised City, New York's Jews 1870-1914* (1962) is a work of high scholarship which helps explain phases of muckraking. Such a work as David H. Grover's *Debaters and Dynamiters: the story of the Haywood Trial* (1964), throws valued light on that significant episode. Among women who can be specifically noted see, first of all *Jane Addams: a Centennial Reader* (1960): a movement in herself, and also Josephine Goldmark's *Impatient Crusader: Florence Kelley's Life Story* (1953).

Not to be derogated is Leo Katcher's *The Big Bankroll: the Life and Times of Arnold Rothstein* (1959): popular, well-informed, and concerned for a level of society which can always be better comprehended. To discuss reform without discussing corruption is to work with an infirm equation. Arnold Rothstein succeeded the venal police Lieutenant Charles Becker as an organizer of criminal pursuits in New York and beyond. He gave form to what had before been a busy assembly of relatively small criminal businesses. Over his dead body grew what journalists quite properly perceived to be criminal "empires." Relevant in this connection is Walter Bean, *Boss Ruef's San Francisco* (1952).

Bela C. and Lola La Follette's *Robert La Follette* (1953) repays reading, and so, still, do William E. Walling's *Progressivism and After* (1914) and Benjamin P. De Witt's *The Progressive Movement* (1915). Louis D. Brandeis is securely put to rest in Alpheus T. Mason's distinguished *Brandeis* (1946), but as significant for muckraking purposes is Mason's *Bureaucracy Convicts Itself: the Ballinger-Pinchot Controversy, 1910, and Its Meaning for Today* (1941). For it was inspired by Harold L. Ickes's article, "Not Guilty!," a tale of an "American Dreyfus" published in the *Saturday Evening Post*, May 25, 1940. The Dreyfus of this case was not Louis R. Glavis or Gifford Pinchot, but Ballinger. The several million Americans who perused the article knew nothing of the battle Ickes was conducting at this time to take the Bureau of Forestry out of the Department of Agriculture and put it into his own Department of the Interior. But such are the facts which give vitality to history. There have been several biographies of Pinchot, and Pinchot's own autobiographical *Breaking New Ground* (1947) to help fill the chasm of misreading and indifference which blurs our vision of the past.

The passing of muckraking continues to want explication, but, at least, we learn a bit more of those who don't care for it. Herbert Croly's *The Promise of American Life* (1909) is by the founder of the *New Republic*, who was also an admirer and biographer of the Republican boss, Mark Hanna. Charles Forcey, *The Crossroads of Liberalism* (1961) deals with Croly and his associates Walter Lippmann and Walter Weyl. David W. Noble, *The Paradox of Progressive Thought* (1958) perceives the Progressives as shallow and confused. Such studies in intellectual thought can be further prosecuted in Morton G. White's *Social Thought in America* (1949) and Henry F. May, *The End of American Innocence* (1959). Helene M. Hooker, ed., *History of the Progressive Party, 1912-1916*, by Amos R. E. Pinchot (1958) helps explain much about the conflicting interests which brought on the Progressive debacle.

Immigration certainly has something to do with muckraking —it has to do with everything else—but just what has yet to be determined. The better-known writings on this subject do not fathom it. It involves an expose of actual conditions among the immigrants— their failures and faults as well as their flattering features. It involves also a clarification of their relationship to the rest of us immigrants. The muckraking era produced notable volumes in the "Americanization of—" genre, but life-stories of Jacob A. Riis, Edward W. Bok, Mary Antin, and the like do not constitute muckraking. An expose of slums, factory exploitation, political trickery, and under-representation of minorities does, when it puts the particular immigrant groups in perspective, and some muckraking did; see my pages 116-9 for suggestions along this line.

Related to immigration and muckraking is the story of labor, which needs to be especially developed since it became as officially successful as it did. Bernard Mandel's lengthy and outstanding *Samuel Gompers* (1963) demands notice in this connection because of what it *does not* find it necessary to discuss, with respect to muckraking. The subject is complex. It merits close, unglib consideration. One place to start might be with Ralph Chaplin's *Wobbly* (1948), by a man who had fought bitter labor wars during the muckraking era, and whose *Solidarity Forever* had an overtone of social permanency about it. Chaplin could hardly have been accused of "selling out" to anyone, yet his memoirs, repudiating violence and communism had been aided by a Newberry Fellowship in Midwestern Studies, and published by the University of Chicago Press.

Like immigration, the Negroes are relevant to everything, and have now received their due portion of the total American story. I offer my chapter on the Negroes and muckraking, and will gladly offer more. There are materials in August Meier's *Negro Thought in America, 1880-1915* (1963) which bear on the topic, as do several biographies of W. E. B. DuBois, especially as he inter-related with such figures as Oswald Garrison Villard and with the National Association for the Advancement of Colored People. Gilbert Osofsky's work in the field and that of other academics is yet to be geared to the larger movements of the time, involving the entire population of minorities.

Momentous in this area is the question of Progressivism and the South, which southerners, at least, tend to believe is over-simplified into Solid South formulas and a concentration upon Negro civil rights. I note *Tom Watson's Magazine* (p. 258). Watson—a tragic figure, so far as American hopes for popular decency are concerned— is all too typical of what southern "muckraking" had to offer. Yet southern Progressivism must be studied and understood. William D. Miller's *Memphis During the Progressive Era, 1900-1917* (1957) merits study in this connection. Dewey W. Grantham's *The Democratic South* (1963) is more philosophically couched than some persons concerned for democratic vistas in their own lifetimes might prefer, but it suggests a more complex South than they often perceive, and it offers a bibliography for people who read as well as hope.

Other aspects of Progressivism—including concomitant muckraking—are being exploited. Roy Lubove, *The Progressives and the Slums* (1962) deals with the New York experience, and James H. Timberlake's *Prohibition and the Progressive Movement* (1963) breaks ground in that profound American problem. Oscar E. Anderson, *The Health of a Nation: Harvey W. Wiley and the Fight for Pure Food* (1958) reminds me that we may have to reconsider our assumptions about American objectives. We have assumed that Americans desire health. Apparently they did. But do they? Who leads the fight to curb cigarette advertising and use? We will know more about these and equally vital questions with time, but not before a fresh and seeking literature more thoroughly and intelligently investigates historical reality in the area, and probes its modern implications.

Finally, the debacle. World War I channeled the muckrakers into an apparently higher and more significant sphere of influence.

Ray Stannard Baker reported the spirit of England under wartime conditions. Edwin Markham's war poems were translated into French. Charles Edward Russell was sent as Wilson's emissary to revolutionary Russia. Yet all such deeds and glories dwindle into forgetfulness. Events with impact took place elsewhere. Howard K. Beale's *Theodore Roosevelt and the Rise of America to World Power* (1956) takes us into a field where Americans rate as only one unit, and muckrakers are presently all but lost in that. William Leuchtenburg's "Progressivism and Imperialism: the Progressive Movement and American Foreign Policy, 1898-1916," *Mississippi Valley Historical Review*, December, 1952, deals with a subject which should engage many and varied energies. The same may be said of Walter I. Trattner, "Progressivism and World War I: a Reappraisal," *Mid-America*, July, 1962.

But perhaps enough has been said for present purposes to suggest the lines of inquiry which require extension, and something of the fashion in which they influence one another. The Nonpartisan League of the late 1910's and early 1920's, urban reform as compared with rural reform, the problem of our geographical sections, and first of all the South, which Grantham, at least, believes has served, "however unwittingly, as the nation's political conscience" (*The Democratic South*, p. 97), all of these areas want probing and perspective. Such particular areas as social work, housing, economic opportunity, health, education—these and other reforms vitally concern the content of muckraking. But muckraking was first of all communication, and it involved advertising, banking, entertainment. We will never be able to *use* its experience so long as we think of it in the abstract. There is vitality in such a personal account of the crash and disappearance of a multi-million-dollar periodical as Paul C. Smith's "The Collier's Affair: A Rueful Memoir," *Esquire*, September, 1964—much more vitality than there is in a hundred general essays about what journalism ought to be.

Since the above was written (in 1964) much has been published, but sadly little which probes the dimensions and uses of Progressivism. Such a book as Simon Lazarus's *The Genteel Populists* (1974) by a follower of Ralph Nader is an essentially frivolous work which seeks a "people's" mandate by working up gimmicks which will protect their consumer interests. It imagines that Populism was gimmicks, rather than people, and that a "new"

Populism can be administered by Harvard-trained lawyers—of course, in the masses' best interests. It is to be hoped that the actual people will disappoint their pretensions.

Several works—among them, Arthur A. Ekirch's *Progressivism in America* (1974); David M. Chalmers's combination of text and readings, *The Muckrake Years* (1974); and *Muckraking: Past, Present, and Future*, edited by John M. Harrison and Harry H. Stein (1973)—have been forthright in their research and contribute to an urgently needed dialogue, though one is not apparent in this moment of time. My own Bowker bibliography in one section discusses "Work that Needs to Be Done": a topic which can itself be extended as required and, one hopes, will be.

The years have seen Progressivism subjected to severe and often senseless blows. Loose charges of racism and imperialism have been "established" as fact in academic circles, if nowhere else. It has been tragic to note that *anti*-racism and *anti*-imperialism have *not* been highlighted as Progressive. Vann Woodward, the biographer of the Georgia Populist and racist Tom Watson, has been regrettably outstanding in treating Watson as having been a typical Progressive who invoked Lynch Law in the somber murder of the maligned Leo Frank in 1915. Woodward would have been wiser, and been more accurate, and done more for the Yale University tradition to have cited as Progressive the noble Georgia governor of the time, John M. Slaton, who commuted Frank's death sentence, only to be flouted by a respectable mob, by no means composed of Progressives.

Efforts to identify Senator Joseph McCarthy of Wisconsin as a product of Progressivism have been subjected to research and repudiation. What remains to be gathered is research explaining the compulsion of "liberal" intellectuals to perpetrate such malefic theories in books and articles. Adlai E. Stevenson and Estes Kefauver would have seemed better candidates for inheriting the Progressive tradition. John F. Kennedy fingered verbalists for his administration, rather than professionals of social service—as distinguished from "social activists." Kennedy did have connections with Progressive concerns, as in his *A Nation of Immigrants* (1964). But he and his circle were so deep in politics as to offer little directly for the rebuilding of Progressive ideals.

Muckraking, as distinguished from Progressivism, has continued more alive than ever in the work of Drew Pearson, Jack Anderson, I. F. Stone, and the Daniel Ellsberg of the Pentagon papers. Muckraking has been critical of national leaders and administrations, of corporate under-the-table contrivings, of the status of women, youth, "gays," and sexual mores and their social implications in general. Incidentally, it is mightily important to keep in mind at all times that women ultimately determine all decisions in society; and that the matter in which they will assess "woman's lib," for example, will help define any Progressivism of the future.

The problem with muckraking has been to determine what social philosophy guides the various investigations, how they are to be distinguished from mere sensationalism, and what they contribute to the world's real concerns. There has been a need for clarifying through muckraking differences between freedom and anarchy, rights and desires, and above all social responsibility and irresponsibility. With the decline of the magazines, television has become a key communication instrument, and many people seem reconciled to it as preeminent in its field. More needs to be done to define television's role and potential in instigating and illuminating social debates.

What is certain is that there will be no better television than there is a public. And it may well be that, with the decline of a narcissistic writing and fascination with the irrational in literature, magazines and books will resume their once distinguished place in our Progressive tradition.

(1976)

INDEX

Library of Congress Cataloging-in-Publication Data

Filler, Louis
  The muckrakers / Louis Filler. — New and enl. ed. of Crusaders
for American liberalism.
        p.   cm.
  Originally published: 1968. With new preface.
  Includes bibliographical references and index.
  ISBN 0-8047-2236-6 (pb.)
    1. United States—Social conditions—20th century.   2. Social
problems.   3. Social reformers—United States.   I. Title.
HN57.F47   1993
306'.0973—dc20   93-30381
                                                        CIP

⊗ This book is printed on acid-free paper.